W9-BWV-395

The Desire of Ages

BOOK II

E. G. White

FH3
Family Heritage Books
Thomaston, GA 30286

The bracketed numbers at the foot of each page coordinate this edition with the pagination of the standard hardback printings published under the title, *The Desire of Ages.*

Cover design by Kim Justinen and Merwin Stewart
Interior design by Gena Cowen, Dan Willett, & C. David Wingate
All photographs & artwork supplied by Pacific Press Publishing Association
Type set: 10/11.5 Times Roman
Printed on acid free paper

Printed in U.S.A. by Pacific Press Publishing Association

FHB Cataloging Service

White, Ellen G., 1827-1915
   The Desire of Ages, Book 2

   1. History, Christ   2. Jesus' Ministry
I. Title

ISBN 0-8163-1017-3

Contents

Section VIII. The Crucified.

Section IX. To The Father's Throne.

Ministry

The entire night had been passed in the mountain; and as the sun arose, Jesus and His disciples descended to the plain. Absorbed in thought, the disciples were awed and silent. Even Peter had not a word to say. Gladly would they have lingered in that holy place which had been touched with the light of heaven, and where the Son of God had manifested His glory; but there was work to be done for the people, who were already searching far and near for Jesus.

At the foot of the mountain a large company had gathered, led hither by the disciples who had remained behind, but who knew whither Jesus had resorted. As the Saviour drew near, He charged His three companions to keep silence concerning what they had witnessed, saying, "Tell the vision to no man, until the Son of man be risen again from the dead." The revelation made to the disciples was to be pondered in their own hearts, not to be published abroad. To relate it to the multitudes would excite only ridicule or idle wonder And even the nine apostles would not understand the scene until after Christ had risen from the dead. How slow of comprehension even the three favored disciples were, is seen in the fact that notwithstanding all that Christ had said of what was before Him, they queried among themselves what the rising from the dead should mean. Yet they asked no explanation from Jesus. His words in regard to the future had filled them with sorrow; they sought no further revelation concerning that which they were fain to believe might never come to pass.

As the people on the plain caught sight of Jesus, they ran to meet Him, greeting Him with expressions of reverence and joy. Yet His quick eye discerned that they were in great perplexity. The disciples appeared troubled. A circumstance had just occurred that had caused them bitter disappointment and humiliation.

While they were waiting at the foot of the mountain, a father had brought to them his son, to be delivered from a dumb spirit that tormented him. Authority over unclean spirits, to cast them out, had been conferred on the disciples when Jesus sent out the Twelve to preach through Galilee. As they went forth strong in faith, the evil spirits had obeyed their word. Now in the name of Christ they commanded the torturing spirit to leave his victim; but the demon only mocked them by a fresh display of his power. The disciples, unable to account for their defeat, felt that they were bringing dishonor upon themselves and their Master. And in the crowd there were scribes who made the most of this opportunity to humiliate them. Pressing around the disciples, they plied them with questions, seeking to prove that they and their Master were deceivers. Here, the rabbis triumphantly declared, was an evil spirit that neither the disciples nor Christ Himself could conquer. The people were inclined to side with the scribes, and a feeling of contempt and scorn pervaded the crowd.

But suddenly the accusations ceased. Jesus and the three disciples were seen approaching, and with a quick revulsion of feeling the people turned to meet them. The night of communion with the heavenly glory had left its trace upon the Saviour and His companions. Upon their countenances was a light that awed the beholders. The scribes drew back in fear, while the people welcomed Jesus.

As if He had been a witness of all that had occurred, the Saviour came to the scene of conflict, and fixing His gaze on the scribes inquired, "What question ye with them?"

But the voices so bold and defiant before, were now silent. A hush had fallen upon the entire company. Now the afflicted father made his way through the crowd, and falling at the feet of Jesus, poured out the story of his trouble and disappointment.

"Master," he said, "I have brought unto Thee my son, which hath a dumb spirit; and wheresoever he taketh him, he teareth him: . . . and I spake to Thy disciples that they should cast him out; and they could not."

Jesus looked about Him upon the awe-stricken multitude, the caviling scribes, the perplexed disciples. He read the unbelief in every heart; and in a voice filled with sorrow He exclaimed, "O faithless generation, how long shall I be with you? how long shall I suffer you?" Then He bade the distressed father, "Bring thy son hither."

"In Christ, God has provided means for . . . resisting every temptation, however strong. . . . He who healed the sick and cast out demons . . . is the same mighty Redeemer today . . . Cast yourself at His feet with the cry, 'Lord, I believe; help *Thou* mine unbelief.' You can never perish while you do this—never."

The boy was brought, and as the Saviour's eyes fell upon him, the evil spirit cast him to the ground in convulsions of agony. He lay wallowing and foaming, rending the air with unearthly shrieks.

Again the Prince of life and the prince of the powers of darkness had met on the field of battle, — Christ in fulfillment of His mission to "preach deliverance to the captives, . . . to set at liberty them that are bruised" (Luke 4:18), Satan seeking to hold his victim under his control. Angels of light and the hosts of evil angels, unseen, were pressing near to behold the conflict. For a moment, Jesus permitted the evil spirit to display his power, that the beholders might comprehend the deliverance about to be wrought.

The multitude looked on with bated breath, the father in an agony of hope and fear. Jesus asked, "How long is it ago since this came unto him?" The father told the story of long years of suffering, and then, as if he could endure no more, exclaimed, "If Thou canst do anything, have compassion on us, and help us." "If Thou canst!" Even now the father questioned the power of Christ.

Jesus answers, "If thou canst believe, all things are possible to him that believeth." There is no lack of power on the part of Christ; the healing of the son depends upon the father's faith. With a burst of tears, realizing his own weakness, the father casts himself upon Christ's mercy, with the cry, "Lord, I believe; help Thou mine unbelief."

Jesus turns to the suffering one, and says, "Thou dumb and deaf spirit, I charge thee, come out of him, and enter no more into him." There is a cry, an agonized struggle. The demon, in passing, seems about to rend the life from his victim. Then the boy lies motionless, and apparently lifeless. The multitude whisper, "He is dead." But Jesus takes him by the hand, and lifting him up, presents him, in perfect soundness of mind and body, to his father. Father and son praise the name of their Deliverer. The multitude are "amazed at the mighty power of God," while the scribes, defeated and crestfallen, turn sullenly away.

"If Thou canst do anything, have compassion on us, and help us." How many a sin-burdened soul has echoed that prayer. And to all, the pitying Saviour's answer is, "If thou canst believe, all things are possible to him that believeth." It is faith that connects us with heaven, and brings us strength for coping with the powers of darkness. In Christ, God has provided means for subduing every sinful trait, and resisting every temptation, however strong. But many feel that they lack faith, and therefore they remain away from Christ. Let these souls, in their helpless unworthiness, cast themselves upon the mercy of their compassionate Saviour. Look not to self, but to Christ. He who healed the sick and cast out demons when He walked among men, is the same mighty Redeemer today. Faith comes by the word of God. Then grasp His promise, "Him that cometh to Me I will in no wise cast out." John 6:37. Cast yourself at His feet with the cry, "Lord, I believe; help *Thou* mine unbelief." You can never perish while you do this — never.

In a brief space of time the favored disciples have beheld the extreme of glory and of humiliation. They have seen humanity as transfigured into the image of God, and as debased into the likeness of Satan. From the mountain where He has talked with the heavenly messengers, and has been proclaimed the Son of God by the voice from the radiant glory they have seen Jesus descend to meet that most distressing and revolting spectacle, the maniac boy, with distorted countenance, gnashing his teeth in spasms of agony that no human power could relieve. And this mighty Redeemer, who but a few hours before stood glorified before His wondering disciples, stoops to lift the victim of Satan from the earth where he is wallowing, and in health of mind and body restores him to his father and his home.

It was an object lesson of redemption, — the Divine One from the Father's glory stooping to save the lost. It represented also the disciples' mission. Not alone upon the mountaintop with Jesus, in hours of spiritual illumination, is the life of Christ's servants to be spent. There is work for them down in the plain. Souls whom Satan has enslaved, are waiting for the word of faith and prayer to set them free.

The nine disciples were yet pondering upon the bitter fact of their own failure; and when Jesus was once more alone with them, they questioned, "Why could not we cast him out?" Jesus answered them, "Because of your unbelief; for verily I say unto you, If ye have faith as a grain of mustard seed, ye shall say unto this mountain, Remove hence to yonder place, and it shall remove; and nothing shall be impossible unto you. Howbeit this kind goeth not out but by prayer and fasting." Their unbelief, that shut them out from deeper sympathy with Christ, and the carelessness with which they regarded the sacred work committed to them, had caused their failure in the conflict with the powers of darkness.

The words of Christ pointing to His death, had brought sadness and doubt. And the selection of the three disciples to accompany Jesus to the mountain had excited the jealousy of the nine. Instead of strengthening their faith by prayer and meditation on the words of Christ, they had been dwelling on their discouragements and personal grievances. In this state of darkness they had undertaken the conflict with Satan.

In order to succeed in such a conflict they must come to the work in a different spirit. Their faith must be strengthened by fervent prayer and fasting, and humiliation of heart. They must be emptied of self, and be filled with the Spirit and power of God. Earnest, persevering supplication to God in faith, — faith that leads to entire dependence upon God, and unreserved consecration to His work, — can alone avail to bring men the Holy Spirit's aid in the battle against principalities and powers, the rulers of the darkness of this world, and wicked spirits in high places.

"If ye have faith as a grain of mustard seed," said Jesus, "ye shall say unto this mountain, Remove hence to yonder place; and it shall remove." Though the grain of mustard seed is so small, it contains that same mysterious life principle which produces growth in the loftiest tree. When the mustard seed is cast into the ground, the tiny germ lays hold of every element that God has provided for its nutriment, and it speedily develops a sturdy growth. If you have faith like this, you will lay hold upon God's word, and upon all the helpful agencies He has appointed. Thus your faith will strengthen, and will bring to your aid the power of heaven. The obstacles that are piled by Satan across your path, though apparently as insurmountable as the eternal hills, shall disappear before the demand of faith. "Nothing shall be impossible unto you."

"Who Is the Greatest?"

On returning to Capernaum, Jesus did not repair to the well-known resorts where He had taught the people, but with His disciples quietly sought the house that was to be His temporary home. During the remainder of His stay in Galilee it was His object to instruct the disciples rather than to labor for the multitudes.

On the journey through Galilee, Christ had again tried to prepare the minds of His disciples for the scenes before Him. He told them that He was to go up to Jerusalem to be put to death and to rise again. And He added the strange and solemn announcement that He was to be betrayed into the hands of His enemies. The disciples did not even now comprehend His words. Although the shadow of a great sorrow fell upon them, a spirit of rivalry found a place in their hearts. They disputed among themselves which should be accounted greatest in the kingdom. This strife they thought to conceal from Jesus, and they did not, as usual, press close to His side, but loitered behind, so that He was in advance of them as they entered Capernaum. Jesus read their thoughts, and He longed to counsel and instruct them. But for this He awaited a quiet hour, when their hearts should be open to receive His words.

Soon after they reached the town, the collector of the temple revenue came to Peter with the question, "Doth not your Master pay tribute?" This tribute was not a civil tax, but a religious contribution, which every Jew was required to pay annually for the support of the temple. A refusal to pay the tribute would be regarded as disloyalty to the temple, — in the estimation of the rabbis a most grievous sin. The Saviour's attitude toward the rabbinical laws, and His plain reproofs to the defenders of tradition, afforded a pretext for the charge that He was seeking to overthrow the temple service. Now His enemies saw an opportunity of casting discredit upon Him. In the collector of the tribute they found a ready ally.

Peter saw in the collector's question an insinuation touching Christ's loyalty to the temple. Zealous for his Master's honor, he hastily answered, without consulting Him, that Jesus would pay the tribute.

But Peter only partially comprehended the purpose of his questioner. There were some classes who were held to be exempt from the payment of the tribute. In the time of Moses, when the Levites were set apart for the service of the sanctuary, they were given no inheritance among the people. The Lord said, "Levi hath no part nor inheritance with his brethren; the Lord is his inheritance." Deuteronomy 10:9. In the days of Christ the priests and Levites were still regarded as especially devoted to the temple, and were not required to make the annual contribution for its support. Prophets also were exempted from this payment. In requiring the tribute from Jesus, the rabbis were setting aside His claim as a prophet or teacher, and were dealing with Him as with any commonplace person. A refusal on His part to pay the tribute would be represented as disloyalty to the temple; while, on the other hand, the payment of it would be taken as justifying their rejection of Him as a prophet.

Only a little before, Peter had acknowledged Jesus as the Son of God; but he now missed an opportunity of setting forth the character of his Master. By his answer to the collector, that Jesus would pay the tribute, he had virtually sanctioned the false conception of Him to which the priests and rulers were trying to give currency.

When Peter entered the house, the Saviour made no reference to what had taken place, but inquired, "What thinkest thou, Simon? of whom do the kings of the earth

This chapter is based on Matthew 17:22-27; 18:1-20; Mark 9:30-50; Luke 9:46-48.

take custom or tribute? of their own children, or of strangers?" Peter answered, "Of strangers." And Jesus said, "Then are the children free." While the people of a country are taxed for the maintenance of their king, the monarch's own children are exempt. So Israel, the professed people of God, were required to maintain His service; but Jesus, the Son of God, was under no such obligation. If priests and Levites were exempt because of their connection with the temple, how much more He to whom the temple was His Father's house.

If Jesus had paid the tribute without a protest, He would virtually have acknowledged the justice of the claim, and would thus have denied His divinity. But while He saw good to meet the demand, He denied the claim upon which it was based. In providing for the payment of the tribute He gave evidence of His divine character. It was made manifest that He was one with God, and therefore was not under tribute as a mere subject of the kingdom.

"Go thou to the sea," He directed Peter, "and cast an hook, and take up the fish that first cometh up; and when thou hast opened his mouth, thou shalt find a piece of money: that take, and give unto them for Me and thee."

Though He had clothed His divinity with humanity, in this miracle He revealed His glory. It was evident that this was He who through David had declared, "Every beast of the forest is Mine, and the cattle upon a thousand hills. I know all the fowls of the mountains; and the wild beasts of the field are Mine. If I were hungry, I would not tell thee; for the world is Mine, and the fullness thereof." Psalms 50:10-12.

While Jesus made it plain that He was under no obligation to pay the tribute, He entered into no controversy with the Jews in regard to the matter; for they would have misinterpreted His words, and turned them against Him. Lest He should give offense by withholding the tribute, He did that which He could not justly be required to do. This lesson would be of great value to His disciples. Marked changes were soon to take place in their relation to the temple service, and Christ taught them not to place themselves needlessly in antagonism to established order. So far as possible, they were to avoid giving occasion for misinterpretation of their faith. While Christians are not to sacrifice one principle of truth, they should avoid controversy whenever it is possible to do so.

When Christ and the disciples were alone in the house, while Peter was gone to the sea, Jesus called the others to Him, and asked, "What was it that ye disputed among yourselves by the way?" The presence of Jesus, and His question, put the matter in an entirely different light from that in which it had appeared to them while they were contending by the way. Shame and self-condemnation kept them silent. Jesus had told them that He was to die for their sake, and their selfish ambition was in painful contrast to His unselfish love.

When Jesus told them that He was to be put to death and to rise again, He was trying to draw them into conversation in regard to the great test of their faith. Had they been ready to receive what He desired to make known to them, they would have been saved bitter anguish and despair. His words would have brought consolation in the hour of bereavement and disappointment. But although He had spoken so plainly of what awaited Him, His mention of the fact that He was soon to go to Jerusalem, again kindled their hope that the kingdom was about to be set up. This had led to questioning as to who should fill the highest offices. On Peter's return from the sea, the disciples told him of the Saviour's question, and at last one ventured to ask Jesus, "Who is the greatest in the kingdom of heaven?"

The Saviour gathered His disciples about Him, and said to them, "If any man desire to be first, the same shall be last of all, and servant of all." There was in these words a solemnity and impressiveness which the disciples were far from comprehending. That which Christ discerned, they could not see. They did not understand the nature of Christ's kingdom, and this ignorance was the apparent cause of their contention. But the real cause lay deeper. By explaining the nature of the kingdom, Christ might for the time have quelled their strife; but this would not have touched the underlying cause. Even after they had received the fullest knowledge, any question of precedence might have renewed the trouble. Thus disaster would have been brought to the church after Christ's departure. The strife for the highest place was the outworking of that same spirit which was the beginning of the great controversy in the worlds above, and which had brought Christ from heaven to die. There rose up before Him a vision of Lucifer, the "son of the morning," in glory surpassing all the angels that surround the throne, and united in closest ties to the Son of God. Lucifer had said, "I will be like the Most High;" (Isaiah 14:12, 14.) and the desire for self-exaltation had brought strife into the heavenly courts, and had banished a multitude of the hosts of God. Had Lucifer really desired to be like the Most High, he would never have deserted his appointed place in heaven; for the spirit of the Most High is manifested in unselfish ministry. Lucifer desired God's power, but not His character. He sought for himself the highest place, and every being who is actuated by his spirit will do the same. Thus alienation, discord, and strife will be inevitable. Dominion becomes the prize of the strongest. The kingdom of Satan is a kingdom of force; every individual regards every other as an obstacle in the way of his own advancement, or a steppingstone on which he himself may climb to a higher place.

While Lucifer counted it a thing to be grasped to be equal with God, Christ, the Exalted One, "made Himself of no reputation, and took upon Him the form of a servant, and was made in the likeness of men. And being found in fashion as a man, He humbled Himself, and became obedient unto death, even the death of the cross." Philippians 2:7, 8. Now the cross was just before Him; and His own disciples were so filled with self-seeking—the very principle of Satan's kingdom—that they could not enter into sympathy with their Lord, or even understand Him as He spoke of His humiliation for them.

Very tenderly, yet with solemn emphasis, Jesus tried to correct the evil. He showed what is the principle that bears sway in the kingdom of heaven, and in what true greatness consists, as estimated by the standard of the courts above. Those who were actuated by pride and love of distinction, were thinking of themselves, and of the rewards they were to have, rather than how they were to render back to God the gifts they had received. They would have no place in the kingdom of heaven, for they were identified with the ranks of Satan.

Before honor is humility. To fill a high place before men, Heaven chooses the worker who, like John the Baptist, takes a lowly place before God. The most childlike disciple is the most efficient in labor for God. The heavenly intelligences can co-operate with him who is seeking, not to exalt self, but to save souls. He who feels most deeply his need of divine aid will plead for it; and the Holy Spirit will give unto him glimpses of Jesus that will strengthen and uplift the soul. From communion with Christ he will go forth to work for those who are perishing in their sins. He is anointed for his mission; and he succeeds where many of the learned and intellectually wise would fail.

But when men exalt themselves, feeling that they are a necessity for the success of God's great plan, the Lord causes them to be set aside. It is made evident that the Lord is not dependent upon them. The work does not stop because of their removal from it, but goes forward with greater power.

It was not enough for the disciples of Jesus to be instructed as to the nature of His kingdom. What they needed was a change of heart that would bring them into harmony with its principles. Calling a little child to Him, Jesus set him in the midst of them; then tenderly folding the little one in His arms He said, "Except ye be converted, and become as little children, ye shall not enter into the kingdom of heaven." The simplicity, the self-forgetfulness, and the confiding love of a little child are the attributes that Heaven values. These are the characteristics of real greatness.

Again Jesus explained to the disciples that His kingdom is not characterized by earthly dignity and display. At the feet of Jesus all these distinctions are forgotten. The rich and the poor, the learned and the ignorant, meet together, with no thought of caste or worldly preeminence. All meet as blood-bought souls, alike dependent upon One who has redeemed them to God.

The sincere, contrite soul is precious in the sight of God. He places His own signet upon men, not by their rank, not by their wealth, not by their intellectual greatness, but by their oneness with Christ. The Lord of glory is satisfied with those who are meek and lowly in heart. "Thou hast also given me," said David, "the shield of Thy salvation:

. . . and Thy gentleness"—as an element in the human character— "hath made me great." Psalms 18:35.

"Whosoever shall receive one of such children in My name," said Jesus, "receiveth Me. And whosoever shall receive Me, receiveth not Me, but Him that sent Me." "Thus saith the Lord: The heaven is My throne, and the earth is My footstool; . . . but to this man will I look, even to him that is poor and of a contrite spirit, and trembleth at My word." Isaiah 66:1, 2.

"The sincere, contrite soul is precious in the sight of God. He places His own signet upon men, not by their rank, not by their wealth, not by their intellectual greatness, but by their oneness with Christ. The Lord of glory is satisfied with those who are meek and lowly in heart."

The Saviour's words awakened in the disciples a feeling of self-distrust. No one had been specially pointed out in the reply; but John was led to question whether in one case his action had been right. With the spirit of a child he laid the matter before Jesus. "Master," he said, "we saw one casting out devils in Thy name, and he followeth not us, and we forbade him, because he followeth not us."

James and John had thought that in checking this man they had had in view their Lord's honor; they began to see that they were jealous for their own. They acknowledged their error, and accepted the reproof of Jesus, "Forbid him not; for there is no man which shall do a miracle in My name, that can lightly speak evil of Me." None who showed themselves in any way friendly to Christ were to be repulsed. There were many who had been deeply moved by the character and the work of Christ, and whose hearts were opening to Him in faith; and the disciples, who could not read motives, must be careful not to discourage these souls. When Jesus was no longer personally among them, and the work was left in their hands, they must not indulge a narrow, exclusive spirit, but manifest the same far-reaching sympathy which they had seen in their Master.

The fact that one does not in all things conform to our personal ideas or opinions, will not justify us in forbidding him to labor for God. Christ is the great Teacher; we are not to judge or to command, but in humility each is to sit at the feet of Jesus, and learn of Him. Every soul whom God has made willing, is a channel through which Christ will reveal His pardoning love. How careful we should be lest we discourage one of God's light bearers, and thus intercept the rays that He would have shine to the world.

Harshness or coldness shown by a disciple toward one whom Christ was drawing, — such an act as that of John in forbidding one to work miracles in Christ's name, — might result in turning the feet into the path of the enemy, and causing the loss of a soul. Rather than for one to do this, said Jesus, "It is better for him that a millstone were hanged about his neck, and he were cast into the sea." And He added, "If thy hand cause thee to stumble, cut it off: it is good for thee to enter into life maimed, rather than having thy two hands to go into hell, into the unquenchable fire. And if thy foot cause thee to stumble, cut it off: it is good for thee to enter into life halt, rather than having thy two feet to be cast into hell." Mark 9:43-45, R. V.

Why this earnest language, than which none can be stronger? — Because "the Son of man is come to save that which was lost." Shall His disciples show less regard for the souls of their fellow men than the Majesty of heaven has shown? Every soul has cost an infinite price, and how terrible is the sin of turning one soul away from Christ, so that for him the Saviour's love and humiliation and agony shall have been in vain.

"Woe unto the world because of occasions of stumbling! for it must needs be that the occasions come" Matthew 18:7, R. V. The world, inspired by Satan, will surely oppose the followers of Christ, and seek to destroy their faith; but woe to him who has taken Christ's name, and yet is found doing this work. Our Lord is put to shame by those who claim to serve Him, but who misrepresent His character; and multitudes are deceived, and led into false paths.

Any habit or practice that would lead into sin, and bring dishonor upon Christ, would better be put away, whatever the sacrifice. That which dishonors God cannot benefit the soul. The blessing of heaven cannot attend any man in violating the eternal principles of right. And one sin cherished is sufficient to work the degradation of the character, and to mislead others. If the foot or the hand would be cut off, or even the eye would be plucked out, to save the body from death, how much more earnest should we be to put away sin, that brings death to the soul.

In the ritual service, salt was added to every sacrifice. This, like the offering of incense, signified that only the righteousness of Christ could make the service acceptable to God. Referring to this practice, Jesus said, "Every sacrifice shall be salted with salt." "Have salt in yourselves, and have peace one with another." All who would present themselves "a living sacrifice, holy, acceptable unto God," (Romans 12:1.) must receive the saving salt, the righteousness of our Saviour. Then they become "the salt of the earth," (Matthew 5:13.) restraining evil among men, as salt preserves from corruption. But if the salt has lost its savor; if there is only a profession of godliness, without the love of Christ, there is no power for good. The life can exert no saving influence upon the world. Your energy and efficiency in the upbuilding of My kingdom, Jesus says, depend upon your receiving of My Spirit. You must be partakers of My grace, in order to be a savor of life unto life. Then there will be no rivalry, no self-seeking, no desire for the highest place. You will have that love which seeks not her own, but another's wealth.

Let the repenting sinner fix his eyes upon "the Lamb of God, which taketh away the sin of the world;" and by beholding, he becomes changed. His fear is turned to joy, his doubts to hope. Gratitude springs up. The stony heart is broken. A tide of love sweeps into the soul. Christ is in him a well of water springing up unto everlasting life. When we see Jesus, a Man of sorrows and acquainted with grief, working to save the lost, slighted, scorned, derided, driven from city to city till His mission was accomplished; when we behold Him in Gethsemane, sweating great drops of blood, and on the cross dying in agony, — when we see this, self will no longer clamor to be recognized. Looking unto Jesus, we shall be ashamed of our coldness, our lethargy, our self-seeking. We shall be willing to be anything or nothing, so that we may do heart service for the Master. We shall rejoice to bear the cross after Jesus, to endure trial, shame, or persecution for His dear sake.

"We then that are strong ought to bear the infirmities of the weak, and not to please ourselves." Romans 15:1. No soul who believes in Christ, though his faith may be weak, and his steps wavering as those of a little child, is to be lightly esteemed. By all that has given us advantage over another, — be it education and refinement, nobility of character, Christian training, religious experience, — we are in debt to those less favored; and, so far as lies in our power, we are to minister unto them. If we are strong, we are to stay up the hands of the weak. Angels of glory, that do always behold the face of the Father in heaven, joy in ministering to His little ones. Trembling souls, who have many objectionable traits of character, are their special charge. Angels are ever present where they are most needed, with those who have the hardest battle with self to fight, and whose surroundings are the most discouraging. And in this ministry Christ's true followers will cooperate.

If one of these little ones shall be overcome, and commit a wrong against you, then it is your work to seek his restoration. Do not wait for him to make the first effort for reconciliation. "How think ye?" said Jesus; "if a man have an hundred sheep, and one of them be gone astray, doth he not leave the ninety and nine, and goeth into the mountains, and seeketh that which is gone astray? And if so be that he find it, verily I say unto you, he rejoiceth more of that sheep, than of the ninety and nine which went not astray. Even so it is not the will of your Father which is in heaven that one of these little ones should perish."

In the spirit of meekness, "considering thyself, lest thou also be tempted," (Galations 6:1.) go to the erring one, and "tell him his fault between thee and him alone." Do not put him to shame by exposing his fault to others, nor bring dishonor upon Christ by making public the sin or error of one who bears His name. Often the truth must be plainly spoken to the erring; he must be led to see his error, that he may reform. But you are not to judge or to condemn. Make no attempt at self-justification. Let all your effort be for his recovery. In treating the wounds of the soul, there is need of the most delicate touch, the finest sensibility. Only the love that flows from the suffering One of Calvary can avail here. With pitying tenderness, let brother deal with brother, knowing that if you succeed, you will "save a soul from death," and "hide a multitude of sins." James 5:20.

But even this effort may be unavailing. Then, said Jesus, "take with thee one or two more." It may be that their united influence will prevail where that of the first was unsuccessful. Not being parties to the trouble, they will be more likely to act impartially, and this fact will give their counsel greater weight with the erring one.

If he will not hear them, then, and not till then, the matter is to be brought before the whole body of believers. Let the members of the church, as the representatives of Christ, unite in prayer and loving entreaty that the offender may be restored. The Holy Spirit will speak through His servants, pleading with the wanderer to return to God. Paul the apostle, speaking by inspiration, says, "As though God did beseech you by us, we pray you in Christ's stead, be ye reconciled to God." 2 Corinthians 5:20. He who rejects this united overture, has broken the tie that binds him to Christ, and thus has severed himself from the fellowship of the church. Henceforth, said Jesus, "let him be unto thee as an heathen man and a publican." But he is not to be regarded as cut off from the mercy of God. Let him not be despised or neglected by his former brethren, but be treated with tenderness and compassion, as one of the lost sheep that Christ is still seeking to bring to His fold.

Christ's instruction as to the treatment of the erring repeats in more specific form the teaching given to Israel through Moses: "Thou shalt not hate thy brother in thine heart; thou shalt in any wise rebuke thy neighbor, that thou bear not sin for him." Leviticus 19:17, margin. That is, if one neglects the duty Christ has enjoined, of trying to restore those who are in error and sin, he becomes a partaker in the sin. For evils that we might have checked, we are just as responsible as if we were guilty of the acts ourselves.

But it is to the wrongdoer himself that we are to present the wrong. We are not to make it a matter of comment and criticism among ourselves; nor even after it is told to the church, are we at liberty to repeat it to others. A knowledge of the faults of Christians will be only a cause of stumbling to the unbelieving world; and by dwelling upon these things, we ourselves can receive only harm; for it is by beholding that we become changed. While we seek to correct the errors of a brother, the Spirit of Christ will lead us to shield him, as far as possible, from the criticism of even his own brethren, and how much more from the censure of the unbelieving world. We ourselves are erring, and need Christ's pity and forgiveness, and just as we wish Him to deal with us, He bids us deal with one another.

"Whatsoever ye shall bind on earth shall be bound in heaven; and whatsoever ye shall loose on earth shall be loosed in heaven." You are acting as the ambassadors of heaven, and the issues of your work are for eternity.

But we are not to bear this great responsibility alone. Wherever His word is obeyed with a sincere heart, there Christ abides. Not only is He present in the assemblies of the church, but wherever disciples, however few, meet in His name, there also He will be. And He says, "If two of you shall agree on earth as touching anything that they shall ask, it shall be done for them of My Father which is in heaven."

Jesus says, "*My* Father which is in heaven," as reminding His disciples that while by His humanity He is linked with them, a sharer in their trials, and sympathizing with them in their sufferings, by His divinity He is connected with the throne of the Infinite. Wonderful assurance! The heavenly intelligences unite with men in sympathy and labor for the saving of that which was lost. And all the power of heaven is brought to combine with human ability in drawing souls to Christ.

At the
Feast of Tabernacles

Three times a year the Jews were required to assemble at Jerusalem for religious purposes. Enshrouded in the pillar of cloud, Israel's invisible Leader had given the directions in regard to these gatherings. During the captivity of the Jews, they could not be observed; but when the people were restored to their own land, the observance of these memorials was once more begun. It was God's design that these anniversaries should call Him to the minds of the people. But with few exceptions, the priests and leaders of the nation had lost sight of this purpose. He who had ordained these national assemblies and understood their significance, witnessed their perversion.

The Feast of Tabernacles was the closing gathering of the year. It was God's design that at this time the people should reflect on His goodness and mercy. The whole land had been under His guidance, receiving His blessing. Day and night His watchcare had continued. The sun and rain had caused the earth to produce her fruits. From the valleys and plains of Palestine the harvest had been gathered. The olive berries had been picked, and the precious oil stored in bottles. The palm had yielded her store. The purple clusters of the vine had been trodden in the wine press.

The feast continued for seven days, and for its celebration the inhabitants of Palestine, with many from other lands, left their homes, and came to Jerusalem. From far and near the people came, bringing in their hands a token of rejoicing. Old and young, rich and poor, all brought some gift as a tribute of thanksgiving to Him who had crowned the year with His goodness, and made His paths drop fatness. Everything that could please the eye, and give expression to the universal joy, was brought from the woods; the city bore the appearance of a beautiful forest.

This feast was not only the harvest thanksgiving, but the memorial of God's protecting care over Israel in the wilderness. In commemoration of their tent life, the Israelites during the feast dwelt in booths or tabernacles of green boughs. These were erected in the streets, in the courts of the temple, or on the housetops. The hills and valleys surrounding Jerusalem were also dotted with these leafy dwellings, and seemed to be alive with people.

With sacred song and thanksgiving the worshipers celebrated this occasion. A little before the feast was the day of atonement, when, after confession of their sins, the people were declared to be at peace with Heaven. Thus the way was prepared for the rejoicing of the feast. "O give thanks unto the Lord; for He is good; for His mercy endureth forever," (Psalms 106:1) rose triumphantly, while all kinds of music, mingled with shouts of hosanna, accompanied the united singing. The temple was the center of the universal joy. Here was the pomp of the sacrificial ceremonies. Here, ranged on either side of the white marble steps of the sacred building, the choir of Levites led the service of song. The multitude of worshipers, waving their branches of palm and myrtle, took up the strain, and echoed the chorus; and again the melody was caught up by voices near and afar off, till the encircling hills were vocal with praise.

At night the temple and its court blazed with artificial light. The music, the waving of palm branches, the glad hosannas, the great concourse of people, over whom the light streamed from the hanging lamps, the array of the priests, and the majesty of the ceremonies, combined to make a scene that deeply impressed the beholders. But the most impressive ceremony of the feast, one that called

This chapter is based on John 7:1-15,37-39.

forth greatest rejoicing, was one commemorating an event in the wilderness sojourn.

At the first dawn of day, the priests sounded a long, shrill blast upon their silver trumpets, and the answering trumpets, and the glad shouts of the people from their booths, echoing over hill and valley, welcomed the festal day. Then the priest dipped from the flowing waters of the Kedron a flagon of water, and, lifting it on high, while the trumpets were sounding, he ascended the broad steps of the temple, keeping time with the music with slow and measured tread, chanting meanwhile, "Our feet shall stand within thy gates, O Jerusalem." Psalms 122:2.

He bore the flagon to the altar, which occupied a central position in the court of the priests. Here were two silver basins, with a priest standing at each one. The flagon of water was poured into one, and a flagon of wine into the other; and the contents of both flowed into a pipe which communicated with the Kedron, and was conducted to the Dead Sea. This display of the consecrated water represented the fountain that at the command of God had gushed from the rock to quench the thirst of the children of Israel. Then the jubilant strains rang forth, "The Lord Jehovah is my strength and my song;" "therefore with joy shall ye draw water out of the wells of salvation." Isaiah 12:2, 3.

As the sons of Joseph made preparation to attend the Feast of Tabernacles, they saw that Christ made no movement signifying His intention of attending. They watched Him with anxiety. Since the healing at Bethesda He had not attended the national gatherings. To avoid useless conflict with the leaders at Jerusalem, He had restricted His labors to Galilee. His apparent neglect of the great religious assemblies, and the enmity manifested toward Him by the priests and rabbis, were a cause of perplexity to the people about Him, and even to His own disciples and His kindred. In His teachings He had dwelt upon the blessings of obedience to the law of God, and yet He Himself seemed to be indifferent to the service which had been divinely established. His mingling with publicans and others of ill repute, His disregard of the rabbinical observances, and the freedom with which He set aside the traditional requirements concerning the Sabbath, all seeming to place Him in antagonism to the religious authorities, excited much questioning. His brothers thought it a mistake for Him to alienate the great and learned men of the nation. They felt that these men must be in the right, and that Jesus was at fault in placing Himself in antagonism to them. But they had witnessed His blameless life, and though they did not rank themselves with His disciples, they had been deeply impressed by His works. His popularity in Galilee was gratifying to their ambition; they still hoped that He would give an evidence of His power which would lead the Pharisees to see that He was what He claimed to be. What if He were the Messiah, the Prince of Israel! They cherished this thought with proud satisfaction.

So anxious were they about this, that they urged Christ to go to Jerusalem. "Depart hence," they said, "and go into Judea, that Thy disciples also may see the works that Thou doest. For there is no man that doeth anything in secret, and he himself seeketh to be known openly. If Thou do these things, show Thyself to the world." The "if" expressed doubt and unbelief. They attributed cowardice and weakness to Him. If He knew that He was the Messiah,

---

"Jesus knew the wants of the soul. Pomp, riches, and honor cannot satisfy the heart. 'If any man thirst, let him come unto Me.' . . . He promises to relieve the burdened mind, to comfort the sorrowing, and to give hope to the despondent. . . . The cry of Christ to the thirsty soul is still going forth, and it appeals to us with even greater power . . . The fountain is open for all."

---

why this strange reserve and inaction? If He really possessed such power, why not go boldly to Jerusalem, and assert His claims? Why not perform in Jerusalem the wonderful works reported of Him in Galilee? Do not hide in secluded provinces, they said, and perform your mighty works for the benefit of ignorant peasants and fishermen. Present yourself at the capital, win the support of the priests and rulers, and unite the nation in establishing the new kingdom.

These brothers of Jesus reasoned from the selfish motive so often found in the hearts of those ambitious for display. This spirit was the ruling spirit of the world. They were offended because, instead of seeking a temporal throne, Christ had declared Himself to be the Bread of Life. They were greatly disappointed when so many of His disciples forsook Him. They themselves turned from Him to escape the cross of acknowledging what His works revealed — that He was the Sent of God.

"Then Jesus said unto them, My time is not yet come: but your time is alway ready. The world cannot hate you; but Me it hateth, because I testify of it, that the works thereof are evil. Go ye up unto this feast: I go not up yet unto this feast; for My time is not yet full come. When He had said these words unto them, He abode still in Galilee." His brothers had spoken to Him in a tone of authority, prescribing the course He should pursue. He cast their rebuke back to them, classing them not with His self-denying disciples, but with the world. "The world cannot hate you," He said, "but Me it hateth, because I testify of it, that the works thereof are evil." The world does not hate those who are like it in spirit; it loves them as its own.

The world for Christ was not a place of ease and self-aggrandizement. He was not watching for an opportunity to seize its power and its glory. It held out no such prize for Him. It was the place into which His Father had sent Him. He had been given for the life of the world, to work out the great plan of redemption. He was accomplishing His work for the fallen race. But He was not to be presumptuous, not to rush into danger, not to hasten a crisis. Each event in His work had its appointed hour. He must wait patiently. He knew that He was to receive the world's hatred; He knew that His work would result in His death; but to prematurely expose Himself would not be the will of His Father.

From Jerusalem the report of Christ's miracles had spread wherever the Jews were dispersed; and although for many months He had been absent from the feasts, the interest in Him had not abated. Many from all parts of the world had come up to the Feast of Tabernacles in the hope of seeing Him. At the beginning of the feast many inquiries were made for Him. The Pharisees and rulers looked for Him to come, hoping for an opportunity to condemn Him. They anxiously inquired, "Where is He?" but no one knew. The thought of Him was uppermost in all minds. Through fear of the priests and rulers, none dared acknowledge Him as the Messiah, but everywhere there was quiet yet earnest discussion concerning Him. Many defended Him as one sent from God, while others denounced him as a deceiver of the people.

Meanwhile Jesus had quietly arrived at Jerusalem. He had chosen an unfrequented route by which to go, in order to avoid the travelers who were making their way to the city from all quarters. Had He joined any of the caravans that went up to the feast, public attention would have been attracted to Him on His entrance into the city, and a popular demonstration in His favor would have aroused the authorities against Him. It was to avoid this that He chose to make the journey alone.

In the midst of the feast, when the excitement concerning Him was at its height, He entered the court of the temple in the presence of the multitude. Because of His absence from the feast, it had been urged that He dared not place Himself in the power of the priests and rulers. All were surprised at His presence. Every voice was hushed. All wondered at the dignity and courage of His bearing in the midst of powerful enemies who were thirsting for His life.

Standing thus, the center of attraction to that vast throng, Jesus addressed them as no man had ever done. His words showed a knowledge of the laws and institutions of Israel, of the sacrificial service and the teachings of the prophets, far exceeding that of the priests and rabbis. He broke through the barriers of formalism and tradition. The scenes of the future life seemed outspread before Him. As one who beheld the Unseen, He spoke of the earthly and the heavenly, the human and the divine, with positive authority. His words were most clear and convincing; and again, as at Capernaum, the people were astonished at His teaching; "for His word was with power." Luke 4:32. Under a variety of representations He warned His hearers of the calamity that would follow all who rejected the blessings He came to bring them. He had given them every possible proof that He came forth from God, and made every possible effort to bring them to repentance. He would not be rejected and murdered by His own nation if He could save them from the guilt of such a deed.

All wondered at His knowledge of the law and the prophecies; and the question passed from one to another, "How knoweth this man letters, having never learned?" No one was regarded as qualified to be a religious teacher unless he had studied in the rabbinical schools, and both Jesus and John the Baptist had been represented as ignorant because they had not received this training. Those who heard them were astonished at their knowledge of the Scriptures, "having never learned." Of men they had not, truly; but the God of heaven was their teacher, and from Him they had received the highest kind of wisdom.

As Jesus spoke in the temple court, the people were held spellbound. The very men who were the most violent against Him felt themselves powerless to do Him harm. For the time, all other interests were forgotten.

Day after day He taught the people, until the last, "that great day of the feast." The morning of this day found the people wearied from the long season of festivity. Suddenly Jesus lifted up His voice, in tones that rang through the courts of the temple: —

"If any man thirst, let him come unto Me, and drink. He that believeth on Me, as the Scripture hath said, out of his belly shall flow rivers of living water." The condition of the people made this appeal very forcible. They had been engaged in a continued scene of pomp and festivity, their eyes had been dazzled with light and color, and their ears regaled with the richest music; but there had been nothing in all this round of ceremonies to meet the wants of the spirit, nothing to satisfy the thirst of the soul for that which perishes not. Jesus invited them to come and drink of the fountain of life, of that which would be in them a well of water, springing up unto everlasting life.

The priest had that morning performed the ceremony which commemorated the smiting of the rock in the wilderness. That rock was a symbol of Him who by His death would cause living streams of salvation to flow to all who are athirst. Christ's words were the water of life. There in the presence of the assembled multitude He set Himself apart to be smitten, that the water of life might flow to the world. In smiting Christ, Satan thought to destroy the Prince of life; but from the smitten rock there flowed living water. As Jesus thus spoke to the people, their hearts thrilled with a strange awe, and many were ready to exclaim, with the woman of Samaria, "Give me of this water, that I thirst not."

Jesus knew the wants of the soul. Pomp, riches, and honor cannot satisfy the heart. "If any man thirst, let him come unto Me." The rich, the poor, the high, the low, are alike welcome. He promises to relieve the burdened mind, to comfort the sorrowing, and to give hope to the despondent. Many of those who heard Jesus were mourners over disappointed hopes, many were nourishing a secret grief, many were seeking to satisfy their restless longing with the things of the world and the praise of men; but when all was gained, they found that they had toiled only to reach a broken cistern, from which they could not quench their thirst. Amid the glitter of the joyous scene they stood, dissatisfied and sad. That sudden cry, "If any man thirst," startled them from their sorrowful meditation, and as they listened to the words that followed, their minds kindled with a new hope. The Holy Spirit presented the symbol before them until they saw in it the offer of the priceless gift of salvation.

The cry of Christ to the thirsty soul is still going forth, and it appeals to us with even greater power than to those who heard it in the temple on that last day of the feast. The fountain is open for all. The weary and exhausted ones are offered the refreshing draught of eternal life. Jesus is still crying, "If any man thirst, let him come unto Me, and drink." "Let him that is athirst come. And whosoever will, let him take of the water of life freely." "Whosoever drinketh of the water that I shall give him, shall never thirst; but the water that I shall give him shall be in him a well of water, springing up into everlasting life." Revelation 22:17; John 4:14.

Among Snares

All the while Jesus was at Jerusalem during the feast He was shadowed by spies. Day after day new schemes to silence Him were tried. The priests and rulers were watching to entrap Him. They were planning to stop Him by violence. But this was not all. They wanted to humble this Galilean Rabbi before the people.

On the first day of His presence at the feast, the rulers had come to Him, demanding by what authority He taught. They wished to divert attention from Him to the question of His right to teach, and thus to their own importance and authority.

"My teaching is not Mine," said Jesus, "but His that sent Me. If any man willeth to do His will, he shall know of the teaching, whether it be of God, or whether I speak from Myself." John 7:16, 17, R. V. The question of these cavilers Jesus met, not by answering the cavil, but by opening up truth vital to the salvation of the soul. The perception and appreciation of truth, He said, depends less upon the mind than upon the heart. Truth must be received into the soul; it claims the homage of the will. If truth could be submitted to the reason alone, pride would be no hindrance in the way of its reception. But it is to be received through the work of grace in the heart; and its reception depends upon the renunciation of every sin that the Spirit of God reveals. Man's advantages for obtaining a knowledge of the truth, however great these may be, will prove of no benefit to him unless the heart is open to receive the truth, and there is a conscientious surrender of every habit and practice that is opposed to its principles. To those who thus yield themselves to God, having an honest desire to know and to do His will, the truth is revealed as the power of God for their salvation. These will be able to distinguish between him who speaks for God, and him who speaks merely from himself. The Pharisees had not put their will on the side of God's will. They were not seeking to know the truth, but to find some excuse for evading it; Christ showed that this was why they did not understand His teaching.

He now gave a test by which the true teacher might be distinguished from the deceiver: "He that speaketh from himself, seeketh his own glory, but he that seeketh the glory of Him that sent him, the same is true, and no unrighteousness is in him." John 7:18, R. V. He that seeketh his own glory is speaking only from himself. The spirit of self-seeking betrays its origin. But Christ was seeking the glory of God. He spoke the words of God. This was the evidence of His authority as a teacher of the truth.

Jesus gave the rabbis an evidence of His divinity by showing that He read their hearts. Ever since the healing at Bethesda they had been plotting His death. Thus they were themselves breaking the law which they professed to be defending. "Did not Moses give you the law," He said, "and yet none of you keepeth the law? Why do ye about to kill Me?"

Like a swift flash of light these words revealed to the rabbis the pit of ruin into which they were about to plunge. For an instant they were filled with terror. They saw that they were in conflict with infinite power. But they would not be warned. In order to maintain their influence with the people, their murderous designs must be concealed. Evading the question of Jesus, they exclaimed, "Thou hast a devil; who goeth about to kill Thee?" They insinuated that the wonderful words of Jesus were instigated by an evil spirit.

To this insinuation Christ gave no heed. He went on to show that His work of healing at Bethesda was in harmony

This chapter is based on John 7:16-36, 40-53; 8:11-11.

with the Sabbath law, and that it was justified by the interpretation which the Jews themselves put upon the law. He said, "Moses therefore gave unto you circumcision; ... and ye on the Sabbath day circumcise a man." According to the law, every child must be circumcised on the eighth day. Should the appointed time fall upon the Sabbath, the rite must then be performed. How much more must it be in harmony with the spirit of the law to make a man "every whit whole on the Sabbath day." And He warned them to "judge not according to the appearance, but judge righteous judgment."

The rulers were silenced; and many of the people exclaimed, "Is not this He whom they seek to kill? But lo, He speaketh boldly, and they say nothing unto Him. Do the rulers know indeed that this is the very Christ?"

Many among Christ's hearers who were dwellers at Jerusalem, and who were not ignorant of the plots of the rulers against Him, felt themselves drawn to Him by an irresistible power. The conviction pressed upon them that He was the Son of God. But Satan was ready to suggest doubt; and for this the way was prepared by their own erroneous ideas of the Messiah and His coming. It was generally believed that Christ would be born at Bethlehem, but that after a time He would disappear, and at His second appearance none would know whence He came. There were not a few who held that the Messiah would have no natural relationship to humanity. And because the popular conception of the glory of the Messiah was not met by Jesus of Nazareth, many gave heed to the suggestion, "Howbeit, we know this man whence he is; but when Christ cometh, no man knoweth whence He is."

While they were thus wavering between doubt and faith, Jesus took up their thoughts and answered them: "Ye both know Me, and ye know whence I am; and I am not come of Myself, but He that sent Me is true, whom ye know not." They claimed a knowledge of what the origin of Christ should be, but they were in utter ignorance of it. If they had lived in accordance with the will of God, they would have known His Son when He was manifested to them.

The hearers could not but understand Christ's words. Clearly they were a repetition of the claim He had made in the presence of the Sanhedrim many months before, when He declared Himself the Son of God. As the rulers then tried to compass His death, so now they sought to take Him; but they were prevented by an unseen power, which put a limit to their rage, saying to them, Thus far shalt thou go, and no farther.

Among the people many believed on Him, and they said, "When Christ cometh, will He do more miracles than these which this man hath done?" The leaders of the Pharisees, who were anxiously watching the course of events, caught the expressions of sympathy among the throng. Hurrying away to the chief priests, they laid their plans to arrest Him. They arranged, however, to take Him when He was alone; for they dared not seize Him in the presence of the people. Again Jesus made it manifest that He read their purpose.

"Yet a little while am I with you," He said, "and then I go unto Him that sent Me. Ye shall seek Me, and shall not find Me; and where I am, thither ye cannot come." Soon He would find a refuge beyond the reach of their scorn and hate. He would ascend to the Father, to be again the Adored of the angels; and thither His murderers could never come.

Sneeringly the rabbis said, "Whither will He go, that we shall not find Him? Will He go unto the dispersed among the Gentiles, and teach the Gentiles?" Little did these cavilers dream that in their mocking words they were picturing the mission of the Christ! All day long He had stretched forth His hands unto a disobedient and gainsaying people; yet He would be found of them that sought Him not; among a people that had not called upon His name He would be manifest. Romans 10:20, 21.

Many who were convinced that Jesus was the Son of God were misled by the false reasoning of the priests and rabbis. These teachers had repeated with great effect the prophecies concerning the Messiah, that He would "reign in Mount Zion, and in Jerusalem, and before His ancients gloriously;" that He would "have dominion also from sea to sea, and from the river unto the ends of the earth." Isaiah 24:23; Psalms 72:8. Then they made contemptuous comparisons between the glory here pictured and the humble appearance of Jesus. The very words of prophecy were so perverted as to sanction error. Had the people in sincerity studied the word for themselves, they would not have been misled. The sixty-first chapter of Isaiah testifies that Christ was to do the very work He did. Chapter fifty-three sets forth His rejection and sufferings in the world, and chapter fifty-nine describes the character of the priests and rabbis.

God does not compel men to give up their unbelief. Before them are light and darkness, truth and error. It is for them to decide which they will accept. The human mind is endowed with power to discriminate between right and wrong. God designs that men shall not decide from impulse, but from weight of evidence, carefully comparing scripture with scripture. Had the Jews laid by their prejudice and compared written prophecy with the facts characterizing the life of Jesus, they would have perceived a beautiful harmony between the prophecies and their fulfillment in the life and ministry of the lowly Galilean.

Many are deceived today in the same way as were the Jews. Religious teachers read the Bible in the light of their own understanding and traditions; and the people do not search the Scriptures for themselves, and judge for themselves as to what is truth; but they yield up their judgment, and commit their souls to their leaders. The preaching and teaching of His word is one of the means that God has ordained for diffusing light; but we must bring every man's teaching to the test of Scripture. Whoever will prayerfully study the Bible, desiring to know the truth, that he may obey it, will receive divine enlightenment. He will understand the Scriptures. "If any man willeth to do His will, he shall know of the teaching." John 7:17, R. V.

On the last day of the feast, the officers sent out by the priests and rulers to arrest Jesus, returned without Him. They were angrily questioned, "Why have ye not brought Him?" With solemn countenance they answered, "Never man spake like this man."

Hardened as were their hearts, they were melted by His words. While He was speaking in the temple court, they had lingered near, to catch something that might be turned

> **"Jesus looked for a moment upon the scene,—the trembling victim in her shame, the hard-faced dignitaries, devoid of even human pity. His spirit of stainless purity shrank from the spectacle. Well He knew for what purpose this case had been brought to Him. . . . Giving no sign that He had heard their question, He stooped, and fixing His eyes upon the ground, began to write in the dust."**

against Him. But as they listened, the purpose for which they had been sent was forgotten. They stood as men entranced. Christ revealed Himself to their souls. They saw that which priests and rulers would not see,—humanity flooded with the glory of divinity. They returned, so filled with this thought, so impressed by His words, that to the inquiry, "Why have ye not brought Him?" they could only reply, "Never man spake like this man."

The priests and rulers, on first coming into the presence of Christ, had felt the same conviction. Their hearts were deeply moved, and the thought was forced upon them, "Never man spake like this man." But they had stifled the conviction of the Holy Spirit. Now, enraged that even the instruments of the law should be influenced by the hated Galilean, they cried, "Are ye also deceived? Have any of the rulers or of the Pharisees believed on Him? But this people who knoweth not the law are cursed."

Those to whom the message of truth is spoken, seldom ask, "Is it true?" but, "By whom is it advocated?" Multitudes estimate it by the numbers who accept it; and the question is still asked, "Have any of the learned men or religious leaders believed?" Men are no more favorable to real godliness now than in the days of Christ. They are just as intently seeking earthly good, to the neglect of the eternal riches; and it is not an argument against the truth, that large numbers are not ready to accept it, or that it is not received by the world's great men, or even by the religious leaders.

Again the priests and rulers proceeded to lay plans for arresting Jesus. It was urged that if He were longer left at liberty, He would draw the people away from the established leaders, and the only safe course was to silence Him without delay. In the full tide of their discussion, they were suddenly checked. Nicodemus questioned, "Doth our law judge any man, before it hear him, and know what he doeth?" Silence fell on the assembly. The words of Nicodemus came home to their consciences. They could not condemn a man unheard. But it was not for this reason alone that the haughty rulers remained silent, gazing at him who had dared to speak in favor of justice. They were startled and chagrined that one of their own number had been so far impressed by the character of Jesus as to speak a word in His defense. Recovering from their astonishment, they addressed Nicodemus with cutting sarcasm, "Art thou also of Galilee? Search and look: for out of Galilee ariseth no prophet."

Yet the protest resulted in staying the proceedings of the council. The rulers were unable to carry out their purpose and condemn Jesus without a hearing. Defeated for the time, "every man went unto his own house. Jesus went unto the Mount of Olives."

From the excitement and confusion of the city, from the eager crowds and the treacherous rabbis, Jesus turned away to the quiet of the olive groves, where He could be alone with God. But in the early morning He returned to the temple, and as the people gathered about Him, He sat down and taught them.

He was soon interrupted. A group of Pharisees and scribes approached Him, dragging with them a terror-stricken woman, whom with hard, eager voices they accused of having violated the seventh commandment. Having pushed her into the presence of Jesus, they said to Him, with a hypocritical show of respect, "Moses in the law commanded us, that such should be stoned; but what sayest Thou?"

Their pretended reverence veiled a deep-laid plot for His ruin. They had seized upon this opportunity to secure His condemnation, thinking that whatever decision He might make, they would find occasion to accuse Him. Should He acquit the woman, He might be charged with despising the law of Moses. Should He declare her worthy of death, He could be accused to the Romans as one who was assuming authority that belonged only to them.

Jesus looked for a moment upon the scene,—the trembling victim in her shame, the hard-faced dignitaries, devoid of even human pity. His spirit of stainless purity shrunk from the spectacle. Well He knew for what purpose this case had been brought to Him. He read the heart, and knew the character and life history of every one in His presence. These would-be guardians of justice had themselves led their victim into sin, that they might lay a snare for Jesus. Giving no sign that He had heard their question, He stooped, and fixing His eyes upon the ground, began to write in the dust.

Impatient at His delay and apparent indifference, the accusers drew nearer, urging the matter upon His attention. But as their eyes, following those of Jesus, fell upon the pavement at His feet, their countenances changed. There, traced before them, were the guilty secrets of their own lives. The people, looking on, saw the sudden change of expression, and pressed forward to discover what it was that they were regarding with such astonishment and shame.

With all their professions of reverence for the law, these rabbis, in bringing the charge against the woman, were disregarding its provisions. It was the husband's duty to take action against her, and the guilty parties were to be punished equally. The action of the accusers was wholly unauthorized. Jesus, however, met them on their own ground. The law specified that in punishment by stoning, the witnesses in the case should be the first to cast a stone. Now rising, and fixing His eyes upon the plotting elders, Jesus said, "He that is without sin among you, let him first cast a stone at her." And stooping down, He continued writing on the ground.

He had not set aside the law given through Moses, not infringed upon the authority of Rome. The accusers had been defeated. Now, their robe of pretended holiness torn from them, they stood, guilty and condemned, in the presence of infinite purity. They trembled lest the hidden iniquity of their lives should be laid open to the multitude; and one by one, with bowed heads and downcast eyes, they stole away, leaving their victim with the pitying Saviour.

Jesus arose, and looking at the woman said, "Woman, where are those thine accusers? hath no man condemned thee? She said, No man, Lord. And Jesus said unto her, Neither do I condemn thee. Go, and sin no more."

The woman had stood before Jesus, cowering with fear. His words, "He that is without sin among you, let him first cast a stone," had come to her as a death sentence. She dared not lift her eyes to the Saviour's face, but silently awaited her doom. In astonishment she saw her accusers depart speechless and confounded; then those words of hope fell upon her ear, "Neither do I condemn thee. Go, and sin no more." Her heart was melted, and she cast herself at the feet of Jesus, sobbing out her grateful love, and with bitter tears confessing her sins.

This was to her the beginning of a new life, a life of purity and peace, devoted to the service of God. In the uplifting of this fallen soul, Jesus performed a greater miracle than in healing the most grievous physical disease; He cured the spiritual malady which is unto death everlasting. This penitent woman became one of His most steadfast followers. With self-sacrificing love and devotion she repaid His forgiving mercy.

In His act of pardoning this woman and encouraging her to live a better life, the character of Jesus shines forth in the beauty of perfect righteousness. While He does not palliate sin, nor lessen the sense of guilt, He seeks not to condemn, but to save. The world had for this erring woman only contempt and scorn; but Jesus speaks words of comfort and hope. The Sinless One pities the weakness of the sinner, and reaches to her a helping hand. While the hypocritical Pharisees denounce, Jesus bids her, "Go, and sin no more."

It is not Christ's follower that, with averted eyes, turns from the erring, leaving them unhindered to pursue their downward course. Those who are forward in accusing others, and zealous in bringing them to justice, are often in their own lives more guilty than they. Men hate the sinner, while they love the sin. Christ hates the sin, but loves the sinner. This will be the spirit of all who follow Him. Christian love is slow to censure, quick to discern penitence, ready to forgive, to encourage, to set the wanderer in the path of holiness, and to stay his feet therein.

"The Light of Life"

hen spake Jesus again unto them, saying, I am the light of the world; he that followeth Me shall not walk in darkness, but shall have the light of life."

When He spoke these words, Jesus was in the court of the temple specially connected with the services of the Feast of Tabernacles. In the center of this court rose two lofty standards, supporting lampstands of great size. After the evening sacrifice, all the lamps were kindled, shedding their light over Jerusalem. This ceremony was in commemoration of the pillar of light that guided Israel in the desert, and was also regarded as pointing to the coming of the Messiah. At evening when the lamps were lighted, the court was a scene of great rejoicing. Gray-haired men, the priests of the temple and the rulers of the people, united in the festive dances to the sound of instrumental music and the chants of the Levites.

In the illumination of Jerusalem, the people expressed their hope of the Messiah's coming to shed His light upon Israel. But to Jesus the scene had a wider meaning. As the radiant lamps of the temple lighted up all about them, so Christ, the source of spiritual light, illumines the darkness of the world. Yet the symbol was imperfect. That great light which His own hand had set in the heavens was a truer representation of the glory of His mission.

It was morning; the sun had just risen above the Mount of Olives, and its rays fell with dazzling brightness on the marble palaces, and lighted up the gold of the temple walls, when Jesus, pointing to it, said, "I am the Light of the world."

By one who listened to these words, they were long afterward re-echoed in that sublime passage, "In Him was life; and the life was the light of men. And the light shineth in the darkness; and the darkness apprehended it not."

"That was the true light, which lighteth every man that cometh into the world. " John 1:4, 5. R. V., 9. And long after Jesus had ascended to heaven, Peter also, writing under the illumination of the divine Spirit, recalled the symbol Christ had used: "We have also a more sure word of prophecy; whereunto ye do well that ye take heed (as unto a light that shineth in a dark place, until the day dawn, and the day star arise) in your hearts." 2 Peter 1:19.

In the manifestation of God to His people, light had ever been a symbol of His presence. At the creative word in the beginning, light had shone out of darkness. Light had been enshrouded in the pillar of cloud by day and the pillar of fire by night, leading the vast armies of Israel. Light blazed with awful grandeur about the Lord on Mount Sinai. Light rested over the mercy seat in the tabernacle. Light filled the temple of Solomon at its dedication. Light shone on the hills of Bethlehem when the angels brought the message of redemption to the watching shepherds.

God is light; and in the words, "I am the Light of the world," Christ declared His oneness with God, and His relation to the whole human family. It was He who at the beginning had caused "the light to shine out of darkness." 2 Corinthians 4:6. He is the light of sun and moon and star. He was the spiritual light that in symbol and type and prophecy had shone upon Israel. But not to the Jewish nation alone was the light given. As the sunbeams penetrate to the remotest corners of the earth, so does the light of the Sun of Righteousness shine upon every soul.

"That was the true light, which lighteth every man that cometh into the world." The world has had its great teachers, men of giant intellect and wonderful research, men whose utterances have stimulated thought, and opened to view vast fields of knowledge; and these men

This chapter is based on John 8:12-59; 9.   (463-464)

have been honored as guides and benefactors of their race. But there is One who stands higher than they. "As many as received Him, to them gave He power to become the sons of God." "No man hath seen God at any time; the only-begotten Son, which is in the bosom of the Father, He hath declared Him." John 1:12, 18. We can trace the line of the world's great teachers as far back as human records extend; but the Light was before them. As the moon and the stars of the solar system shine by the reflected light of the sun, so, as far as their teaching is true, do the world's great thinkers reflect the rays of the Sun of Righteousness. Every gem of thought, every flash of the intellect, is from the Light of the world. In these days we hear much about "higher education." The true "higher education" is that imparted by Him "in whom are hid all the treasures of wisdom and knowledge." "In Him was life, and the life was the light of men." Colossians 2:3; John 1:4. "He that followeth Me," said Jesus, "shall not walk in darkness, but shall have the light of life."

In the words, "I am the Light of the world," Jesus declared Himself the Messiah. The aged Simeon, in the temple where Christ was now teaching, had spoken of Him as "a light to lighten the Gentiles, and the glory of Thy people Israel." Luke 2:32. In these words he was applying to Him a prophecy familiar to all Israel. By the prophet Isaiah, the Holy Spirit had declared, "It is too light a thing that Thou shouldst be My servant to raise up the tribes of Jacob, and to restore the preserved of Israel; I will also give Thee for a light to the Gentiles, that Thou mayest be My salvation unto the end of the earth." Isaiah 49:6, R. V. This prophecy was generally understood as spoken of the Messiah, and when Jesus said, "I am the Light of the world," the people could not fail to recognize His claim to be the Promised One.

To the Pharisees and rulers this claim seemed an arrogant assumption. That a man like themselves should make such pretensions they could not tolerate. Seeming to ignore His words, they demanded, "Who art Thou?" They were bent upon forcing Him to declare Himself the Christ. His appearance and His work were so at variance with the expectations of the people, that, as His wily enemies believed, a direct announcement of Himself as the Messiah would cause Him to be rejected as an impostor.

But to their question, "Who art Thou?" Jesus replied, "Even that which I have also spoken unto you from the beginning." John 8:25, R. V. That which had been revealed in His words, was revealed also in His character. He was the embodiment of the truths He taught. "I do nothing of Myself," He continued; "but as My Father hath taught Me, I speak these things. And He that sent Me is with Me; the Father hath not left Me alone; for I do always those things that please Him." He did not attempt to prove His Messianic claim, but showed His unity with God. If their minds had been open to God's love, they would have received Jesus.

Among His hearers many were drawn to Him in faith, and to them He said, "if ye continue in My words, then are ye My disciples indeed; and ye shall know the truth, and the truth shall make you free."

These words offended the Pharisees. The nation's long subjection to a foreign yoke, they disregarded, and angrily exclaimed, "We be Abraham's seed, and were never in bondage to any man; how sayest Thou, Ye shall be made

---

❝The world has had its great teachers, men of giant intellect and wonderful research, men whose utterances have stimulated thought, . . . and these men have been honored as guides and benefactors of their race. But there is One who stands higher than they.❞

---

free?" Jesus looked upon these men, the slaves of malice, whose thoughts were bent upon revenge, and sadly answered, "Verily, verily, I say unto you, Whosoever committeth sin is the servant of sin." They were in the worst kind of bondage,—ruled by the spirit of evil.

Every soul that refuses to give himself to God, is under the control of another power. He is not his own. He may talk of freedom, but he is in the most abject slavery. He is not allowed to see the beauty of truth, for his mind is under the control of Satan. While he flatters himself that he is following the dictates of his own judgment, he obeys the will of the prince of darkness. Christ came to break the shackles of sin-slavery from the soul. "If the Son therefore shall make you free, ye shall be free indeed." "The law of the Spirit of life in Christ Jesus" sets us "free from the law of sin and death." Romans 8:2.

In the work of redemption there is no compulsion. No external force is employed. Under the influence of the Spirit of God, man is left free to choose whom he will serve. In the change that takes place when the soul surrenders to Christ, there is the highest sense of freedom. The expulsion of sin is the act of the soul itself. True, we have no power to free ourselves from Satan's control; but when we desire to be set free from sin, and in our great need cry out for a power out of and above ourselves, the powers of the soul are imbued with the divine energy of the Holy Spirit, and they obey the dictates of the will in fulfilling the will of God.

The only condition upon which the freedom of man is possible, is that of becoming one with Christ. "The truth shall make you free;" and Christ is the truth. Sin can triumph only by enfeebling the mind, and destroying the liberty of the soul. Subjection to God is restoration to one's self, — to the true glory and dignity of man. The divine law, to which we are brought into subjection, is "the law of liberty." James 2:12.

The Pharisees had declared themselves the children of Abraham. Jesus told them that this claim could be established only by doing the works of Abraham. The true children of Abraham would live, as he did, a life of obedience to God. They would not try to kill One who was speaking the truth that was given Him from God. In plotting against Christ, the rabbis were not doing the works of Abraham. A mere lineal descent from Abraham was of no value. Without a spiritual connection with him, which would be manifested in possessing the same spirit, and doing the same works, they were not his children.

This principle bears with equal weight upon a question that has long agitated the Christian world, — the question of apostolic succession. Descent from Abraham was proved, not by name and lineage, but by likeness of character. So the apostolic succession rests not upon the transmission of ecclesiastical authority, but upon spiritual relationship. A life actuated by the apostles' spirit, the belief and teaching of the truth they taught, this is the true evidence of apostolic succession. This is what constitutes men the successors of the first teachers of the gospel.

Jesus denied that the Jews were children of Abraham. He said, "Ye do the deeds of your father." In mockery they answered, "*We* be not born of fornication; we have one Father, even God." These words, in allusion to the circumstances of His birth, were intended as a thrust against Christ in the presence of those who were beginning to believe on Him. Jesus gave no heed to the base insinuation, but said, "If God were your Father, ye would love Me; for I proceeded forth and came from God."

Their works testified of their relationship to him who was a liar and a murderer. "Ye are of your father the devil," said Jesus, "and the lusts of your father it is your will to do. He was a murderer from the beginning, and stood not in the truth, because there is no truth in him. . . . Because I say the truth, ye believe Me not." The fact that Jesus spoke the truth, and that with certainty, was why He was not received by the Jewish leaders. It was the truth that offended these self-righteous men. The truth exposed the fallacy of error; it condemned their teaching and practice, and it was unwelcome. They would rather close their eyes to the truth than humble themselves to confess that they had been in error. They did not love the truth. They did not desire it, even though it was truth.

"Which of you convicteth (R. V.) Me of sin? And if I say the truth, why do ye not believe Me?" Day by day for three years His enemies had been following Christ, trying to find some stain in His character. Satan and all the confederacy of evil had been seeking to overcome Him; but they had found nothing in Him by which to gain an advantage. Even the devils were forced to confess, "Thou art the Holy One of God." Mark 1:24. Jesus lived the law in the sight of heaven, in the sight of unfallen worlds, and in the sight of sinful men. Before angels, men, and demons, He had spoken, unchallenged, words that from any other lips would have been blasphemy: "I do always those things that please Him."

The fact that although they could find no sin in Christ, the Jews would not receive Him, proved that they themselves had no connection with God. They did not recognize His voice in the message of His Son. They thought themselves passing judgment on Christ; but in rejecting Him they were pronouncing sentence upon themselves. "He that is of God," said Jesus, "heareth God's words; ye therefore hear them not, because ye are not of God."

The lesson is true for all time. Many a man who delights to quibble, to criticize, seeking for something to question in the word of God, thinks that he is thereby giving evidence of independence of thought, and mental acuteness. He supposes that he is sitting in judgment on the Bible, when in truth he is judging himself. He makes it manifest that he is incapable of appreciating truths that originate in heaven, and that compass eternity. In presence of the great mountain of God's righteousness, his spirit is not awed. He busies himself with hunting for sticks and straws, and in this betrays a narrow and earthly nature, a heart that is fast losing its capacity to appreciate God. He whose heart has responded to the divine touch will be seeking for that which will increase his knowledge of God, and will refine and elevate the character. As a flower turns to the sun, that the bright rays may touch it with tints of beauty, so will the soul turn to the Sun of Righteousness, that heaven's light may beautify the character with the graces of the character of Christ.

Jesus continued, drawing a sharp contrast between the position of the Jews and that of Abraham: "Your father Abraham rejoiced to see My day: and he saw it, and was glad."

Abraham had greatly desired to see the promised Saviour. He offered up the most earnest prayer that before his death he might behold the Messiah. And he saw Christ. A supernatural light was given him, and he acknowledged Christ's divine character. He saw His day, and was glad. He was given a view of the divine sacrifice for sin. Of this sacrifice he had an illustration in his own experience. The command came to him, "Take now thy son, thine only son Isaac, whom thou lovest, . . . and offer him . . . for a burnt offering." Genesis 22:2. Upon the altar of sacrifice he laid

the son of promise, the son in whom his hopes were centered. Then as he waited beside the altar with knife upraised to obey God, he heard a voice from heaven saying, "Lay not thine hand upon the lad, neither do thou anything unto him; for now I know that thou fearest God, seeing that thou hast not withheld thy son, thine only son, from Me." Genesis 22:2. This terrible ordeal was imposed upon Abraham that he might see the day of Christ, and realize the great love of God for the world, so great that to raise it from its degradation, He gave His only-begotten Son to a most shameful death.

Abraham learned of God the greatest lesson ever given to mortal. His prayer that he might see Christ before he should die was answered. He saw Christ; he saw all that mortal can see, and live. By making an entire surrender, he was able to understand the vision of Christ, which had been given him. He was shown that in giving His only-begotten Son to save sinners from eternal ruin, God was making a greater and more wonderful sacrifice than ever man could make.

Abraham's experience answered the question: "Wherewith shall I come before the Lord, and bow myself before the high God? shall I come before Him with burnt offerings, with calves of a year old? Will the Lord be pleased with thousands of rams, or with ten thousands of rivers of oil? shall I give my first-born for my transgression, the fruit of my body for the sin of my soul?" Micah 6:6, 7. In the words of Abraham, "My son, God will provide Himself a lamb for a burnt offering," (Genesis 22:8.) and in God's provision of a sacrifice instead of Isaac, it was declared that no man could make expiation for himself. The pagan system of sacrifice was wholly unacceptable to God. No father was to offer up his son or his daughter for a sin offering. The Son of God alone can bear the guilt of the world.

Through his own suffering, Abraham was enabled to behold the Saviour's mission of sacrifice. But Israel would not understand that which was so unwelcome to their proud hearts. Christ's words concerning Abraham conveyed to His hearers no deep significance. The Pharisees saw in them only fresh ground for caviling. They retorted with a sneer, as if they would prove Jesus to be a madman, "Thou art not yet fifty years old, and hast Thou seen Abraham?"

With solemn dignity Jesus answered, "Verily, verily, I say unto you, Before Abraham was, I AM."

Silence fell upon the vast assembly. The name of God, given to Moses to express the idea of the eternal presence, had been claimed as His own by this Galilean rabbi. He had announced Himself to be the self-existent One, He who had been promised to Israel, "whose goings forth have been from of old, from the days of eternity." Micah 5:2, margin.

Again the priests and rabbis cried out against Jesus as a blasphemer. His claim to be one with God had before stirred them to take His life, and a few months later they plainly declared, "For a good work we stone Thee not, but for blasphemy; and because that Thou, being a man, makest Thyself God." John 10:33. Because He was, and avowed Himself to be, the Son of God, they were bent on destroying Him. Now many of the people, siding with the priests and rabbis, took up stones to cast at Him. "But Jesus hid Himself, and went out of the temple, going through the midst of them, and so passed by."

The Light was shinning in darkness; but "the darkness apprehended it not." John 1:5, R. V.

"As Jesus passed by, He saw a man which was blind from his birth. And His disciples asked Him, saying, Master, who did sin, this man, or his parents, that he was born blind? Jesus answered, Neither hath this man sinned, nor his parents: but that the works of God should be made manifest in him. . . . When He had thus spoken, He spat on the ground, and made clay of the spittle, and He anointed the eyes of the blind man with the clay, and He said unto him, Go, wash in the pool of Siloam, (which is by interpretation, Sent). He went his way therefore, and washed, and came seeing."

It was generally believed by the Jews that sin is punished in this life. Every affliction was regarded as the penalty of some wrongdoing, either of the sufferer himself or of his parents. It is true that all suffering results from the transgression of God's law, but this truth had become perverted. Satan, the author of sin and all its results, had led men to look upon disease and death as proceeding from God, — as punishment arbitrarily inflicted on account of sin. Hence one upon whom some great affliction or calamity had fallen, had the additional burden of being regarded as a great sinner.

Thus the way was prepared for the Jews to reject Jesus. He who "hath borne our griefs and carried our sorrows," was looked upon by the Jews as "stricken, smitten of God, and afflicted;" and they hid their faces from Him. Isaiah 53:4, 3.

God had given a lesson designed to prevent this. The history of Job had shown that suffering is inflicted by Satan, and is overruled by God for purposes of mercy. But Israel did not understand the lesson. The same error for which God had reproved the friends of Job was repeated by the Jews in their rejection of Christ.

The belief of the Jews in regard to the relation of sin and suffering was held by Christ's disciples. While Jesus corrected their error, He did not explain the cause of the man's affliction, but told them what would be the result. Because of it the works of God would be made manifest. "As long as I am in the world," He said, "I am the Light of the world." Then having anointed the eyes of the blind man, He sent him to wash in the pool of Siloam, and the man's sight was restored. Thus Jesus answered the question of the disciples in a practical way, as He usually answered questions put to Him from curiosity. The disciples were not called upon to discuss the question as to who had sinned or had not sinned, but to understand the power and mercy of God in giving sight to the blind. It was evident that there was no healing virtue in the clay, or in the pool wherein the blind man was sent to wash, but that the virtue was in Christ.

The Pharisees could not but be astonished at the cure. Yet they were more than ever filled with hatred; for the miracle had been performed on the Sabbath day.

The neighbors of the young man, and those who knew him before in his blindness, said, "Is not this he that sat

> "To the Saviour's question, 'Dost thou believe on the Son of God?' the blind man replied by asking, 'Who is He, Lord, that I might believe on Him?' And Jesus said, 'Thou hast both seen Him, and it is He that talketh with thee.' The man cast himself at the Saviour's feet in worship. Not only had his natural sight been restored, but Christ had been revealed to his soul, and he received Him."

and begged?" They looked upon him with doubt; for when his eyes were opened, his countenance was changed and brightened, and he appeared like another man. From one to another the question passed. Some said, "This is he;" others, "He is like him." But he who had received the great blessing settled the question by saying, "I am he." He then told them of Jesus, and by what means he had been healed, and they inquired, "Where is He? He said, I know not."

Then they brought him before a council of the Pharisees. Again the man was asked how he had received his sight. "He said unto them, He put clay upon mine eyes, and I washed, and do see. Therefore said some of the Pharisees, This man is not of God, because He keepeth not the Sabbath day." The Pharisees hoped to make Jesus out to be a sinner, and therefore not the Messiah. They knew not that it was He who had made the Sabbath and knew all its

obligation, who had healed the blind man. They appeared wonderfully zealous for the observance of the Sabbath, yet were planning murder on that very day. But many were greatly moved at hearing of this miracle, and were convicted that He who had opened the eyes of the blind was more than a common man. In answer to the charge that Jesus was a sinner because He kept not the Sabbath day, they said, "How can a man that is a sinner do such miracles?"

Again the rabbis appealed to the blind man, "What sayest thou of Him, that He hath opened thine eyes? He said, He is a prophet." The Pharisees then asserted that he had not been born blind and received his sight. They called for his parents, and asked them, saying, "Is this your son, who ye say was born blind?"

There was the man himself, declaring that he had been blind, and had had his sight restored; but the Pharisees would rather deny the evidence of their own senses than admit that they were in error. So powerful is prejudice, so distorting is Pharisaical righteousness.

The Pharisees had one hope left, and that was to intimidate the man's parents. With apparent sincerity they asked. "How then doth he now see?" The parents feared to compromise themselves; for it had been declared that whoever should acknowledge Jesus as the Christ should be "put out of the synagogue;" that is, should be excluded from the synagogue for thirty days. During this time no child could be circumcised nor dead be lamented in the offender's home. The sentence was regarded as a great calamity; and if it failed to produce repentance, a far heavier penalty followed. The great work wrought for their son had brought conviction to the parents, yet they answered, "We know that this is our son, and that he was born blind; but by what means he now seeth, we know not; or who hath opened his eyes, we know not: he is of age; ask him: he shall speak for himself." Thus they shifted all responsibility from themselves to their son; for they dared not confess Christ.

The dilemma in which the Pharisees were placed, their questioning and prejudice, their unbelief in the facts of the case, were opening the eyes of the multitude, especially of the common people. Jesus had frequently wrought His miracles in the open street, and His work was always of a character to relieve suffering. The question in many minds was, Would God do such mighty works through an impostor, as the Pharisees insisted that Jesus was? The controversy was becoming very earnest on both sides.

The Pharisees saw that they were giving publicity to the work done by Jesus. They could not deny the miracle. The blind man was filled with joy and gratitude; he beheld the wondrous things of nature, and was filled with delight at the beauty of earth and sky. He freely related his experience, and again they tried to silence him, saying, "Give God the praise; we know that this man is a sinner." That is, Do not say again that this man gave you sight; it is God who has done this.

The blind man answered "Whether He be a sinner or no, I know not: one thing I know, that, whereas I was blind, now I see"

Then they questioned again, "What did He to thee? how opened He thine eyes?" With many words they tried to confuse him, so that he might think himself deluded. Satan and his evil angels were on the side of the Pharisees, and united their energies and subtlety with man's reasoning in order to counteract the influence of Christ. They blunted the convictions that were deepening in many minds. Angels of God were also on the ground to strengthen the man who had had his sight restored.

The Pharisees did not realize that they had to deal with any other than the uneducated man who had been born blind; they knew not Him with whom they were in controversy. Divine light shone into the chambers of the blind man's soul. As these hypocrites tried to make him disbelieve, God helped him to show, by the vigor and pointedness of his replies, that he was not to be ensnared. He answered, "I have told you already, and ye did not hear; wherefore would ye hear it again? will ye also be His disciples? Then they reviled him, and said, Thou art His disciple; but we are Moses' disciples. We know that God spake unto Moses: as for this fellow, we know not from whence He is."

The Lord Jesus knew the ordeal through which the man was passing, and He gave him grace and utterance, so that he became a witness for Christ. He answered the Pharisees in words that were cutting rebuke to his questioners. They claimed to be the expositors of Scripture, the religious guides of the nation; and yet here was One performing miracles, and they were confessedly ignorant as to the source of His power, and as to His character and claims. "Why herein is a marvelous thing," said the man, "that ye know not from whence He is, and yet He hath opened mine eyes. Now we know that God heareth not sinners; but if any man be a worshiper of God, and doeth His will, him He heareth. Since the world began was it not heard that any man opened the eyes of one that was born blind. If this man were not of God, He could do nothing."

The man had met his inquisitors on their own ground. His reasoning was unanswerable. The Pharisees were astonished, and they held their peace, — spellbound before his pointed, determined words. For a few moments there was silence. Then the frowning priests and rabbis gathered about them their robes, as though they feared contamination from contact with him; they shook off the dust from their feet, and hurled denunciations against him, — "Thou wast altogether born in sins, and dost thou teach *us*?" And they excommunicated him.

Jesus heard what had been done; and finding him soon after, He said, "Dost thou believe on the Son of God?"

For the first time the blind man looked upon the face of his Restorer. Before the council he had seen his parents troubled and perplexed; he had looked upon the frowning faces of the rabbis; now his eyes rested upon the loving, peaceful countenance of Jesus. Already, at great cost to himself, he had acknowledged Him as a delegate of divine power; now a higher revelation was granted him.

To the Savior's question, "Dost thou believe on the Son of God?" the blind man replied by asking, "Who is He, Lord, that I might believe on Him?" And Jesus said, "Thou hast both seen Him, and it is He that talketh with thee." The man cast himself at the Saviour's feet in worship. Not only had his natural sight been restored, but the eyes of his understanding had been opened. Christ had been revealed to his soul, and he received Him as the Sent of God.

A group of Pharisees had gathered near, and the sight of them brought to the mind of Jesus the contrast ever manifest in the effect of His words and works. He said, "For judgment I am come into this world, that they which see not might see; and that they which see might be made blind." Christ had come to open the blind eyes, to give light to them that sit in darkness. He had declared Himself to be the Light of the world, and the miracle just performed was in attestation of His mission. The people who beheld the Saviour, at His advent were favored with a fuller manifestation of the divine presence than the world had ever enjoyed before. The knowledge of God was revealed more perfectly. But in this very revelation, judgment was passing upon men. Their character was tested, their destiny determined.

The manifestation of divine power that had given to the blind man both natural and spiritual sight, had left the Pharisees in yet deeper darkness. Some of His hearers, feeling that Christ's words applied to them, inquired, "Are we blind also?" Jesus answered, "If ye were blind, ye should have no sin." If God had made it impossible for you to see the truth, your ignorance would involve no guilt. "But now ye say, We see." You believe yourselves able to see, and reject the means through which alone you could receive sight. To all who realized their need, Christ came with infinite help. But the Pharisees would confess no need; they refused to come to Christ, and hence they were left in blindness, — a blindness for which they were themselves guilty. Jesus said, "Your sin remaineth."

The Divine Shepherd

I am the good Shepherd: the good shepherd giveth his life for the sheep." "I am the good Shepherd, and know My sheep, and am known of Mine. As the Father knoweth Me, even so know I the Father: and I lay down My life for the sheep."

Again Jesus found access to the minds of His hearers by the pathway of their familiar associations. He had likened the Spirit's influence to the cool, refreshing water. He had represented Himself as the light, the source of life and gladness to nature and to man. Now in a beautiful pastoral picture He represents His relation to those that believe on Him. No picture was more familiar to His hearers than this, and Christ's words linked it forever with Himself. Never could the disciples look on the shepherds tending their flocks without recalling the Saviour's lesson. They would see Christ in each faithful shepherd. They would see themselves in each helpless and dependent flock.

This figure the prophet Isaiah had applied to the Messiah's mission, in the comforting words, "O Zion, that bringest good tidings, get thee up into the high mountain; O Jerusalem, that bringest good tidings, lift up thy voice with strength; lift it up, be not afraid; say unto the cities of Judah, Behold your God. . . . He shall feed His flock like a shepherd; He shall gather the lambs with His arm, and carry them in His bosom." Isaiah 40:9-11. David had sung, "The Lord is my shepherd: I shall not want." And the Holy Spirit through Ezekiel had declared: "I will set up one Shepherd over them, and He shall feed them;" "I will seek that which was lost, and bring again that which was driven away, and will bind up that which was broken, and will strengthen that which was sick." "And I will make with them a covenant of peace." "And they shall no more be a prey to the heathen; . . . but they shall dwell safely, and

none shall make them afraid." Psalms 23:1; Ezekiel 34:23, 16, 25, 28.

Christ applied these prophecies to Himself, and He showed the contrast between His own character and that of the leaders in Israel. The Pharisees had just driven one from the fold, because he dared to bear witness to the power of Christ. They had cut off a soul whom the true Shepherd was drawing to Himself. In this they had shown themselves ignorant of the work committed to them, and unworthy of their trust as shepherds of the flock. Jesus now set before them the contrast between them and the good Shepherd, and He pointed to Himself as the real keeper of the Lord's flock. Before doing this, however, He speaks of Himself under another figure.

He said, "He that entereth not by the door into the sheepfold, but climbeth up some other way, the same is a thief and a robber. But he that entereth in by the door is the shepherd of the sheep." The Pharisees did not discern that these words were spoken against them. When they reasoned in their hearts as to the meaning, Jesus told them plainly, "I am the door; by Me if any man enter in, he shall be saved, and shall go in and out, and find pasture. The thief cometh not, but for to steal, and to kill, and to destroy; I am come that they might have life, and that they might have it more abundantly."

Christ is the door to the fold of God. Through this door all His children, from the earliest times, have found entrance. In Jesus, as shown in types, as shadowed in symbols, as manifested in the revelation of the prophets, as unveiled in the lessons given to His disciples, and in the miracles wrought for the sons of men, they have beheld "the Lamb of God, which taketh away the sin of the world," (John 1:29), and through Him they are brought

This chapter is based on John 10:1-30.

I am the good shepherd: the good shepherd giveth His life for His sheep . . . I am the good shephard, and know My sheep, and am known of Mine. As the Father knoweth Me, even so know I the Father: and I lay down My life for the sheep. And other sheep I have, which are not of this fold: them also I must bring, and they shall hear My voice; and there shall be one fold, and one shepherd . . . My sheep hear my voice, and I know them, and they follow Me: And I give unto them eternal life; and they shall never perish, neither shall any man pluck them out of My hand.

John 10:11, 14-16, 27, 28

within the fold of His grace. Many have come presenting other objects for the faith of the world; ceremonies and systems have been devised by which men hope to receive justification and peace with God, and thus find entrance to His fold. But the only door is Christ, and all who have interposed something to take the place of Christ, all who have tried to enter the fold in some other way, are thieves and robbers.

The Pharisees had not entered by the door. They had climbed into the fold by another way than Christ, and they were not fulfilling the work of the true shepherd. The priests and rulers, the scribes and Pharisees, destroyed the living pastures, and defiled the wellsprings of the water of life. Faithfully do the words of inspiration describe those false shepherds: "The diseased have ye not strengthened, neither have ye healed that which was sick, neither have ye bound up that which was broken, neither have ye brought again that which was driven away, . . . but with force and with cruelty have ye ruled them." Ezekiel 34:4.

In all ages, philosophers and teachers have been presenting to the world theories by which to satisfy the soul's need. Every heathen nation has had its great teachers and religious systems offering some other means of redemption than Christ, turning the eyes of men away from the Father's face, and filling their hearts with fear of Him who has given them only blessing. The trend of their work is to rob God of that which is His own, both by creation and by redemption. And these false teachers rob man as well. Millions of human beings are bound down under false religions, in the bondage of slavish fear, of stolid indifference, toiling like beasts of burden, bereft of hope or joy or aspiration here, and with only a dull fear of the hereafter. It is the gospel of the grace of God alone that can uplift the soul. The contemplation of the love of God manifested in His Son, will stir the heart and arouse the powers of the soul as nothing else can. Christ came that He might recreate the image of God in man; and whoever turns men away from Christ, is turning them away from the source of true development; he is defrauding them of the hope and purpose and glory of life. He is a thief and a robber.

"He that entereth in by the door is the shepherd of the sheep." Christ is both the Door and the Shepherd. He enters in by Himself. It is through His own sacrifice that He becomes the shepherd of the sheep. "To Him the porter openeth; and the sheep hear His voice; and He calleth His own sheep by name, and leadeth them out. And when He putteth forth His own sheep, He goeth before them, and the sheep follow Him; for they know His voice."

Of all creatures the sheep is one of the most timid and helpless, and in the East the shepherd's care for his flock is untiring and incessant. Anciently as now there was little security outside of the walled towns. Marauders from the roving border tribes, or beasts of prey from their hiding-places in the rocks, lay in wait to plunder the flocks. The shepherd watched his charge, knowing that it was at the peril of his own life. Jacob, who kept the flocks of Laban in the pasture grounds of Haran, describing his own unwearied labor, said, "In the day the drought consumed me, and the frost by night; and my sleep departed from mine eyes." Genesis 31:40. And it was while guarding his father's sheep, that the boy David, singlehanded, encountered the lion and the bear, and rescued from their teeth the stolen lamb.

As the shepherd leads his flock over the rocky hills, through forest and wild ravines, to grassy nooks by the riverside; as he watches them on the mountains through the lonely night, shielding from robbers, caring tenderly for the sickly and feeble, his life comes to be one with theirs. A strong and tender attachment unites him to the objects of his care. However large the flock, the shepherd knows every sheep. Every one has its name, and responds to the name at the shepherd's call.

As an earthly shepherd knows his sheep, so does the divine Shepherd know His flock that are scattered throughout the world. "Ye My flock, the flock of My pasture, are men, and I am your God, saith the Lord God." Jesus says, "I have called thee by thy name; thou art Mine." "I have graven thee upon the palms of My hands." Ezekiel 34:31; Isaiah 43:1; 49:16.

Jesus knows us individually, and is touched with the feeling of our infirmities. He knows us all by name. He knows the very house in which we live, the name of each occupant. He has at times given directions to His servants to go to a certain street in a certain city, to such a house, to find one of His sheep.

Every soul is as fully known to Jesus as if he were the only one for whom the Saviour died. The distress of every one touches His heart. The cry for aid reaches His ear. He came to draw all men unto Himself. He bids them, "Follow Me," and His Spirit moves upon their hearts to draw them to come to Him. Many refuse to be drawn. Jesus knows who they are. He also knows who gladly hear His call, and are ready to come under His pastoral care. He says, "My sheep hear My voice, and I know them, and they follow Me." He cares for each one as if there were not another on the face of the earth.

"He calleth His own sheep by name, and leadeth them out, . . . and the sheep follow Him; for they know His voice." The Eastern shepherd does not drive his sheep. He depends not upon force or fear; but going before, he calls them. They know his voice, and obey the call. So does the Saviour-Shepherd with His sheep. The Scripture says, "Thou leddest Thy people like a flock by the hand of Moses and Aaron." Through the prophet, Jesus declares, "I have loved thee with an everlasting love; therefore with loving-kindness have I drawn thee." He compels none to follow Him. "I drew them," He says, "with cords of a man, with bands of love." Psalms 77:20; Jeremiah 31: 3; Hosea 11:4.

It is not the fear of punishment, or the hope of everlasting reward, that leads the disciples of Christ to follow Him. They behold the Saviour's matchless love, revealed throughout His pilgrimage on earth, from the manger of Bethlehem to Calvary's cross, and the sight of Him attracts, it softens and subdues the soul. Love awakens in the heart of the beholders. They hear His voice, and they follow Him.

As the shepherd goes before his sheep, himself first encountering the perils of the way, so does Jesus with His people. "When He putteth forth His own sheep, He goeth before them." The way to heaven is consecrated by the Saviour's footprints. The path may be steep and rugged, but Jesus has traveled that way; His feet have pressed down the cruel thorns, to make the pathway easier for us. Every burden that we are called to bear, He Himself has borne.

Though now He has ascended to the presence of God, and shares the throne of the universe, Jesus has lost none of His compassionate nature. Today the same tender, sympathizing heart is open to all the woes of humanity. Today the hand that was pierced is reached forth to bless more abundantly His people that are in the world. "And they shall never perish; neither shall any man pluck them out of My hand." The soul that has given himself to Christ is more precious in His sight than the whole world. The Saviour would have passed through the agony of Calvary, that one might be saved in His kingdom. He will never abandon one for whom He has died. Unless His followers choose to leave Him, He will hold them fast.

Through all our trials we have a never-failing Helper. He does not leave us alone to struggle with temptation, to battle with evil, and be finally crushed with burdens and sorrow. Though now He is hidden from mortal sight, the ear of faith can hear His voice saying, Fear not; I am with you. "I am He that liveth, and was dead; and, behold, I am alive forevermore." Revelation 1:18. I have endured your sorrows, experienced your struggles, encountered your temptations. I know your tears; I also have wept. The griefs that lie too deep to be breathed into any human ear, I know. Think not that you are desolate and forsaken. Though your pain touch no responsive chord in any heart on earth, look unto Me, and live. "The mountains shall depart, and the hills be removed; but My kindness shall not depart from thee, neither shall the covenant of My peace be removed, saith the Lord that hath mercy on thee." Isaiah 54:10.

However much a shepherd may love his sheep, he loves his sons and daughters more. Jesus is not only our shepherd; He is our "everlasting Father." And He says, "I know Mine own, and Mine own know Me, even as the Father knoweth Me, and I know the Father." John 10:14, 15, R. V. What a statement is this! — the only-begotten Son, He who is in the bosom of the Father, He whom God has declared to be "the Man that is My fellow," (Zechariah 13:7.) — the communion between Him and the eternal God is taken to represent the communion between Christ and His children on the earth!

Because we are the gift of His Father, and the reward of His work, Jesus loves us. He loves us as His children. Reader, He loves you. Heaven itself can bestow nothing greater, nothing better. Therefore trust.

Jesus thought upon the souls all over the earth who were misled by false shepherds. Those whom He longed to gather as the sheep of His pasture were scattered among wolves, and he said, "Other sheep I have, which are not of this fold; them also I must bring, and they shall hear My voice; and they shall become one flock, one shepherd." John 10:16, R. V.

"Therefore doth My Father love Me, because I lay down My life, that I might take it again." That is, My Father has so loved you, that He even loves Me more for giving My life to redeem you. In becoming your substitute and surety, by surrendering My life, by taking your liabilities, your transgressions, I am endeared to My Father.

"I lay down My life, that I might take it again. No man taketh it from Me, but I lay it down of Myself. I have power to lay it down, and I have power to take it again." While as a member of the human family He was mortal, as God He was the fountain of life for the world. He could have withstood the advances of death, and refused to come under its dominion; but voluntarily He laid down His life, that He might bring life and immortality to light. He bore the sin of the world, endured its curse, yielded up His life as a sacrifice, that men might not eternally die. "Surely He hath borne our griefs, and carried our sorrows. . . . He was wounded for our transgressions, He was bruised for our iniquities; the chastisement of our peace was upon Him; and with His stripes we are healed. All we like sheep have gone astray; we have turned every one to his own way; and the Lord hath laid on Him the iniquity of us all." Isaiah 53:4-6.

The Last Journey From Galilee

As the close of His ministry drew near, there was a change in Christ's manner of labor. Heretofore He had sought to shun excitement and publicity. He had refused the homage of the people, and had passed quickly from place to place when the popular enthusiasm in His favor seemed kindling beyond control. Again and again He had commanded that none should declare Him to be the Christ.

At the time of the Feast of Tabernacles His journey to Jerusalem was made swiftly and secretly. When urged by His brothers to present Himself publicly as the Messiah, His answer was, "My time is not yet come." John 7:6. He made His way to Jerusalem unobserved, and entered the city unannounced, and unhonored by the multitude. But not so with His last journey. He had left Jerusalem for a season because of the malice of the priests and rabbis. But He now set out to return, traveling in the most public manner, by a circuitous route, and preceded by such an announcement of His coming as He had never made before. He was going forward to the scene of His great sacrifice, and to this the attention of the people must be directed.

"As Moses lifted up the serpent in the wilderness, even so must the Son of man be lifted up." John 3:14. As the eyes of all Israel had been directed to the uplifted serpent, the symbol appointed for their healing, so all eyes must be drawn to Christ, the sacrifice that brought salvation to the lost world.

It was a false conception of the Messiah's work, and a lack of faith in the divine character of Jesus, that had led His brothers to urge Him to present Himself publicly to the people at the Feast of Tabernacles. Now, in a spirit akin to this, the disciples would have prevented Him from making the journey to Jerusalem. They remembered His words concerning what was to befall Him there, they knew the deadly hostility of the religious leaders, and they would fain have dissuaded their Master from going thither.

To the heart of Christ it was a bitter task to press His way against the fears, disappointment, and unbelief of His beloved disciples. It was hard to lead them forward to the anguish and despair that awaited them at Jerusalem. And Satan was at hand to press his temptations upon the Son of man. Why should He now go to Jerusalem, to certain death? All around Him were souls hungering for the bread of life. On every hand were suffering ones waiting for His word of healing. The work to be wrought by the gospel of His grace was but just begun. And He was full of the vigor of manhood's prime. Why not go forward to the vast fields of the world with the words of His grace, the touch of His healing power? Why not take to Himself the joy of giving light and gladness to those darkened and sorrowing millions? Why leave the harvest gathering to His disciples, so weak in faith, so dull of understanding, so slow to act? Why face death now, and leave the work in its infancy? The foe who in the wilderness had confronted Christ, assailed Him now with fierce and subtle temptations. Had Jesus yielded for a moment, had He changed His course in the least particular to save Himself, Satan's agencies would have triumphed, and the world would have been lost.

But Jesus had "steadfastly set His face to go to Jerusalem." The one law of His life was the Father's will. In the visit to the temple in His boyhood, He had said to Mary, "Wist ye not that I must be about My Father's business?" Luke 2:49. At Cana, when Mary desired Him to reveal His miraculous power, His answer was, "Mine hour is not yet

This chapter is based on Luke 9:51-56; 10:1-24.

come." John 2:4. With the same words He replied to His brothers when they urged Him to go to the feast. But in God's great plan the hour had been appointed for the offering of Himself for the sins of men, and that hour was soon to strike. He would not fail nor falter. His steps are turned toward Jerusalem, where His foes have long plotted to take His life; now He will lay it down. He set His face steadfastly to go to persecution, denial, rejection, condemnation, and death.

And He "sent messengers before His face; and they went, and entered into a village of the Samaritans, to make ready for Him." But the people refused to receive Him, because He was on His way to Jerusalem. This they interpreted as meaning that Christ showed a preference for the Jews, whom they hated with intense bitterness. Had He come to restore the temple and worship upon Mount Gerizim, they would gladly have received Him; but He was going to Jerusalem, and they would show Him no hospitality. Little did they realize that they were turning from their doors the best gift of heaven. Jesus invited men to receive Him, He asked favors at their hands, that He might come near to them, to bestow the richest blessings. For every favor manifested toward Him, He requited a more precious grace. But all was lost to the Samaritans because of their prejudice and bigotry.

James and John, Christ's messengers, were greatly annoyed at the insult shown to their Lord. They were filled with indignation because He had been so rudely treated by the Samaritans whom He was honoring by His presence. They had recently been with Him on the mount of transfiguration, and had seen Him glorified by God, and honored by Moses and Elijah. This manifest dishonor on the part of the Samaritans, should not, they thought, be passed over without marked punishment.

Coming to Christ, they reported to Him the words of the people, telling Him that they had even refused to give Him a night's lodging. They thought that a grievous wrong had been done Him, and seeing Mount Carmel in the distance, where Elijah had slain the false prophets, they said, "Wilt Thou that we command fire to come down from heaven, and consume them, even as Elias did?" They were surprised to see that Jesus was pained by their words, and still more surprised as His rebuke fell upon their ears, "Ye know not what manner of spirit ye are of. For the Son of man is not come to destroy men's lives, but to save them." And He went to another village.

It is no part of Christ's mission to compel men to receive Him. It is Satan, and men actuated by his spirit, that seek to compel the conscience. Under a pretense of zeal for righteousness, men who are confederate with evil angels bring suffering upon their fellow men, in order to convert them to their ideas of religion; but Christ is ever showing mercy, ever seeking to win by the revealing of His love. He can admit no rival in the soul, nor accept of partial service; but He desires only voluntary service, the willing surrender of the heart under the constraint of love. There can be no more conclusive evidence that we possess the spirit of Satan than the disposition to hurt and destroy those who do not appreciate our work, or who act contrary to our ideas.

Every human being, in body, soul, and spirit, is the property of God. Christ died to redeem all. Nothing can be more offensive to God than for men, through religious bigotry, to bring suffering upon those who are the purchase of the Saviour's blood.

"Satan was at hand to press his temptations upon the Son of man. Why should He now go to Jerusalem, to certain death? . . . Why not go forward to the vast fields of the world with the words of His grace, the touch of His healing power? . . . Why face death now? . . . Had Jesus yielded for a moment, had He changed His course in the least particular to save Himself . . . the world would have been lost."

"And He arose from thence, and cometh into the coasts of Judea by the farther side of Jordan; and the people resort unto Him again; and, as He was wont, He taught them again." Mark 10:1.

A considerable part of the closing months of Christ's ministry was spent in Perea, the province on "the farther side of Jordan" from Judea. Here the multitude thronged His steps, as in His early ministry in Galilee, and much of His former teaching was repeated.

As He had sent out the Twelve, so He "appointed seventy others, and sent them two and two before His face into every city and place, whither He Himself was about to come." Luke 10:1, R. V. These disciples had been for some time with Him, in training for their work. When the

Twelve were sent out on their first separate mission, other disciples accompanied Jesus in His journey through Galilee. Thus they had the privilege of intimate association with Him, and direct personal instruction. Now this larger number also were to go forth on a separate mission.

The directions to the Seventy were similar to those that had been given to the Twelve; but the command to the Twelve, not to enter into any city of the Gentiles or of the Samaritans, was not given to the Seventy. Though Christ had just been repulsed by the Samaritans, His love toward them was unchanged. When the seventy went forth in His name, they visited, first of all, the cities of Samaria.

The Saviour's own visit to Samaria, and later, the commendation of the good Samaritan, and the grateful joy of that leper, a Samaritan, who alone of the ten returned to give thanks to Christ, were full of significance to the disciples. The lesson sunk deep into their hearts. In His commission to them, just before His ascension, Jesus mentioned Samaria with Jerusalem and Judea as the places where they were first to preach the gospel. This commission His teaching had prepared them to fulfill. When in their Master's name they went to Samaria, they found the people ready to receive them. The Samaritans had heard of Christ's words of commendation and His works of mercy for men of their nation. They saw that notwithstanding their rude treatment of Him, He had only thoughts of love toward them, and their hearts were won. After His ascension they welcomed the Saviour's messengers, and the disciples gathered a precious harvest from among those who had once been their bitterest enemies. "A bruised reed shall He not break, and the dimly burning flax shall He not quench; He shall bring forth judgment unto truth." "And in His name shall the Gentiles trust." Isaiah 42:3, margin; Matthew 12:21.

In sending out the Seventy, Jesus bade them, as He had bidden the Twelve, not to urge their presence where they were unwelcome. "Into whatsoever city ye enter, and they receive you not," He said, "go your ways out into the streets of the same, and say, Even the very dust of your city, which cleaveth on us, we do wipe off against you: notwithstanding be ye sure of this, that the kingdom of God is come nigh unto you." They were not to do this from motives of resentment or through wounded dignity, but to show how grievous a thing it is to refuse the Lord's message or His messengers. To reject the Lord's servants is to reject Christ Himself.

"I say unto you," Jesus added, "that it shall be more tolerable in that day for Sodom, than for that city." Then His mind reverted to the Galilean towns where so much of His ministry had been spent. In deeply sorrowful accents He exclaimed, "Woe unto thee, Chorazin! woe unto thee, Bethsaida! for if the mighty works had been done in Tyre and Sidon, which have been done in you, they had a great while ago repented, sitting in sackcloth and ashes. But it shall be more tolerable for Tyre and Sidon at the judgment,

than for you. And thou, Capernaum, which art exalted to heaven, shalt be thrust down to hell."

To those busy towns about the Sea of Galilee, heaven's richest blessings had been freely offered. Day after day the Prince of life had gone in and out among them. The glory of God, which prophets and kings had longed to see, had shone upon the multitudes that thronged the Saviour's steps. Yet they had refused the heavenly Gift.

With a great show of prudence the rabbis had warned the people against receiving the new doctrines taught by this new teacher; for His theories and practices were contrary to the teachings of the fathers. The people gave credence to what the priests and Pharisees taught, in place of seeking to understand the word of God for themselves. They honored the priests and rulers instead of honoring God, and rejected the truth that they might keep their own traditions. Many had been impressed and almost persuaded; but they did not act upon their convictions, and were not reckoned on the side of Christ. Satan presented his temptations, until the light appeared as darkness. Thus many rejected the truth that would have proved the saving of the soul.

The True Witness says, "Behold, I stand at the door, and knock." Revelation 3:20. Every warning, reproof, and entreaty in the word of God or through His messengers is a knock at the door of the heart. It is the voice of Jesus asking for entrance. With every knock unheeded, the disposition to open becomes weaker. The impressions of the Holy Spirit, if disregarded today, will not be as strong tomorrow. The heart becomes less impressible, and lapses into a perilous unconsciousness of the shortness of life, and of the great eternity beyond. Our condemnation in the Judgment will not result from the fact that we have been in error, but from the fact that we have neglected heaven-sent opportunities for learning what is truth.

Like the apostles, the Seventy had received supernatural endowments as a seal of their mission. When their work was completed, they returned with joy, saying, "Lord, even the devils are subject unto us through Thy name." Jesus answered, "I beheld Satan as lightning fall from heaven."

The scenes of the past and the future were presented to the mind of Jesus. He beheld Lucifer as he was first cast out from the heavenly places. He looked forward to the scenes of His own agony, when before all the worlds the character of the deceiver should be unveiled. He heard the cry, "It is finished," (John 19:30), announcing that the redemption of the lost race was forever made certain, that heaven was made eternally secure against the accusations, the deceptions, the pretensions, that Satan would instigate.

Beyond the cross of Calvary, with its agony and shame, Jesus looked forward to the great final day, when the prince of the power of the air will meet his destruction in the earth so long marred by his rebellion. Jesus beheld the work of evil forever ended, and the peace of God filling heaven and earth.

Henceforward Christ's followers were to look upon Satan as a conquered foe. Upon the cross, Jesus was to gain the victory for them; that victory He desired them to accept as their own. "Behold," He said, "I give unto you power to tread on serpents and scorpions, and over all the power of the enemy; and nothing shall by any means hurt you."

The omnipotent power of the Holy Spirit is the defense of every contrite soul. Not one that in penitence and faith has claimed His protection will Christ permit to pass under

---

"Every warning, reproof, and entreaty in the word of God or through His messengers is a knock at the door of the heart. It is the voice of Jesus asking for entrance. With every knock unheeded, the disposition to open becomes weaker. The impressions of the Holy Spirit if disregarded today, will not be as strong tomorrow."

---

the enemy's power. The Saviour is by the side of His tempted and tried ones. With Him there can be no such thing as failure, loss, impossibility, or defeat; we can do all things through Him who strengthens us. When temptations and trials come, do not wait to adjust all the difficulties, but look to Jesus, your helper.

There are Christians who think and speak altogether too much about the power of Satan. They think of their adversary, they pray about him, they talk about him, and he looms up greater and greater in their imagination. It is true that Satan is a powerful being; but thank God, we have a mighty Saviour, who cast out the devil one from heaven. Satan is pleased when we magnify his power. Why not talk of Jesus? Why not magnify His power and His love?

The rainbow of promise encircling the throne on high is an everlasting testimony that "God so loved the world, that He gave His only-begotten Son, that whosoever believeth in Him should not perish, but have everlasting life." John 3:16. It testifies to the universe that God will never forsake His people in their struggle with evil. It is an assurance to us of strength and protection as long as the throne itself shall endure.

Jesus added, "Notwithstanding in this rejoice not, that the spirits are subject unto you; but rather rejoice, because your names are written in heaven." Rejoice not in the possession of power, lest you lose sight of your dependence upon God. Be careful lest self-sufficiency come in, and you work in your own strength, rather than in the spirit and strength of your Master. Self is ever ready to take the credit if any measure of success attends the work. Self is flattered and exalted, and the impression is not made upon other minds that God is all and in all. The apostle Paul says, "When I am weak, then am I strong." 2 Corinthians 12:10. When we have a realization of our weakness, we learn to depend upon a power not inherent. Nothing can take so strong a hold on the heart as the abiding sense of our responsibility to God. Nothing reaches so fully down to the deepest motives of conduct as a sense of the pardoning love of Christ. We are to come in touch with God, then we shall be imbued with His Holy Spirit, that enables us to come in touch with our fellow men. Then rejoice that through Christ you have become connected with God, members of the heavenly family. While you look higher than yourself, you will have a continual sense of the weakness of humanity. The less you cherish self, the more distinct and full will be your comprehension of the excellence of your Saviour. The more closely you connect yourself with the source of light and power, the greater light will be shed upon you, and the greater power will be yours to work for God. Rejoice that you are one with God, one with Christ, and with the whole family of heaven.

As the Seventy listened to the words of Christ, the Holy Spirit was impressing their minds with living realities, and writing truth upon the tablets of the soul. Though multitudes surrounded them, they were as though shut in with God.

Knowing that they had caught the inspiration of the hour, Jesus "rejoiced in spirit, and said, I thank Thee, O Father, Lord of heaven and earth, that Thou hast hid these things from the wise and prudent, and hast revealed them unto babes. Even so, Father, for so it seemed good in Thy sight. All things are delivered to Me of My Father, and no man knoweth who the Son is, but the Father; and who the Father is, but the Son, and he to whom the Son will reveal Him."

The honored men of the world, the so-called great and wise men, with all their boasted wisdom, could not comprehend the character of Christ. They judged Him from outward appearance, from the humiliation that came upon Him as a human being. But to fishermen and publicans it had been given to see the Invisible. Even the disciples failed of understanding all that Jesus desired to reveal to them; but from time to time, as they surrendered themselves to the Holy Spirit's power, their minds were illuminated. They realized that the mighty God, clad in the garb of humanity, was among them. Jesus rejoiced that though this knowledge was not possessed by the wise and prudent, it had been revealed to these humble men. Often as He had presented the Old Testament Scriptures, and showed their application to Himself and His work of atonement, they had been awakened by His Spirit, and lifted into a heavenly atmosphere. Of the spiritual truths spoken by the prophets they had a clearer understanding than had the original writers themselves. Hereafter they would read the Old Testament Scriptures, not as the doctrines of the scribes and Pharisees, not as the utterances of wise men who were dead, but as a new revelation from God. They beheld Him "whom the world cannot receive, because it seeth Him not, neither knoweth Him; but ye know Him; for He dwelleth with you, and shall be in you." John 14:17.

The only way in which we can gain a more perfect apprehension of truth is by keeping the heart tender and subdued by the Spirit of Christ. The soul must be cleansed from vanity and pride, and vacated of all that has held it in possession, and Christ must be enthroned within. Human science is too limited to comprehend the atonement. The plan of redemption is so far-reaching that philosophy cannot explain it. It will ever remain a mystery that the most profound reasoning cannot fathom. The science of salvation cannot be explained; but it can be known by experience. Only he who sees his own sinfulness can discern the preciousness of the Saviour.

Full of instruction were the lessons which Christ taught as He slowly made his way from Galilee toward Jerusalem. Eagerly the people listened to His words. In Perea as in Galilee the people were less under the control of Jewish bigotry than in Judea, and His teaching found a response in their hearts.

During these last months of His ministry, many of Christ's parables were spoken. The priests and rabbis pursued Him with ever-increasing bitterness, and His warnings to them He veiled in symbols. They could not mistake His meaning, yet they could find in His words nothing on which to ground an accusation against Him. In the parable of the Pharisee and the publican, the self-sufficient prayer, "God, I thank Thee that I am not as the rest of men," stood out in sharp contrast to the penitent's plea, "Be merciful to me the sinner." Luke 18:11, 13, R. V., margin. Thus Christ rebuked the hypocrisy of the Jews. And under the figures of the barren fig tree and the great supper He foretold the doom about to fall upon the impenitent nation. Those who had scornfully rejected the invitation to the gospel feast heard His warning words: "I say unto you, That none of those men which were bidden shall taste of My supper." Luke 14:24.

Very precious was the instruction given to the disciples. The parable of the importunate widow and the friend asking for bread at midnight, gave new force to His words, "Ask, and it shall be given you; seek, and ye shall find; knock, and it shall be opened unto you." Luke 11:9. And often their wavering faith was strengthened by the memory that Christ had said, "Shall not God do justice for His elect, which cry to Him day and night, and He is longsuffering over them? I say unto you, that He will do them justice speedily." Luke 18:7, 8, R. V., margin.

The beautiful parable of the lost sheep Christ repeated. And He carried its lesson still farther, as He told of the lost piece of silver and the prodigal son. The force of these lessons the disciples could not then fully appreciate; but after the outpouring of the Holy Spirit, as they saw the ingathering of the Gentiles and the envious anger of the Jews, they better understood the lesson of the prodigal son, and could enter into the joy of Christ's words, "It was meet that we should make merry and be glad;" "for this my son was dead, and is alive again; he was lost, and is found." Luke 15:32, 24. And as they went out in their Master's name, facing reproach and poverty and persecution, they often strengthened their hearts by repeating His injunction, spoken on this last journey, "Fear not, little flock; for it is your Father's good pleasure to give you the kingdom. Sell that ye have, and give alms; provide yourselves bags which wax not old, a treasure in the heavens that faileth not, where no thief approacheth, neither moth corrupteth. For where your treasure is, there will your heart be also." Luke 12:32-34.

The Good Samaritan

In the story of the good Samaritan, Christ illustrates the nature, of true religion. He shows that it consists not in systems, creeds, or rites, but in the performance of loving deeds, in bringing the greatest good to others, in genuine goodness.

As Christ was teaching the people, "a certain lawyer stood up, and tempted Him, saying, Master, what shall I do to inherit eternal life?" With breathless attention the large congregation awaited the answer. The priests and rabbis had thought to entangle Christ by having the lawyer ask this question. But the Saviour entered into no controversy. He required the answer from the questioner himself. "What is written in the law?" He said; "how readest thou?" The Jews still accused Jesus of lightly regarding the law given from Sinai; but He turned the question of salvation upon the keeping of God's commandments.

The lawyer said, "Thou shalt love the Lord thy God with all thy heart, and with all thy soul, and with all thy strength, and with all thy mind; and thy neighbor as thyself." Jesus said, "Thou hast answered right; this do, and thou shalt live."

The lawyer was not satisfied with the position and works of the Pharisees. He had been studying the Scriptures with a desire to learn their real meaning. He had a vital interest in the matter, and had asked in sincerity, "what shall I do?" In his answer as to the requirements of the law, he passed by all the mass of ceremonial and ritualistic precepts. For these he claimed no value, but presented the two great principles on which hang all the law and the prophets. This answer, being commended by Christ, placed the Saviour on vantage ground with the rabbis. They could not condemn Him for sanctioning that which had been advanced by an expositor of the law.

"This do, and thou shalt live," Jesus said. He presented the law as a divine unity, and in this lesson taught that it is not possible to keep one precept, and break another; for the same principle runs through them all. Man's destiny will be determined by his obedience to the whole law. Supreme love to God and impartial love to man are the principles to be wrought out in the life.

The lawyer found himself a lawbreaker. He was convicted under Christ's searching words. The righteousness of the law, which he claimed to understand, he had not practiced. He had not manifested love toward his fellow man. Repentance was demanded; but instead of repenting, he tried to justify himself. Rather than acknowledge the truth, he sought to show how difficult of fulfillment the commandment is. Thus he hoped both to parry conviction and to vindicate himself in the eyes of the people. The Saviour's words had shown that his question was needless, since he had been able to answer it himself. Yet he put another question, saying, "Who is my neighbor?"

Among the Jews this question caused endless dispute. They had no doubt as to the heathen and the Samaritans; these were strangers and enemies. But where should the distinction be made among the people of their own nation, and among the different classes of society? Whom should the priest, the rabbi, the elder, regard as neighbor? They spent their lives in a round of ceremonies to make themselves pure. Contact with the ignorant and careless multitude, they taught, would cause defilement that would require wearisome effort to remove. Were they to regard the "unclean" as neighbors?

Again Jesus refused to be drawn into controversy. He did not denounce the bigotry of those who were watching to condemn Him. But by a simple story He held up before

This chapter is based on Luke 10:25-37.

His hearers such a picture of the outflowing of heaven-born love as touched all hearts, and drew from the lawyer a confession of the truth.

The way to dispel darkness is to admit light. The best way to deal with error is to present truth. It is the revelation of God's love that makes manifest the deformity and sin of the heart centered in self.

"A certain man," said Jesus, "was going down from Jerusalem to Jericho; and he fell among robbers, which both stripped him and beat him, and departed, leaving him half dead. And by a chance a certain priest was going down that way; and when he saw him, he passed by on the other side. And in like manner a Levite also, when he came to the place, and saw him, passed by on the other side." Luke 10:30-32, R. V. This was no imaginary scene, but an actual occurrence, which was known to be exactly as represented. The priest and the Levite who had passed by on the other side were in the company that listened to Christ's words.

In journeying from Jerusalem to Jericho, the traveler had to pass through a portion of the wilderness of Judea. The road led down a wild, rocky ravine, which was infested by robbers, and was often the scene of violence. It was here that the traveler was attacked, stripped of all that was valuable, wounded and bruised, and left half dead by the wayside. As he lay thus, the priest came that way; but he merely glanced toward the wounded man. Then the Levite appeared. Curious to know what had happened, he stopped and looked at the sufferer. He was convicted of what he ought to do; but it was not an agreeable duty. He wished that he had not come that way, so that he need not have seen the wounded man. He persuaded himself that the case was no concern of his.

Both these men were in sacred office, and professed to expound the Scriptures. They were of the class specially chosen to be representatives of God to the people. They were to "have compassion on the ignorant, and on them that are out of the way," (Hebrews 5:2), that they might lead men to understand God's great love toward humanity. The work they were called to do was the same that Jesus had described as His own when He said, "The Spirit of the Lord is upon Me, because He hath anointed Me to preach the gospel to the poor; He hath sent Me to heal the brokenhearted, to preach deliverance to the captives, and recovering of sight to the blind, to set at liberty them that are bruised." Luke 4:18.

The angels of heaven look upon the distress of God's family upon the earth, and they are prepared to co-operate with men in relieving oppression and suffering. God in His providence had brought the priest and the Levite along the road where the wounded sufferer lay, that they might see his need of mercy and help. All heaven watched to see if the hearts of these men would be touched with pity for human woe. The Saviour was the One who had instructed the Hebrews in the wilderness; from the pillar of cloud and of fire He had taught a very different lesson from that which the people were now receiving from their priests and teachers. The merciful provisions of the law extended even to the lower animals, which cannot express in words their want and suffering. Directions had been given to Moses for the children of Israel to this effect: "If thou meet thine enemy's ox or his ass going astray, thou shalt surely bring it back to him again. If thou see the ass of him that hateth thee lying under his burden, and wouldst forbear to help him, thou shalt surely help with him." Exodus 23:4, 5. But in the man wounded by robbers, Jesus presented the case of a brother in suffering. How much more should their hearts have been moved with pity for him than for a beast of burden! The message had been given them through Moses that the Lord their God, "a great God, a mighty, and a terrible," "doth execute the judgment of the fatherless and widow, and loveth the stranger." Wherefore He commanded, "Love ye therefore the stranger." "Thou shalt love him as thyself." Deuteronomy 10:17-19; Leviticus 19:34.

Job had said, "The stranger did not lodge in the street; but I opened my doors to the traveler." And when the two angels in the guise of men came to Sodom, Lot bowed himself with his face toward the ground, and said, "Behold now, my lords, turn in, I pray you, into your servant's house, and tarry all night." Job 31:32; Genesis 19:2. With all these lessons the priest and the Levite were familiar, but they had not brought them into practical life. Trained in the school of national bigotry, they had become selfish, narrow, and exclusive. When they looked upon the wounded man, they could not tell whether he was of their nation or not. They thought he might be of the Samaritans, and they turned away.

In their action, as Christ had described it, the lawyer saw nothing contrary to what he had been taught concerning the requirements of the law. But now another scene was presented: —

A certain Samaritan, in his journey, came where the sufferer was, and when he saw him, he had compassion on him. He did not question whether the stranger was a Jew or a Gentile. If a Jew, the Samaritan well knew that, were their condition reversed, the man would spit in his face, and pass him by with contempt. But he did not hesitate on account of this. He did not consider that he himself might be in danger of violence by tarrying in the place. It was enough that there was before him a human being in need and suffering. He took off his own garment with which to cover him. The oil and wine provided for his own journey he used to heal and refresh the wounded man. He lifted him on his own beast, and moved slowly along with even pace, so that the stranger might not be jarred, and made to suffer increased pain. He brought him to an inn, and cared for him through the night, watching him tenderly. In the morning, as the sick man had improved, the Samaritan ventured to go on his way. But before doing this, he placed him in the care of the innkeeper, paid the charges, and left a deposit for his benefit; and not satisfied even with this, he made provision for any further need, saying to the host, "Take care of him; and whatsoever thou spendest more, when I come again, I will repay thee."

The story ended, Jesus fixed His eyes upon the lawyer, in a glance that seemed to read his soul, and said, "Which of these three, thinkest *thou*, proved neighbor unto him that fell among the robbers?" Luke 10:36, R. V.

The lawyer would not, even now, take the name Samaritan upon his lips, and he made answer, "He that showed mercy on him." Jesus said, "Go, and do *thou* likewise."

Thus the question, "Who is my neighbor? is forever answered. Christ has shown that our neighbor does not mean merely one of the church or faith to which we belong. It has no reference to race, color, or class distinction. Our neighbor is every person who needs our help. Our neighbor is every soul who is wounded and bruised by the adversary. Our neighbor is every one who is the property of God.

In the story of the good Samaritan, Jesus gave a picture of Himself and His mission. Man had been deceived, bruised, robbed, and ruined by Satan, and left to perish; but the Saviour had compassion on our helpless condition. He left His glory, to come to our rescue. He found us ready to die, and He undertook our case. He healed our wounds. He covered us with His robe of righteousness. He opened to us a refuge of safety, and made complete provision for us at His own charges. He died to redeem us. Pointing to His own example, He says to His followers, "These things I command you, that ye love one another." "As I have loved you, that ye also love one another." John 15:17; 13:34.

The lawyer's question to Jesus had been, "What shall I do?" And Jesus, recognizing love to God and man as the sum of righteousness, had said, "This do, and thou shalt live." The Samaritan had obeyed the dictates of a kind and loving heart, and in this had proved himself a doer of the law. Christ bade the lawyer, "Go, and do thou likewise." Doing, and not saying merely, is expected of the children of God. "He that saith he abideth in Him ought himself also so to walk, even as He walked." 1 John 2:6.

The lesson is no less needed in the world today than when it fell from the lips of Jesus. Selfishness and cold formality have well-nigh extinguished the fire of love, and dispelled the graces that should make fragrant the character. Many who profess His name have lost sight of that fact that Christians are to represent Christ. Unless there is practical self-sacrifice for the good of others, in the family circle, in the neighborhood, in the church, and wherever we may be, then whatever our profession, we are not Christians.

Christ has linked His interest with that of humanity, and He asks us to become one with Him for the saving of humanity. "Freely ye have received," He says, "freely give." Matthew 10:8. Sin is the greatest of all evils, and it is ours to pity and help the sinner. There are many who err, and who feel their shame and their folly. They are hungry for words of encouragement. They look upon their mistakes and errors, until they are driven almost to desperation. These souls we are not to neglect. If we are Christians, we shall not pass by on the other side, keeping as far as possible from the very ones who most need our help. When we see human beings in distress, whether through affliction or through sin, we shall never say, This does not concern me.

"Ye which are spiritual, restore such a one in the spirit of meekness." Galatians 6:1. By faith and prayer press back the power of the enemy. Speak words of faith and courage that will be as a healing balsam to the bruised and wounded one. Many, many, have fainted and become discouraged in the great struggle of life, when one word of kindly cheer would have strengthened them to overcome. Never should we pass by one suffering soul without seeking to impart to him of the comfort wherewith we are comforted of God.

All this is but a fulfillment of the principle of the law,—the principle that is illustrated in the story of the good Samaritan, and made manifest in the life of Jesus. His character reveals the true significance of the law, and shows what is meant by loving our neighbor as ourselves. And when the children of God manifest mercy, kindness, and love toward all men, they also are witnessing to the character of the statutes of heaven. They are bearing testimony to the fact that "the law of the Lord is perfect, converting the soul." Psalms 19:7. And whoever fails to manifest this love is breaking the law which he professes to revere. For the spirit we manifest toward our brethren, declares what is our spirit toward God. The love of God in the heart is the only spring of love toward our neighbor. "If a man say, I love God, and hateth his brother, he is a liar; for he that loveth not his brother whom he hath seen, how can he love God whom he hath not seen?" Beloved, "if we love one another, God dwelleth in us, and His love is perfected in us." John 4:20, 12.

Not With Outward Show

Some of the Pharisees had come to Jesus demanding "when the kingdom of God should come." More than three years had passed since John the Baptist gave the message that like a trumpet call had sounded through the land, "The kingdom of heaven is at hand." Matthew 3:2. And as yet these Pharisees saw no indication of the establishment of the kingdom. Many of those who rejected John, and at every step had opposed Jesus, were insinuating that His mission had failed.

Jesus answered, "The kingdom of God cometh not with outward show (margin): neither shall they say, Lo here! or, lo there! for, behold, the kingdom of God is within you." The kingdom of God begins in the heart. Look not here or there for manifestations of earthly power to mark its coming.

"The days will come," He said, turning to His disciples, "when ye shall desire to see one of the days of the Son of man, and ye shall not see it." Because it is not attended by worldly pomp, you are in danger of failing to discern the glory of My mission. You do not realize how great is your present privilege in having among you, though veiled in humanity, Him who is the life and the light of men. The days will come when you will look back with longing upon the opportunities you now enjoy to walk and talk with the Son of God.

Because of their selfishness and earthliness, even the disciples of Jesus could not comprehend the spiritual glory which He sought to reveal unto them. It was not until after Christ's ascension to His Father, and the outpouring of the Holy Spirit upon the believers, that the disciples fully appreciated the Saviour's character and mission. After they had received the baptism of the Spirit, they began to realize that they had been in the very presence of the Lord of glory. As the sayings of Christ were brought to their remembrance, their minds were opened to comprehend the prophecies, and to understand the miracles which He had wrought. The wonders of His life passed before them, and they were as men awakened from a dream. They realized that "the Word was made flesh, and dwelt among us, (and we beheld His glory, the glory as of the Only-begotten of the Father,) full of grace and truth." John 1:14. Christ had actually come from God to a sinful world to save the fallen sons and daughters of Adam. The disciples now seemed, to themselves, of much less importance than before they realized this. They never wearied of rehearsing His words and works. His lessons, which they had but dimly understood, now came to them as a fresh revelation. The Scriptures became to them a new book.

As the disciples searched the prophecies that testified of Christ, they were brought into fellowship with the Deity, and learned of Him who had ascended to heaven to complete the work He had begun on earth. They recognized the fact that in Him dwelt knowledge which no human being, unaided by divine agency, could comprehend. They needed the help of Him whom kings, prophets, and righteous men had foretold. With amazement they read and reread the prophetic delineations of His character and work. How dimly had they comprehended the prophetic scriptures; how slow they had been in taking in the great truths which testified of Christ. Looking upon Him in His humiliation, as He walked a man among men, they had not understood the mystery of His incarnation, the dual character of His nature. Their eyes were holden, so that they did not fully recognize divinity in humanity. But after they were illuminated by the Holy Spirit, how they longed to see Him again, and to place themselves at His feet. How they wished that they might come to Him, and have Him explain the scriptures which they could not comprehend. How attentively would they listen to His words. What had Christ meant when He said, "I have yet many things to say unto you, but ye cannot bear them now"? John 16:12. How eager they were to know it all. They grieved that their faith had been so feeble, that their ideas had been so wide of the mark, that they had so failed of comprehending the reality.

"Today in the religious world there are multitudes who . . . are working for the establishment of the kingdom of Christ as an earthly dominion. They desire to make our Lord the ruler of the kingdoms of this world . . . They expect Him to rule through legal enactments, enforced by human authority. . . . The establishment of such a kingdom is what the Jews desired . . . But He said, 'My kingdom is not of this world.' He would not accept the earthly throne."

A herald had been sent from God to proclaim the coming of Christ, and to call the attention of the Jewish nation and of the world to His mission, that men might prepare for His reception. The wonderful personage whom John had announced had been among them for more than thirty years, and they had not really known Him as the One sent from God. Remorse took hold of the disciples because they had allowed the prevailing unbelief to leaven their opinions and becloud their understanding. The Light of this dark world had been shining amid its gloom, and they had failed to comprehend whence were its beams. They asked themselves why they had pursued a course that made it necessary for Christ to reprove them. They often repeated His conversations, and said, Why did we allow earthly considerations and the opposition of priests and rabbis to confuse our senses, so that we did not comprehend that a greater than Moses was among us, that One wiser than Solomon was instructing us? How dull were our ears! how feeble was our understanding!

Thomas would not believe until he had thrust his finger into the wound made by the Roman soldiers. Peter had denied Him in His humiliation and rejection. These painful remembrances came before them in distinct lines. They had been with Him, but they had not known or appreciated Him. But how these things now stirred their hearts as they recognized their unbelief!

As priests and rulers combined against them, and they were brought before councils and thrust into prison, the followers of Christ rejoiced "that they were counted worthy to suffer shame for His name." Acts 5:41. They rejoiced to prove, before men and angels, that they recognized the glory of Christ, and chose to follow Him at the loss of all things.

It is as true now as in apostolic days, that without the illumination of the divine Spirit, humanity cannot discern the glory of Christ. The truth and the work of God are unappreciated by a world-loving and compromising Christianity. Not in the ways of ease, of earthly honor or worldly conformity, are the followers of the Master found. They are far in advance, in the paths of toil, and humiliation, and reproach, in the front of the battle "against the principalities, against the powers, against the world rulers of this darkness, against the spiritual hosts of wickedness in the heavenly places." Ephesians 6:12, R. V. And now, as in Christ's day, they are misunderstood and reproached and oppressed by the priests and Pharisees of their time.

The kingdom of God comes not with outward show. The gospel of the grace of God, with its spirit of self-abnegation, can never be in harmony with the spirit of the world. The two principles are antagonistic. "The natural man receiveth not the things of the Spirit of God: for they are foolishness unto him: neither can he know them, because they are spiritually discerned." 1 Corinthians 2:14.

But today in the religious world there are multitudes who, as they believe, are working for the establishment of the kingdom of Christ as an earthly and temporal dominion. They desire to make our Lord the ruler of the kingdoms of this world, the ruler in its courts and camps, its legislative halls, its palaces and market places. They expect Him to rule through legal enactments, enforced by human authority. Since Christ is not now here in person, they themselves will undertake to act in His stead, to execute the laws of His kingdom. The establishment of such a kingdom is what the Jews desired in the days of Christ. They would have received Jesus, had He been willing to establish a temporal dominion, to enforce what they regarded as the laws of God, and to make them the expositors of His will and the agents of His authority. But He said, "My kingdom is not of this world." John 18:36. He would not accept the earthly throne.

The government under which Jesus lived was corrupt and oppressive; on every hand were crying abuses, — extortion, intolerance, and grinding cruelty. Yet the Saviour attempted no civil reforms. He attacked no national abuses, nor condemned the national enemies. He did not interfere with the authority or administration of those in power. He who was our example kept aloof from earthly governments. Not because He was indifferent to the woes of men, but because the remedy did not lie in merely human and external measures. To be efficient, the cure must reach men individually, and must regenerate the heart.

Not by the decisions of courts or councils or legislative assemblies, not by the patronage of worldly great men, is the kingdom of Christ established, but by the implanting of Christ's nature in humanity through the work of the Holy Spirit. "As many as received Him, to them gave He power to become the sons of God, even to them that believe on His name; which were born, not of blood, nor of the will of the flesh, nor of the will of man, but of God." John 1:12, 13. Here is the only power that can work the uplifting of mankind. And the human agency for the accomplishment of this work is the teaching and practicing of the word of God.

When the apostle Paul began his ministry in Corinth, that populous, wealthy, and wicked city, polluted by the nameless vices of heathenism, he said, "I determined not to know anything among you, save Jesus Christ, and Him crucified." 1 Corinthians 2:2. Writing afterward to some of those who had been corrupted by the foulest sins, he could say, "But ye are washed, but ye are sanctified, but ye are justified in the name of the Lord Jesus, and by the Spirit of our God." "I thank my God always on your behalf, for the grace of God which is given you by Jesus Christ." 1 Corinthians 6:11; 1:4.

Now, as in Christ's day, the work of God's kingdom lies not with those who are clamoring for recognition and support by earthly rulers and human laws, but with those who are declaring to the people in His name those spiritual truths that will work in the receivers the experience of Paul: "I am crucified with Christ: nevertheless I live; yet not I, but Christ liveth in me." Galatians 2:20. Then they will labor as did Paul for the benefit of men. He said, "Now then we are ambassadors for Christ, as though God did beseech you by us; we pray you in Christ's stead, be ye reconciled to God." 2 Corinthians 5:20.

Blessing the Children

Jesus was ever a lover of children. He accepted their childish sympathy and their open, unaffected love. The grateful praise from their pure lips was music in His ears, and refreshed His spirit when oppressed by contact with crafty and hypocritical men. Wherever the Saviour went, the benignity of His countenance, and His gentle, kindly manner won the love and confidence of children.

Among the Jews it was customary for children to be brought to some rabbi, that he might lay his hands upon them in blessing; but the Saviour's disciples thought His work too important to be interrupted in this way. When the mothers came to Him with their little ones, the disciples looked on them with disfavor. They thought these children too young to be benefited by a visit to Jesus, and concluded that He would be displeased at their presence. But it was the disciples with whom He was displeased. The Saviour understood the care and burden of the mothers who were seeking to train their children according to the word of God. He had heard their prayers. He Himself had drawn them into His presence.

One mother with her child had left her home to find Jesus. On the way she told a neighbor her errand, and the neighbor wanted to have Jesus bless her children. Thus several mothers came together, with their little ones. Some of the children had passed beyond the years of infancy to childhood and youth. When the mothers made known their desire, Jesus heard with sympathy the timid, tearful request. But He waited to see how the disciples would treat them. When He saw them send the mothers away, thinking to do Him a favor, He showed them their error, saying, "Suffer the little children to come unto Me, and forbid them not; for of such is the kingdom of God." He took the children in His arms, He laid His hands upon them, and gave them the blessing for which they came.

The mothers were comforted. They returned to their homes strengthened and blessed by the words of Christ. They were encouraged to take up their burden with new cheerfulness, and to work hopefully for their children. The mothers of today are to receive His words with the same faith. Christ is as verily a personal Saviour today as when He lived a man among men. He is as verily the helper of mothers today as when He gathered the little ones to His arms in Judea. The children of our hearths are as much the purchase of His blood as were the children of long ago.

Jesus knows the burden of every mother's heart. He who had a mother that struggled with poverty and privation, sympathizes with every mother in her labors. He who made a long journey in order to relieve the anxious heart of a Canaanite woman, will do as much for the mothers of today. He who gave back to the widow of Nain her only son, and who in His agony upon the cross remembered His own mother, is touched today by the mother's sorrow. In every grief and every need He will give comfort and help.

Let mothers come to Jesus with their perplexities. They will find grace sufficient to aid them in the management of their children. The gates are open for every mother who would lay her burdens at the Saviour's feet. He who said, "Suffer the little children to come unto Me, and forbid them not," still invites the mothers to lead up their little ones to be blessed by Him. Even the babe in its mother's arms may dwell as under the shadow of the Almighty through the faith of the praying mother. John the Baptist was filled with the Holy Spirit from his birth. If we will live in communion with God, we too may expect the divine

This chapter is based on Matthew 19:13-15; Mark 10:13-16; Luke 18:15-17.

Spirit to mold our little ones, even from their earliest moments.

In the children who were brought in contact with Him, Jesus saw the men and women who should be heirs of His grace and subjects of His kingdom, and some of whom would become martyrs for His sake. He knew that these children would listen to Him and accept Him as their Redeemer far more readily than would grown-up people, many of whom were the worldly-wise and hardhearted. In His teaching He came down to their level. He, the Majesty of heaven, did not disdain to answer their questions, and simplify His important lessons to meet their childish understanding. He planted in their minds the seeds of truth, which in after years would spring up, and bear fruit unto eternal life.

It is still true that children are the most susceptible to the teachings of the gospel; their hearts are open to divine influences, and strong to retain the lessons received. The little children may be Christians, having an experience in accordance with their years. They need to be educated in spiritual things, and parents should give them every advantage, that they may form characters after the similitude of the character of Christ.

Fathers and mothers should look upon their children as younger members of the Lord's family, committed to them to educate for heaven. The lessons that we ourselves learn from Christ we should give to our children, as the young minds can receive them, little by little opening to them the beauty of the principles of heaven. Thus the Christian home becomes a school, where the parents serve as underteachers, while Christ Himself is the chief instructor.

In working for the conversion of our children, we should not look for violent emotion as the essential evidence of conviction of sin. Nor is it necessary to know the exact time when they are converted. We should teach them to bring their sins to Jesus, asking His forgiveness, and believing that He pardons and receives them as He received the children when He was personally on earth.

As the mother teaches her children to obey her because they love her, she is teaching them the first lessons in the Christian life. The mother's love represents to the child the love of Christ, and the little ones who trust and obey their mother, are learning to trust and obey the Saviour.

Jesus was the pattern for children, and He was also the father's example. He spoke as one having authority, and His word was with power; yet in all His intercourse with rude and violent men He did not use one unkind or discourteous expression. The grace of Christ in the heart will impart a heaven-born dignity and sense of propriety. It will soften whatever is harsh, and subdue all that is coarse and unkind. It will lead fathers and mothers to treat their children as intelligent beings, as they themselves would like to be treated.

Parents, in the training of your children, study the lessons that God has given in nature. If you would train a pink, or rose, or lily, how would you do it? Ask the gardener by what process he makes every branch and leaf to flourish so beautifully, and to develop in symmetry and loveliness. He will tell you that it was by no rude touch, no violent effort; for this would only break the delicate stems. It was by little attentions, often repeated. He moistened the soil, and protected the growing plants from the fierce blasts and from the scorching sun, and God caused them to flourish and to blossom into loveliness. In dealing with your children, follow the method of the gardener. By gentle touches, by loving ministrations, seek to fashion their characters after the pattern of the character of Christ.

"Jesus knows the burden of every mother's heart. He who had a mother that struggled with poverty and privation sympathizes with every mother in her labors. . . . In every grief and every need He will give comfort and help."

Encourage the expression of love toward God and toward one another. The reason why there are so many hardhearted men and women in the world is that true affection has been regarded as weakness, and has been discouraged and repressed. The better nature of these persons was stifled in childhood; and unless the light of divine love shall melt away their cold selfishness, their happiness will be forever ruined. If we wish our children to possess the tender spirit of Jesus, and the sympathy that angels manifest for us, we must encourage the generous, loving impulses of childhood.

Teach the children to see Christ in nature. Take them out into the open air, under the noble trees, into the garden; and in all the wonderful works of creation teach them to see an expression of His love. Teach them that He made the laws which govern all living things, that He has made laws for us, and that these laws are for our happiness and joy. Do not weary them with long prayers and tedious exhortations, but through nature's object lessons teach them obedience to the law of God.

As you win their confidence in you as followers of Christ, it will be easy to teach them of the great love wherewith He has loved us. As you try to make plain the truths of salvation, and point the children to Christ as a personal Saviour, angels will be by your side. The Lord will give to fathers and mothers grace to interest their little ones in the precious story of the Babe of Bethlehem, who is indeed the hope of the world.

When Jesus told the disciples not to forbid the children to come to Him, He was speaking to His followers in all ages, — to officers of the church, to ministers, helpers, and all Christians. Jesus is drawing the children, and He bids us, "Suffer them to come;" as if He would say, They will come if you do not hinder them.

Let not your unchristlike character misrepresent Jesus. Do not keep the little ones away from Him by your coldness and harshness. Never give them cause to feel that heaven will not be a pleasant place to them if you are there. Do not speak of religion as something that children cannot understand, or act as if they were not expected to accept Christ in their childhood. Do not give them the false impression that the religion of Christ is a religion of gloom, and that in coming to the Saviour they must give up all that makes life joyful.

As the Holy Spirit moves upon the hearts of the children, co-operate with His work. Teach them that the Saviour is calling them, that nothing can give Him greater joy than for them to give themselves to Him in the bloom and freshness of their years.

The Saviour regards with infinite tenderness the souls whom He has purchased with His own blood. They are the claim of His love. He looks upon them with unutterable longing. His heart is drawn out, not only to the best-behaved children, but to those who have by inheritance objectionable traits of character. Many parents do not understand how much they are responsible for these traits in their children. They have not the tenderness and wisdom to deal with the erring ones whom they have made what they are. But Jesus looks upon these children with pity. He traces from cause to effect.

The Christian worker may be Christ's agent in drawing these children to the Saviour. By wisdom and tact he may bind them to his heart, he may give them courage and hope, and through the grace of Christ may see them transformed in character, so that of them it may be said, "Of such is the kingdom of God."

"One Thing Thou Lackest"

A nd when He was gone forth into the way, there came one running, and kneeled to Him, and asked Him, Good Master, what shall I do that I may inherit eternal life?"

The young man who asked this question was a ruler. He had great possessions, and occupied a position of responsibility. He saw the love that Christ manifested toward the children brought to Him; he saw how tenderly He received them, and took them up in His arms, and his heart kindled with love for the Saviour. He felt a desire to be His disciple. He was so deeply moved that as Christ was going on His way, he ran after Him, and kneeling at His feet, asked with sincerity and earnestness the question so important to his soul and to the soul of every human being, "Good Master, what shall I do that I may inherit eternal life?"

"Why callest thou Me good?" said Christ, "there is none good but one, that is, God." Jesus desired to test the ruler's sincerity, and to draw from him the way in which he regarded Him as good. Did he realize that the one to whom he was speaking was the Son of God? What was the true sentiment of his heart?

This ruler had a high estimate of his own righteousness. He did not really suppose that he was defective in anything, yet he was not altogether satisfied. He felt the want of something that he did not possess. Could not Jesus bless him as He blessed the little children, and satisfy his soul-want?

In reply to this question Jesus told him that obedience to the commandments of God was necessary if he would obtain eternal life; and He quoted several of the commandments which show man's duty to his fellow men. The ruler's answer was positive: "All these things have I kept from my youth up. What lack I yet?"

Christ looked into the face of the young man, as if reading his life and searching his character. He loved him, and He hungered to give him that peace and grace and joy which would materially change his character. "One thing thou lackest," He said; "go thy way, sell whatsoever thou hast, and give to the poor, and thou shalt have treasure in heaven; and come, take up the cross, and follow Me."

Christ was drawn to this young man. He knew him to be sincere in his assertion, "All these things have I kept from my youth." The Redeemer longed to create in him that discernment which would enable him to see the necessity of heart devotion and Christian goodness. He longed to see in him a humble and contrite heart, conscious of the supreme love to be given to God, and hiding its lack in the perfection of Christ.

Jesus saw in this ruler just the help He needed if the young man would become a colaborer with Him in the work of salvation. If he would place himself under Christ's guidance, he would be a power for good. In a marked degree the ruler could have represented Christ; for he possessed qualifications, which, if he were united with the Saviour, would enable him to become a divine force among men. Christ, seeing into his character, loved him. Love for Christ was awakening in the ruler's heart; for love begets love. Jesus longed to see him a co-worker with Him. He longed to make him like Himself, a mirror in which the likeness of God would be reflected. He longed to develop the excellence of his character, and sanctify it to the Master's use. If the ruler had then given himself to Christ, he would have grown in the atmosphere of His presence.

If he had made this choice, how different would have been his future.

"One thing thou lackest," Jesus said. "If thou wilt be perfect, go and sell that thou hast, and give to the poor, and thou shalt have treasure in heaven, and come and follow Me." Christ read the ruler's heart. Only one thing he lacked, but that was a vital principle. He needed the love of God in the soul. This lack, unless supplied, would prove fatal to him; his whole nature would become corrupted. By indulgence, selfishness would strengthen. That he might receive the love of God, his supreme love of self must be surrendered.

Christ gave this man a test. He called upon him to choose between the heavenly treasure and worldly greatness. The heavenly treasure was assured him if he would follow Christ. But self must yield; his will must be given into Christ's control. The very holiness of God was offered to the young ruler. He had the privilege of becoming a son of God, and a coheir with Christ to the heavenly treasure. But he must take up the cross, and follow the Saviour in the path of self-denial.

Christ's words were verily to the ruler the invitation, "Choose you this day whom ye will serve." Joshua 24:15. The choice was left with him. Jesus was yearning for his conversion. He had shown him the plague spot in his character, and with what deep interest He watched the issue as the young man weighed the question. If he decided to follow Christ, he must obey His words in everything. He must turn from his ambitious projects. With what earnest, anxious longing, what soul hunger, did the Saviour look at the young man, hoping that he would yield to the invitation of the Spirit of God.

Christ made the only terms which could place the ruler where he would perfect a Christian character. His words were words of wisdom, though they appeared severe and exacting. In accepting and obeying them was the ruler's only hope of salvation. His exalted position and his possessions were exerting a subtle influence for evil upon his character. If cherished, they would supplant God in his affections. To keep back little or much from God was to retain that which would lessen his moral strength and efficiency; for if the things of this world are cherished, however uncertain and unworthy they may be, they will become all-absorbing.

The ruler was quick to discern all that Christ's words involved, and he became sad. If he had realized the value of the offered gift, quickly would he have enrolled himself as one of Christ's followers. He was a member of the honored council of the Jews, and Satan was tempting him with flattering prospects of the future. He wanted the heavenly treasure, but he wanted also the temporal advantages his riches would bring him. He was sorry that such conditions existed; he desired eternal life; but he was not willing to make the sacrifice. The cost of eternal life seemed too great, and he went away sorrowful; "for he had great possessions."

His claim that he had kept the law of God was a deception. He showed that riches were his idol. He could not keep the commandments of God while the world was first in his affections. He loved the gifts of God more than he loved the Giver. Christ had offered the young man fellowship with Himself. "Follow Me," He said. But the Saviour was not so much to him as his own name among men or his possessions. To give up his earthly treasure, that was seen, for the heavenly treasure, that was unseen, was too great a risk. He refused the offer of eternal life, and went away, and ever after the world was to receive his worship.

> **❝**Only those who will become co-workers with Christ, only those who will say, Lord, all I have and all I am is Thine, will be acknowledged as sons and daughters of God. All should consider what it means to desire heaven, and yet to turn away . . . Think of what it means to say 'No' to Christ. The ruler said, No, I cannot give You all. Do we say the same?**❞**

Thousands are passing through this ordeal, weighing Christ against the world; and many choose the world. Like the young ruler, they turn from the Saviour, saying in their hearts, I will not have this man as my leader.

Christ's dealing with the young man is presented as an object lesson. God has given us the rule of conduct which every one of His servants must follow. It is obedience to His law, not merely a legal obedience, but an obedience which enters into the life, and is exemplified in the character. God has set His own standard of character for all who would become subjects of His kingdom. Only those who will become co-workers with Christ, only those who will say, Lord, all I have and all I am is Thine, will be acknowledged as sons and daughters of God. All should consider what it means to desire heaven, and yet to turn away because of the conditions laid down. Think of what it means to say "No" to Christ. The ruler said, No, I cannot give you all. Do we say the same? The Saviour offers to share with us the work God has given us to do. He offers to use the means God has given us, to carry forward His work in the world. Only in this way can He save us.

The ruler's possessions were entrusted to him that he might prove himself a faithful steward; he was to dispense these goods for the blessing of those in need. So God now entrusts men with means, with talents and opportunities, that they may be His agents in helping the poor and the suffering. He who uses his entrusted gifts as God designs, becomes a co-worker with the Saviour. He wins souls to Christ, because he is a representative of His character.

To those who, like the young ruler, are in high positions of trust and have great possessions, it may seem too great a sacrifice to give up all in order to follow Christ. But this is the rule of conduct for all who would become His disciples. Nothing short of obedience can be accepted. Self-surrender is the substance of the teachings of Christ. Often it is presented and enjoined in language that seems authoritative, because there is no other way to save man than to cut away those things which, if entertained, will demoralize the whole being.

When Christ's followers give back to the Lord His own, they are accumulating treasure which will be given to them when they shall hear the words, "Well done, good and faithful servant; . . . enter thou into the joy of thy Lord." "Who for the joy that was set before Him endured the cross, despising the shame, and is set down at the right hand of the throne of God." Matthew 25:33; Hebrews 12:2. The joy of seeing souls redeemed, souls eternally saved, is the reward of all that put their feet in the footprints of Him who said, "Follow Me."

"Lazarus, Come Forth"

Among the most steadfast of Christ's disciples was Lazarus of Bethany. From their first meeting his faith in Christ had been strong; his love for Him was deep, and he was greatly beloved by the Saviour. It was for Lazarus that the greatest of Christ's miracles was performed. The Saviour blessed all who sought His help; He loves all the human family; but to some He is bound by peculiarly tender associations. His heart was knit by a strong bond of affection to the family at Bethany, and for one of them His most wonderful work was wrought.

At the home of Lazarus, Jesus had often found rest. The Saviour had no home of His own; He was dependent on the hospitality of His friends and disciples; and often, when weary, thirsting for human fellowship, He had been glad to escape to this peaceful household, away from the suspicion and jealousy of the angry Pharisees. Here He found a sincere welcome, and pure, holy friendship. Here He could speak with simplicity and perfect freedom, knowing that His words would be understood and treasured.

Our Saviour appreciated a quiet home and interested listeners. He longed for human tenderness, courtesy, and affection. Those who received the heavenly instruction He was always ready to impart, were greatly blessed. As the multitudes followed Christ through the open fields, He unfolded to them the beauties of the natural world. He sought to open the eyes of their understanding, that they might see how the hand of God upholds the world. In order to call out an appreciation of God's goodness and benevolence, He called the attention of His hearers to the gently falling dew, to the soft showers of rain and the bright sunshine, given alike to good and evil. He desired men to realize more fully the regard that God bestows on the human instrumentalities He has created. But the multitudes were slow of hearing, and in the home at Bethany Christ found rest from the weary conflict of public life. Here He opened to an appreciative audience the volume of Providence. In these private interviews He unfolded to His hearers that which He did not attempt to tell to the mixed multitude. He needed not to speak to His friends in parables.

As Christ gave His wonderful lessons, Mary sat at His feet, a reverent and devoted listener. On one occasion, Martha, perplexed with the care of preparing the meal, went to Christ, saying, "Lord, dost Thou not care that my sister hath left me to serve alone? bid her therefore that she help me." This was the time of Christ's first visit to Bethany. The Saviour and His disciples had just made the toilsome journey on foot from Jericho. Martha was anxious to provide for their comfort, and in her anxiety she forgot the courtesy due to her Guest. Jesus answered her with mild and patient words, "Martha, Martha, thou art careful and troubled about many things; but one thing is needful; and Mary hath chosen that good part, which shall not be taken away from her." Mary was storing her mind with the precious words falling from the Saviour's lips, words that were more precious to her than earth's most costly jewels.

The "one thing" that Martha needed was a calm, devotional spirit, a deeper anxiety for knowledge concerning the future, immortal life, and the graces necessary for spiritual advancement. She needed less anxiety for the things which pass away, and more for those things which endure forever. Jesus would teach His children to seize every opportunity of gaining that knowledge which will make them wise unto salvation. The cause of Christ needs

This chapter is based on Luke 10:38-42; John 11:1-44.

careful, energetic workers. There is a wide field for the Marthas, with their zeal in active religious work. But let them first sit with Mary at the feet of Jesus. Let diligence, promptness, and energy be sanctified by the grace of Christ; then the life will be an unconquerable power for good.

Sorrow entered the peaceful home where Jesus had rested. Lazarus was stricken with sudden illness, and his sisters sent to the Saviour, saying, "Lord, behold, he whom Thou lovest is sick." They saw the violence of the disease that had seized their brother, but they knew that Christ had shown Himself able to heal all manner of diseases. They believed that He would sympathize with them in their distress; therefore they made no urgent demand for His immediate presence, but sent only the confiding message, "He whom Thou lovest is sick." They thought that He would immediately respond to their message, and be with them as soon as He could reach Bethany.

Anxiously they waited for a word from Jesus. As long as the spark of life was yet alive in their brother, they prayed and watched for Jesus to come. But the messenger returned without Him. Yet he brought the message, "This sickness is not unto death," and they clung to the hope that Lazarus would live. Tenderly they tried to speak words of hope and encouragement to the almost unconscious sufferer. When Lazarus died, they were bitterly disappointed; but they felt the sustaining grace of Christ, and this kept them from reflecting any blame on the Saviour.

When Christ heard the message, the disciples thought He received it coldly. He did not manifest the sorrow they expected Him to show. Looking up to them, He said, "This sickness is not unto death, but for the glory of God, that the Son of God might be glorified thereby." For two days He remained in the place where He was. This delay was a mystery to the disciples. What a comfort His presence would be to the afflicted household, they thought. His strong affection for the family at Bethany, was well known to the disciples, and they were surprised that He did not respond to the sad message, "He whom Thou lovest is sick."

During the two days Christ seemed to have dismissed the message from His mind; for He did not speak of Lazarus. The disciples thought of John the Baptist, the forerunner of Jesus. They had wondered why Jesus, with the power to perform wonderful miracles, had permitted John to languish in prison, and to die a violent death. Possessing such power, why did not Christ save John's life? This question had often been asked by the Pharisees, who presented it as an unanswerable argument against Christ's claim to be the Son of God. The Saviour had warned His disciples of trials, losses, and persecution. Would He forsake them in trial? Some questioned if they had mistaken His mission. All were deeply troubled.

After waiting for two days, Jesus said to the disciples, "Let us go into Judea again." The disciples questioned why, if Jesus were going to Judea, He had waited two days.

But anxiety for Christ and for themselves was now uppermost in their minds. They could see nothing but danger in the course He was about to pursue. "Master," they said, "the Jews of late sought to stone Thee; and goest Thou thither again? Jesus answered, Are there not twelve hours in the day?" I am under the guidance of My Father; as long as I do His will, My life is safe. My twelve hours of day are not yet ended. I have entered upon the last remnant of My day; but while any of this remains, I am safe.

"If any man walk in the day," He continued, "he stumbleth not, because he seeth the light of this world." He who does the will of God, who walks in the path that God has marked out, cannot stumble and fall. The light of God's guiding Spirit gives Him a clear perception of his duty, and leads him aright till the close of his work. "But if a man walk in the night, he stumbleth, because there is no light in him." He who walks in a path of his own choosing, where God has not called him, will stumble. For him day is turned into night, and wherever he may be, he is not secure.

"These things said He: and after that He saith unto them, Our friend Lazarus sleepeth; but I go that I may awake him out of sleep." "Our friend Lazarus sleepeth." How touching the words! how full of sympathy! In the thought of the peril their Master was about to incur by going to Jerusalem, the disciples had almost forgotten the bereaved family at Bethany. But not so Christ. The disciples felt rebuked. They had been disappointed because Christ did not respond more promptly to the message. They had been tempted to think that He had not the tender love for Lazarus and his sisters that they had thought He had, or He would have hastened back with the messenger. But the words, "Our friend Lazarus sleepeth," awakened right feelings in their minds. They were convinced that Christ had not forgotten His suffering friends.

"Then said His disciples, Lord, if he sleep, he shall do well. Howbeit Jesus spake of his death: but they thought that He had spoken of taking of rest in sleep." Christ represents death as a sleep to His believing children. Their life is hid with Christ in God, and until the last trump shall sound, those who die will sleep in Him.

"Then said Jesus unto them plainly, Lazarus is dead. And I am glad for your sakes that I was not there, to the intent ye may believe; nevertheless let us go unto him." Thomas could see nothing but death in store for his Master if he went to Judea; but he girded up his spirit, and said to the other disciples, "Let us also go, that we may die with Him." He knew the hatred of the Jews toward Christ. It was their purpose to compass His death, but this purpose had not succeeded. because some of His allotted time still remained. During this time Jesus had the guardianship of heavenly angels; and even in the regions of Judea, where the rabbis were plotting how they might take Him and put Him to death, no harm could come to Him.

The disciples marveled at Christ's words when He said, "Lazarus is dead. And I am glad . . . that I was not there."

Did the Saviour by His own choice avoid the home of His suffering friends? Apparently Mary and Martha and the dying Lazarus were left alone. But they were not alone. Christ beheld the whole scene, and after the death of Lazarus the bereaved sisters were upheld by His grace. Jesus witnessed the sorrow of their rent hearts, as their brother wrestled with his strong foe, death. He felt every pang of anguish, as He said to His disciples, "Lazarus is dead." But Christ had not only the loved ones at Bethany to think of; He had the training of His disciples to consider. They were to be His representatives to the world, that the Father's blessing might embrace all. For their sake He permitted Lazarus to die. Had He restored him from illness to health, the miracle that is the most positive evidence of His divine character, would not have been performed.

Had Christ been in the sickroom, Lazarus would not have died; for Satan would have had no power over him. Death could not have aimed his dart at Lazarus in the presence of the Life-giver. Therefore Christ remained away. He suffered the enemy to exercise his power, that He might drive him back, a conquered foe. He permitted Lazarus to pass under the dominion of death; and the suffering sisters saw their brother laid in the grave. Christ knew that as they looked on the dead face of their brother their faith in their Redeemer would be severely tried. But He knew that because of the struggle through which they were now passing, their faith would shine forth with far greater power. He suffered every pang of sorrow that they endured. He loved them no less because He tarried; but He knew that for them, for Lazarus, for Himself, and for His disciples, a victory was to be gained.

"For your sakes," "to the intent ye may believe." To all who are reaching out to feel the guiding hand of God, the moment of greatest discouragement is the time when divine help is nearest. They will look back with thankfulness upon the darkest part of their way. "The Lord knoweth how to deliver the godly." 2 Peter 2:9. From every temptation and every trial He will bring them forth with firmer faith and a richer experience.

In delaying to come to Lazarus, Christ had a purpose of mercy toward those who had not received Him. He tarried, that by raising Lazarus from the dead He might give to His stubborn, unbelieving people another evidence that He was indeed "the resurrection and the life." He was loath to give up all hope of the people, the poor, wandering sheep of the house of Israel. His heart was breaking because of their impenitence. In His mercy He purposed to give them one more evidence that He was the Restorer, the One who alone could bring life and immortality to light. This was to be an evidence that the priests could not misinterpret. This was the reason of His delay in going to Bethany. This crowning miracle, the raising of Lazarus, was to set the seal of God on His work and on His claim to divinity.

On His journey to Bethany, Jesus, according to His custom, ministered to the sick and the needy. Upon reaching the town He sent a messenger to the sisters with the tidings of His arrival. Christ did not at once enter the house, but remained in a quiet place by the wayside. The great outward display observed by the Jews at the death of friends or relatives was not in harmony with the spirit of Christ. He heard the sound of wailing from the hired mourners, and He did not wish to meet the sisters in the scene of confusion. Among the mourning friends were relatives of the family, some of whom held high positions of responsibility in Jerusalem. Among these were some of Christ's bitterest enemies. Christ knew their purposes, and therefore He did not at once make Himself known.

The message was given to Martha so quietly that others in the room did not hear. Absorbed in her grief, Mary did not hear the words. Rising at once, Martha went out to meet her Lord, but thinking that she had gone to the place where Lazarus was buried, Mary sat still in her sorrow, making no outcry.

Martha hastened to meet Jesus, her heart agitated by conflicting emotions. In His expressive face she read the same tenderness and love that had always been there. Her confidence in Him was unbroken, but she thought of her dearly loved brother, whom Jesus also had loved. With grief surging in her heart because Christ had not come before, yet with hope that even now He would do something to comfort them, she said, "Lord, if thou hadst been here, my brother had not died." Over and over again, amid the tumult made by the mourners, the sisters had repeated these words.

With human and divine pity Jesus looked into her sorrowful, careworn face. Martha had no inclination to recount the past; all was expressed by the pathetic words, "Lord, if thou hadst been here, my brother had not died." But looking into that face of love, she added, "I know, that even now, whatsoever Thou wilt ask of God, God will give it Thee."

Jesus encouraged her faith, saying, "Thy brother shall rise again." His answer was not intended to inspire hope of an immediate change. He carried Martha's thoughts beyond the present restoration of her brother, and fixed them upon the resurrection of the just. This He did that she might see in the resurrection of Lazarus a pledge of the resurrection of all the righteous dead, and an assurance that it would be accomplished by the Saviour's power.

Martha answered, "I know that he shall rise again in the resurrection at the last day."

Still seeking to give a true direction to her faith, Jesus declared, "I am the resurrection, and the life." In Christ is life, original, unborrowed, underived. "He that hath the Son hath life." 1 John 5:12. The divinity of Christ is the believer's assurance of eternal life. "He that believeth in Me," said Jesus, "though he were dead, yet shall he live; and whosoever liveth and believeth in Me shall never die. Believest thou this?" Christ here looks forward to the time of His second coming. Then the righteous dead shall be raised incorruptible, and the living righteous shall be translated to heaven without seeing death. The miracle which

Christ was about to perform, in raising Lazarus from the dead, would represent the resurrection of all the righteous dead. By His word and His works He declared Himself the Author of the resurrection. He who Himself was soon to die upon the cross, stood with the keys of death, a conqueror of the grave, and asserted His right and power to give eternal life.

To the Saviour's words, "Believest thou?" Martha responded, "Yea, Lord; I believe that Thou art the Christ, the Son of God, which should come into the world." She did not comprehend in all their significance the words spoken by Christ, but she confessed her faith in His divinity, and her confidence that He was able to perform whatever it pleased Him to do.

"And when she had so said, she went her way, and called Mary her sister, secretly, saying, The Master is come, and calleth for thee." She delivered her message as quietly as possible; for the priests and rulers were prepared to arrest Jesus when opportunity offered. The cries of the mourners prevented her words from being heard.

On hearing the message, Mary rose hastily, and with an eager look on her face left the room. Thinking that she had gone to the grave to weep, the mourners followed her. When she reached the place where Jesus was waiting, she knelt at His feet, and said with quivering lips, "Lord, if Thou hadst been here, my brother had not died." The cries of the mourners were painful to her; for she longed for a few quiet words alone with Jesus. But she knew of the envy and jealousy cherished in the hearts of some present against Christ, and she was restrained from fully expressing her grief.

"When Jesus therefore saw her weeping, and the Jews also weeping which came with her, He groaned in the spirit, and was troubled." He read the hearts of all assembled. He saw that with many, what passed as a demonstration of grief was only pretense. He knew that some in the company, now manifesting hypocritical sorrow, would ere long be planning the death, not only of the mighty miracle worker, but of the one to be raised from the dead. Christ could have stripped from them their robe of pretended sorrow. But He restrained His righteous indignation. The words He could in all truth have spoken, He did not speak, because of the loved one kneeling at His feet in sorrow, who truly believed in Him.

"Where have ye laid him?" He asked, "They said unto Him, Lord, come and see." Together they proceeded to the grave. It was a mournful scene. Lazarus had been much beloved, and his sisters wept for him with breaking hearts, while those who had been his friends mingled their tears with those of the bereaved sisters. In view of this human distress, and of the fact that the afflicted friends could mourn over the dead while the Saviour of the world stood by,—"Jesus wept." Though He was the Son of God, yet He had taken human nature upon Him, and He was moved by human sorrow. His tender, pitying heart is ever awakened to sympathy by suffering. He weeps with those that weep, and rejoices with those that rejoice.

But it was not only because of His human sympathy with Mary and Martha that Jesus wept. In His tears there was a sorrow as high above human sorrow as the heavens are higher than the earth. Christ did not weep for Lazarus; for He was about to call him from the grave. He wept because many of those now mourning for Lazarus would soon plan the death of Him who was the resurrection and the life. But how unable were the unbelieving Jews rightly to interpret His tears! Some, who could see nothing more than the outward circumstances of the scene before Him as a cause for His grief, said softly, "Behold how He loved him." Others, seeking to drop the seed of unbelief into the hearts of those present, said derisively, "Could not this man, which opened the eyes of the blind, have caused that even this man should not have died?" If it were in Christ's power to save Lazarus, why then did He suffer him to die?

With prophetic eye Christ saw the enmity of the Pharisees and the Sadducees. He knew that they were premeditating His death. He knew that some of those now apparently so sympathetic would soon close against themselves the door of hope and the gates of the city of God. A scene was about to take place, in His humiliation and crucifixion, that would result in the destruction of Jerusalem, and at that time none would make lamentation for the dead. The retribution that was coming upon Jerusalem was plainly portrayed before Him. He saw Jerusalem compassed by the Roman legions. He knew that many now weeping for Lazarus would die in the siege of the city, and in their death there would be no hope.

It was not only because of the scene before Him that Christ wept. The weight of the grief of ages was upon Him. He saw the terrible effects of the transgression of God's law. He saw that in the history of the world, beginning with the death of Abel, the conflict between good and evil had been unceasing. Looking down the years to come, He saw the suffering and sorrow, tears and death, that were to be the lot of men. His heart was pierced with the pain of the human family of all ages and in all lands. The woes of the sinful race were heavy upon His soul, and the fountain of His tears was broken up as He longed to relieve all their distress.

"Jesus therefore again groaning in Himself cometh to the grave." Lazarus had been laid in a cave in a rock, and a massive stone had been placed before the entrance. "Take ye away the stone," Christ said. Thinking that He only wished to look upon the dead, Martha objected, saying that the body had been buried four days, and corruption had already begun its work. This statement, made before the raising of Lazarus, left no room for Christ's enemies to say that a deception had been practiced. In the past the Pharisees had circulated false statements regarding the most wonderful manifestations of the power of God. When Christ raised to life the daughter of Jairus, He had said, "The damsel is not dead, but sleepeth." Mark 5:39. As she had been sick only a short time, and was raised immediately after death, the Pharisees declared that the child had not been dead; that Christ Himself had said she was only asleep. They had tried to make it appear that Christ could not cure disease, that there was foul play about His miracles. But in this case, none could deny that Lazarus was dead.

When the Lord is about to do a work, Satan moves upon some one to object. "Take ye away the stone," Christ said. As far as possible, prepare the way for My work. But Martha's positive and ambitious nature asserted itself. She was unwilling that the decomposing body should be brought to view. The human heart is slow to understand Christ's words, and Martha's faith had not grasped the true meaning of His promise.

Christ reproved Martha, but His words were spoken with the utmost gentleness. "Said I not unto thee, that, if thou wouldst believe, thou shouldst see the glory of God?" Why should you doubt in regard to My power? Why reason in opposition to My requirements? You have My word. If you will believe, you shall see the glory of God. Natural impossibilities cannot prevent the work of the Omnipotent One. Skepticism and unbelief are not humility. Implicit belief in Christ's word is true humility, true self-surrender.

"Take ye away the stone." Christ could have commanded the stone to remove, and it would have obeyed His voice. He could have bidden the angels who were close by His side to do this. At His bidding, invisible hands would have removed the stone. But it was to be taken away by human hands. Thus Christ would show that humanity is to co-operate with divinity. What human power can do, divine power is not summoned to do. God does not dispense with man's aid. He strengthens him, co-operating with him as he uses the powers and capabilities given him.

The command is obeyed. The stone is rolled away. Everything is done openly and deliberately. All are given a chance to see that no deception is practiced. There lies the body of Lazarus in its rocky grave, cold and silent in death. The cries of the mourners are hushed. Surprised and expectant, the company stand around the sepulcher, waiting to see what is to follow.

Calmly Christ stands before the tomb. A sacred solemnity rests upon all present. Christ steps closer to the sepulcher. Lifting His eyes to heaven, He says, "Father, I thank Thee that Thou hast heard Me." Not long before this, Christ's enemies had accused Him of blasphemy, and had taken up stones to cast at Him because He claimed to be the Son of God. They accused Him of performing miracles by the power of Satan. But here Christ claims God as His Father, and with perfect confidence declares that He is the Son of God.

In all that He did, Christ was co-operating with His Father. Ever He had been careful to make it evident that He did not work independently; it was by faith and prayer that He wrought His miracles. Christ desired all to know His relationship with His Father. "Father," He said, "I thank Thee that Thou hast heard Me. And I knew that Thou hearest Me always; but because of the people which stand by I said it, that they may believe that Thou hast sent Me." Here the disciples and the people were to be given the most convincing evidence in regard to the relationship existing between Christ and God. They were to be shown that Christ's claim was not a deception.

"And when He thus had spoken, He cried with a loud voice, Lazarus, come forth." His voice, clear and penetrating, pierces the ear of the dead. As he speaks, divinity flashes through humanity. In His face, which is lighted up by the glory of God, the people see the assurance of His power. Every eye is fastened on the entrance to the cave. Every ear is bent to catch the slightest sound. With intense and painful interest all wait for the test of Christ's divinity, the evidence that is to substantiate His claim to be the Son of God, or to extinguish the hope forever.

There is a stir in the silent tomb, and he who was dead stands at the door of the sepulcher. His movements are impeded by the grave clothes in which he was laid away, and Christ says to the astonished spectators, "Loose him, and let him go." Again they are shown that the human worker is to co-operate with God. Humanity is to work for humanity. Lazarus is set free, and stands before the company, not as one emaciated from disease, and with feeble, tottering limbs, but as a man in the prime of life, and in the vigor of a noble manhood. His eyes beam with intelligence and with love for his Saviour. He casts himself in adoration at the feet of Jesus.

The beholders are at first speechless with amazement. Then there follows an inexpressible scene of rejoicing and thanksgiving. The sisters receive their brother back to life as the gift of God, and with joyful tears they brokenly express their thanks to the Saviour. But while brother, sisters, and friends are rejoicing in this reunion, Jesus withdraws from the scene. When they look for the Lifegiver, He is not to be found.

Priestly Plottings

Bethany was so near Jerusalem that the news of the raising of Lazarus was soon carried to the city. Through spies who had witnessed the miracle the Jewish rulers were speedily in possession of the facts. A meeting of the Sanhedrim was at once called to decide as to what should be done. Christ had now fully made manifest His control of death and the grave. That mighty miracle was the crowning evidence offered by God to men that He had sent His Son into the world for their salvation. It was a demonstration of divine power sufficient to convince every mind that was under the control of reason and enlightened conscience. Many who witnessed the resurrection of Lazarus were led to believe on Jesus. But the hatred of the priests against Him was intensified. They had rejected all lesser evidence of His divinity, and they were only enraged at this new miracle. The dead had been raised in the full light of day, and before a crowd of witnesses. No artifice could explain away such evidence. For this very reason the enmity of the priests grew deadlier. They were more than ever determined to put a stop to Christ's work.

The Sadducees, though not favorable to Christ, had not been so full of malignity toward Him as were the Pharisees. Their hatred had not been so bitter. But they were now thoroughly alarmed. They did not believe in a resurrection of the dead. Producing so-called science, they had reasoned that it would be an impossibility for a dead body to be brought to life. But by a few words from Christ their theory had been overthrown. They were shown to be ignorant both of the Scriptures and of the power of God. They could see no possibility of removing the impression made on the people by the miracle. How would men be turned away from Him who had prevailed to rob the grave of its dead? Lying reports were put in circulation, but the miracle could not be denied, and how to counteract its effect they knew not. Thus far the Sadducees had not encouraged the plan of putting Christ to death. But after the resurrection of Lazarus they decided that only by His death could His fearless denunciations against them be stopped.

The Pharisees believed in the resurrection, and they could not but see that this miracle was an evidence that the Messiah was among them. But they had ever opposed Christ's work. From the first they had hated Him because He had exposed their hypocritical pretensions. He had torn aside the cloak of rigorous rites under which their moral deformity was hidden. The pure religion that He taught had condemned their hollow professions of piety. They thirsted to be revenged upon Him for His pointed rebukes. They had tried to provoke Him to say or do something that would give them occasion to condemn Him. Several times they had attempted to stone Him, but He had quietly withdrawn, and they had lost sight of Him.

The miracles He performed on the Sabbath were all for the relief of the afflicted, but the Pharisees had sought to condemn Him as a Sabbathbreaker. They had tried to arouse the Herodians against Him. They represented that He was seeking to set up a rival kingdom, and consulted with them how to destroy Him. To excite the Romans against Him, they had represented Him as trying to subvert their authority. They had tried every pretext to cut Him off from influencing the people. But so far their attempts had been foiled. The multitudes who witnessed His works of mercy and heard His pure and holy teachings knew that these were not the deeds and words of a Sabbathbreaker or blasphemer. Even the officers sent by the Pharisees had been so influenced by His words that they could not lay hands on Him. In desperation the Jews had finally passed an edict that any man who professed faith in Jesus, should be cast out of the synagogue.

So, as the priests, the rulers, and the elders gathered for consultation, it was their fixed determination to silence Him who did such marvelous works that all men wondered. Pharisees and Sadducees were more nearly united than ever before. Divided hitherto, they became one in their opposition to Christ. Nicodemus and Joseph had, in former councils, prevented the condemnation of Jesus, and for this reason they were not now summoned. There were present at the council other influential men who believed on Jesus, but their influence prevailed nothing against that of the malignant Pharisees.

Yet the members of the council were not all agreed. The Sanhedrin was not at this time a legal assembly. It existed only by tolerance. Some of its number questioned the wisdom of putting Christ to death. They feared that this would excite an insurrection among the people, causing the Romans to withhold further favors from the priesthood, and to take from them the power they still held. The Sadducees were united in their hatred of Christ, yet they were inclined to be cautious in their movements, fearing that the Romans would deprive them of their high standing.

In this council, assembled to plan the death of Christ, the Witness was present who heard the boastful words of Nebuchadnezzar, who witnessed the idolatrous feast of Belshazzar, who was present when Christ in Nazareth announced Himself the Anointed One. This Witness was now impressing the rulers with the work they were doing. Events in the life of Christ rose up before them with a distinctness that alarmed them. They remembered the scene in the temple, when Jesus, then a child of twelve, stood before the learned doctors of the law, asking them questions at which they wondered. The miracle just performed bore witness that Jesus was none other than the Son of God. In their true significance, the Old Testament Scriptures regarding Christ flashed before their minds. Perplexed and troubled, the rulers asked, "What do we?" There was a division in the council. Under the impression of the Holy Spirit, the priests and rulers could not banish the conviction that they were fighting against God.

While the council was at the height of its perplexity, Caiaphas the high priest arose. Caiaphas was a proud and cruel man, overbearing and intolerant. Among his family connections were Sadducees, proud, bold, reckless, full of ambition and cruelty, which they hid under a cloak of pretended righteousness. Caiaphas had studied the prophecies, and although ignorant of their true meaning, he spoke with great authority and assurance: "Ye know nothing at all, nor consider that it is expedient for us, that one man should die for the people, and that the whole nation perish not." Even if Jesus were innocent, urged the high priest, He must be put out of the way. He was troublesome,

drawing the people to Himself, and lessening the authority of the rulers. He was only one; it was better that He should die than that the authority of the rulers should be weakened. If the people were to lose confidence in their rulers, the national power would be destroyed. Caiaphas urged that after this miracle the followers of Jesus would likely rise in revolt. The Romans will then come, he said, and will close our temple, and abolish our laws, destroying us as a nation. What is the life of this Galilean worth in

"Jesus had now given three years of public labor to the world. His example of self-denial and disinterested benevolence was before them. His life of purity, of suffering and devotion, was known to all. Yet this short period of three years was as long as the world could endure the presence of its Redeemer."

comparison with the life of the nation? If He stands in the way of Israel's well-being, is it not doing God a service to remove Him? Better than one man perish than that the whole nation be destroyed.

In declaring that one man should die for the nation, Caiaphas indicated that he had some knowledge of the prophecies, although it was very limited. But John, in his account of this scene, takes up the prophecy, and shows its broad and deep significance. He says, "And not for that nation only, but that also He should gather together in one the children of God that were scattered abroad." How blindly did the haughty Caiaphas acknowledge the Saviour's mission!

On the lips of Caiaphas this most precious truth was turned into a lie. The policy he advocated was based on a principle borrowed from heathenism. Among the heathen, the dim consciousness that one was to die for the human race, had led to the offering of human sacrifices. So Caiaphas proposed by the sacrifice of Jesus to save the guilty nation, not from transgression, but in transgression, that they might continue in sin. And by his reasoning he thought to silence the remonstrances of those who might dare to say that as yet nothing worthy of death had been found in Jesus.

At this council Christ's enemies had been deeply convicted. The Holy Spirit had impressed their minds. But Satan strove to gain control of them. He urged upon their notice the grievances they had suffered on account of Christ. How little He had honored their righteousness. He presented a righteousness far greater, which all who would be children of God must possess. Taking no notice of their forms and ceremonies, He had encouraged sinners to go directly to God as a merciful Father, and make known their wants. Thus, in their opinion, He had set aside the priesthood. He had refused to acknowledge the theology of the rabbinical schools. He had exposed the evil practices of the priests, and had irreparably hurt their influence. He had injured the effect of their maxims and traditions, declaring that though they strictly enforced the ritual law, they made void the law of God. All this Satan now brought to their minds.

Satan told them that in order to maintain their authority, they must put Jesus to death. This counsel they followed. The fact that they might lose the power they then exercised, was, they thought, sufficient reason for coming to some decision. With the exception of a few who dared not speak their minds, the Sanhedrim received the words of Caiaphas as the words of God. Relief came to the council; the discord ceased. They resolved to put Christ to death at the first favorable opportunity. In rejecting the proof of the divinity of Jesus, these priests and rulers had locked themselves in impenetrable darkness. They had come wholly under the sway of Satan, to be hurried by him over the brink of eternal ruin. Yet such was their deception that they were well pleased with themselves. They regarded themselves as patriots, who were seeking the nation's salvation.

The Sanhedrim feared, however, to take rash measures against Jesus, lest the people should become incensed, and the violence meditated toward Him should fall upon themselves. On this account the council delayed to execute the sentence they had pronounced. The Saviour understood the plotting of the priests. He knew that they longed to remove Him, and that their purpose would soon be accomplished. But it was not His place to hasten the crisis, and He withdrew from that region, taking the disciples with Him. Thus by His own example Jesus again enforced the instruction He had given to the disciples, "When they persecute you in this city, flee ye into another." Matthew 10:23. There was a wide field in which to work for the salvation of souls; and unless loyalty to Him required it, the Lord's servants were not to imperil their lives.

Jesus had now given three years of public labor to the world. His example of self-denial and disinterested benevolence was before them. His life of purity, of suffering and devotion, was known to all. Yet this short period of three years was as long as the world could endure the presence of its Redeemer.

His life had been one of persecution and insult. Driven from Bethlehem by a jealous king, rejected by His own people at Nazareth, condemned to death without a cause at Jerusalem, Jesus, with His few faithful followers, found a temporary asylum in a strange city. He who was ever touched by human woe, who healed the sick, restored sight to the blind, hearing to the deaf, and speech to the dumb, who fed the hungry and comforted the sorrowful, was driven from the people He had labored to save. He who walked upon the heaving billows, and by a word silenced their angry roaring, who cast out devils that in departing acknowledged Him to be the Son of God, who broke the slumbers of the dead, who held thousands entranced by His words of wisdom, was unable to reach the hearts of those who were blinded by prejudice and hatred, and who stubbornly rejected the light.

The Law of the New Kingdom

The time of the Passover was drawing near, and again Jesus turned toward Jerusalem. In His heart was the peace of perfect oneness with the Father's will, and with eager steps He pressed on toward the place of sacrifice. But a sense of mystery, of doubt and fear, fell upon the disciples. The Saviour "went before them, and they were amazed, and as they followed, they were afraid."

Again Christ called the Twelve about Him, and with greater definiteness than ever before, He opened to them His betrayal and sufferings. "Behold," He said, "we go up to Jerusalem, and all things that are written by the prophets concerning the Son of man shall be accomplished. For He shall be delivered unto the Gentiles, and shall be mocked, and spitefully entreated, and spitted on; and they shall scourge Him, and put Him to death; and the third day He shall rise again. And they understood none of these things; and this saying was hid from them, neither knew they the things which were spoken."

Had they not just before proclaimed everywhere, "The kingdom of heaven is at hand"? Had not Christ Himself promised that many should sit down with Abraham and Isaac and Jacob in the kingdom of God? Had He not promised to all who had left aught for His sake a hundredfold in this life, and a part in His kingdom? And had He not given to the Twelve the special promise of positions of high honor in His kingdom, — to sit on thrones judging the twelve tribes of Israel? Even now He had said that all things written in the prophets concerning Him should be fulfilled. And had not the prophets foretold the glory of the Messiah's reign? In the light of these thoughts, His words in regard to betrayal, persecution, and death, seemed vague and shadowy. Whatever difficulties might intervene, they believed that the kingdom was soon to be established.

John, the son of Zebedee, had been one of the first two disciples who had followed Jesus. He and his brother James had been among the first group who had left all for His service. Gladly they had forsaken home and friends that they might be with Him; they had walked and talked with Him; they had been with Him in the privacy of the home, and in the public assemblies. He had quieted their fears, delivered them from danger, relieved their sufferings, comforted their grief, and with patience and tenderness had taught them, till their hearts seemed linked with His, and in the ardor of their love they longed to be nearest to Him in His kingdom. At every possible opportunity, John took his place next the Saviour, and James longed to be honored with as close connection with Him.

Their mother was a follower of Christ, and had ministered to Him freely of her substance. With a mother's love and ambition for her sons, she coveted for them the most honored place in the new kingdom. For this she encouraged them to make request.

Together the mother and her sons came to Jesus, asking that He would grant a petition on which their hearts were set.

"What would ye that I should do for you?" He questioned.

The mother answered, "Grant that these my two sons may sit, the one on Thy right hand, and the other on the left, in Thy kingdom."

Jesus bears tenderly with them, not rebuking their selfishness in seeking preference above their brethren. He reads their hearts, He knows the depth of their attachment to Him. Their love is not a mere human affection; though defiled by the earthliness of its human channel, it is an outflowing from the fountain of His own redeeming love. He will not rebuke, but deepen and purify. He said, "Are ye able to drink of the cup that I shall drink of, and to be baptized with the baptism that I am baptized with?" They recall His mysterious words, pointing to trial and suffering, yet answer confidently, "We are able." They would count it highest honor to prove their loyalty by sharing all that is to befall their Lord.

"The one who stands nearest to Christ will be he who on earth has drunk most deeply of the spirit of His self-sacrificing love, . . . love that moves the disciple, as it moved our Lord, to give all, to live and labor and sacrifice, even unto death, for the saving of humanity."

"Ye shall drink indeed of My cup, and be baptized with the baptism that I am baptized with," He said; before Him a cross instead of a throne, two malefactors His companions at His right hand and His left. John and James were to share with their Master in suffering; the one, first of the brethren to perish with the sword; the other, longest of all to endure toil, and reproach, and persecution.

"But to sit on My right hand, and on My left" He continued, "is not Mine to give, but it shall be given to them for whom it is prepared of My Father." In the kingdom of God, position is not gained through favoritism. It is not earned, nor is it received through an arbitrary bestowal. It is the result of character. The crown and the throne are the tokens of a condition attained; they are the tokens of self-conquest through our Lord Jesus Christ.

Long afterward, when the disciple had been brought into sympathy with Christ through the fellowship of His sufferings, the Lord revealed to John what is the condition of nearness in His kingdom. "To him that overcometh," Christ said, "will I grant to sit with Me in My throne, even as I also overcame, and am set down with My Father in His throne." "Him that overcometh will I make a pillar in the temple of My God, and he shall go no more out: and I will write upon him the name of My God, . . . and I will write upon him My new name." Revelation 3:21, 12. So Paul the apostle wrote, "I am now ready to be offered, and the time of my departure is at hand. I have fought a good fight, I have finished my course, I have kept the faith: henceforth there is laid up for me a crown of righteousness, which the Lord, the righteous Judge, shall give me at that day." 2 Timothy 4:6-8.

The one who stands nearest to Christ will be he who on earth has drunk most deeply of the spirit of His self-sacrificing love,—love that "vaunteth not itself, is not puffed up, . . . seeketh not her own, is not easily provoked, thinketh no evil," (1 Corinthians 13:4, 5.)—love that moves the disciple, as it moved our Lord, to give all, to live and labor and sacrifice, even unto death, for the saving of humanity. This spirit was made manifest in the life of Paul. He said, "For to me to live is Christ;" for his life revealed Christ to men; "and to die is gain,"—gain to Christ; death itself would make manifest the power of His grace, and gather souls to Him. "Christ shall be magnified in my body," he said, "whether it be by life or by death." Philippians 1:21, 20.

When the ten heard of the request of James and John, they were much displeased. The highest place in the kingdom was just what every one of them was seeking for himself, and they were angry that the two disciples had gained a seeming advantage over them.

Again the strife as to which should be greatest seemed about to be renewed, when Jesus, calling them to Him, said to the indignant disciples, "Ye know that they which are accounted to rule over the Gentiles exercise lordship over them; and their great ones exercise authority upon them. But so shall it not be among you."

In the kingdoms of the world, position meant self-aggrandizement. The people were supposed to exist for the benefit of the ruling classes. Influence, wealth, education, were so many means of gaining control of the masses for the use of the leaders. The higher classes were to think, decide, enjoy, and rule; the lower were to obey and serve. Religion, like all things else, was a matter of authority. The people were expected to believe and practice as their superiors directed. The right of man as man, to think and act for himself, was wholly unrecognized.

Christ was establishing a kingdom on different principles. He called men, not to authority, but to service, the strong to bear the infirmities of the weak. Power, position, talent, education, placed their possessor under the greater obligation to serve his fellows. To even the lowliest of Christ's disciples it is said, "All things are for your sakes." 2 Corinthians 4:15.

"The Son of man came not to be ministered unto, but to minister, and to give His life a ransom for many." Among His disciples Christ was in every sense a caretaker, a burden bearer. He shared their poverty, He practiced self-denial on their account, He went before them to smooth the more difficult places, and soon He would consummate His work on earth by laying down His life. The principle on which Christ acted is to actuate the members of the church which is His body. The plan and ground of salvation is love. In the kingdom of Christ those are greatest who follow the example He has given, and act as shepherds of His flock.

The words of Paul reveal the true dignity and honor of the Christian life: "Though I be free from all men, yet have I made myself servant unto all," "not seeking mine own profit, but the profit of many, that they may be saved." 1 Corinthians 9:19; 10:33.

In matters of conscience, the soul must be left untrammeled. No one is to control another's mind, to judge for another, or to prescribe his duty. God gives to every soul freedom to think, and to follow his own convictions. "Every one of us shall give account of himself to God." Romans 14:12. No one has a right to merge his own individuality in that of another. In all matters where principle is involved, "let every man be fully persuaded in his own mind." Romans 14:5. In Christ's kingdom there is no lordly oppression, no compulsion of manner. The angels of heaven do not come to the earth to rule, and to exact homage, but as messengers of mercy, to co-operate with men in uplifting humanity.

The principles and the very words of the Saviour's teaching, in their divine beauty, dwelt in the memory of the beloved disciple. To his latest days the burden of John's testimony to the churches was, "This is the message that ye heard from the beginning, that we should love one another." "Hereby perceive we the love of God, because He laid down His life for us: and we ought to lay down our lives for the brethren." 1 John 3:11, 16.

This was the spirit that pervaded the early church. After the outpouring of the Holy Spirit, "the multitude of them that believed were of one heart and of one soul; neither said any of them that aught of the things which He possessed was his own." "Neither was there any among them that lacked." "And with great power gave the apostles witness of the resurrection of the Lord Jesus; and great grace was upon them all." Acts 4:32, 34, 33.

Zaccheus

On the way to Jerusalem, "Jesus entered and passed through Jericho." A few miles from the Jordan, on the western edge of the valley that here spread out into a plain, the city lay in the midst of tropic verdure, and luxuriance of beauty. With its palm trees and rich gardens watered by living springs, it gleamed like an emerald in the setting of limestone hills and desolate ravines that interposed between Jerusalem and the city of the plain.

Many caravans on their way to the feast passed through Jericho. Their arrival was always a festive season, but now a deeper interest stirred the people. It was known that the Galilean rabbi who had so lately brought Lazarus to life, was in the throng; and though whispers were rife as to the plottings of the priests, the multitudes were eager to do Him homage.

Jericho was one of the cities anciently set apart for the priest, and at this time large numbers of priests had their residence there. But the city had also a population of a widely different character. It was a great center of traffic, and Roman officials and soldiers, with strangers from different quarters, were found there, while the collection of customs made it the home of many publicans.

"The chief among the publicans," Zaccheus, was a Jew, and detested by his countrymen. His rank and wealth were the reward of a calling they abhorred, and which was regarded as another name for injustice and extortion. Yet the wealthy customs officer was not altogether the hardened man of the world that he seemed. Beneath the appearance of worldliness and pride was a heart susceptible to divine influences. Zaccheus had heard of Jesus. The report of One who had borne Himself with kindness and courtesy toward the proscribed classes, had spread far and wide. In this chief of the publicans was awakened a longing for a better life. Only a few miles from Jericho, John the Baptist had preached at the Jordan, and Zaccheus had heard of the call to repentance. The instruction to the publicans, "Exact no more than that which is appointed you," (Luke 3:13), though outwardly disregarded, had impressed his mind. He knew the Scriptures, and was convicted that his practice was wrong. Now, hearing the words reported to have come from the great Teacher, he felt that he was a sinner in the sight of God. Yet what he had heard of Jesus kindled hope in his heart. Repentance, reformation of life, was possible, even to him; was not one of the new Teacher's most trusted disciples a publican? Zaccheus began at once to follow the conviction that had taken hold upon him, and to make restitution to those whom he had wronged.

Already he had begun thus to retrace his steps, when the news sounded through Jericho that Jesus was entering the town. Zaccheus determined to see Him. He was beginning to realize how bitter are the fruits of sin, and how difficult the path of him who tries to return from a course of wrong. To be misunderstood, to be met with suspicion and distrust in the effort to correct his errors, was hard to bear. The chief publican longed to look upon the face of Him whose words had brought hope to his heart.

The streets were crowded, and Zaccheus, who was small of stature, could see nothing over the heads of the people. None would give way for him; so, running a little in advance of the multitude, to where a wide-branching fig tree hung over the way, the rich tax collector climbed to a seat among the boughs, whence he could survey the procession as it passed below. The crowd comes near, it is going by, and Zaccheus scans with eager eyes to discern the one figure he longs to see.

This chapter is based on Luke 19:1-10.

Above the clamor of priests and rabbis and the shouts of welcome from the multitude, that unuttered desire of the chief publican spoke to the heart of Jesus. Suddenly, just beneath the fig tree, a group halts, the company before and behind come to a standstill, and One looks upward whose glance seems to read the soul. Almost doubting his senses, the man in the tree hears the words, "Zaccheus, make haste, and come down; for today I must abide at thy house."

The multitude give way, and Zaccheus, walking as in a dream, leads the way toward his own home. But the rabbis look on with scowling faces, and murmur in discontent and scorn, "that He was gone to be a guest with a man that is a sinner."

Zaccheus had been overwhelmed, amazed, and silenced, at the love and condescension of Christ in stooping to him, so unworthy. Now love and loyalty to his new-found Master unseal his lips. He will make public his confession and his repentance.

In the presence of the multitude, "Zaccheus stood, and said unto the Lord, Behold, Lord, the half of my goods I give to the poor; and if I have taken anything from any man by false accusation, I restore him fourfold.

"And Jesus said unto him, This day is salvation come to this house, forsomuch as he also is a son of Abraham."

When the rich young ruler had turned away from Jesus, the disciples had marveled at their Master's saying, "How hard is it for them that trust in riches to enter into the kingdom of God." They had exclaimed one to another, "Who then can be saved?" Now they had a demonstration of the truth of Christ's words, "The things which are impossible with men are possible with God." Mark 10:24, 26; Luke 18:27. They saw how, through the grace of God, a rich man could enter into the kingdom.

Before Zaccheus had looked upon the face of Christ, he had begun the work that made him manifest as a true penitent. Before being accused by man, he had confessed his sin. He had yielded to the conviction of the Holy Spirit, and had begun to carry out the teaching of the words written for ancient Israel as well as for ourselves. The Lord had said long before, "If thy brother be waxen poor, and fallen in decay with thee; then thou shalt relieve him: yea, though he be a stranger or a sojourner; that he may live with thee. Take thou no usury of him, or increase: but fear thy God; that thy brother may live with thee. Thou shalt not give him thy money upon usury, nor lend him thy victuals for increase." "Ye shall not therefore oppress one another; but thou shalt fear thy God." Leviticus 25:35-37, 17. These words had been spoken by Christ Himself when He was enshrouded in the pillar of cloud, and the very first response of Zaccheus to the love of Christ was in manifesting compassion toward the poor and suffering.

Among the publicans there was a confederacy, so that they could oppress the people, and sustain one another in their fraudulent practices. In their extortion they were but carrying out what had become an almost universal custom. Even the priests and rabbis who despised them were guilty of enriching themselves by dishonest practices under cover of their sacred calling. But no sooner did Zaccheus yield to the influence of the Holy Spirit than he cast aside every practise contrary to integrity.

No repentance is genuine that does not work reformation. The righteousness of Christ is not a cloak to cover unconfessed and unforsaken sin; it is a principle of life that transforms the character and controls the conduct. Holiness is wholeness for God; it is the entire surrender of heart and life to the indwelling of the principles of heaven.

The Christian in his business life is to represent to the world the manner in which our Lord would conduct business enterprises. In every transaction he is to make it manifest that God is his teacher. "Holiness unto the Lord," is to be written upon day books and ledgers, on deeds, receipts, and bills of exchange. Those who profess to be followers of Christ, and who deal in an unrighteous manner, are bearing false witness against the character of a holy, just, and merciful God. Every converted soul will, like Zaccheus, signalize the entrance of Christ into his heart by an abandonment of the unrighteous practices that have marked his life. Like the chief publican, he will give proof of his sincerity by making restitution. The Lord says, "If the wicked restore the pledge, give again that he had robbed, walk in the statutes of life, without committing iniquity; . . . none of his sins that he hath committed shall be mentioned unto him. . . . He shall surely live." Ezekiel 33:15, 16.

If we have injured others through any unjust business transaction, if we have overreached in trade, or defrauded any man, even though it be within the pale of the law, we should confess our wrong, and make restitution as far as lies in our power. It is right for us to restore not only that which we have taken, but all that it would have accumulated if put to a right and wise use during the time it has been in our possession.

To Zaccheus the Saviour said, "This day is salvation come to this house." Not only was Zaccheus himself blessed, but all his household with him. Christ went to his home to give him lessons of truth, and to instruct his household in the things of the kingdom. They had been shut out from the synagogues by the contempt of rabbis and worshipers; but now, the most favored household in all Jericho, they gathered in their own home about the divine Teacher, and heard for themselves the words of life.

It is when Christ is received as a personal Saviour that salvation comes to the soul. Zaccheus had received Jesus, not merely as a passing guest in his home, but as One to abide in the soul temple. The scribes and Pharisees accused him as a sinner, they murmured against Christ for becoming his guest, but the Lord recognized him as a son of Abraham. For "they which are of faith, the same are the children of Abraham." Galatians 3:7.

The Feast at Simon's House

Simon of Bethany was accounted a disciple of Jesus. He was one of the few Pharisees who had openly joined Christ's followers. He acknowledged Jesus as a teacher, and hoped that He might be the Messiah, but he had not accepted Him as a Saviour. His character was not transformed; his principles were unchanged.

Simon had been healed of the leprosy, and it was this that had drawn him to Jesus. He desired to show his gratitude, and at Christ's last visit to Bethany he made a feast for the Saviour and His disciples. This feast brought together many of the Jews. There was at this time much excitement at Jerusalem. Christ and His mission were attracting greater attention than ever before. Those who had come to the feast closely watched His movements, and some of them with unfriendly eyes.

The Saviour had reached Bethany only six days before the Passover, and according to His custom had sought rest at the home of Lazarus. The crowds of travelers who passed on to the city, spread the tidings that He was on His way to Jerusalem, and that He would rest over the Sabbath at Bethany. Among the people there was great enthusiasm. Many flocked to Bethany, some out of sympathy with Jesus, and others from curiosity to see one who had been raised from the dead.

Many expected to hear from Lazarus a wonderful account of scenes witnessed after death. They were surprised that he told them nothing. He had nothing of this kind to tell. Inspiration declares, "The dead know not anything. . . . Their love, and their hatred, and their envy is now perished." Ecclesiastes 9:5, 6. But Lazarus did have a wonderful testimony to bear in regard to the work of Christ. He had been raised from the dead for this purpose. With assurance and power he declared that Jesus was the Son of God.

The reports carried back to Jerusalem by the visitors to Bethany increased the excitement. The people were eager to see and hear Jesus. There was a general inquiry as to whether Lazarus would accompany Him to Jerusalem, and if the prophet would be crowned king at the Passover. The priests and rulers saw that their hold upon the people was still weakening, and their rage against Jesus grew more bitter. They could hardly wait for the opportunity of removing Him forever from their way. As time passed, they began to fear that after all He might not come to Jerusalem. They remembered how often He had baffled their murderous designs, and they were fearful that He had now read their purposes against Him, and would remain away. They could ill conceal their anxiety, and questioned among themselves, "What think ye, that He will not come to the feast?"

A council of the priests and Pharisees was called. Since the raising of Lazarus the sympathies of the people were so fully with Christ that it would be dangerous to seize upon Him openly. So the authorities determined to take Him secretly, and carry on the trial as quietly as possible. They hoped that when His condemnation became known, the fickle tide of public opinion would set in their favor.

Thus they proposed to destroy Jesus. But so long as Lazarus lived, the priests and rabbis knew that they were not secure. The very existence of a man who had been four days in the grave, and who had been restored by a word from Jesus, would sooner or later cause a reaction. The people would be avenged on their leaders for taking the life of One who could perform such a miracle. The Sanhedrin therefore decided that Lazarus also must die.

To such lengths do envy and prejudice lead their slaves. The hatred and unbelief of the Jewish leaders had increased until they would even take the life of one whom infinite power had rescued from the grave.

While this plotting was going on at Jerusalem, Jesus and His friends were invited to Simon's feast. At the table the Saviour sat with Simon, whom He had cured of a loathsome disease, on one side, and Lazarus, whom He had raised from the dead, on the other. Martha served at the table, but Mary was earnestly listening to every word from the lips of Jesus. In His mercy, Jesus had pardoned her sins, He had called forth her beloved brother from the grave, and Mary's heart was filled with gratitude. She had heard Jesus speak of His approaching death, and in her deep love and sorrow she had longed to show Him honor. At great personal sacrifice she had purchased an alabaster box of "ointment of spikenard, very costly," with which to anoint His body. But now many were declaring that He was about to be crowned king. Her grief was turned to joy, and she was eager to be first in honoring her Lord. Breaking her box of ointment, she poured its contents upon the head and feet of Jesus; then, as she knelt weeping, moistening them with her tears, she wiped His feet with her long, flowing hair.

She had sought to avoid observation, and her movements might have passed unnoticed, but the ointment filled the room with its fragrance, and published her act to all present. Judas looked upon this act with great displeasure. Instead of waiting to hear what Christ would say of the matter, he began to whisper his complaints to those near him, throwing reproach upon Christ for suffering such waste. Craftily he made suggestions that would be likely to cause disaffection.

Judas was treasurer for the disciples, and from their little store he had secretly drawn for his own use, thus narrowing down their resources to a meager pittance. He was eager to put into the bag all that he could obtain. The treasure in the bag was often drawn upon to relieve the poor; and when something that Judas did not think essential was bought, he would say, Why is this waste? why was not the cost of this put into the bag that I carry for the poor? Now the act of Mary was in such marked contrast to his selfishness that he was put to shame; and according to his custom, he sought to assign a worthy motive for his objection to her gift. Turning to the disciples, he asked: "Why was not this ointment sold for three hundred pence, and given to the poor? This he said, not that he cared for the poor; but because he was a thief, and had the bag, and bare what was put therein." Judas had no heart for the poor. Had Mary's ointment been sold, and the proceeds fallen into his possession, the poor would have received no benefit.

Judas had a high opinion of his own executive ability. As a financier he thought himself greatly superior to his fellow disciples, and he had led them to regard him in the same light. He had gained their confidence, and had a strong influence over them. His professed sympathy for the poor deceived them, and his artful insinuation caused them to look distrustfully upon Mary's devotion. The murmur passed round the table, "To what purpose is this waste? for this ointment might have been sold for much, and given to the poor."

Mary heard the words of criticism. Her heart trembled within her. She feared that her sister would reproach her for extravagance. The Master, too, might think her im-

---

❝Christ values acts of heartfelt courtesy. When anyone did Him a favor, with heavenly politeness He blessed the actor. He did not refuse the simplest flower plucked by the hand of a child, and offered to Him in love. . . . Acts of love and reverence for Jesus are an evidence of faith in Him as the Son of God.❞

---

provident. Without apology or excuse she was about to shrink away, when the voice of her Lord was heard, "Let her alone; why trouble ye her?" He saw that she was embarrassed and distressed. He knew that in this act of service she had expressed her gratitude for the forgiveness of her sins, and He brought relief to her mind. Lifting His voice above the murmur of criticism, He said, "She hath wrought a good work on Me. For ye have the poor with you always, and whensoever ye will ye may do them good; but Me ye have not always. She hath done what she could; she is come aforehand to anoint My body to the burying."

The fragrant gift which Mary had thought to lavish upon the dead body of the Saviour, she poured upon His living form. At the burial its sweetness could only have pervaded the tomb, now it gladdened His heart with the assurance of her faith and love. Joseph of Arimathea and Nicodemus offered not their gift of love to Jesus in His life. With bitter tears they brought their costly spices for His cold, unconscious form. The women who bore spices to the tomb found their errand in vain, for He had risen. But Mary, pouring out her love upon the Saviour while He was conscious of her devotion, was anointing Him for the burial. And as He went down into the darkness of His great trial, He carried with Him the memory of that deed, an earnest of the love that would be His from His redeemed ones forever.

Many there are who bring their precious gifts for the dead. As they stand about the cold, silent form, words of love are freely spoken. Tenderness, appreciation, devotion, all are lavished upon one who sees not nor hears. Had these words been spoken when the weary spirit needed them so much; when the ear could hear, and the heart could feel, how precious would have been their fragrance.

Mary knew not the full significance of her deed of love. She could not answer her accusers. She could not explain why she had chosen that occasion for anointing Jesus. The Holy Spirit had planned for her, and she had obeyed His promptings. Inspiration stoops to give no reason. As unseen presence, it speaks to mind and soul, and moves the heart to action. It is its own justification.

Christ told Mary the meaning of her act, and in this He gave her more than He had received. "In that she hath poured this ointment on My body," He said, "she did it for My burial." As the alabaster box was broken, and filled the whole house with its fragrance, so Christ was to die, His body was to be broken; but He was to rise from the tomb, and the fragrance of His life was to fill the earth. Christ "hath loved us, and hath given Himself for us an offering and a sacrifice to God for a sweet-smelling savor." Ephesians 5:2.

"Verily I say unto you," Christ declared, "wheresoever this gospel shall be preached throughout the whole world, this also that she hath done shall be spoken of for a memorial of her." Looking into the future, the Saviour spoke with certainty concerning His gospel. It was to be preached throughout the world. And as far as the gospel extended, Mary's gift would shed its fragrance, and hearts would be blessed through her unstudied act. Kingdoms would rise and fall; the names of monarchs and conquerors would be forgotten; but this woman's deed would be immortalized upon the pages of sacred history. Until time should be no more, that broken alabaster box would tell the story of the abundant love of God for a fallen race.

Mary's act was in marked contrast with that which Judas was about to do. What a sharp lesson Christ might have given him who had dropped the seed of criticism and evil thinking into the minds of the disciples. How justly the accuser might have been accused. He who reads the motives of every heart, and understands every action, might have opened before those at the feast dark chapters in the experience of Judas. The hollow pretense on which the traitor based his words might have been laid bare; for instead of sympathizing with the poor, he was robbing them of the money intended for their relief. Indignation might have been excited against him for his oppression of the widow, the orphan, and the hireling. But had Christ unmasked Judas, this would have been urged as a reason for the betrayal. And though charged with being a thief, Judas would have gained sympathy, even among the disciples. The Saviour reproached him not, and thus avoided giving him an excuse for his treachery.

But the look which Jesus cast upon Judas convinced him that the Saviour penetrated his hypocrisy, and read his base, contemptible character. And in commending Mary's action, which had been so severely condemned, Christ had rebuked Judas. Prior to this, the Saviour had never given him a direct rebuke. Now the reproof rankled in his heart. He determined to be revenged. From the supper he went directly to the palace, of the high priest, where he found the council assembled, and he offered to betray Jesus into their hands.

The priests were greatly rejoiced. These leaders of Israel had been given the privilege of receiving Christ as their Saviour, without money and without price. But they refused the precious gift offered them in the most tender spirit of constraining love. They refused to accept that salvation which is of more value than gold, and bought their Lord for thirty pieces of silver.

Judas had indulged avarice until it overpowered every good trait of his character. He grudged the offering made to Jesus. His heart burned with envy that the Saviour should be the recipient of a gift suitable for the monarchs of the earth. For a sum far less than the box of ointment cost, he betrayed his Lord.

The disciples were not like Judas. They loved the Saviour. But they did not rightly appreciate His exalted character. Had they realized what He had done for them, they would have felt that nothing bestowed upon Him was wasted. The wise men from the East, who knew so little of Jesus, had shown a truer appreciation of the honor due Him. They brought precious gifts to the Saviour, and bowed in homage before Him, when he was but a babe, and cradled in a manger.

Christ values acts of heartfelt courtesy. When any one did Him a favor, with heavenly politeness He blessed the actor. He did not refuse the simplest flower plucked by the hand of a child, and offered to Him in love. He accepted the offerings of children, and blessed the givers, inscribing their names in the book of life. In the Scriptures, Mary's anointing of Jesus is mentioned as distinguishing her from the other Marys. Acts of love and reverence for Jesus are an evidence of faith in Him as the Son of God. And the holy Spirit mentions, as evidences of woman's loyalty to Christ: "If she have washed the saints' feet, if she have relieved the afflicted, if she have diligently followed every good work." 1 Timothy 5:10.

Christ delighted in the earnest desire of Mary to do the will of her Lord. He accepted the wealth of pure affection which His disciples did not, would not understand. The desire that Mary had to do this service for her Lord was of more value to Christ than all the precious ointment in the world, because it expressed her appreciation of the world's

Redeemer. It was the love of Christ that constrained her. The matchless excellence of the character of Christ filled her soul. That ointment was a symbol of the heart of the giver. It was the outward demonstration of a love fed by heavenly streams until it overflowed.

The work of Mary was just the lesson the disciples needed to show them that the expression of their love for Him would be pleasing to Christ. He had been everything to them, and they did not realize that soon they would be deprived of His presence, that soon they could offer Him no token of their gratitude for His great love. The loneliness of Christ, separated from the heavenly courts, living

> **"Jesus knows the circumstances of every soul. You may say, I am sinful, very sinful. You may be; but the worse you are, the more you need Jesus. He turns no weeping, contrite one away."**

the life of humanity, was never understood or appreciated by the disciples as it should have been. He was often grieved because His disciples did not give Him that which He should have received from them. He knew that if they were under the influence of the heavenly angels that accompanied Him, they too would think no offering of sufficient value to declare the heart's spiritual affection.

Their after knowledge gave them a true sense of the many things they might have done for Jesus expressive of the love and gratitude of their hearts, while they were near him. When Jesus was no longer with them, and they felt indeed as sheep without a shepherd, they began to see how they might have shown Him attentions that would have brought gladness to His heart. They no longer cast blame upon Mary, but upon themselves. O, if they could have taken back their censuring, their presenting the poor as more worthy of the gift than was Christ! They felt the reproof keenly as they took from the cross the bruised body of their Lord.

The same want is evident in our world today. But few appreciate all that Christ is to them. If they did, the great love of Mary would be expressed, the anointing would be freely bestowed. The expensive ointment would not be called a waste. Nothing would be thought too costly to give

for Christ, no self-denial or self-sacrifice too great to be endured for His sake.

The words spoken in indignation, "To what purpose in this waste?" brought vividly before Christ the greatest sacrifice ever made, — the gift of Himself as the propitiation for a lost world. The Lord would be so bountiful to His human family that it could not be said of Him that He could do more. In the gift of Jesus, God gave all heaven. From a human point of view, such a sacrifice was a wanton waste. To human reasoning the whole plan of salvation is a waste of mercies and resources. Self-denial and whole-hearted sacrifice meet us everywhere. Well may the heavenly host look with amazement upon the human family who refuse to be uplifted and enriched with the boundless love expressed in Christ. Well may they exclaim, Why this great waste?

But the atonement for a lost world was to be full, abundant, and complete. Christ's offering was exceedingly abundant to reach every soul that God had created. It could not be restricted so as not to exceed the number who would accept the great Gift. All men are not saved; yet the plan of redemption is not a waste because it does not accomplish all that its liberality has provided for. There must be enough and to spare.

Simon the host had been influenced by the criticism of Judas upon Mary's gift, and he was surprised at the conduct of Jesus. His Pharisaic pride was offended. He knew that many of his guests were looking upon Christ with distrust and displeasure. Simon said in his heart, "This man, if He were a prophet, would have known who and what manner of woman this is that toucheth Him; for she is a sinner."

By curing Simon of leprosy, Christ had saved him from a living death. But now Simon questioned whether the Saviour were a prophet. Because Christ allowed this woman to approach Him, because He did not indignantly spurn her as one whose sins were too great to be forgiven, because He did not show that He realized she had fallen, Simon was tempted to think that He was not a prophet. Jesus knows nothing of this woman who is so free in her demonstrations, he thought, or He would not allow her to touch Him.

But it was Simon's ignorance of God and of Christ that led him to think as he did. He did not realize that God's Son must act in God's way, with compassion, tenderness, and mercy. Simon's way was to take no notice of Mary's penitent service. Her act of kissing Christ's feet and anointing them with ointment was exasperating to his hard-heartedness. He thought that if Christ were a prophet, He would recognize sinners and rebuke them.

To this unspoken thought the Saviour answered: "Simon, I have somewhat to say unto thee. . . . There was a certain creditor which had two debtors; the one owed five hundred pence and the other fifty. And when they had nothing to pay, he frankly forgave them both. Tell Me therefore, which of them will love him most? Simon answered and said, I suppose that he, to whom he forgave most. And He said unto him, Thou hast rightly judged."

As did Nathan with David, Christ concealed His home thrust under the veil of a parable. He threw upon His host the burden of pronouncing sentence upon himself. Simon had led into sin the woman he now despised. She had been deeply wronged by him. By the two debtors of the parable, Simon and the woman were represented. Jesus did not design to teach that different degrees of obligation should be felt by the two persons, for each owed a debt of gratitude that never could be repaid. But Simon felt himself more righteous than Mary, and Jesus desired him to see how great his guilt really was. He would show him that his sin was greater than hers, as much greater as a debt of five hundred pence exceeds a debt of fifty pence.

Simon now began to see himself in a new light. He saw how Mary was regarded by One who was more than a prophet. He saw that with keen prophetic eye Christ read her heart of love and devotion. Shame seized upon him, and he realized that he was in the presence of One superior to himself.

"I entered into thine house," Christ continued, "thou gavest Me no water for My feet;" but with tears of repentance, prompted by love, Mary hath washed My feet, and wiped them with the hair of her head. "Thou gavest Me no kiss; but this woman," whom you despise, "since the time I came in hath not ceased to kiss My feet." Christ recounted the opportunities Simon had had to show his love for his Lord, and his appreciation of what had been done for him. Plainly, yet with delicate politeness, the Saviour assured His disciples that His heart is grieved when His children neglect to show their gratitude to Him by words and deeds of love.

The Heart searcher read the motive that led to Mary's action, and He saw also the spirit that prompted Simon's words. "Seest thou this woman?" He said to him. She is a sinner. "I say unto thee, her sins, which are many, are forgiven; for she loved much: but to whom little is forgiven, the same loveth little."

Simon's coldness and neglect toward the Saviour showed how little he appreciated the mercy he had received. He had thought he honored Jesus by inviting Him to his house. But he now saw himself as he really was. While he thought himself reading his Guest, his Guest had been reading him. He saw how true Christ's judgment of him was. His religion had been a robe of Pharisaism. He had despised the compassion of Jesus. He had not recognized Him as the representative of God. While Mary was a sinner pardoned, he was a sinner unpardoned. The rigid rule of justice he had desired to enforce against her, condemned him.

Simon was touched by the kindness of Jesus in not openly rebuking him before the guests. He had not been treated as he desired Mary to be treated. He saw that Jesus did not wish to expose his guilt to others, but sought by a true statement of the case to convince his mind, and by pitying kindness to subdue his heart. Stern denunciation would have hardened Simon against repentance, but patient admonition convinced him of his error. He saw the magnitude of the debt which he owed his Lord. His pride was humbled, he repented, and the proud Pharisee became a lowly, self-sacrificing disciple.

Mary had been looked upon as a great sinner, but Christ knew the circumstances that had shaped her life. He might have extinguished every spark of hope in her soul, but He did not. It was He who had lifted her from despair and ruin. Seven times she had heard His rebuke of the demons that controlled her heart and mind. She had heard His strong cries to the Father in her behalf. She knew how offensive is sin to His unsullied purity, and in His strength she had overcome.

When to human eyes her case appeared hopeless, Christ saw in Mary capabilities for good. He saw the better traits of her character. The plan of redemption has invested humanity with great possibilities, and in Mary these possibilities were to be realized. Through His grace she became a partaker of the divine nature. The one who had fallen, and whose mind had been a habitation of demons, was brought very near to the Saviour in fellowship and ministry. It was Mary who sat at His feet and learned of Him. It was Mary who poured upon His head the precious anointing oil, and bathed His feet with her tears. Mary stood beside the cross, and followed Him to the sepulcher. Mary was first at the tomb after His resurrection. It was Mary who first proclaimed a risen Saviour.

Jesus knows the circumstances of every soul. You may say, I am sinful, very sinful. You may be; but the worse you are, the more you need Jesus. He turns no weeping, contrite one away. He does not tell to any all that He might reveal, but He bids every trembling soul take courage. Freely will He pardon all who come to Him for forgiveness and restoration.

Christ might commission the angels of heaven to pour out the vials of His wrath on our world, to destroy those who are filled with hatred of God. He might wipe this dark spot from His universe. But He does not do this. He is today standing at the altar of incense, presenting before God the prayers of those who desire His help.

The souls that turn to Him for refuge, Jesus lifts above the accusing and the strife of tongues. No man or evil angel can impeach these souls. Christ unites them to His own divine-human nature. They stand beside the great Sinbearer, in the light proceeding from the throne of God. "Who shall lay anything to the charge of God's elect? It is God that justifieth. Who is he that condemneth? It is Christ that died; yea rather, that is risen again, who is even at the right hand of God, who also maketh intercession for us." Romans 8:33, 34.

"Thy King Cometh"

Rejoice greatly, O daughter of Zion; shout, O daughter of Jerusalem. Behold, thy King cometh unto thee; He is just, and having salvation; lowly, and riding upon an ass, and upon a colt, the foal of an ass." Zechariah 9:9.

Five hundred years before the birth of Christ, the prophet Zechariah thus foretold the coming of the King to Israel. This prophecy is now to be fulfilled. He who has so long refused royal honors, now comes to Jerusalem as the promised heir to David's throne.

It was on the first day of the week that Christ made His triumphal entry into Jerusalem. Multitudes who had flocked to see Him at Bethany, now accompanied Him, eager to witness His reception. Many people were on their way to the city to keep the Passover, and these joined the multitude attending Jesus. All nature seemed to rejoice. The trees were clothed with verdure, and their blossoms shed a delicate fragrance on the air. A new life and joy animated the people. The hope of the new kingdom was again springing up.

Purposing to ride into Jerusalem, Jesus had sent two of His disciples to bring to Him an ass and its colt. At His birth the Saviour was dependent upon the hospitality of strangers. The manger in which He lay, was a borrowed resting place. Now, although the cattle on a thousand hills are His, He is dependent on a stranger's kindness for an animal on which to enter Jerusalem as its King. But again His divinity is revealed, even in the minute directions given His disciples for this errand. As He foretold, the plea, "The Lord hath need of them," was readily granted. Jesus chose for His use the colt on which never man had sat. The disciples, with glad enthusiasm, spread their garments on the beast, and seated their Master upon it. Heretofore Jesus had always traveled on foot, and the disciples had at first wondered that He should now choose to ride. But hope brightened in their hearts with the joyous thought that He was about to enter the capital, proclaim Himself King, and assert His royal power. While on their errand they communicated their glowing expectations to the friends of Jesus, and the excitement spread far and near, raising the expectations of the people to the highest pitch.

Christ was following the Jewish custom for a royal entry. The animal on which He rode was that ridden by the kings of Israel, and prophecy had foretold that thus the Messiah should come to His kingdom. No sooner was he seated upon the colt than a loud shout of triumph rent the air. The multitude hailed Him as Messiah, their King. Jesus now accepted the homage which He had never before permitted, and the disciples received this as proof that their glad hopes were to be realized by seeing Him established on the throne. The multitude were convinced that the hour of their emancipation was at hand. In imagination they saw the Roman armies driven from Jerusalem, and Israel once more an independent nation. All were happy and excited; the people vied with one another in paying Him homage. They could not display outward pomp and splendor, but they gave Him the worship of happy hearts. They were unable to present Him with costly gifts, but they spread their outer garments as a carpet in His path, and they also strewed the leafy branches of the olive and the palm in the way. They could lead the triumphal procession with no royal standards, but they cut down the spreading palm boughs, Nature's emblem of victory, and waved them aloft with loud acclamations and hosannas.

As they proceeded, the multitude was continually increased by those who had heard of the coming of Jesus and

This chapter is based on Matthew 21:1-11; Mark 11:1-10; Luke 19: 29-44; John 12:12-19. (569-570)

hastened to join the procession. Spectators were constantly mingling with the throng, and asking, Who is this? What does all this commotion signify? They had all heard of Jesus, and expected Him to go to Jerusalem; but they knew that He had heretofore discouraged all effort to place Him on the throne, and they were greatly astonished to learn that this was He. They wondered what could have wrought this change in Him who had declared that His kingdom was not of this world.

Their questionings are silenced by a shout of triumph. Again and again it is repeated by the eager throng; it is taken up by the people afar off, and echoed from the surrounding hills and valleys. And now the procession is joined by crowds from Jerusalem. From the multitudes gathered to attend the Passover, thousands go forth to welcome Jesus. They greet Him with the waving of palm branches and a burst of sacred song. The priests at the temple sound the trumpet for evening service, but there are few to respond, and the rulers say to one another in alarm, "The world has gone after Him."

Never before His earthly life had Jesus permitted such a demonstration. He clearly foresaw the result. It would bring Him to the cross. But it was His purpose thus publicly to present Himself as the Redeemer. He desired to call attention to the sacrifice that was to crown His mission to a fallen world. While the people were assembling at Jerusalem to celebrate the Passover, He, the antitypical Lamb, by a voluntary act set Himself apart as an oblation. It would be needful for His church in all succeeding ages to make His death for the sins of the world a subject of deep thought and study. Every fact connected with it should be verified beyond a doubt. It was necessary, then, that the eyes of all people should now be directed to Him; the events which preceded His great sacrifice must be such as to call attention to the sacrifice itself. After such a demonstration as that attending His entry into Jerusalem, all eyes would follow His rapid progress to the final scene.

The events connected with this triumphal ride would be the talk of every tongue, and would bring Jesus before every mind. After His crucifixion, many would recall these events in their connection with His trial and death. They would be led to search the prophecies, and would be convinced that Jesus was the Messiah; and in all lands converts to the faith would be multiplied.

In this one triumphant scene of His early life, the Saviour might have appeared escorted by heavenly angels, and heralded by the trump of God; but such a demonstration would have been contrary to the purpose of His mission, contrary to the law which had governed His life. He remained true to the humble lot He had accepted. The burden of humanity He must bear until His life was given for the life of the world.

This day, which seemed to the disciples the crowning day of their lives, would have been shadowed with gloomy clouds had they known that this scene of rejoicing was but a prelude to the suffering and death of their Master.

Although He had repeatedly told them of His certain sacrifice, yet in the glad triumph of the present they forgot His sorrowful words, and looked forward to His prosperous reign on David's throne.

New accessions were made continually to the procession, and, with few exceptions, all who joined it caught the inspiration of the hour, and helped to swell the hosannas that echoed and re-echoed from hill to hill and from valley to valley. The shouts went up continually, "Hosanna to the Son of David! Blessed is He that cometh in the name of the Lord! Hosanna in the highest!"

Never before had the world seen such a triumphal procession. It was not like that of the earth's famous conquerors. No train of mourning captives, as trophies of kingly valor, made a feature of that scene. But about the Saviour were the glorious trophies of His labors of love for sinful man. There were the captives whom He had rescued from Satan's power, praising God for their deliverance. The blind whom He had restored to sight, were leading the way. The dumb whose tongues He had loosed, shouted the loudest hosannas. The cripples whom He had healed, bounded with joy, and were the most active in breaking the palm branches and waving them before the Saviour. Widows and orphans were exalting the name of Jesus for His works of mercy to them. The lepers whom He had cleansed, spread their untainted garments in His path, and hailed Him as the King of Glory. Those whom His voice had awakened from the sleep of death were in that throng. Lazarus, whose body had seen corruption in the grave, but who now rejoiced in the strength of glorious manhood, led the beast on which the Saviour rode.

Many Pharisees witnessed the scene, and, burning with envy and malice, sought to turn the current of popular feeling. With all their authority they tried to silence the people; but their appeals and threats only increased the enthusiasm. They feared that this multitude, in the strength of their numbers, would make Jesus king. As a last resort they pressed through the crowd to where the Saviour was, and accosted Him with reproving and threatening words: "Master, rebuke thy disciples." They declared that such noisy demonstrations were unlawful, and would not be permitted by the authorities. But they were silenced by the reply of Jesus, "I tell you that, if these should hold their peace, the stones would immediately cry out." That scene of triumph was of God's own appointing. It had been foretold by the prophet, and man was powerless to turn aside God's purpose. Had men failed to carry out His plan, He would have given a voice to the inanimate stones, and they would have hailed His Son with acclamations of praise. As the silenced Pharisees drew back, the words of Zechariah were taken up by hundreds of voices: "Rejoice greatly, O daughter of Zion; shout, O daughter of Jerusalem. Behold, thy King cometh unto thee; He is just, and having salvation; lowly, and riding upon an ass, and upon a colt, the foal of an ass."

When the procession reached the brow of the hill, and was about to descend into the city, Jesus halted, and all the multitude with him. Before them lay Jerusalem in its glory, now bathed in the light of the declining sun. The temple attracted all eyes. In stately grandeur it towered above all else, seeming to point toward heaven as if directing the people to the only true and living God. The temple had long been the pride and glory of the Jewish nation. The Romans also prided themselves in its magnificence. A king appointed by the Romans had united with the Jews to rebuild and embellish it, and the emperor of Rome had enriched it with his gifts. Its strength, richness, and magnificence had made it one of the wonders of the world.

While the westering sun was tinting and gilding the heavens, its resplendent glory lighted up the pure white marble of the temple walls, and sparkled on its gold-capped pillars. From the crest of the hill where Jesus and His followers stood, it had the appearance of a massive structure of snow, set with golden pinnacles. At the entrance to the temple was a vine of gold and silver, with green leaves and massive clusters of grapes executed by the most skillful artists. This design represented Israel as a prosperous vine. The gold, silver, and living green were combined with rare taste and exquisite workmanship; as it twined gracefully about the white and glistening pillars, clinging with shining tendrils to their golden ornaments, it caught the splendor of the setting sun, shining as if with a glory borrowed from heaven.

Jesus gazes upon the scene, and the vast multitude hush their shouts, spellbound by the sudden vision of beauty. All eyes turn upon the Saviour, expecting to see in His countenance the admiration they themselves feel. But instead of this they behold a cloud of sorrow. They are surprised and disappointed to see His eyes fill with tears, and His body rock to and fro like a tree before the tempest, while a wail of anguish bursts from His quivering lips, as if from the depths of a broken heart. What a sight was this for angels to behold! their loved Commander in an agony of tears! What a sight was this for the glad throng that with shouts of triumph and the waving of palm branches were escorting Him to the glorious city, where they fondly hoped He was about to reign. Jesus had wept at the grave of Lazarus, but it was in a Godlike grief in sympathy with human woe. But this sudden sorrow was like a note of wailing in a grand triumphal chorus. In the midst of a scene of rejoicing, where all were paying Him homage, Israel's King was in tears; not silent tears of gladness, but tears and groans of insuppressible agony. The multitude were struck with a sudden gloom. Their acclamations were silenced. Many wept in sympathy with a grief they could not comprehend.

The tears of Jesus were not in anticipation of His own suffering. Just before Him was Gethsemane, where soon the horror of a great darkness would overshadow Him. The sheep gate also was in sight, through which for centuries the beasts for sacrificial offerings had been led. This gate was soon to open for Him, the great Antitype, toward whose sacrifice for the sins of the world all these offerings had pointed. Near by was Calvary, the scene of His approaching agony. Yet it was not because of these reminders of His cruel death that the Redeemer wept and groaned in anguish of spirit. His was no selfish sorrow. The thought of His own agony did not intimidate that noble, self-sacrificing soul. It was the sight of Jerusalem that pierced the heart of Jesus, — Jerusalem that had rejected the Son of God and scorned His love, that refused to be convinced by His mighty miracles, and was about to take His life. He saw what she was in her guilt of rejecting her Redeemer, and what she might have been had she accepted Him who alone could heal her wound. He had come to save her; how could He give her up?

Israel had been a favored people; God had made their temple His habitation; it was "beautiful for situation, the joy of the whole earth." Psalms 48:2. The record of more than a thousand years of Christ's guardian care and tender love, such as a father bears his only child, was there. In the temple the prophets had uttered their solemn warnings. There had the burning censers waved, while incense, mingled with the prayers of the worshipers, had ascended to God. There the blood of beasts had flowed, typical of the blood of Christ. There Jehovah had manifested His glory above the mercy seat. There the priests had officiated, and the pomp of symbol and ceremony had gone on for ages. But all this must have an end.

Jesus raised His hand, — that had so often blessed the sick and suffering, — and waving it toward the doomed city, in broken utterances of grief exclaimed: "If thou hadst known, even thou, at least in this thy day, the things which belong unto thy peace! — " Here the Saviour paused, and left unsaid what might have been the condition of Jerusalem, had she accepted the help that God desired to give her, — the gift of His beloved Son. If Jerusalem had known what it was her privilege to know, and had heeded the light which Heaven had sent her, she might have stood forth in the pride of posterity, the queen of kingdoms, free in the strength of her God-given power. There would have been no armed soldiers standing at her gates, no Roman banners waving from her walls. The glorious destiny that might have blessed Jerusalem, had she accepted her Redeemer, rose before the Son of God. He saw that she might through Him have been healed of her grievous malady, liberated from bondage, and established as the mighty metropolis of the earth. From her walls the dove of peace would have gone forth to all nations. She would have been the world's diadem of glory.

But the bright picture of what Jerusalem might have been fades from the Saviour's sight. He realizes what she now is under the Roman yoke, bearing the frown of God, doomed to His retributive judgment. He takes up the broken thread of His lamentation: "But now they are hid from thine eyes. For the days shall come upon thee, that thine enemies shall cast a trench about thee, and compass thee round, and keep thee in on every side, and shall lay thee even with the ground, and thy children within thee; and they shall not leave in thee one stone upon another; because thou knewest not the time of thy visitation."

Christ came to save Jerusalem with her children; but Pharisaical pride, hypocrisy, jealousy, and malice had prevented Him from accomplishing His purpose. Jesus knew the terrible retribution which would be visited upon the doomed city. He saw Jerusalem encompassed with armies, the besieged inhabitants driven to starvation and death, mothers feeding upon the dead bodies of their own children, and both parents and children snatching the last morsel of food from one another, natural affection being destroyed by the gnawing pangs of hunger. He saw that the stubbornness of the Jews, as evinced in their rejection of His salvation, would also lead them to refuse submission to the invading armies. He beheld Calvary, on which He was to be lifted up, set with crosses as thickly as forest trees. He saw the wretched inhabitants suffering torture on the rack, and by crucifixion, the beautiful palaces destroyed, the temple in ruins, and of its massive walls not one stone left upon another, while the city was plowed like a field. Well might the Saviour weep in agony in view of that fearful scene.

Jerusalem had been the child of His care, and as a tender father mourns over a wayward son, so Jesus wept over the beloved city. How can I give thee up? How can I see thee devoted to destruction? Must I let thee go to fill up the cup of thine iniquity? One soul is of such value that, in comparison with it, worlds sink into insignificance; but here was a whole nation to be lost. When the fast westering sun should pass from sight in the heavens, Jerusalem's day of grace would be ended. While the procession was halting on the brow of Olivet, it was not yet too late for Jerusalem to repent. The angel of mercy was then folding her wings to step down from the golden throne to give place to justice and swift-coming judgment. But Christ's great heart of love still pleaded for Jerusalem, that had scorned His mercies, despised His warnings, and was about to imbrue her hands in His blood. If Jerusalem would but repent, it was not yet too late. While the last rays of the setting sun were lingering on temple, tower, and pinnacle, would not some good angel lead her to the Saviour's love, and avert

her doom? Beautiful and unholy city, that had stoned the prophets, that had rejected the Son of God, that was locking herself by her impenitence in fetters of bondage, — her day of mercy was almost spent!

Yet again the Spirit of God speaks to Jerusalem. Before the day is done, another testimony is borne to Christ. The voice of witness is lifted up, responding to the call from a prophetic past. If Jerusalem will hear the call, if she will receive the Saviour who is entering her gates, she may yet be saved.

Reports have reached the rulers in Jerusalem that Jesus is approaching the city with a great concourse of people. But they have no welcome for the Son of God. In fear they go out to meet Him, hoping to disperse the throng. As the procession is about to descend the Mount of Olives, it is intercepted by the rulers. They inquire the cause of the tumultuous rejoicing. As they question, "Who is this?" the disciples, filled with the spirit of inspiration, answer this question. In eloquent strains they repeat the prophecies concerning Christ: —

Adam will tell you, It is the seed of the woman that shall bruise the serpent's head.

Ask Abraham, he will tell you, It is "Melchizedek, King of Salem," Genesis 14:18. King of Peace.

Jacob will tell you, He is Shiloh of the tribe of Judah.

Isaiah will tell you, "Immanuel," "Wonderful, Counselor, the mighty God, the everlasting Father, the Prince of Peace." Isaiah 7:14;9:6.

Jeremiah will tell you, The Branch of David, "the Lord our Righteousness." Jeremiah 23:6.

Daniel will tell you, He is the Messiah.

Hosea will tell you, He is "the Lord God of hosts ; the Lord is His memorial." Hosea 12:5.

John the Baptist will tell you, He is "the Lamb of God, which taketh away the sin of the world." John 1:29.

The great Jehovah has proclaimed from His throne, "This is My beloved Son." Matthew 3:17.

We, His disciples, declare, This is Jesus, the Messiah, the Prince of life, the Redeemer of the world.

And the price of the powers of darkness acknowledges Him, saying, "I know Thee who Thou art, the Holy One of God." Mark 1:24.

A Doomed People

The triumphal ride of Christ into Jerusalem was the dim foreshadowing of His coming in the clouds of heaven with power and glory, amid the triumph of angels and the rejoicing of the saints. Then will be fulfilled the words of Christ to the priests and Pharisees: "Ye shall not see Me henceforth, till ye shall say, Blessed is He that cometh in the name of the Lord." Matthew 23:29. In prophetic vision Zechariah was shown that day of final triumph; and he beheld also the doom of those who at the first advent had rejected Christ: "They shall look upon Me whom they have pierced, and they shall mourn for Him, as one mourneth for his only son, and shall be in bitterness for Him, as one that is in bitterness for his first-born." Zechariah 12:10. This scene Christ foresaw when He beheld the city and wept over it. In the temporal ruin of Jerusalem He saw the final destruction of that people who were guilty of the blood of the Son of God.

The disciples saw the hatred of the Jews to Christ, but they did not yet see to what it would lead. They did not yet understand the true condition of Israel, nor comprehend the retribution that was to fall upon Jerusalem. This Christ opened to them by a significant object lesson.

The last appeal to Jerusalem had been in vain. The priests and rulers had heard the prophetic voice of the past echoed by the multitude, in answer to the question, "Who is this?" but they did not accept it as the voice of inspiration. In anger and amazement they tried to silence the people. There were Roman officers in the throng, and to them His enemies denounced Jesus as the leader of a rebellion. They represented that He was about to take possession of the temple, and reign as king in Jerusalem.

But the calm voice of Jesus hushed for a moment the clamorous throng as He again declared that He had not come to establish a temporal rule; He should soon ascend to His Father, and His accusers would see Him no more until He should come again in glory. Then, too late for their salvation, they would acknowledge Him. These words Jesus spoke with sadness and with singular power. The Roman officers were silenced and subdued. Their hearts, though strangers to divine influence, were moved as they had never been moved before. In the calm, solemn face of Jesus they read love, benevolence, and quiet dignity. They were stirred by a sympathy they could not understand. Instead of arresting Jesus, they were more inclined to pay Him homage. Turning upon the priests and rulers, they charged them with creating the disturbance. These leaders, chagrined and defeated, turned to the people with their complaints, and disputed angrily among themselves.

Meanwhile Jesus passed unnoticed to the temple. All was quiet there, for the scene upon Olivet had called away the people. For a short time Jesus remained at the temple, looking upon it with sorrowful eyes. Then He withdrew with His disciples, and returned to Bethany. When the people sought for Him to place Him on the throne, He was not to be found.

The entire night Jesus spent in prayer, and in the morning He came again to the temple. On the way He passed a fig orchard. He was hungry, "and seeing a fig tree afar off having leaves, He came, if haply He might find anything thereon; and when He came to it, He found nothing but leaves; for the time of figs was not yet."

It was not the season for ripe figs, except in certain localities; and on the highlands about Jerusalem it might truly be said, "The time of figs was not yet." But in the orchard to which Jesus came, one tree appeared to be in advance of all the others. It was already covered with

This chapter is based on Mark 11:11-14, 20, 21; 17-19.

leaves. It is the nature of the fig tree that before the leaves open, the growing fruit appears. Therefore this tree in full leaf gave promise of well-developed fruit. But its appearance was deceptive. Upon searching its branches, from the lowest bough to the topmost twig, Jesus found "nothing but leaves." It was a mass of pretentious foliage, nothing more.

Christ uttered against it a withering curse. "No man eat fruit of thee hereafter forever," He said. The next morning, as the Saviour and His disciples were again on their way to the city, the blasted branches and drooping leaves attracted their attention. "Master," said Peter. "behold, the fig tree which Thou cursedst is withered away."

Christ's act in cursing the fig tree had astonished the disciples. It seemed to them unlike His ways and works. Often they had heard Him declare that He came not to condemn the world, but that the world through Him might be saved. They remembered His words, "The Son of man is not come to destroy men's lives, but to save them." Luke 9:56. His wonderful works had been done to restore, never to destroy. The disciples had known Him only as the Restorer, the Healer. This act stood alone. What was its purpose? they questioned.

God "delighteth in mercy." "As I live, saith the Lord God, I have no pleasure in the death of the wicked," Micah 7:18; Ezekiel 33:11. To Him the work of destruction and the denunciation of judgment is a "strange work." Isaiah 28:21. But it is in mercy and love that He lifts the veil from the future, and reveals to men the results of a course of sin.

The cursing of the fig tree was an acted parable. That barren tree, flaunting its pretentious foliage in the very face of Christ, was a symbol of the Jewish nation. The Saviour desired to make plain to His disciples the cause and the certainty of Israel's doom. For this purpose He invested the tree with moral qualities, and made it the expositor of divine truth. The Jews stood forth distinct from all other nations, professing allegiance to God. They had been specially favored by Him, and they laid claim to righteousness above every other people. But they were corrupted by the love of the world and the greed of gain. They boasted of their knowledge, but they were ignorant of the requirements of God, and were full of hypocrisy. Like the barren tree, they spread their pretentious branches aloft, luxuriant in appearance, and beautiful to the eye, but they yielded "nothing but leaves." The Jewish religion, with its magnificent temple, its sacred altars, its mitred priests and impressive ceremonies, was indeed fair in outward appearance, but humility, love, and benevolence were lacking.

All the trees in the fig orchard were destitute of fruit; but the leafless trees raised no expectation, and caused no disappointment. By these trees the Gentiles were represented. They were as destitute as were the Jews of godliness; but they had not professed to serve God. They made no boastful pretensions to goodness. They were blind to the works and ways of God. With them the time of figs was not yet. They were still waiting for a day which would bring them light and hope. The Jews, who had received greater blessings from God, were held accountable for their abuse of these gifts. The privileges of which they boasted, only increased their guilt.

Jesus had come to the fig tree hungry, to find food. So He had come to Israel, hungering to find in them the fruits of righteousness. He had lavished on them His gifts, that they might bear fruit for the blessing of the world. Every opportunity and privilege had been granted them, and in return He sought their sympathy and co-operation in His work of grace. He longed to see in them self-sacrifice and compassion, zeal for God, and a deep yearning of soul for the salvation of their fellow men. Had they kept the law of God, they would have done the same unselfish work that Christ did. But love to God and man was eclipsed by pride and self-sufficiency. They brought ruin upon themselves by refusing to minister to others. The treasures of truth which God had committed to them, they did not give to the world. In the barren tree they might read both their sin and its punishment. Withered beneath the Saviour's curse, standing forth sere and blasted, dried up by the roots, the fig tree showed what the Jewish people would be when the grace of God was removed from them. Refusing to impart blessing, they would no longer receive it. "O Israel," the Lord says, "thou hast destroyed thyself." Hosea 13:9.

The warning is for all time. Christ's act in cursing the tree which His own power had created, stands as a warning to all churches and to all Christians. No one can live the law of God without ministering to others. But there are many who do not live out Christ's merciful, unselfish life. Some who think themselves excellent Christians do not understand what constitutes service for God. They plan and study to please themselves. They act only in reference to self. Time is of value to them only as they can gather for themselves. In all the affairs of life this is their object. Not for others but for themselves do they minister. God created them to live in a world where unselfish service must be performed. He designed them to help their fellow men in every possible way. But self is so large that they cannot see anything else. They are not in touch with humanity. Those who thus live for self are like the fig tree, which made every pretension, but was fruitless. They observe the forms of worship, but without repentance or faith. In profession they honor the law of God, but obedience is lacking. They say, but do not. In the sentence pronounced on the fig tree Christ demonstrates how hateful in His eyes is this vain pretense. He declares that the open sinner is less guilty than is he who professes to serve God, but who bears no fruit to His glory.

The parable of the fig tree, spoken before Christ's visit to Jerusalem, had a direct connection with the lesson He taught in cursing the fruitless tree. For the barren tree of the parable the gardener pleaded, Let it alone this year, until I shall dig about it and dress it; and if it bear fruit, well; but if not, then after that thou shalt cut it down.

Increased care was to be given the unfruitful tree. It was to have every advantage. But if it remained fruitless, nothing could save it from destruction. In the parable the result of the gardener's work was not foretold. It depended upon that people to whom Christ's words were spoken. They were represented by the fruitless tree, and it rested with them to decide their own destiny. Every advantage that Heaven could bestow was given them, but they did not profit by their increased blessings. By Christ's act in cursing the barren fig tree, the result was shown. They had determined their own destruction.

For more than a thousand years the Jewish nation had abused God's mercy and invited His judgments. They had rejected His warnings and slain His prophets. For these sins the people of Christ's day made themselves responsible by following the same course. In the rejection of their present mercies and warnings lay the guilt of that generation. The fetters which the nation had for centuries been forging, the people of Christ's day were fastening upon themselves.

In every age there is given to men their day of light and privilege, a probationary time in which they may become reconciled to God. But there is a limit to this grace. Mercy may plead for years and be slighted and rejected; but there comes a time when mercy makes her last plea. The heart becomes so hardened that it ceases to respond to the Spirit of God. Then the sweet, winning voice entreats the sinner no longer, and reproofs and warnings cease.

That day had come to Jerusalem. Jesus wept in anguish over the doomed city, but He could not deliver her. He had exhausted every resource. In rejecting the warnings of God's Spirit, Israel had rejected the only means of help. There was no other power by which they could be delivered.

The Jewish nation was a symbol of the people of all ages who scorn the pleadings of Infinite Love. The tears of Christ when He wept over Jerusalem were for the sins of all time. In the judgments pronounced upon Israel, those who reject the reproofs and warnings of God's Holy Spirit, may read their own condemnation.

In this generation there are many who are treading on the same ground as were the unbelieving Jews. They have witnessed the manifestation of the power of God; the Holy Spirit has spoken to their hearts; but they cling to their unbelief and resistance. God sends them warnings and reproof, but they are not willing to confess their errors, and they reject His message and His messenger. The very means He uses for their recovery becomes to them a stone of stumbling.

The prophets of God were hated by apostate Israel because through them their hidden sins were brought to light. Ahab regarded Elijah as his enemy because the prophet was faithful to rebuke the king's secret iniquities. So today the servant of Christ, the reprover of sin, meets with scorn and rebuffs. Bible truth, the religion of Christ, struggles against a strong current of moral impurity. Prejudice is even stronger in the hearts of men now than in Christ's day. Christ did not fulfill men's expectations; His life was a rebuke to their sins, and they rejected Him. So now the truth of God's word does not harmonize with men's practices and their natural inclination, and thousands reject its light. Men prompted by Satan, cast doubt upon God's word, and choose to exercise their independent judgment. They choose darkness rather than light, but they do it at the peril of their souls. Those who caviled at the words of Christ, found ever-increased cause for cavil, until they turned from the Truth and the Life. So it is now. God does not propose to remove every objection which the carnal heart may bring against His truth. To those who refuse the precious rays of light which would illuminate the darkness, the mysteries of God's word remain such forever. From them the truth is hidden. They walk blindly, and know not the ruin before them.

Christ overlooked the world and all ages from the height of Olivet; and His words are applicable to every soul who slights the pleadings of divine mercy. Scorner of His love, He addresses you today. It is "thou, even thou," who shouldst know the things that belong to thy peace. Christ is shedding bitter tears for you, who have no tears to shed for yourself. Already that fatal hardness of heart which destroyed the Pharisees is manifest in you. And every evidence of the grace of God, every ray of divine light, is either melting and subduing the soul, or confirming it in hopeless impenitence.

Christ foresaw that Jerusalem would remain obdurate and impenitent; yet all the guilt, all the consequences of rejected mercy, lay at her own door. Thus it will be with every soul who is following the same course. The Lord declares, "O Israel, thou hast destroyed thyself." "Hear, O earth: behold, I will bring evil upon this people, even the fruit of their thoughts, because they have not hearkened unto My words, nor to My law, but rejected it." Hosea 13:9; Jeremiah 6:19.

The Temple Cleansed Again

At the beginning of His ministry, Christ had driven from the temple those who defiled it by their unholy traffic; and His stern and Godlike demeanor had struck terror to the hearts of the scheming traders. At the close of His mission He came again to the temple, and found it still desecrated as before. The condition of things was even worse than before. The outer court of the temple was like a vast cattle yard. With the cries of the animals and the sharp chinking of coin was mingled the sound of angry altercation between traffickers, and among them were heard the voices of men in sacred office. The dignitaries of the temple were themselves engaged in buying and selling and the exchange of money. So completely were they controlled by their greed of gain, that in the sight of God they were no better than thieves.

Little did the priests and rulers realize the solemnity of the work which it was theirs to perform. At every Passover and Feast of Tabernacles, thousands of animals were slain, and their blood was caught by the priests and poured upon the altar. The Jews had become familiar with the offering of blood , and had almost lost sight of the fact that it was sin which made necessary all this shedding of the blood of beasts. They did not discern that it prefigured the blood of God's dear Son, which was to be shed for the life of the world, and that by the offering of sacrifices men were to be diverted to a crucified Redeemer.

Jesus looked upon the innocent victims of sacrifice, and saw how the Jews had made these great convocations scenes of bloodshed and cruelty. In place of humble repentance of sin, they had multiplied the sacrifice of beasts, as if God could be honored by a heartless service. The priests and rulers had hardened their hearts through selfishness and avarice. The very symbols pointing to the Lamb of God they had made a means of getting gain. Thus in the eyes of the people the sacredness of the sacrificial service had been in a great measure destroyed. The indignation of Jesus was stirred; He knew that His blood, so soon to be shed for the sins of the world, would be as little appreciated by the priests and elders as was the blood of beasts which they kept incessantly flowing.

Against these practices Christ had spoken through the prophets. Samuel had said, "Hath the Lord as great delight in burnt offerings and sacrifices, as in obeying the voice of the Lord? Behold, to obey is better than sacrifice, and to hearken than the fat of rams." And Isaiah, seeing in prophetic vision the apostasy of the Jews, addressed them as rulers of Sodom and Gomorrah: "Hear the word of the Lord, ye rulers of Sodom; give ear unto the law of our God, ye people of Gomorrah. To what purpose is the multitude of your sacrifices unto Me? saith the Lord, I am full of the burnt offerings of rams, and the fat of fed beasts; and I delight not in the blood of bullocks, or of lambs, or of he goats. When ye come to appear before Me, who hath required this at your hand, to tread My courts?" "Wash you; make you clean; put away the evil of your doings from before Mine eyes; cease to do evil; learn to do well; seek judgment, relieve the oppressed, judge the fatherless, plead for the widow." 1 Samuel 15:22; Isaiah 1:10-12, 16,17.

He who had Himself given these prophecies, now for the last time repeated the warning. In fulfillment of prophecy the people had proclaimed Jesus king of Israel. He had received their homage, and accepted the office of king. In this character He must act. He knew that His efforts to reform a corrupt priesthood would be in vain; nevertheless

This chapter is based on Matthew 21:12-16, 23-46; Mark 11:15-19, 27-33; 12:1-12; Luke 19:45-48; 20:1-19.

His work must be done; to an unbelieving people the evidence of His divine mission must be given.

Again the piercing look of Jesus swept over the desecrated court of the temple. All eyes were turned toward Him. Priest and ruler, Pharisee and Gentile, looked with astonishment and awe upon Him who stood before them with the majesty of heaven's King. Divinity flashed through humanity, investing Christ with a dignity and glory He had never manifested before. Those standing nearest Him drew as far away as the crowd would permit. Except for a few of His disciples, the Saviour stood alone. Every sound was hushed. The deep silence seemed unbearable. Christ spoke with a power that swayed the people like a mighty tempest: "It is written, My house shall be called the house of prayer; but ye have made it a den of thieves." His voice sounded like a trumpet through the temple. The displeasure of His countenance seemed like consuming fire. With authority He commanded, "Take these things hence."

Three years before, the rulers of the temple had been ashamed of their flight before the command of Jesus. They had since wondered at their own fears, and their unquestioning obedience to a single humble man. They had felt that it was impossible for their undignified surrender to be repeated. Yet they were now more terrified than before, and in greater haste to obey His command. There were none who dared question His authority. Priests and traders fled from His presence, driving their cattle before them.

On the way from the temple they were met by a throng who came with their sick inquiring for the great Healer. The report given by the fleeing people caused some of these to turn back. They feared to meet One so powerful, whose very look had driven the priests and rulers from His presence. But a large number pressed through the hurrying crowd, eager to reach Him who was their only hope. When the multitude fled from the temple, many had remained behind. These were now joined by the newcomers. Again the temple court was filled by the sick and the dying, and once more Jesus ministered to them.

After a season the priests and rulers ventured back to the temple. When the panic had abated, they were seized with anxiety to know what would be the next movement of Jesus. They expected Him to take the throne of David. Quietly returning to the temple, they heard the voices of men, women, and children praising God. Upon entering, they stood transfixed before the wonderful scene. They saw the sick healed, the blind restored to sight, and deaf receive their hearing, and the crippled leap for joy. The children were foremost in the rejoicing. Jesus had healed their maladies; He had clasped them in His arms, received their kisses of grateful affection, and some of them had fallen asleep upon His breast as He was teaching the people. Now with glad voices the children sounded His praise. They repeated the hosannas of the day before, and waved palm branches triumphantly before the Saviour. The temple echoed and re-echoed with their acclamations,

"Blessed be He that cometh in the name of the Lord!" "Behold, thy King cometh unto thee; He is just, and having salvation!" Psalms 118:26; Zechariah 9:9. "Hosanna to the Son of David!"

The sound of these happy, unrestrained voices was an offense to the rulers of the temple. They set about putting a stop to such demonstrations. They represented to the people that the house of God was desecrated by the feet of the children and the shouts of rejoicing. Finding that their

---

"In infinite wisdom, God chose the foundation stone, and laid it Himself. . . . The entire world may lay upon it their burdens and griefs; it can endure them all. . . . Christ is a 'tried stone.' Those who trust in Him, He never disappoints. He has borne every test. . . . He has borne the burdens cast upon Him by every repenting sinner. . . . He is the sure foundation."

---

words made no impression on the people, the rulers appealed to Christ: "Hearest Thou what these say? and Jesus saith unto them, Yea; have ye never read, Out of the mouth of babes and sucklings Thou hast perfected praise?" Prophecy had foretold that Christ should be proclaimed as king, and that word must be fulfilled. The priests and rulers of Israel refused to herald His glory, and God moved upon the children to be His witnesses. Had the voices of the children been silent, the very pillars of the temple would have sounded the Saviour's praise.

The Pharisees were utterly perplexed and disconcerted. One whom they could not intimidate was in command. Jesus had taken His position as guardian of the temple. Never before had He assumed such kingly authority. Never before had His words and works possessed so great power. He had done marvelous works throughout Jerusalem, but never before in a manner so solemn and impressive. In presence of the people who had witnessed His wonderful works, the priests and rulers dared not show Him open hostility. Though enraged and confounded by His answer, they were unable to accomplish anything further that day.

The next morning the Sanhedrin again considered what course to pursue toward Jesus. Three years before, they had demanded a sign of His Messiahship. Since that time He had wrought mighty works throughout the land. He had healed the sick, miraculously fed thousands of people, walked upon the waves, and spoken peace to the troubled sea. He had repeatedly read the hearts of men as an open book; He had cast out demons, and raised the dead. The rulers had before them the evidences of His Messiahship. They now decided to demand no sign of His authority, but to draw out some admission or declaration by which He might be condemned.

Repairing to the temple where He was teaching, they proceeded to question Him: "By what authority doest Thou these things? and who gave Thee this authority?" They expected Him to claim that His authority was from God. Such an assertion they intended to deny. But Jesus met them with a question apparently pertaining to another subject, and He made His reply to them conditional on their answering this question. "The baptism of John," He said, "whence was it? from heaven, or of men?"

The priests saw that they were in a dilemma from which no sophistry could extricate them. If they said that John's baptism was from heaven, their inconsistency would be made apparent. Christ would say, Why have ye not then believed on him? John had testified of Christ, "Behold the Lamb of God, which taketh away the sin of the world." John 1:29. If the priests believed John's testimony, how could they deny the Messiahship of Christ? If they declared their real belief, that John's ministry was of men, they would bring upon themselves a storm of indignation; for the people believed John to be a prophet.

With intense interest the multitude awaited the decision. They knew that the priests had professed to accept the ministry of John, and they expected them to acknowledge without a question that he was sent from God. But after conferring secretly together, the priests decided not to commit themselves. Hypocritically professing ignorance, they said, "We cannot tell." "Neither tell I you," said Christ, "by what authority I do these things."

Scribes, priests, and rulers were all silenced. Baffled and disappointed, they stood with lowering brows, not daring to press further questions upon Christ. By their cowardice and indecision they had in a great measure forfeited the respect of the people, who now stood by, amused to see these proud, self-righteous men defeated.

All these sayings and doings of Christ were important, and their influence was to be felt in an ever-increasing degree after His crucifixion and ascension. Many of those who had anxiously awaited the result of the questioning of Jesus, were finally to become His disciples, first drawn toward Him by His words on that eventful day. The scene in the temple court was never to fade from their minds. The contrast between Jesus and the high priest as they talked together was marked. The proud dignitary of the temple was clothed in rich and costly garments. Upon his head was a glittering tiara. His bearing was majestic, his hair and his long flowing beard were silvered by age. His appearance awed the beholders. Before this august personage stood the Majesty of heaven, without adornment or display. His garments were travel stained; His face was pale, and expressed a patient sadness; yet written there were dignity and benevolence that contrasted strangely with the proud, self-confident, and angry air of the high priest. Many of those who witnessed the words and deeds of Jesus in the temple, from that time enshrined Him in their hearts as a prophet of God. But as the popular feeling turned in His favor, the hatred of the priests toward Jesus increased. The wisdom by which He escaped the snares set for His feet, being a new evidence of His divinity, added fuel to their wrath.

In His contest with the rabbis, it was not Christ's purpose to humiliate His opponents. He was not glad to see them in a hard place. He had an important lesson to teach. He had mortified His enemies by allowing them to be entangled in the net they had spread for Him. Their acknowledged ignorance in regard to the character of John's baptism gave Him an opportunity to speak, and He improved the opportunity by presenting before them their real position, adding another warning to the many already given.

"What think ye?" He said. "A certain man had two sons, and he came to the first, and said, Son, go work today in my vineyard. He answered and said, I will not; but afterward he repented and went. And he came to the second, and said likewise. And he answered and said, I go, sir, and went not. Whether of them twain did the will of his father?"

This abrupt question threw His hearers off their guard. They had followed the parable closely, and now immediately answered, "The first." Fixing His steady eye upon them, Jesus responded in stern and solemn tones: "Verily I say unto you, That the publicans and the harlots go into the kingdom of God before you. For John came unto you in the way of righteousness, and ye believed him not; but the publicans and the harlots believed him; and ye, when ye had seen it, repented not afterward, that ye might believe him."

The priests and rulers could not but give a correct answer to Christ's question, and thus He obtained their opinion in favor of the first son. This son represented the publicans, those who were despised and hated by the Pharisees. The publicans had been grossly immoral. They had indeed been transgressors of the law of God, showing in their lives an absolute resistance to His requirements. They had been unthankful and unholy; when told to go and work in the

Lord's vineyard, they had given a contemptous refusal. But when John came, preaching repentance and baptism, the publicans received his message and were baptized.

The second son represented the leading men of the Jewish nation. Some of the Pharisees had repented and received the baptism of John; but the leaders would not acknowledge that he came from God. His warnings and denunciations did not lead them to reformation. They "rejected the counsel of God against themselves, being not baptized of him." They treated his message with disdain. Like the second son, who, when called, said, "I go, sir," but went not, the priests and rulers professed obedience, but acted disobedience. They made great professions of piety, they claimed to be obeying the law of God, but they rendered only a false obedience. The publicans were denounced and cursed by the Pharisees as infidels; but they showed by their faith and works that they were going into the kingdom of heaven before those self-righteous men who had been given great light, but whose works did not correspond to their profession of godliness.

The priests and rulers were unwilling to bear these searching truths; they remained silent, however, hoping that Jesus would say something which they could turn against Him; but they had still more to bear.

"Hear another parable," Christ said: "There was a certain householder, which planted a vineyard, and hedged it round about, and digged a wine press in it, and built a tower, and let it out to husbandmen, and went into a far country. And when the time of the fruit drew near, he sent his servants to the husbandmen, that they might receive the fruits of it. And the husbandmen took his servants, and beat one, and killed another, and stoned another. Again, he sent other servants more than the first; and they did unto them likewise. But last of all he sent unto them his son, saying, They will reverence my son; but when the husbandmen saw the son, they said among themselves, This is the heir, come, let us kill him, and let us seize on his inheritance. And they caught him, and cast him out of the vineyard, and slew him. When the lord therefore of the vineyard cometh, what will he do unto those husbandmen?"

Jesus addressed all the people present; but the priests and rulers answered. "He will miserably destroy those wicked men," they said, "and will let out his vineyard unto other husbandmen, which shall render him the fruits in their seasons." The speakers had not at first perceived the application of the parable, but they now saw that they had pronounced their own condemnation. In the parable the householder represented God, the vineyard the Jewish nation, and the hedge the divine law which was their protection. The tower was a symbol of the temple. The lord of the vineyard had done everything needful for its prosperity "What could have been done more to my vineyard," he says, "that I have not done in it." Isaiah 5:4. Thus was represented God's unwearied care for Israel. And as the husbandmen were to return to the lord a due proportion of the fruits of the vineyard, so God's people were to honor Him by a life corresponding to their sacred privileges. But as the husbandmen had killed the servants whom the master sent to them for fruit, so the Jews had put to death the prophets whom God sent to call them to repentance. Messenger after messenger had been slain. Thus far the application of the parable could not be questioned, and in what followed it was not less evident. In the beloved son whom the lord of the vineyard finally sent to his disobedient servants, and whom they seized and slew, the priests and rulers saw a distinct picture of Jesus and His impending fate. Already they were planning to slay Him whom the Father had sent to them as a last appeal. In the retribution inflicted upon the ungrateful husbandmen was portrayed the doom of those who should put Christ to death.

Looking with pity upon them, the Saviour continued, "Did ye never read in the Scriptures, The stone which the builders rejected, the same is become the head of the corner: this is the Lord's doing, and it is marvelous in our eyes? Therefore say I unto you, The kingdom of God shall be taken from you, and given to a nation bringing forth the fruits thereof. And whosoever shall fall on this stone shall be broken; but on whomsoever it shall fall, it will grind him to powder."

This prophecy the Jews had often repeated in the synagogues, applying it to the coming Messiah. Christ was the cornerstone of the Jewish economy, and of the whole plan of salvation. This foundation stone the Jewish builders, the priests and rulers of Israel, were now rejecting. The Saviour called their attention to the prophecies that would show them their danger. By every means in His power He sought to make plain to them the nature of the deed they were about to do.

And His words had another purpose. In asking the question, "When the lord therefore of the vineyard cometh, what will he do unto those husbandmen?" Christ designed that the Pharisees should answer as they did. He designed that they should condemn themselves. His warnings, failing to arouse them to repentance, would seal their doom, and He wished them to see that they had brought ruin on themselves. He designed to show them the justice of God in the withdrawal of their national privileges, which had already begun, and which would end, not only in the destruction of their temple and their city, but in the dispersion of the nation.

The hearers recognized the warning. But notwithstanding the sentence they themselves had pronounced, the priests and rulers were ready to fill out the picture by saying, "This is the heir; come, let us kill him." "But when they sought to lay hands on Him, they feared the multitude," for the public sentiment was in Christ's favor.

In quoting the prophecy of the rejected stone, Christ referred to an actual occurrence in the history of Israel. The incident was connected with the building of the first temple. While it had a special application at the time of Christ's first advent, and should have appealed with spe-

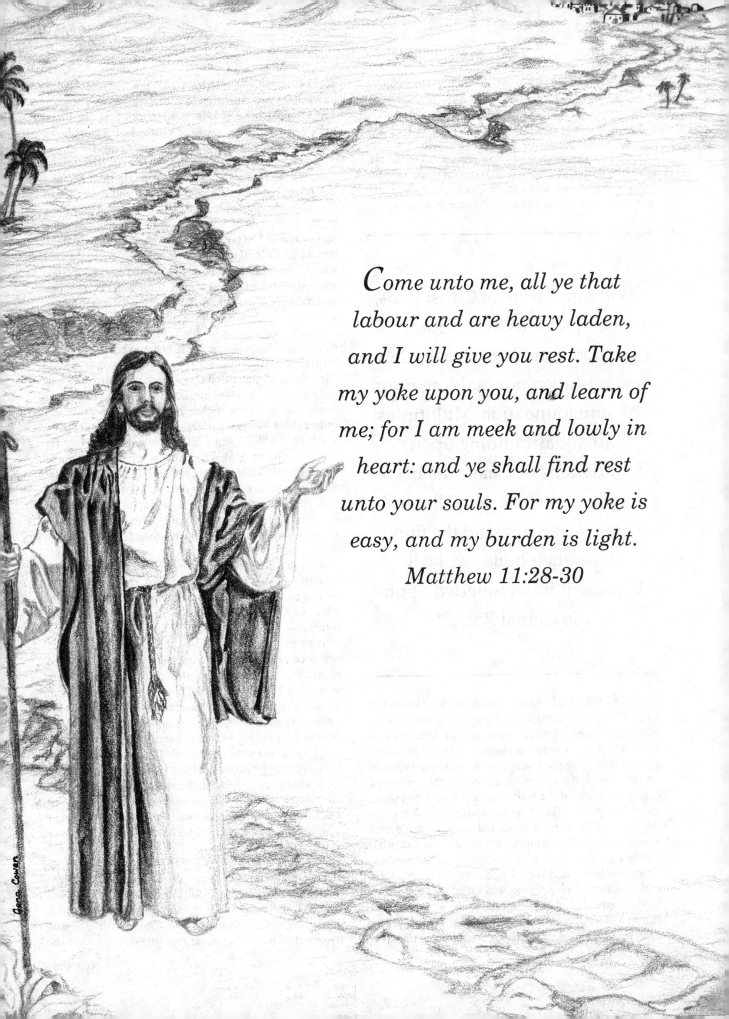

Come unto me, all ye that labour and are heavy laden, and I will give you rest. Take my yoke upon you, and learn of me; for I am meek and lowly in heart: and ye shall find rest unto your souls. For my yoke is easy, and my burden is light.
Matthew 11:28-30

cial force to the Jews, it has also a lesson for us. When the temple of Solomon was erected, the immense stones for the walls and the foundation were entirely prepared at the quarry; after they were brought to the place of building, not an instrument was to be used upon them; the workmen had only to place them in position. For use in the foundation, one stone of unusual size and peculiar shape had been brought; but the workmen could find no place for it, and would not accept it. It was an annoyance to them as it lay

"Without the life of Christ in us, we cannot withstand the storms of temptation. Our eternal safety depends upon our building upon the sure foundation. Multitudes are today building upon foundations that have not been tested. When the rain falls, and the tempest rages, and the floods come, their house will fall, because it is not founded upon the eternal Rock."

unused in their way. Long it remained a rejected stone. But when the builders came to the laying of the corner, they searched for a long time to find a stone of sufficient size and strength, and of the proper share, to take that particular place, and bear the great weight which would rest upon it. Should they make an unwise choice for this important place, the safety of the entire building would be endangered. They must find a stone capable of resisting the influence of the sun, of frost, and of tempest. Several stones had at different times been chosen, but under the pressure of immense weights they had crumbled to pieces. Others could not bear the test of the sudden atmospheric changes. But at last attention was called to the stone so long rejected. It had been exposed to the air, to sun and storm, without revealing the slightest crack. The builders examined this stone. It had borne every test but one. If it

could bear the test of severe pressure, they decided to accept it for the cornerstone. The trial was made. The stone was accepted, brought to its assigned position, and found to be an exact fit. In prophetic vision, Isaiah was shown that this stone was a symbol of Christ. He says: —

"Sanctify the Lord of hosts Himself; and let Him be your fear, and let Him be your dread. And He shall be for a sanctuary; but for a stone of stumbling and for a rock of offense to both the houses of Israel, for a gin and for a snare to the inhabitants of Jerusalem. And many among them shall stumble, and fall, and be broken, and be snared, and be taken." Carried down in prophetic vision to the first advent, the prophet is shown that Christ is to bear trials and tests of which the treatment of the chief cornerstone in the temple of Solomon was symbolic. "Therefore thus saith the Lord God, Behold, I lay in Zion for a foundation a stone, a tried stone, a precious cornerstone, a sure foundation; he that believeth shall not make haste." Isaiah 8:13-15; 28:16.

In infinite wisdom, God chose the foundation stone, and laid it Himself. He called it "a sure foundation." The entire world may lay upon it their burdens and griefs; it can endure them all. With perfect safety they may build upon it. Christ is a "tried stone." Those who trust in Him, He never disappoints. He has borne every test. He has endured the pressure of Adam's guilt, and the guilt of his posterity, and has come off more than conqueror of the powers of evil. He has borne the burdens cast upon Him by every repenting sinner. In Christ the guilty heart has found relief. He is the sure foundation. All who make Him their dependence, rest in perfect security.

In Isaiah's prophecy, Christ is declared to be both a sure foundation and a stone of stumbling. The apostle Peter, writing by inspiration of the Holy Spirit, clearly shows to whom Christ is a foundation stone, and to whom a rock of offense: —

"If so be ye have tasted that the Lord is gracious, to whom coming, as unto a living stone, disallowed indeed of men, but chosen of God, and precious, ye also, as lively stones, are built up a spiritual house, an holy priesthood, to offer up spiritual sacrifices, acceptable to God by Jesus Christ. Wherefore also it is contained in the Scripture, Behold, I lay in Sion a Chief Cornerstone, elect, precious; and he that believeth on Him shall not be confounded. Unto you therefore which believe He is precious; but unto them which be disobedient, the stone which the builders disallowed, the same is made the head of the corner, and a stone of stumbling, and a rock of offense, even to them which stumble at the word, being disobedient." 1 Peter 2:3-8.

To those who believe, Christ is the sure foundation. These are they who fall upon the Rock and are broken. Submission to Christ and faith in Him are here represented. To fall upon the Rock and be broken is to give up our self-righteousness, and to go to Christ with the humility of a child, repenting of our transgressions, and believing in His forgiving love. And so also it is by faith and obedience that we build on Christ as our foundation.

Upon this living stone, Jews and Gentiles alike may build. This is the only foundation upon which we may securely build. It is broad enough for all, and strong enough to sustain the weight and burden of the whole world. And by connection with Christ, the living stone, all who build upon this foundation become living stones. Many persons are by their own endeavors hewn, polished, and beautified; but they cannot become "living stones," because they are not connected with Christ. Without this connection, no man can be saved. Without the life of Christ in us, we cannot withstand the storms of temptation. Our eternal safety depends upon our building upon the sure foundation. Multitudes are today building upon foundations that have not been tested. When the rain falls, and the tempest rages, and the floods come, their house will fall, because it is not founded upon the eternal Rock, the Chief Cornerstone Christ Jesus.

"To them which stumble at the word, being disobedient," Christ is a rock of offense. But "the stone which the builders disallowed, the same is made the head of the corner." Like the rejected stone, Christ in His earthly mission had borne neglect and abuse. He was "despised and rejected of men; a Man of Sorrows, and acquainted with grief: . . . He was despised, and we esteemed Him not." Isaiah 53:3. But the time was near when He would be glorified. By the resurrection from the dead He would be "declared the Son of God with power." Romans 1:4. At His second coming He would be revealed as Lord of heaven and earth. Those who were now about to crucify Him, would recognize His greatness. Before the universe the rejected stone would become the head of the corner.

And on "whomsoever it shall fall, it will grind him to powder." The people who rejected Christ, were soon to see their city and their nation destroyed. Their glory would be broken, and scattered as the dust before the wind. And what was it that destroyed the Jews? It was the rock which, had they built upon it, would have been their security. It was the goodness of God despised, the righteousness spurned, the mercy slighted. Men set themselves in opposition to God, and all that would have been their salvation was turned to their destruction. All that God ordained unto life, they found to be unto death. In the Jews' crucifixion of Christ was involved the destruction of Jerusalem. The blood shed upon Calvary was the weight that sunk them to ruin for this world and for the world to come. So it will be in the great final day, when judgment shall fall upon the rejecters of God's grace. Christ, their Rock of offense, will then appear to them as an avenging mountain. The glory of His countenance, which to the righteous is life, will be to the wicked a consuming fire. Because of love rejected, grace despised, the sinner will be destroyed.

By many illustrations and repeated warnings, Jesus showed what would be the result to the Jews of rejecting the Son of God. In these words He was addressing all in every age who refuse to receive Him as their Redeemer. Every warning is for them. The desecrated temple, the disobedient son, the false husbandmen, the contemptuous builders, have their counterpart in the experience of every sinner. Unless he repent, the doom which they foreshadowed will be his.

Controversy

The priests and rulers had listened in silence to Christ's pointed rebukes. They could not refute His charges. But they were only the more determined to entrap Him, and with this object they sent to Him spies, "which should feign themselves just men, that they might take hold of His words, that so they might deliver Him unto the power and authority of the governor." They did not send the old Pharisees whom Jesus had often met, but young men, who were ardent and zealous, and whom, they thought, Christ did not know. These were accompanied by certain of the Herodians, who were to hear Christ's words, that they might testify against Him at His trial. The Pharisees and Herodians had been bitter enemies, but they were now one in enmity to Christ.

The Pharisees had ever chafed under the exaction of tribute by the Romans. The payment of tribute they held to be contrary to the law of God. Now they saw opportunity to lay a snare for Jesus. The spies came to Him, and with apparent sincerity, as though desiring to know their duty, said, "Master, we know that Thou sayest and teachest rightly, neither acceptest Thou the person of any, but teachest the way of God truly: is it lawful for us to give tribute unto Caesar, or no?"

The words, "We know that Thou sayest and teachest rightly," had they been sincere, would have been a wonderful admission. But they were spoken to deceive; nevertheless their testimony was true. The Pharisees did know that Christ said and taught rightly, and by their own testimony will they be judged.

Those who put the question to Jesus thought that they had sufficiently disguised their purpose; but Jesus read their hearts as an open book, and sounded their hypocrisy. "Why tempt ye Me?" He said; thus giving them a sign they had not asked, by showing that He read their hidden purpose. They were still more confused when He added, "Show Me a penny." They brought it, and He asked them, "Whose image and superscription hath it? They answered and said, Caesar's." Pointing to the inscription on the coin, Jesus said, "Render therefore unto Caesar the things which are Caesar's; and unto God the things that are God's."

The spies had expected Jesus to answer their question directly, in one way or the other. If He should say, It is unlawful to give tribute to Caesar, He would be reported to the Roman authorities and arrested for inciting rebellion. But in case He should pronounce it lawful to pay the tribute, they designed to accuse Him to the people as opposing the law of God. Now they felt themselves baffled and defeated. Their plans were disarranged. The summary manner in which their question had been settled left them nothing further to say.

Christ's reply was no evasion, but a candid answer to the question. Holding in His hand the Roman coin, upon which were stamped the name and image of Caesar, He declared that since they were living under the protection of the Roman power, they should render to that power the support it claimed, so long as this did not conflict with a higher duty. But while peaceably subject to the laws of the land, they should at all times give their first allegiance to God.

The Saviour's words, "Render . . . unto God the things that are God's," were a severe rebuke to the intriguing Jews. Had they faithfully fulfilled their obligations to God, they would not have become a broken nation, subject to a foreign power. No Roman ensign would have waved over Jerusalem, no Roman sentinel would have stood at her gates, no Roman governor would have ruled within her

This chapter is based on Matthew 22:15-46; Mark 12:13-40; Luke 20:20-47.

walls. The Jewish nation was then paying the penalty of its apostasy from God.

When the Pharisees heard Christ's answer, "they marveled, and left Him, and went their way." He had rebuked their hypocrisy and presumption, and in doing this He had stated a great principle, a principle that clearly defines the limits of man's duty to the civil government and his duty to God. In many minds a vexed question had been settled. Ever after they held to the right principle. And although many went away dissatisfied, they saw that the principle underlying the question had been clearly set forth, and they marveled at Christ's far-seeing discernment.

No sooner were the Pharisees silenced, than the Sadducees came forward with their artful questions. The two parties stood in bitter opposition to each other. The Pharisees were rigid adherents to tradition. They were exact in outward ceremonies, diligent in washings, fastings, and long prayers, and ostentatious in almsgiving. But Christ declared that they made void the law of God by teaching for doctrines the commandments of men. As a class they were bigoted and hypocritical; yet among them were persons of genuine piety, who accepted Christ's teachings and became His disciples. The Sadducees rejected the traditions of the Pharisees. They professed to believe the greater portion of the Scriptures, and to regard them as the rule of action; but practically they were skeptics and materialists.

The Sadducees denied the existence of angels, the resurrection of the dead, and the doctrine of a future life, with its rewards and punishments. On all these points they differed with the Pharisees. Between the two parties the resurrection was especially a subject of controversy. The Pharisees had been firm believers in the resurrection, but in these discussions their views in regard to the future state became confused. Death became to them an inexplicable mystery. Their inability to meet the arguments of the Sadducees gave rise to continual irritation. The discussions between the two parties usually resulted in angry disputes, leaving them farther apart than before.

In numbers the Sadducees fell far below their opponents, and they had not so strong a hold upon the common people; but many of them were wealthy, and they had the influence which wealth imparts. In their ranks were included most of the priests, and from among them the high priest was usually chosen. This was, however, with the express stipulation that their skeptical opinions should not be made prominent. On account of the numbers and popularity of the Pharisees, it was necessary for the Sadducees to concede outwardly to their doctrines when holding any priestly office; but the very fact that they were eligible to such office gave influence to their errors.

The Sadducees rejected the teaching of Jesus; He was animated by a spirit which they would not acknowledge as manifesting itself thus; and His teaching in regard to God and the future life contradicted their theories. They believed in God as the only being superior to man; but they

argued that an overruling providence and a divine foresight would deprive man of free moral agency, and degrade him to the position of a slave. It was their belief, that, having created man, God had left him to himself, independent of a higher influence. They held that man was free to control his own life and to shape the events of the world; that his destiny was in his own hands. They denied that the Spirit of God works through human efforts or natural means. Yet they still held that, through the proper employment of his natural powers, man could become elevated and enlightened; that by rigorous and austere exactions his life could be purified.

Their ideas of God molded their own character. As in their view He had no interest in man, so they had little regard for one another; there was little union among them. Refusing to acknowledge the influence of the Holy Spirit upon human action, they lacked His power in their lives. Like the rest of the Jews, they boasted much of their birthright as children of Abraham, and of their strict adherence to the requirements of the law; but of the true spirit of the law and the faith and benevolence of Abraham, they were destitute. Their natural sympathies were brought within a narrow compass. They believed it possible for all men to secure the comforts and blessings of life; and their hearts were not touched by the wants and sufferings of others. They lived for themselves.

By His words and His works, Christ testified to a divine power that produces supernatural results, to a future life beyond the present, to God as a Father of the children of men, ever watchful of their true interests. He revealed the working of divine power in benevolence and compassion that rebuked the selfish exclusiveness of the Sadducees. He taught that both for man's temporal and for his eternal good, God moves upon the heart by the Holy Spirit. He showed the error of trusting to human power for that transformation of character which can be wrought only by the Spirit of God.

This teaching the Sadducees were determined to discredit. In seeking a controversy with Jesus, they felt confident of bringing Him into disrepute, even if they could not secure His condemnation. The resurrection was the subject on which they chose to question Him. Should He agree with them, He would give still further offense to the Pharisees. Should He differ with them, they designed to hold His teaching up to ridicule.

The Sadducees reasoned that if the body is to be composed of the same particles of matter in its immortal as in its mortal state, then when raised from the dead it must have flesh and blood, and must resume in the eternal world the life interrupted on earth. In that case they concluded that earthly relationships would be resumed, husband and wife would be reunited, marriages consummated, and all things go on the same as before death, the frailties and passions of this life being perpetuated in the life beyond.

In answer to their questions, Jesus lifted the veil from the future life. "In the resurrection," He said, "they neither marry nor are given in marriage, but are as the angels of God in heaven." He showed that the Sadducees were wrong in their belief. Their premises were false. "Ye do err," He added, "not knowing the Scriptures nor the power of God." He did not charge them, as He had charged the Pharisees, with hypocrisy, but with error of belief.

The Sadducees had flattered themselves that they of all men adhered most strictly to the Scriptures. But Jesus showed that they had not known their true meaning. That

---

"The first four of the Ten Commandments are summed up in the one great precept, 'Thou shalt love the Lord thy God with all thy heart.' The last six are included in the other, 'Thou shalt love thy neighbor as thyself.' Both these commandments are an expression of the principle of love."

---

knowledge must be brought home to the heart by the enlightenment of the Holy Spirit. Their ignorance of the Scriptures and the power of God He declared to be the cause of their confusion of faith and darkness of mind. They were seeking to bring the mysteries of God within the compass of their finite reasoning. Christ called upon them to open their minds to those sacred truths that would broaden and strengthen the understanding. Thousands become infidels because their finite minds cannot comprehend the mysteries of God. They cannot explain the wonderful exhibition of divine power in His providences, therefore they reject the evidences of such power, attributing them to natural agencies which they can comprehend still less. The only key to the mysteries that surround us is to acknowledge in them all, the presence and power of God. Men need to recognize God as the Creator of the universe, One who commands and executes all things. They need a broader view of His character, and of the mystery of His agencies.

Christ declared to His hearers that if there were no resurrection of the dead, the Scriptures which they professed to believe would be of no avail. He said, "But as touching the resurrection of the dead, have ye not read that which was spoken unto you by God, saying, I am the God of Abraham, and the God of Isaac, and the God of Jacob? God is not the God of the dead, but of the living." God counts the things that are not, as though they were. He sees the end from the beginning, and beholds the result of His work as though it were now accomplished. The precious dead, from Adam down to the last saint who dies, will hear the voice of the Son of God, and will come forth from the grave to immortal life. God will be their God, and they shall be His people. There will be a close and tender relationship between God and the risen saints. This condition, which is anticipated in His purpose, He beholds as if it were already existing. The dead live unto Him.

By the words of Christ the Sadducees were put to silence. They could not answer Him. Not a word had been spoken of which the least advantage could be taken for His condemnation. His adversaries had gained nothing but the contempt of the people.

The Pharisees, however, did not yet despair of driving Him to speak that which they could use against Him. They prevailed upon a certain learned scribe to question Jesus as to which of the ten precepts of the law was of the greatest importance.

The Pharisees had exalted the first four commandments, which point out the duty of man to his Maker, as of far greater consequence than the other six, which define man's duty to his fellow man. As the result they greatly failed of practical godliness. Jesus had shown the people their great deficiency, and had taught the necessity of good works, declaring that the tree is known by its fruits. For this reason He had been charged with exalting the last six commandments above the first four.

The lawyer approached Jesus with a direct question, "Which is the first commandment of all?" The answer of Christ is direct and forcible: "The first of all the commandments is, Hear, O Israel, the Lord our God is one Lord: and thou shalt love the Lord thy God with all thy heart, and with all thy soul, and with all thy mind, and with all thy strength: this is the first commandment." The second is like the first, said Christ; for it flows out of it, "Thou shalt love thy neighbor as thyself. There is none other commandment greater than these." "On these two commandments hang all the law and the prophets."

The first four of the ten commandments are summed up in the one great precept, "Thou shalt love the Lord thy God with all thy heart." The last six are included in the other, "Thou shalt love thy neighbor as thyself." Both these commandments are an expression of the principle of love. The first cannot be kept and the second broken, nor can the second be kept while the first is broken. When God has His rightful place on the throne of the heart, the right place will be given to our neighbor. We shall love him as ourselves. And only as we love God supremely is it possible to love our neighbor impartially.

And since all the commandments are summed up in love to God and man, it follows that not one precept can be broken without violating this principle. Thus Christ taught His hearers that the law of God is not so many separate precepts, some of which are of great importance, while others are of small importance, and may with impunity be ignored. Our Lord presents the first four and the last six commandments as a divine whole, and teaches that love to God will be shown by obedience to all His commandments.

The scribe who had questioned Jesus was well read in the law, and he was astonished at His words. He did not expect Him to manifest so deep and thorough a knowledge of the Scriptures. He had gained a broader view of the principles underlying the sacred precepts. Before the assembled priests and rulers he honestly acknowledged that Christ had given the right interpretation to the law, saying, —

"Well, Master, Thou hast said the truth; for there is one God, and there is none other but He. And to love Him with all the heart, and with all the understanding, and with all the soul, and with all the strength, and to love his neighbor as himself, is more than all whole burnt offerings and sacrifices."

The wisdom of Christ's answer had convicted the scribe. He knew that the Jewish religion consisted in outward ceremonies rather than inward piety. He had some sense of the worthlessness of mere ceremonial offerings, and the faithless shedding of blood for expiation of sin. Love and obedience to God, and unselfish regard for man, appeared to him of more value than all these rites. The readiness of this man to acknowledge the correctness of Christ's reasoning, and his decided and prompt response before the people, manifested a spirit entirely different from that of the priests and rulers. The heart of Jesus went out in pity to the honest scribe who had dared to face the frowns of the priests and the threats of the rulers to speak the convictions of his heart. "And when Jesus saw that he answered discreetly, He said unto him, Thou art not far from the kingdom of God."

The scribe was near to the kingdom of God, in that he recognized deeds of righteousness as more acceptable to God than burnt offerings and sacrifices. But he needed to recognize the divine character of Christ, and through faith in Him receive power to do the works of righteousness. The ritual service was of no value, unless connected with Christ by living faith. Even the moral law fails of its purpose, unless it is understood in its relation to the Saviour. Christ had repeatedly shown that His Father's law contained something deeper than mere authoritative commands. In the law is embodied the same principle that is revealed in the gospel. The law points out man's duty and shows him his guilt. To Christ he must look for pardon and for power to do what the law enjoins.

The Pharisees had gathered close about Jesus as He answered the question of the scribe. Now turning He put a question to them: "What think ye of Christ? whose son is He?" This question was designed to test their belief concerning the Messiah, — to show whether they regarded Him simply as a man or as the Son of God. A chorus of voices answered, "The Son of David." This was the title which prophecy had given to the Messiah. When Jesus revealed His divinity by His mighty miracles, when He healed the sick and raised the dead, the people had inquired among themselves, "Is not this the Son of David?" The Syro-Phenician woman, blind Bartimeus, and many others had cried to Him for help, "Have mercy on me, O Lord, Thou Son of David." Matthew 15:22. While riding into Jerusalem He had been hailed with the joyful shout, "Hosanna to the Son of David; blessed is He that cometh in the name of the Lord." Matthew 21:9. And the little children in the temple had that day echoed the glad ascription. But many who called Jesus the Son of David did not recognize His divinity. They did not understand that the Son of David was also the Son of God.

In reply to the statement that Christ was the Son of David, Jesus said, "How then doth David in Spirit [the Spirit of inspiration from God] call Him Lord, saying, The Lord said unto my Lord, Sit Thou on My right hand till I make Thine enemies Thy footstool? If David then call Him Lord, how is He his son? And no man was able to answer Him a word, neither durst any man from that day forth ask Him any more questions."

Woes on the Pharisees

It was the last day of Christ's teaching in the temple. Of the vast throngs that were gathered at Jerusalem, the attention of all had been attracted to Him; the people had crowded the temple courts, watching the contest that had been in progress, and they eagerly caught every word that fell from His lips. Never before had such a scene been witnessed. There stood the young Galilean, bearing no earthly honor or royal badge. Surrounding Him were priests in their rich apparel, rulers with robes and badges significant of their exalted station, and scribes with scrolls in their hands, to which they made frequent reference. Jesus stood calmly before them, with the dignity of a king. As one invested with the authority of heaven, He looked unflinchingly upon His adversaries, who had rejected and despised His teachings, and who thirsted for His life. They had assailed Him in great numbers, but their schemes to ensnare and condemn Him had been in vain. Challenge after challenge He had met, presenting the pure, bright truth in contrast to the darkness and errors of the priests and Pharisees. He had set before these leaders their real condition, and the retribution sure to follow persistence in their evil deeds. The warning had been faithfully given. Yet another work remained for Christ to do. Another purpose was still to be accomplished.

The interest of the people in Christ and His work had steadily increased. They were charmed with His teaching, but they were also greatly perplexed. They had respected the priests and rabbis for their intelligence and apparent piety. In all religious matters they had ever yielded implicit obedience to their authority. Yet they now saw these men trying to cast discredit upon Jesus, a teacher whose virtue and knowledge shone forth the brighter from every assault. They looked upon the lowering countenances of the priests and elders, and there saw discomfiture and confusion. They marveled that the rulers would not believe on Jesus, when His teachings were so plain and simple. They themselves knew not what course to take. With eager anxiety they watched the movements of those whose counsel they had always followed.

In the parables which Christ had spoken, it was His purpose both to warn the rulers and to instruct the people who were willing to be taught. But there was need to speak yet more plainly. Through their reverence for tradition and their blind faith in a corrupt priesthood, the people were enslaved. These chains Christ must break. The character of the priests, rulers, and Pharisees must be more fully exposed.

"The scribes and the Pharisees," He said, "sit in Moses' seat. All therefore whatsoever they bid you observe, that observe and do; but do not ye after their works; for they say, and do not." The scribes and Pharisees claimed to be invested with divine authority similar to that of Moses. They assumed to take his place as expounders of the law and judges of the people. As such they claimed from the people the utmost deference and obedience. Jesus bade His hearers do that which the rabbis taught according to the law, but not to follow their example. They themselves did not practice their own teaching.

And they taught much that was contrary to the Scriptures. Jesus said, "They bind heavy burdens and grievous to be borne, and lay them on men's shoulders; but they themselves will not move them with one of their fingers." The Pharisees enjoined a multitude of regulations, having their foundation in tradition, and unreasonably restricting personal liberty. And certain portions of the law they so explained as to impose upon the people observances which

This chapter is based on Matthew 23; Mark 12:41-44; Luke 20:45-47; 21:1-4.

they themselves secretly ignored, and from which, when it served their purpose, they actually claimed exemption.

To make a show of their piety was their constant aim. Nothing was held too sacred to serve this end. To Moses God had said concerning His commandments, "Thou shalt bind them for a sign upon thine hand, and they shall be as frontlets between thine eyes." Deuteronomy 6:8. These words have a deep meaning. As the word of God is meditated upon and practiced, the whole man will be ennobled. In righteous and merciful dealing, the hands will reveal, as a signet, the principles of God's law. They will be kept clean from bribes, and from all that is corrupt and deceptive. They will be active in works of love and compassion. The eyes, directed toward a noble purpose, will be clear and true. The expressive countenance, the speaking eye, will testify to the blameless character of him who loves and honors the word of God. But by the Jews of Christ's day all this was undiscerned. The command given to Moses was construed into a direction that the precepts of Scripture should be worn upon the person. They were accordingly written upon strips of parchment, and bound in a conspicuous manner about the head and wrists. But this did not cause the law of God to take a firmer hold of the mind and heart. These parchments were worn merely as badges, to attract attention. They were thought to give the wearers an air of devotion which would command the reverence of the people. Jesus struck a blow at this vain pretense: —

"But all their works they do for to be seen of men; they make broad their phylacteries, and enlarge the borders of their garments, and love the uppermost rooms at feasts, and the chief seats in the synagogues, and greetings in the markets, and to be called of men, Rabbi, Rabbi. But be not ye called Rabbi: for one is your Master, even Christ; and all ye are brethren. And call no man your father upon the earth; for one is your Father, which is in heaven. Neither be ye called masters; for one is your Master, even Christ." In such plain words the Saviour revealed the selfish ambition that was ever reaching for place and power, displaying a mock humility, while the heart was filled with avarice and envy. When persons were invited to a feast, the guests were seated according to their rank, and those who were given the most honorable place received the first attention and special favors. The Pharisees were ever scheming to secure these honors. This practice Jesus rebuked.

He also reproved the vanity shown in coveting the title of rabbi, or master. Such a title, He declared, belonged not to men, but to Christ. Priests, scribes, and rulers, expounders and administrators of the law, were all brethren, children of one Father. Jesus impressed upon the people that they were to give no man a title of honor indicating his control of their conscience or their faith.

If Christ were on earth today, surrounded by those who bear the title of "Reverend" or "Right Reverend," would He not repeat His saying, "Neither be ye called masters; for one is your Master, even Christ"? The Scripture declares of God, "Holy and reverend is His name." Psalms 111:9. To what human being is such a title befitting? How little does man reveal of the wisdom and righteousness it indicates. How many of those who assume this title are misrepresenting the name and character of God. Alas, how often have worldly ambition, despotism, and the basest sins been hidden under the broidered garments of a high and holy office. The Saviour continued: —

"But he that is greatest among you shall be your servant. And whosoever shall exalt himself shall be abased; and he that shall humble himself shall be exalted." Again and again Christ had taught that true greatness is measured by moral worth. In the estimation of heaven, greatness of character consists in living for the welfare of our fellow men, in doing works of love and mercy. Christ, the King of Glory, was a servant to fallen man.

"Woe unto you, scribes and Pharisees, hypocrites," said Jesus; "for ye shut up the kingdom of heaven against men; for ye neither go in yourselves, neither suffer ye them that are entering to go in." By perverting the Scriptures, the priests and lawyers blinded the minds of those who would otherwise have received a knowledge of Christ's kingdom, and that inward, divine life which is essential to true holiness.

"Woe unto You, scribes and Pharisees, hypocrites! for ye devour widows' houses, and for a pretense make long prayer; therefore ye shall receive the greater damnation." The Pharisees had great influence with the people, and of this they took advantage to serve their own interests. They gained the confidence of pious widows, and then represented it as a duty for them to devote their property to religious purposes. Having secured control of their money, the wily schemers used it for their own benefit. To cover their dishonesty, they offered long prayers in public, and made a great show of piety. This hypocrisy Christ declared would bring them the greater damnation. The same rebuke falls upon many in our day who make a high profession of piety. Their lives are stained by selfishness and avarice, yet they throw over it all a garment of seeming purity, and thus for a time deceive their fellow men. But they cannot deceive God. He reads every purpose of the heart, and will judge every man according to his deeds.

Christ unsparingly condemned abuses, but He was careful not to lessen obligation. He rebuked the selfishness that extorted and misapplied the widow's gifts. At the same time He commended the widow who brought her offering for God's treasury. Man's abuse of the gift could not turn God's blessing from the giver.

Jesus was in the court where were the treasure chests, and He watched those who came to deposit their gifts. Many of the rich brought large sums, which they presented with great ostentation. Jesus looked upon them sadly, but made no comment on their liberal offerings. Presently His countenance lighted as He saw a poor widow approach hesitatingly, as though fearful of being observed. As the rich and haughty swept by, to deposit their offerings, she shrank back as if hardly daring to venture farther. And yet she longed to do something, little though it might be, for the cause she loved. She looked at the gift in her hand. It was very small in comparison with the gifts of those around her, yet it was her all. Watching her opportunity, she hurriedly threw in her two mites, and turned to hasten away. But in doing this she caught the eye of Jesus, which was fastened earnestly upon her.

The Saviour called His disciples to Him, and bade them mark the widow's poverty. Then His words of commendation fell upon her ear: "Of a truth I say unto you, that this poor widow hath cast in more than they all." Tears of joy filled her eyes as she felt that her act was understood and appreciated. Many would have advised her to keep her pittance for her own use; given into the hands of the well-fed priests, it would be lost sight of among the many costly gifts brought to the treasury. But Jesus understood her motive. She believed the service of the temple to be of God's appointment, and she was anxious to do her utmost to sustain it. She did what she could, and her act was to be a monument to her memory through all time, and her joy in eternity. Her heart went with her gift; its value was estimated, not by the worth of the coin, but by the love to God and the interest in His work that had prompted the deed.

Jesus said of the poor widow, She "hath cast in more than they all." The rich had bestowed from their abundance, many of them to be seen and honored by men. Their large donations had deprived them of no comfort, or even luxury; they had required no sacrifice, and could not be compared in value with the widow's mite.

It is the motive that gives character to our acts, stamping them with ignominy or with high moral worth. Not the great things which every eye sees and every tongue praises does God account most precious. The little duties cheerfully done, the little gifts which make no show, and which to human eyes may appear worthless, often stand highest in His sight. A heart of faith and love is dearer to God than the most costly gift. The poor widow gave her living to do the little that she did. She deprived herself of food in order to give those two mites to the cause she loved. And she did it in faith, believing that her Heavenly Father would not overlook her great need. It was this unselfish spirit and childlike faith that won the Saviour's commendation.

Among the poor there are many who long to show their gratitude to God for His grace and truth. They greatly desire to share with their more prosperous brethren in sustaining His service. These souls should not be repulsed. Let them lay up their mites in the bank of heaven. If given from a heart filled with love for God, these seeming trifles become consecrated gifts, priceless offerings, which God smiles upon and blesses.

When Jesus said of the widow, She "hath cast in more than they all," His words were true, not only of the motive, but of the results of her gift. The "two mites which make a farthing" have brought to God's treasury an amount of money far greater than the contributions of those rich Jews. The influence of that little gift has been like a stream, small in its beginning, but widening and deepening as it flowed down through the ages. In a thousand ways it has contributed to the relief of the poor and the spread of the gospel. Her example of self-sacrifice has acted and reacted upon thousands of hearts in every land and in every age. It has appealed to both the rich and the poor, and their offerings have swelled the value of her gift. God's blessing

> ❝The Pharisees built the tombs of the prophets, and adorned their sepulchers, and said one to another, If we had lived in the days of our fathers, we would not have united with them in shedding the blood of God's servants. At the same time they were planning to take the life of His Son. This should be a lesson to us.❞

upon the widow's mite has made it the source of great results. So with every gift bestowed and every act performed with a sincere desire for God's glory. It is linked with the purposes of Omnipotence. Its results for good no man can measure.

The Saviour continued His denunciations of the scribes and Pharisees: "Woe unto you, ye blind guides, which say, Whosoever shall swear by the temple, it is nothing; but whosoever shall swear by the gold of the temple, he is a debtor. Ye fools and blind, for whether is greater, the gold, or the temple that sanctifieth the gold? and, Whosoever shall swear by the altar, it is nothing; but whosoever sweareth by the gift that is upon it, he is guilty. Ye fools and blind; for whether is greater, the gift, or the altar that sanctifieth the gift?" The priests interpreted God's requirements according to their own false and narrow standard. They presumed to make nice distinctions as to the comparative guilt of various sins, passing over some lightly, and treating others of perhaps less consequence as unpardonable. For a money consideration they excused persons from their vows. And for large sums of money they sometimes passed over aggravated crimes. At the same time these priests and rulers would in other cases pronounce severe judgment for trivial offenses.

"Woe unto you, scribes and Pharisees, hypocrites! for ye pay tithe of mint and anise and cummin, and have omitted the weightier matters of the law, judgment, mercy, and faith; these ought ye to have done, and not to leave the other undone." In these words Christ again condemns the abuse of sacred obligation. The obligation itself He does not set aside. The tithing system was ordained by God, and it had been observed from the earliest times. Abraham, the father of the faithful, paid tithes of all that he possessed. The Jewish rulers recognized the obligation of tithing, and this was right; but they did not leave the people to carry out their own convictions of duty. Arbitrary rules were laid down for every case. The requirements had become so complicated that it was impossible for them to be fulfilled. None knew when their obligations were met. As God gave it, the system was just and reasonable; but the priests and rabbis had made it a wearisome burden.

All that God commands is of consequence. Christ recognized the payment of tithes as a duty; but He showed that this could not excuse the neglect of other duties. The Pharisees were very exact in tithing garden herbs, such as mint, anise, and rue; this cost them little, and it gave them a reputation for exactness and sanctity. At the same time their useless restrictions oppressed the people and destroyed respect for the sacred system of God's own appointing. They occupied men's minds with trifling distinctions, and turned their attention from essential truths. The weightier matters of the law, justice, mercy, and truth, were neglected. "These," Christ said, "ought ye to have done, and not to leave the other undone."

Other laws had been perverted by the rabbis in like manner. In the directions given through Moses, it was forbidden to eat any unclean thing. The use of swine's flesh, and the flesh of certain other animals, was prohibited, as likely to fill the blood with impurities, and to shorten life. But the Pharisees did not leave these restrictions as God had given them. They went to unwarranted extremes. Among other things the people were required to strain all the water used, lest it should contain the smallest insect, which might be classed with the unclean animals. Jesus, contrasting these trivial exactions with the magnitude of their actual sins, said to the Pharisees, "Ye blind guides, which strain at a gnat, and swallow a camel."

"Woe unto you, scribes and Pharisees, hypocrites! for ye are like unto whited sepulchers, which indeed appear beautiful outward, but are within full of dead men's bones, and of all uncleanness." As the whited and beautifully decorated tomb concealed the putrefying remains within, so the outward holiness of the priests and rulers concealed iniquity. Jesus continued:

"Woe unto you, scribes and Pharisees, hypocrites! because ye build the tombs of the prophets, and garnish the sepulchers of the righteous, and say, If we had been in the days of our fathers, we would not have been partakers with them in the blood of the prophets. Wherefore ye be witnesses unto yourselves, that ye are the children of them which killed the prophets." To show their esteem for the dead prophets, the Jews were very zealous in beautifying their tombs; but they did not profit by their teachings, nor give heed to their reproofs.

In the days of Christ a superstitious regard was cherished for the resting places of the dead, and vast sums of money were lavished upon their decoration. In the sight of God this was idolatry. In their undue regard for the dead, men showed that they did not love God supremely, nor their neighbor as themselves. The same idolatry is carried to great lengths today. Many are guilty of neglecting the widow and the fatherless, the sick and the poor, in order to build expensive monuments for the dead. Time, money, and labor are freely spent for this purpose, while duties to the living — duties which Christ has plainly enjoined — are left undone.

The Pharisees built the tombs of the prophets, and adorned their sepulchers, and said one to another, If we had lived in the days of our fathers, we would not have united with them in shedding the blood of God's servants. At the same time they were planning to take the life of His Son. This should be a lesson to us. It should open our eyes to the power of Satan to deceive the mind that turns from the light of truth. Many follow in the track of the Pharisees. They revere those who have died for their faith. They wonder at the blindness of the Jews in rejecting Christ. Had we lived in His day, they declare, we would gladly have received His teaching; we would never have been partakers in the guilt of those who rejected the Saviour. But when obedience to God requires self-denial and humiliation, these very persons stifle their convictions, and refuse obedience. Thus they manifest the same spirit as did the Pharisees whom Christ condemned.

Little did the Jews realize the terrible responsibility involved in rejecting Christ. From the time when the first innocent blood was shed, when righteous Abel fell by the hand of Cain, the same history had been repeated, with increasing guilt. In every age prophets had lifted up their voices against the sins of kings, rulers, and people, speaking the words which God gave them, and obeying His will at the peril of their lives. From generation to generation there had been heaping up a terrible punishment for the rejecters of light and truth. This the enemies of Christ were now drawing down upon their own heads. The sin of the priests and rulers was greater than that of any preceding generation. By their rejection of the Saviour, they were making themselves responsible for the blood of all the righteous men slain from Abel to Christ. They were about to fill to overflowing their cup of iniquity. And soon it was to be poured upon their heads in retributive justice. Of this, Jesus warned them:

"That upon you may come all the righteous blood shed upon the earth, from the blood of righteous Abel unto the blood of Zacharias son of Barachias, whom ye slew between the temple and the altar. Verily, I say unto you, All these things shall come upon this generation."

The scribes and Pharisees who listened to Jesus knew that His words were true. They knew how the prophet Zacharias had been slain. While the words of warning from God were upon his lips, a Satanic fury seized the apostate king, and at his command the prophet was put to death. His blood had imprinted itself upon the very stones of the temple court, and could not be erased; it remained to bear testimony against apostate Israel. As long as the temple should stand, there would be the stain of that righteous blood, crying to God to be avenged. As Jesus referred to these fearful sins, a thrill of horror ran through the multitude.

Looking forward, Jesus declared that the impenitence of the Jews and their intolerance of God's servants would be the same in the future as it had been in the past:

"Wherefore, behold, I send unto you prophets, and wise men, and scribes: and some of them ye shall kill and crucify; and some of them shall ye scourge in your synagogues, and persecute them from city to city." Prophets and wise men, full of faith and the Holy Ghost, — Stephen, James, and many others, — would be condemned and slain. With hand uplifted to heaven, and a divine light enshrouding His person, Christ spoke as a judge to those before Him. His voice, that had so often been heard in gentleness and entreaty, was now heard in rebuke and condemnation. The listeners shuddered. Never was the impression made by His words and His look to be effaced.

Christ's indignation was directed against the hypocrisy, the gross sins, by which men were destroying their own souls, deceiving the people, and dishonoring God. In the specious, deceptive reasoning of the priests and rulers, He discerned the working of Satanic agencies. Keen and searching had been His denunciation of sin; but He spoke no words of retaliation. He had a holy wrath against the prince of darkness; but He manifested no irritated temper. So the Christian who lives in harmony with God, possessing the sweet attributes of love and mercy, will feel a righteous indignation against sin; but he will not be roused by passion to revile those who revile him. Even in meeting those who are moved by a power from beneath to maintain falsehood, in Christ he will still preserve calmness and self-possession.

Divine pity marked the countenance of the Son of God as He cast one lingering look upon the temple and then upon His hearers. In a voice choked by deep anguish of heart and bitter tears He exclaimed, "O Jerusalem, Jerusalem, thou that killest the prophets, and stonest them which are sent unto thee, how often would I have gathered thy children together, even as a hen gathereth her chickens under her wings, and ye would not!" This is the separation struggle. In the lamentation of Christ the very heart of God is pouring itself forth. It is the mysterious farewell of the longsuffering love of the Deity.

Pharisees and Sadducees were alike silenced. Jesus summoned His disciples, and prepared to leave the temple, not as one defeated and forced from the presence of his adversaries, but as one whose work was accomplished. He retired a victor from the contest.

The gems of truth that fell from Christ's lips on that eventful day were treasured in many hearts. For them new thoughts started into life, new aspirations were awakened, and a new history began. After the crucifixion and resurrection of Christ, these persons came to the front, and fulfilled their divine commission with a wisdom and zeal corresponding to the greatness of the work. They bore a message that appealed to the hearts of men, weakening the old superstitions that had long dwarfed the lives of thousands. Before their testimony human theories and philosophies became as idle fables. Mighty were the results flowing from the words of the Saviour to that wondering, awestruck crowd in the temple at Jerusalem.

But Israel as a nation had divorced herself from God. The natural branches of the olive tree were broken off. Looking for the last time upon the interior of the temple, Jesus said with mournful pathos, "Behold, your house is left unto you desolate. For I say unto you, Ye shall not see Me henceforth, till ye shall say, Blessed is He that cometh in the name of the Lord." Hitherto He had called the temple His Father's house; but now, as the Son of God should pass out from those walls, God's presence would be withdrawn forever from the temple built to His glory. Henceforth its ceremonies would be meaningless, its services a mockery.

In the Outer Court

A nd there were certain Greeks among them that came up to worship at the feast; the same came therefore to Philip, which was of Bethsaida of Galilee, and desired him, saying, Sir, we would see Jesus. Philip cometh and telleth Andrew, and again Andrew and Philip tell Jesus."

At this time Christ's work bore the appearance of cruel defeat. He had been victor in the controversy with the priests and Pharisees, but it was evident that He would never be received by them as the Messiah. The final separation had come. To His disciples the case seemed hopeless. But Christ was approaching the consummation of His work. The great event which concerned not only the Jewish nation, but the whole world, was about to take place. When Christ heard the eager request, "We would see Jesus," echoing the hungering cry of the world, His countenance lighted up, and He said, "The hour is come, that the Son of man should be glorified." In the request of the Greeks He saw an earnest of the results of His great sacrifice.

These men came from the West to find the Saviour at the close of His life, as the wise men had come from the East at the beginning. At the time of Christ's birth the Jewish people were so engrossed with their own ambitious plans that they knew not of His advent. The Magi from a heathen land came to the manger with their gifts, to worship the Saviour. So these Greeks, representing the nations, tribes, and peoples of the world, came to see Jesus. So the people of all lands and all ages would be drawn by the Saviour's cross. So shall many "come from the east and west, and shall sit down with Abraham, and Isaac, and Jacob, in the kingdom of heaven." Matthew 8:11.

The Greeks had heard of Christ's triumphal entry into Jerusalem. Some supposed, and had circulated the report, that He had driven the priests and rulers from the temple, and that He was to take possession of David's throne, and reign as king of Israel. The Greeks longed to know the truth in regard to His mission. "We would see Jesus," they said. Their desire was granted. When the request was brought to Jesus, He was in that part of the temple from which all except Jews were excluded, but He went out to the Greeks in the outer court, and had a personal interview with them.

The hour of Christ's glorification had come. He was standing in the shadow of the cross, and the inquiry of the Greeks showed Him that the sacrifice He was about to make would bring many sons and daughters to God. He knew that the Greeks would soon see Him in a position they did not then dream of. They would see Him placed beside Barabbas, a robber and murderer, who would be chosen for release before the Son of God. They would hear the people, inspired by the priests and rulers, making their choice. And to the question, "What shall I do then with Jesus which is called Christ?" the answer would be given, "Let Him be crucified." Matthew 27:22. By making this propitiation for the sins of men, Christ knew that His kingdom would be perfected, and would extend throughout the world. He would work as the Restorer, and His Spirit would prevail. For a moment He looked into futurity, and heard the voices proclaiming in all parts of the earth, "Behold the Lamb of God, which taketh away the sin of the world." John 1:29. In these strangers He saw the pledge of a great harvest, when the partition wall between Jew and Gentile should be broken down, and all nations, tongues, and peoples should hear the message of salvation. The anticipation of this, the consummation of His hopes, is expressed in the words, "The hour is come, that the Son of man should be glorified." But the way in which this glorification must take place was never absent from Christ's mind. The gathering in of the Gentiles was to follow His approaching death. Only by His death could the world be saved. Like a grain of wheat, the Son of man must be cast into the ground and die, and be buried out of sight; but He was to live again.

Christ presented His future, illustrating it by the things of nature, that the disciples might understand. The true result of His mission was to be reached by His death. "Verily, verily, I say unto you," He said, "Except a corn of wheat fall into the ground and die, it abideth alone; but if it die, it bringeth forth much fruit." When the grain of wheat falls into the ground and dies, it springs up, and bears fruit. So the death of Christ would result in fruit for the kingdom of God. In accordance with the law of the vegetable kingdom, life was to be the result of His death.

Those who till the soil have the illustration ever before them. Year by year man preserves his supply of grain, by apparently throwing away the choicest part. For a time it must be hidden under the furrow, to be watched over by the Lord. Then appears the blade, then the ear, and then the corn in the ear. But this development cannot take place unless the grain is buried out of sight, hidden, and to all appearance, lost.

The seed buried in the ground produces fruit, and in turn this is planted. Thus the harvest is multiplied. So the death of Christ on the cross of Calvary will bear fruit unto eternal life. The contemplation of this sacrifice will be the glory of those who, as the fruit of it, will live through the eternal ages.

The grain of wheat that preserves its own life can produce no fruit. It abides alone. Christ could, if He chose, save Himself from death. But should He do this, He must abide alone. He could bring no sons and daughters to God. Only by yielding up His life could He impart life to humanity. Only by falling into the ground to die could He become the seed of that vast harvest, — the great multitude that out of every nation, and kindred, and tongue, and people, are redeemed to God.

With this truth Christ connects the lesson of self-sacrifice that all should learn: "He that loveth his life shall lose it; and he that hateth his life in this world shall keep it unto life eternal." All who would bring forth fruit as workers together with Christ, must first fall into the ground and die. The life must be cast into the furrow of the world's need. Self-love, self-interest, must perish. And the law of self-sacrifice is the law of self-preservation. The husbandman preserves his grain by casting it away. So in human life. To give is to live. The life that will be preserved is the life that is freely given in service to God and man. Those who for Christ's sake sacrifice their life in this world, will keep it unto life eternal.

The life spent on self is like the grain that is eaten. It disappears, but there is no increase. A man may gather all he can for self; he may live and think and plan for self; but his life passes away, and he has nothing. The law of self-serving is the law of self-destruction.

"If any man serve Me," said Jesus, "let him follow Me; and where I am, there shall also My servant be. If any man serve Me, him will My Father honor." All who have borne with Jesus the cross of sacrifice, will be sharers with Him of His glory. It was the joy of Christ in His humiliation and pain, that His disciples should be glorified with Him. They are the fruit of His self-sacrifice. The outworking in them of His own character and spirit, is His reward, and will be His joy throughout eternity. This joy they share with Him, as the fruit of their labor and sacrifice is seen in other hearts and lives. They are workers together with Christ, and the Father will honor them as He honors His Son.

The message of the Greeks, foreshadowing as it did the gathering in of the Gentiles, brought to the mind of Jesus His entire mission. The work of redemption passed before Him, from the time when in heaven the plan was laid, to the death that was now so near at hand. A mysterious cloud seemed to enshroud the Son of God. Its gloom was felt by those near Him. He sat rapt in thought. At last the silence was broken by His mournful voice, "Now is My soul troubled; and what shall I say? Father, save Me from this hour?" In anticipation Christ was already drinking the cup of bitterness. His humanity shrank from the hour of abandonment, when to all appearance He would be deserted even by God, when all would see Him stricken, smitten of God, and afflicted. He shrank from public exposure, from being treated as the worst of criminals, from a shameful and dishonored death. A foreboding of His conflict with the powers of darkness, a sense of the awful burden of human transgression, and the Father's wrath because of sin, caused the spirit of Jesus to faint, and the pallor of death to overspread His countenance.

Then came divine submission to His Father's will. "For this cause," He said, "came I unto this hour. Father, glorify Thy name." Only through the death of Christ could Satan's kingdom be overthrown. Only thus could man be redeemed, and God be glorified. Jesus consented to the agony, He accepted the sacrifice. The Majesty of heaven consented to suffer as the Sin Bearer. "Father, glorify Thy name," He said. As Christ spoke these words, a response came from the cloud which hovered above His head: "I have both glorified it, and will glorify it again." Christ's whole life, from the manger to the time when these words were spoken, had glorified God; and in the coming trial His divine-human sufferings would indeed glorify His Father's name.

As the voice was heard, a light darted from the cloud, and encircled Christ, as if the arms of Infinite Power were thrown about Him like a wall of fire. The people beheld this scene with terror and amazement. No one dared to speak. With silent lips and bated breath all stood with eyes fixed upon Jesus. The testimony of the Father having been given, the cloud lifted, and scattered in the heavens. For the time the visible communion between the Father and the Son was ended.

"The people therefore, that stood by, and heard it, said that it thundered. Others said, An angel spake to Him." But the inquiring Greeks saw the cloud, heard the voice, comprehended its meaning, and discerned Christ indeed; to them He was revealed as the Sent of God.

The voice of God had been heard at the baptism of Jesus at the beginning of His ministry, and again at His transfiguration on the mount. Now at the close of His ministry it was heard for the third time, by a larger number of persons, and under peculiar circumstances. Jesus had just spoken the most solemn truth regarding the condition of the Jews. He had made His last appeal, and pronounced their doom. Now God again set His seal to the mission of His Son. He recognized the One whom Israel had rejected. "This voice came not because of Me," said Jesus, "but for your sakes." It was the crowning evidence of His Messiahship, the signal from the Father that Jesus had spoken the truth, and was the Son of God.

"Now is the judgment of this world," Christ continued; "now shall the prince of this world be cast out. And I, if I be lifted up from the earth, will draw all unto Me. This He said, signifying what death He should die." This is the crisis of the world. If I become the propitiation for the sins of men, the world will be lighted up. Satan's hold upon the souls of men will be broken. The defaced image of God will be restored in humanity, and a family of believing saints will finally inherit the heavenly home. This is the result of Christ's death. The Saviour is lost in contemplation of the scene of triumph called up before Him. He sees the cross, the cruel, ignominious cross, with all its attending horrors, blazing with glory.

But the work of human redemption is not all that is accomplished by the cross. The love of God is manifested to the universe. The prince of this world is cast out. The accusations which Satan has brought against God are refuted. The reproach which he has cast upon heaven is forever removed. Angels as well as men are drawn to the Redeemer. "I, if I be lifted up from the earth," He said, "will draw all unto Me."

Many people were round about Christ as He spoke these words, and one said, "We have heard out of the law that Christ abideth forever; and how sayest Thou, The Son of man must be lifted up? who is this Son of man? Then Jesus said unto them, Yet a little while is the light with you. Walk while ye have the light, lest darkness come upon you; for he that walketh in darkness knoweth not whither he goeth. While ye have light, believe in the light, that ye may be the children of light."

"But though He had done so many miracles before them, yet they believed not on Him." They had once asked the Saviour, "What sign showest Thou then, that we may see and believe Thee?" John 6:30. Innumerable signs had been given; but they had closed their eyes and hardened their hearts. Now that the Father Himself had spoken, and they could ask for no further sign, they still refused to believe.

"Nevertheless among the chief rulers also many believed on Him; but because of the Pharisees they did not confess Him, lest they should be put out of the synagogue." They loved the praise of men rather than the approval of God. To save themselves from reproach and shame, they denied Christ, and rejected the offer of eternal life. And how many through all the centuries since have been doing the same thing. To them all the Saviour's warning words apply: "He that loveth his life shall lose it." "He that rejected Me," said Jesus, "and receiveth not My words, hath one that judgeth him; the word that I have spoken, the same shall judge him in the last day." John 12:48.

Alas for those who knew not the time of their visitation! Slowly and regretfully Christ left forever the precincts of the temple.

On the Mount of Olives

Christ's words to the priests and rulers, "Behold, your house is left unto you desolate," (Matthew 23:38.) had struck terror to their hearts. They affected indifference, but the question kept rising in their minds as to the import of these words. An unseen danger seemed to threaten them. Could it be that the magnificent temple, which was the nation's glory, was soon to be a heap of ruins? The foreboding of evil was shared by the disciples, and they anxiously waited for some more definite statement from Jesus. As they passed with Him out of the temple, they called His attention to its strength and beauty. The stones of the temple were of the purest marble, of perfect whiteness, and some of them of almost fabulous size. A portion of the wall had withstood the siege by Nebuchadnezzar's army. In its perfect masonry it appeared like one solid stone dug entire from the quarry. How those mighty walls could be overthrown, the disciples could not comprehend.

As Christ's attention was attracted to the magnificence of the temple, what must have been the unuttered thoughts of that Rejected One. The view before Him was indeed beautiful, but He said with sadness, I see it all. The buildings are indeed wonderful. You point to these walls as apparently indestructible; but listen to my words: The day will come when "there shall not be left one stone upon another, that shall not be thrown down."

Christ's words had been spoken in the hearing of a large number of people; but when He was alone, Peter, John, James, and Andrew came to Him as He sat upon the Mount of Olives. "Tell us," they said, "when shall these things be? and what shall be the sign of Thy coming, and of the end of the world?" Jesus did not answer His disciples by taking up separately the destruction of Jerusalem and the great day of His coming. He mingled the description of these two events. Had He opened to His disciples future events as He beheld them, they would have been unable to endure the sight. In mercy to them He blended the description of the two great crises, leaving the disciples to study out the meaning for themselves. When He referred to the destruction of Jerusalem, His prophetic words reached beyond that event to the final conflagration in that day when the Lord shall rise out of His place to punish the world for their iniquity, when the earth shall disclose her blood, and shall no more cover her slain. This entire discourse was given, not for the disciples only, but for those who should live in the last scenes of this earth's history.

Turning to the disciples, Christ said, "Take heed that no man deceive you. For many shall come in My name, saying, I am Christ; and shall deceive many." Many false messiahs will appear, claiming to work miracles, and declaring that the time of the deliverance of the Jewish nation has come. These will mislead many. Christ's words were fulfilled. Between His death and the siege of Jerusalem many false messiahs appeared. But this warning was given also to those who live in this age of the world. The same deceptions practiced prior to the destruction of Jerusalem have been practiced through the ages, and will be practiced again.

"And ye shall hear of wars and rumors of wars; see that ye be not troubled; for all these things must come to pass, but the end is not yet." Prior to the destruction of Jerusalem, men wrestled for the supremacy. Emperors were murdered. Those supposed to be standing next the throne were slain. There were wars and rumors of wars. "All these things must come to pass," said Christ, "but the end [of the

Jewish nation as a nation] is not yet. For nation shall rise against nation, and kingdom against kingdom; and there shall be famines, and pestilences, and earthquakes in divers places. All these are the beginning of sorrows." Christ said, As the rabbis see these signs, they will declare them to be God's judgments upon the nations for holding in bondage His chosen people. They will declare that these signs are the token of the advent of the Messiah. Be not deceived; they are the beginning of His judgments. The people have looked to themselves. They have not repented and been converted that I should heal them. The signs that they represent as tokens of their release from bondage, are signs of their destruction.

"Then shall they deliver you up to be afflicted, and shall kill you; and ye shall be hated of all nations for My name's sake. And then shall many be offended, and shall betray one another, and shall hate one another." All this the Christians suffered. Fathers and mothers betrayed their children. Children betrayed their parents. Friends delivered their friends up to the Sanhedrin. The persecutors wrought out their purpose by killing Stephen, James, and other Christians.

Through His servants, God gave the Jewish people a last opportunity to repent. He manifested Himself through His witnesses in their arrest, in their trial, and in their imprisonment. Yet their judges pronounced on them the death sentence. They were men of whom the world was not worthy, and by killing them the Jews crucified afresh the Son of God. So it will be again. The authorities will make laws to restrict religious liberty. They will assume the right that is God's alone. They will think they can force the conscience, which God alone should control. Even now they are making a beginning; this work they will continue to carry forward till they reach a boundary over which they cannot step. God will interpose in behalf of His loyal, commandment-keeping people.

On every occasion when persecution takes place, those who witness it make decisions either for Christ or against Him. Those who manifest sympathy for the ones wrongly condemned, show their attachment for Christ. Others are offended because the principles of truth cut directly across their practice. Many stumble and fall, apostatizing from the faith they once advocated. Those who apostatize in time of trial, will, to secure their own safety, bear false witness, and betray their brethren. Christ has warned us of this, that we may not be surprised at the unnatural, cruel course of those who reject the light.

Christ gave His disciples a sign of the ruin to come on Jerusalem, and He told them how to escape: "When ye shall see Jerusalem compassed with armies, then know that the desolation thereof is nigh. Then let them which are in Judea flee to the mountains; and let them which are in the midst of it depart out; and let not them that are in the countries enter thereinto. For these be the days of vengeance, that all things which are written may be fulfilled." This warning was given to be heeded forty years after, at the destruction of Jerusalem. The Christians obeyed the warning, and not a Christian perished in the fall of the city.

"Pray ye that your flight be not in the winter; neither on the Sabbath day," Christ said. He who made the Sabbath did not abolish it, nailing it to His cross. The Sabbath was not rendered null and void by His death. Forty years after His crucifixion it was still to be held sacred. For forty years the disciples were to pray that their flight might not be on the Sabbath day.

"Everything in the world is in agitation. The signs of the times are ominous. . . . Who can read the future? Where is security? . . . Rapidly are men ranging themselves under the banner they have chosen. Restlessly are they waiting and watching the movements of their leaders. . . . Few believe with heart and soul that we have a hell to shun and a heaven to win."

From the destruction of Jerusalem, Christ passed on rapidly to the greater event, the last link in the chain of this earth's history, — the coming of the Son of God in majesty and glory. Between these two events, there lay open to Christ's view long centuries of darkness, centuries for His church marked with blood and tears and agony. Upon these scenes His disciples could not then endure to look, and Jesus passed them by with a brief mention. "Then shall be great tribulation," He said, "such as was not since the beginning of the world to this time, no, nor ever shall be. And except those days should be shortened, there should no flesh be saved; but for the elect's sake those days shall be shortened." For more than a thousand years such persecution as the world had never before known was to come upon Christ's followers. Millions upon millions of His faithful witnesses were to be slain. Had not God's hand been stretched out to preserve His people, all would have perished. "But for the elect's sake," He said, "those days shall be shortened."

Now, in unmistakable language, our Lord speaks of His second coming, and He gives warning of dangers to precede His advent to the world. "If any man shall say unto you, Lo, here is Christ, or there; believe it not. For there shall arise false christs and false prophets, and shall show great signs and wonders; insomuch that, if it were possible, they shall deceive the very elect. Behold, I have told you before. Wherefore if they shall say unto you, Behold, He is in the desert; go not forth: behold, He is in the secret chambers; believe it not. For as the lightning cometh out of the east, and shineth even unto the west; so shall also the coming of the Son of man be." As one of the signs of Jerusalem's destruction, Christ had said, "Many false prophets shall rise, and shall deceive many." False prophets did rise, deceiving the people, and leading great numbers into the desert. Magicians and sorcerers, claiming miraculous power, drew the people after them into the mountain solitudes. But this prophecy was spoken also for the last days. This sign is given as a sign of the second advent. Even now false christs and false prophets are showing signs and wonders to seduce His disciples. Do we not hear the cry, "Behold, He is in the desert"? Have not thousands gone forth into the desert, hoping to find Christ? And from thousands of gatherings where men profess to hold communion with departed spirits, is not the call now heard, "Behold, He is in the secret chambers"? This is the very claim that Spiritualism puts forth. But what says Christ? — "Believe it not. For as the lightning cometh out of the east, and shineth even unto the west; so shall also the coming of the Son of man be."

The Saviour gives signs of His coming, and more than this, He fixes the time when the first of these signs shall appear: "Immediately after the tribulation of those days shall the sun be darkened, and the moon shall not give her light, and the stars shall fall from heaven, and the powers of the heavens shall be shaken. And then shall appear the sign of the Son of man in heaven; and then shall all the tribes of the earth mourn, and they shall see the Son of man coming in the clouds of heaven with power and great glory. And He shall send His angels with a great sound of a trumpet, and they shall gather together His elect from the four winds, from one end of heaven to the other."

At the close of the great papal persecution, Christ declared, the sun should be darkened, and the moon should not give her light. Next, the stars should fall from heaven. And He says, "Learn a parable of the fig tree. When his branch is yet tender, and putteth forth leaves, ye know that summer is nigh. So likewise ye, when ye shall see all these things, know that He is near, even at the doors." Matthew 24:32, 33, margin.

Christ has given signs of His coming. He declares that we may know when He is near, even at the doors. He says of those who see these signs, "This generation shall not pass, till all these things be fulfilled." These signs have appeared. Now we know of a surety that the Lord's coming is at hand. "Heaven and earth shall pass away," He says, "but My words shall not pass away."

Christ is coming with clouds and with great glory. A multitude of shining angels will attend Him. He will come to raise the dead, and to change the living saints from glory to glory. He will come to honor those who have loved Him, and kept His commandments, and to take them to Himself. He has not forgotten them nor His promise. There will be a relinking of the family chain. When we look upon our dead, we may think of the morning when the trump of God shall sound, when "the dead shall be raised incorruptible, and we shall be changed." 1 Corinthians 15:52. A little longer, and we shall see the King in His beauty. A little longer, and He will wipe all tears from our eyes. A little longer, and He will present us "faultless before the presence of His glory with exceeding joy." Jude 24. Wherefore, when He gave the signs of His coming He said, "When these things begin to come to pass, then look up, and lift up your heads; for your redemption draweth nigh."

But the day and the hour of His coming Christ has not revealed. He stated plainly to His disciples that He Himself could not make known the day or the hour of His second appearing. Had He been at liberty to reveal this, why need He have exhorted them to maintain an attitude of constant expectancy? There are those who claim to know the very day and hour of our Lord's appearing. Very earnest are they in mapping out the future. But the Lord has warned them off the ground they occupy. The exact time of the second coming of the Son of man is God's mystery.

Christ continues, pointing out the condition of the world at His coming: "As the days of Noah were, so shall also the coming of the Son of man be. For as in the days that were before the flood they were eating and drinking, marrying, and giving in marriage, until the day that Noah entered into the ark, and knew not until the flood came, and took them all away; so shall also the coming of the Son of man be." Christ does not here bring to view a temporal millennium, a thousand years in which all are to prepare for eternity. He tells us that as it was in Noah's day, so will it be when the Son of man comes again.

How was it in Noah's day? — "God saw that the wickedness of man was great in the earth, and that every imagination of the thoughts of his heart was only evil continually." Genesis 6:5. The inhabitants of the antediluvian world turned from Jehovah, refusing to do His holy will. They followed their own unholy imagination and perverted ideas. It was because of their wickedness that they were destroyed; and today the world is following the same way. It presents no flattering signs of millennial glory. The transgressors of God's law are filling the earth with wickedness. Their betting, their horse racing, their gambling, their dissipation, their lustful practices, their untamable passions, are fast filling the world with violence.

In the prophecy of Jerusalem's destruction Christ said, "Because iniquity shall abound, the love of many shall wax cold. But he that shall endure unto the end, the same shall be saved. And this gospel of the kingdom shall be preached in all the world for a witness unto all nations; and then shall the end come." This prophecy will again be fulfilled. The abounding iniquity of that day finds its counterpart in this generation. So with the prediction in regard to the preaching of the gospel. Before the fall of Jerusalem, Paul, writing by the Holy Spirit, declared that the gospel was preached to "every creature which is under heaven." Colossians 1:23. So now, before the coming of the Son of man, the everlasting gospel is to be preached "to every nation, and kindred, and tongue, and people." Revelation 14:6, 14.

God "hath appointed a day, in the which He will judge the world." Acts 17:31. Christ tells us when that day shall be ushered in. He does not say that all the world will be converted, but that "this gospel of the kingdom shall be preached in all the world for a witness unto all nations; and then shall the end come." By giving the gospel to the world it is in our power to hasten our Lord's return. We are not only to look for but to hasten the coming of the day of God. 2 Peter 3:12, margin. Had the church of Christ done her appointed work as the Lord ordained, the whole world would before this have been warned, and the Lord Jesus would have come to our earth in power and great glory.

After He had given the signs of His coming, Christ said. "When ye see these things come to pass, know ye that the kingdom of God is nigh at hand." "Take ye heed, watch and pray." God has always given men warning of coming judgments. Those who had faith in His message for their time, and who acted out their faith, in obedience to His commandments, escaped the judgments that fell upon the disobedient and unbelieving. The word came to Noah, "Come thou and all thy house into the ark; for thee have I seen righteous before Me." Noah obeyed and was saved. The message came to Lot. "Up, get you out of this place; for the Lord will destroy this city." Genesis 7:1; 19:14. Lot placed himself under the guardianship of the heavenly messengers, and was saved. So Christ's disciples were given warning of the destruction of Jerusalem. Those who watched for the sign of the coming ruin, and fled from the city, escaped the destruction. So now we are given warning of Christ's second coming and of the destruction to fall upon the world. Those who heed the warning will be saved.

Because we know not the exact time of His coming, we are commanded to watch. "Blessed are those servants, whom the Lord when He cometh shall find watching." Luke 12:37, 42. Those who watch for the Lord's coming are not waiting in idle expectancy. The expectation of Christ's coming is to make men fear the Lord, and fear His judgments upon transgression. It is to awaken them to the great sin of rejecting His offers of mercy. Those who are watching for the Lord, are purifying their souls by obedience to the truth. With vigilant watching they combine earnest working. Because they know that the Lord is at the door, their zeal is quickened to co-operate with the divine intelligences in working for the salvation of souls. These are the faithful and wise servants who give to the Lord's household "their portion of meat in due season." Luke 12:37, 42. They are declaring the truth that is now specially applicable. As Enoch, Noah, Abraham, and Moses, each declared the truth for his time, so will Christ's servants now give the special warning for their generation.

But Christ brings to view another class: "If that evil servant shall say in his heart, My lord delayeth his coming; and shall begin to smite his fellow servants, and to eat and drink with the drunken, the lord of that servant shall come in a day when he looketh not for him."

The evil servant says in his heart, "My lord delayeth his coming." He does not say that Christ will not come. He does not scoff at the idea of His second coming. But in his heart and by his actions and words he declares that the Lord's coming is delayed. He banishes from the minds of others the conviction that the Lord is coming quickly. His influence leads men to presumptuous, careless delay. They are confirmed in their worldliness and stupor. Earthly passions, corrupt thoughts, take possession of the mind. The evil servant eats and drinks with the drunken, unites with the world in pleasure seeking. He smites his fellow servants, accusing and condemning those who are faithful to their Master. He mingles with the world. Like grows with like in transgression. It is a fearful assimilation. With the world he is taken in the snare. "The lord of that servant shall come.... in an hour that he is not aware of, and shall cut him asunder, and appoint him his portion with the hypocrites."

"If therefore thou shalt not watch, I will come on thee as a thief, and thou shalt not know what hour I will come upon thee." Revelation 3:3. The advent of Christ will surprise the false teachers. They are saying, "Peace and safety." Like the priests and teachers before the fall of Jerusalem, they look for the church to enjoy earthly prosperity and glory. The signs of the times they interpret as foreshadowing this. But what saith the word of Inspiration? — "Sudden destruction cometh upon them." 1 Thessalonians 5:3. Upon all who dwell on the face of the whole earth, upon all who make this world their home, the day of God will come as a snare. It comes to them as a prowling thief.

The world, full of rioting, full of godless pleasure, is asleep, asleep in carnal security. Men are putting afar off the coming of the Lord. They laugh at warnings. The proud boast is made, "All things continue as they were from the beginning." "Tomorrow shall be as this day, and much more abundant." 2 Peter 3:4; Isaiah 56:12. We will go deeper into pleasure loving. But Christ says, "Behold, I come as a thief." Revelation 16:15. At the very time when the world is asking in scorn, "Where is the promise of His coming?" (2 Peter 3:4; Isaiah 56:12.) the signs are fulfilling. While they cry, "Peace and safety," sudden destruction is coming. When the scorner, the rejecter of truth, has become presumptuous; when the routine of work in the various money-making lines is carried on without regard to principle: when the student is eagerly seeking knowledge of everything but his Bible, Christ comes as a thief.

Everything in the world is in agitation. The signs of the times are ominous. Coming events cast their shadows before. The Spirit of God is withdrawing from the earth, and calamity follows calamity by sea and by land. There are tempests, earthquakes, fires, floods, murders of every grade. Who can read the future? Where is security? There is assurance in nothing that is human or earthly. Rapidly are men ranging themselves under the banner they have chosen. Restlessly are they waiting and watching the movements of their leaders. There are those who are waiting and watching and working for our Lord's appearing. Another class are falling into line under the generalship of the first great apostate. Few believe with heart and soul that we have a hell to shun and a heaven to win.

The crisis is stealing gradually upon us. The sun shines in the heavens, passing over its usual round, and the heavens still declare the glory of God. Men are still eating and drinking, planting and building, marrying, and giving in marriage. Merchants are still buying and selling. Men are jostling one against another, contending for the highest place. Pleasure lovers are still crowding to theaters, horse-races, gambling hells. The highest excitement prevails, yet probation's hour is fast closing, and every case is about to be eternally decided. Satan sees that his time is short. He has set all his agencies at work that men may be deceived, deluded, occupied and entranced, until the day of probation shall be ended, and the door of mercy be forever shut.

Solemnly there come to us down through the centuries the warning words of our Lord from the Mount of Olives: "Take heed to yourselves, lest at any time your hearts be overcharged with surfeiting, and drunkenness, and cares of this life, and so that day come upon you unawares." "Watch ye therefore, and pray always, that ye may be accounted worthy to escape all these things that shall come to pass, and to stand before the Son of man."

"The Least of These My Brethren"

When the Son of man shall come in His glory, and all the holy angels with Him, then shall He sit upon the throne of His glory: and before Him shall be gathered all nations: and He shall separate them one from another." Thus Christ on the Mount of Olives pictured to His disciples the scene of the great Judgment day. And He represented its decision as turning upon one point. When the nations are gathered before Him, there will be but two classes, and their eternal destiny will be determined by what they have done or have neglected to do for Him in the person of the poor and the suffering.

In that day Christ does not present before men the great work He has done for them in giving His life for their redemption. He presents the faithful work they have done for Him. To those whom He sets upon His right hand He will say, "Come, ye blessed of My Father, inherit the kingdom prepared for you from the foundation of the world: for I was an hungered, and ye gave Me meat: I was thirsty, and ye gave Me drink: I was a stranger, and ye took Me in: naked, and ye clothed Me: I was sick, and ye visited Me: I was in prison, and ye came unto Me." But those whom Christ commends know not that they have been ministering unto Him. To their perplexed inquiries He answers, "Inasmuch as ye have done it unto one of the least of these My brethren, ye have done it unto Me."

Jesus had told His disciples that they were to be hated of all men, to be persecuted and afflicted. Many would be driven from their homes, and brought to poverty. Many would be in distress through disease and privation. Many would be cast into prison. To all who forsook friends or home for His sake He had promised in this life a hundredfold. Now He assured a special blessing to all who should minister to their brethren. In all who suffer for My name,

said Jesus, you are to recognize Me. As you would minister to Me, so you are to minister to them. This is the evidence that you are My disciples.

All who have been born into the heavenly family are in a special sense the brethren of our Lord. The love of Christ binds together the members of His family, and wherever that love is made manifest, there the divine relationship is revealed. "Every one that loveth is born of God, and knoweth God." 1 John 4:7.

Those whom Christ commends in the Judgment, may have known little of theology, but they have cherished His principles. Through the influence of the divine Spirit they have been a blessing to those about them. Even among the heathen are those who have cherished the spirit of kindness; before the words of life had fallen upon their ears, they have befriended the missionaries, even ministering to them at the peril of their own lives. Among the heathen are those who worship God ignorantly, those to whom the light is never brought by human instrumentality, yet they will not perish. Though ignorant of the written law of God, they have heard His voice speaking to them in nature, and have done the things that the law required. Their works are evidence that the Holy Spirit has touched their hearts, and they are recognized as the children of God.

How surprised and gladdened will be the lowly among the nations, and among the heathen, to hear from the lips of the Saviour, "Inasmuch as ye have done it unto one of the least of these My brethren, ye have done it unto Me." How glad will be the heart of Infinite Love as His followers look up with surprise and joy at His words of approval.

But not to any class is Christ's love restricted. He identifies Himself with every child of humanity. That we might become members of the heavenly family, He became a

This chapter is based on Matthew 25:31-46. (637-638)

member of the earthly family. He is the Son of man, and thus a brother to every son and daughter of Adam. His followers are not to feel themselves detached from the perishing world around them. They are a part of the great web of humanity; and Heaven looks upon them as brothers to sinners as well as to saints. The fallen, the erring, and the sinful, Christ's love embraces; and every deed of kindness done to uplift a fallen soul, every act of mercy, is accepted as done to Him.

The angels of heaven are sent forth to minister to those who shall be heirs of salvation. We know not now who they are; it is not yet made manifest who shall overcome, and share the inheritance of the saints in light; but angels of heaven are passing throughout the length and breadth of the earth, seeking to comfort the sorrowing, to protect the imperiled, to win the hearts of men to Christ. Not one is neglected or passed by. God is no respecter of persons, and He has an equal care for all the souls He has created.

As you open your door to Christ's needy and suffering ones, you are welcoming unseen angels. You invite the companionship of heavenly beings. They bring a sacred atmosphere of joy and peace. They come with praises upon their lips, and an answering strain is heard in heaven. Every deed of mercy makes music there. The Father from His throne numbers the unselfish workers among His most precious treasures.

Those on the left hand of Christ, those who had neglected Him in the person of the poor and the suffering, were unconscious of their guilt. Satan had blinded them; they had not perceived what they owed to their brethren. They had been self-absorbed, and cared not for others' needs.

To the rich, God has given wealth that they may relieve and comfort His suffering children; but too often they are indifferent to the wants of others. They feel themselves superior to their poor brethren. They do not put themselves in the poor man's place. They do not understand the temptations and struggles of the poor, and mercy dies out of their hearts. In costly dwellings and splendid churches, the rich shut themselves away from the poor; the means that God has given to bless the needy, is spent in pampering pride and selfishness. The poor are robbed daily of the education they should have concerning the tender mercies of God; for He has made ample provision that they should be comforted with the necessities of life. They are compelled to feel the poverty that narrows life, and are often tempted to become envious, jealous, and full of evil surmisings. Those who themselves have not endured the pressure of want, too often treat the poor in a contemptuous way, and make them feel that they are looked upon as paupers.

But Christ beholds it all, and He says, It was I who was hungry and thirsty. It was I who was a stranger. It was I who was sick. It was I who was in prison. While you were feasting at your bountifully spread table, I was famishing in the hovel or the empty street. While you were at ease in your luxurious home, I had not where to lay My head.

While you crowded your wardrobe with rich apparel, I was destitute. While you pursued your pleasures, I languished in prison.

When you doled out the pittance of bread to the starving poor, when you gave those flimsy garments to shield them from the biting frost, did you remember that you were giving to the Lord of Glory? All the days of your life I was near you in the person of these afflicted ones, but you did not seek Me. You would not enter into fellowship with Me. I know you not.

"Among the heathen are those who worship God ignorantly, those to whom the light is never brought by human instrumentality, yet they will not perish. Though ignorant of the written law of God, they have heard His voice speaking to them in nature, and have done the things that the law required."

Many feel that it would be a great privilege to visit the scenes of Christ's life on earth, to walk where He trod, to look upon the lake beside which He loved to teach, and the hills and valleys on which His eyes so often rested. But we need not go to Nazareth, to Capernaum, or to Bethany, in order to walk in the steps of Jesus. We shall find His footprints beside the sick bed, in the hovels of poverty, in the crowded alleys of the great city, and in every place where there are human hearts in need of consolation. In doing as Jesus did when on earth, we shall walk in His steps.

All may find something to do. "The poor always ye have with you" (John 12:8), Jesus said, and none need feel that there is no place where they can labor for Him. Millions upon millions of human souls ready to perish, bound in chains of ignorance and sin, have never so much as heard of Christ's love for them. Were our condition and theirs to be reversed, what would we desire them to do for us? All this, so far as lies in our power, we are under the most solemn obligation to do for them. Christ's rule of life, by which every one of us must stand or fall in the Judgment, is, "Whatsoever ye would that men should do to you, do ye even so to them." Matthew 7:12.

The Saviour has given His precious life in order to establish a church capable of caring for sorrowful, tempted souls. A company of believers may be poor, uneducated, and unknown; yet in Christ they may do a work in the home, the neighborhood, the church, and even in "the regions beyond," whose results shall be as far-reaching as eternity.

It is because this work is neglected that so many young disciples never advance beyond the mere alphabet of Christian experience. The light which was glowing in their own hearts when Jesus spoke to them, "Thy sins be forgiven thee," they might have kept alive by helping those in need. The restless energy that is so often a source of danger to the young, might be directed into channels through which it would flow out in streams of blessing. Self would be forgotten in earnest work to do others good.

Those who minister to others will be ministered unto by the Chief Shepherd. They themselves will drink of the living water, and will be satisfied. They will not be longing for exciting amusements, or for some change in their lives. The great topic of interest will be, how to save the souls that are ready to perish. Social intercourse will be profitable. The love of the Redeemer will draw hearts together in unity.

When we realize that we are workers together with God, His promises will not be spoken with indifference. They will burn in our hearts, and kindle upon our lips. To Moses, when called to minister to an ignorant, undisciplined, and rebellious people, God gave the promise, "My presence shall go with thee, and I will give thee rest." And He said, "Certainly I will be with thee." Exodus 33:14; 3:12. This promise is to all who labor in Christ's stead for His afflicted and suffering ones.

Love to man is the earthward manifestation of the love of God. It was to implant this love, to make us children of one family, that the King of Glory became one with us. And when His parting words are fulfilled, "Love one another, as I have loved you" (John 15:12); when we love the world as He has loved it, then for us His mission is accomplished. We are fitted for heaven; for we have heaven in our hearts.

But "if thou forbear to deliver them that are drawn unto death, and those that are ready to be slain; if thou sayest, Behold, we knew it not; doth not He that pondereth the heart consider it? and He that keepeth thy soul, doth not He know it? and shall not He render to every man according to his works?" Proverbs 24:11, 12. In the great Judgment day, those who have not worked for Christ, who have drifted along thinking of themselves, caring for themselves, will be placed by the Judge of the whole earth with those who did evil. They receive the same condemnation.

To every soul a trust is given. Of every one the Chief Shepherd will demand, "Where is the flock that was given thee, thy beautiful flock?" And "what wilt thou say when He shall punish thee?" Jeremiah 13:20, 21.

A Servant of Servants

In the upper chamber of a dwelling at Jerusalem, Christ was sitting at table with His disciples. They had gathered to celebrate the Passover. The Saviour desired to keep this feast alone with the Twelve. He knew that His hour was come; He Himself was the true paschal lamb, and on the day of the Passover was eaten, He was to be sacrificed. He was about to drink the cup of wrath; He must soon receive the final baptism of suffering. But a few quiet hours yet remained to Him, and these were to be spent for the benefit of His beloved disciples.

The whole life of Christ had been a life of unselfish service. "Not to be ministered unto, but to minister" (Matthew 20:28), had been the lesson of His every act. But not yet had the disciples learned the lesson. At this last Passover supper, Jesus repeated His teaching by an illustration that impressed it forever on their minds and hearts.

The interviews between Jesus and His disciples were usually seasons of calm joy, highly prized by them all. The Passover suppers had been scenes of special interest; but upon this occasion Jesus was troubled. His heart was burdened, and a shadow rested upon His countenance. As He met the disciples in the upper chamber, they perceived that something weighed heavily upon His mind, and although they knew not its cause, they sympathized with His grief.

As they were gathered about the table, He said in tones of touching sadness, "With desire I have desired to eat this Passover with you before I suffer; for I say unto you, I will not any more eat thereof, until it be fulfilled in the kingdom of God. And He took the cup, and gave thanks, and said, Take this, and divide it among yourselves; for I say unto you, I will not drink of the fruit of the vine until the kingdom of God shall come."

Christ knew that the time had come for Him to depart out of the world, and go to His Father. And having loved His own that were in the world, He loved them unto the end. He was now in the shadow of the cross, and the pain was torturing His heart. He knew that He would be deserted in the hour of His betrayal. He knew that by the most humiliating process to which criminals were subjected, He would be put to death. He knew the ingratitude and cruelty of those He had come to save. He knew how great the sacrifice that He must make, and for how many it would be in vain. Knowing all that was before Him, He might naturally have been overwhelmed with the thought of His own humiliation and suffering. But He looked upon the Twelve, who had been with Him as His own, and who, after His shame and sorrow and painful usage were over, would be left to struggle in the world. His thoughts of what He Himself must suffer were ever connected with His disciples. He did not think of Himself. His care for them was uppermost in His mind.

On this last evening with His disciples, Jesus had much to tell them. If they had been prepared to receive what He longed to impart, they would have been saved from heartbreaking anguish, from disappointment and unbelief. But Jesus saw that they could not bear what He had to say. As He looked into their faces, the words of warning and comfort were stayed upon His lips. Moments passed in silence. Jesus appeared to be waiting. The disciples were ill at ease. The sympathy and tenderness awakened by Christ's grief seemed to have passed away. His sorrowful words, pointing to His own suffering, had made little impression. The glances they cast upon each other told of jealousy and contention.

When the Son of man shall come in His glory, and all the holy angels with Him, then shall He sit upon the throne of His glory: And before Him shall be gathered all nations: and He shall separate them one from another, as a shepherd divideth His sheep from the goats. And He shall set the sheep on His right hand, but the goats on the left. Then shall the King say unto them on His right hand, Come, ye blessed of my Father, inherit the kingdom prepared for you from the foundation of the world. For I was an hungred, and ye gave me meat: I was thirsty, and ye gave me drink: I was a stranger, and ye took me in: Naked, and ye clothed me: I was sick, and ye visited me: I was in prison, and ye came unto me. Then shall the righteous answer him, saying, Lord, when saw we thee an hungred, and fed thee? or thirsty, and gave thee drink? When saw we thee a stranger, and took thee in? or naked, and clothed thee? Or when saw we thee sick, or in prison, and came unto thee? And the King shall answer and say unto them, Verily I say unto you, Inasmuch as ye have done it unto one of the least of these my brethren, ye have done it unto me.

Matthew 25:31-40

There was "a strife among them, which of them should be accounted the greatest." This contention, carried on in the presence of Christ, grieved and wounded Him. The disciples clung to their favorite idea that Christ would assert His power, and take His position on the throne of David. And in heart each still longed for the highest place in the kingdom. They had placed their own estimate upon themselves and upon one another, and instead of regarding their brethren as more worthy, they had placed themselves first. The request of James and John to sit on the right and left of Christ's throne, had excited the indignation of the others. That the two brothers should presume to ask for the highest position, so stirred the ten that alienation threatened. They felt that they were misjudged, that their fidelity and talents were not appreciated. Judas was the most severe upon James and John.

When the disciples entered the supper room, their hearts were full of resentful feelings. Judas pressed next to Christ on the left side; John was on the right. If there was a highest place, Judas was determined to have it, and that place was thought to be next to Christ. And Judas was a traitor.

Another cause of dissension had arisen. At a feast it was customary for a servant to wash the feet of the guests, and on this occasion preparation had been made for the service. The pitcher, the basin, and the towel were there, in readiness for the feet washing; but no servant was present, and it was the disciples' part to perform it. But each of the disciples, yielding to wounded pride, determined not to act the part of a servant. All manifested a stoical unconcern, seeming unconscious that there was anything for them to do. By their silence they refused to humble themselves.

How was Christ to bring these poor souls where Satan would not gain over them a decided victory? How could He show that a mere profession of discipleship did not make them disciples, or insure them a place in His kingdom? How could He show that it is loving service, true humility, which constitutes real greatness? How was He to kindle love in their hearts, and enable them to comprehend what He longed to tell them?

The disciples made no move toward serving one another. Jesus waited for a time to see what they would do. Then He, the divine Teacher, rose from the table. Laying aside the outer garment that would have impeded His movements, He took a towel, and girded Himself. With surprised interest the disciples looked on, and in silence waited to see what was to follow. "After that He poureth water into a basin, and began to wash the disciples' feet, and to wipe them with the towel wherewith He was girded." This action opened the eyes of the disciples. Bitter shame and humiliation filled their hearts. They understood the unspoken rebuke, and saw themselves in altogether a new light.

So Christ expressed His love for His disciples. Their selfish spirit filled Him with sorrow, but He entered into no controversy with them regarding their difficulty. Instead He gave them an example they would never forget.

His love for them was not easily disturbed or quenched. He knew that the Father had given all things into His hands, and that He came from God, and went to God. He had a full consciousness of His divinity; but He had laid aside His royal crown and kingly robes, and had taken the form of a servant. One of the last acts of His life on earth was to gird Himself as a servant, and perform a servant's part.

Before the Passover Judas had met a second time with the priests and scribes, and had closed the contract to deliver Jesus into their hands. Yet he afterward mingled with the disciples as though innocent of any wrong, and interested in the work of preparing for the feast. The disciples knew nothing of the purpose of Judas. Jesus alone could read his secret. Yet He did not expose him. Jesus hungered for his soul. He felt for him such a burden as for Jerusalem when He wept over the doomed city. His heart was crying, "How can I give thee up?" The constraining power of that love was felt by Judas. When the Saviour's hands were bathing those soiled feet, and wiping them with the towel, the heart of Judas thrilled through and through with the impulse then and there to confess his sin. But he would not humble himself. He hardened his heart against repentance; and the old impulses, for the moment put aside, again controlled him. Judas was now offended at Christ's act in washing the feet of His disciples. If Jesus could so humble Himself, he thought, He could not be Israel's king. All hope of worldly honor in a temporal kingdom was destroyed. Judas was satisfied that there was nothing to be gained by following Christ. After seeing Him degrade Himself, as he thought, he was confirmed in his purpose to disown Him, and confess himself deceived. He was possessed by a demon, and he resolved to complete the work he had agreed to do in betraying his Lord.

Judas, in choosing his position at table, had tried to place himself first, and Christ as a servant served him first. John, toward whom Judas had felt so much bitterness, was left till the last. But John did not take this as a rebuke or slight. As the disciples watched Christ's action, they were greatly moved. When Peter's turn came, he exclaimed with astonishment, "Lord, dost Thou wash my feet?" Christ's condescension broke his heart. He was filled with shame to think that one of the disciples was not performing this service. "What I do," Christ said, "thou knowest not now; but thou shalt know hereafter." Peter could not bear to see his Lord, whom he believed to be the Son of God, acting the part of a servant. His whole soul rose up against this humiliation. He did not realize that for this Christ came into the world. With great emphasis he exclaimed, "Thou shalt never wash my feet."

Solemnly Christ said to Peter, "If I wash thee not, thou hast no part with Me." The service which Peter refused was the type of a higher cleansing. Christ had come to wash the heart from the stain of sin. In refusing to allow Christ to wash his feet, Peter was refusing the higher cleansing included in the lower. He was really rejecting his Lord. It is not humiliating to the Master to allow Him to work for our purification. The truest humility is to receive with thankful heart any provision made in our behalf, and with earnestness do service for Christ.

At the words, "If I wash thee not, thou hast no part with Me," Peter surrendered his pride and self-will. He could not endure the thought of separation from Christ; that would have been death to him. "Not my feet only," he said, "but also my hands and my head. Jesus saith to him, He that is washed needeth not save to wash his feet, but is clean every whit."

These words mean more than bodily cleanliness. Christ is still speaking of the higher cleansing as illustrated by the lower. He who came from the bath was clean, but the sandaled feet soon became dusty, and again needed to be washed. So Peter and his brethren had been washed in the great fountain opened for sin and uncleanness. Christ acknowledged them as His. But temptation had led them into evil, and they still needed His cleansing grace. When Jesus girded Himself with a towel to wash the dust from their feet, He desired by that very act to wash the alienation, jealousy, and pride from their hearts. This was of far more consequence than the washing of their dusty feet. With the spirit they then had, not one of them was prepared for communion with Christ. Until brought into a state of humility and love, they were not prepared to partake of the paschal supper, or to share in the memorial service which Christ was about to institute. Their hearts must be cleansed. Pride and self-seeking create dissension and hatred, but all this Jesus washed away in washing their feet. A change of feeling was brought about. Looking upon them, Jesus could say, "Ye are clean." Now there was union of heart, love for one another. They had become humble and teachable. Except Judas, each was ready to concede to another the highest place. Now with subdued and grateful hearts they could receive Christ's words.

Like Peter and his brethren, we too have been washed in the blood of Christ, yet often through contact with evil the heart's purity is soiled. We must come to Christ for His cleansing grace. Peter shrank from bringing his soiled feet in contact with the hands of his Lord and Master; but how often we bring our sinful, polluted hearts in contact with the heart of Christ. How grievous to Him is our evil temper, our vanity and pride. Yet all our infirmity and defilement we must bring to Him. He alone can wash us clean. We are not prepared for communion with Him unless cleansed by His efficacy.

Jesus said to the disciples, "Ye are clean, but not all." He had washed the feet of Judas, but the heart had not been yielded to Him. It was not purified. Judas had not submitted himself to Christ.

After Christ had washed the disciples' feet, and had taken His garments and sat down again, He said to them, "Know ye what I have done to you? Ye call Me Master and Lord, and ye say well; for so I am. If I then, your Lord and Master, have washed your feet, ye also ought to wash one another's feet; for I have given you an example, that ye should do as I have done to you. Verily, verily, I say unto you, The servant is not greater than his lord; neither he that is sent greater than he that sent him."

Christ would have His disciples understand that although He had washed their feet, this did not in the least detract from His dignity. "Ye call Me Master and Lord, and ye say well; for so I am." And being so infinitely superior, He imparted grace and significance to the service. No one was so exalted as Christ, and yet He stooped to the humblest duty. That His people might not be misled by the selfishness which dwells in the natural heart, and which strengthens by self-serving, Christ Himself set the example of humility. He would not leave this great subject in man's charge. Of so much consequence did He regard it, that He Himself, One equal with God, acted as servant to His disciples. While they were contending for the highest place, He to whom every knee shall bow, He whom the angels of glory count it honor to serve, bowed down to wash the feet of those who called Him Lord. He washed the feet of His betrayer.

In His life and lessons, Christ has given a perfect exemplification of the unselfish ministry which has its origin in God. God does not live for Himself. By creating the world, and by upholding all things, He is constantly ministering for others. "He maketh His sun to rise on the evil and on the good, and sendeth rain on the just and on the unjust." Matthew 5:45. This ideal of ministry God has committed to His Son. Jesus was given to stand at the head of humanity, that by His example He might teach what it means to minister. His whole life was under a law of service. He served all, ministered to all. Thus He lived the law of God, and by His example showed how we are to obey it.

Again and again Jesus had tried to establish this principle among His disciples. When James and John made their request for pre-eminence, He had said, "Whosoever will be great among you, let him be your minister." Matthew 20:26. In My kingdom the principle of preference and supremacy has no place. The only greatness is the greatness of humility. The only distinction is found in devotion to the service of others.

Now, having washed the disciples' feet, He said, "I have given you an example, that ye should do as I have done to you." In these words Christ was not merely enjoining the practice of hospitality. More was meant than the washing of the feet of guests to remove the dust of travel. Christ was here instituting a religious service. By the act of our Lord this humiliating ceremony was made a consecrated ordinance. It was to be observed by the disciples, that they might ever keep in mind His lessons of humility and service.

This ordinance is Christ's appointed preparation for the sacramental service. While pride, variance, and strife for supremacy are cherished, the heart cannot enter into fellowship with Christ. We are not prepared to receive the communion of His body and His blood. Therefore it was that Jesus appointed the memorial of His humiliation to be first observed.

As they come to this ordinance, the children of God should bring to remembrance the words of the Lord of life and glory: "Know ye what I have done to you? Ye call Me Master and Lord, and ye say well; for so I am. If I then, your Lord and Master, have washed your feet, ye also ought to wash one another's feet. For I have given you an example, that ye should do as I have done to you. Verily, verily, I say unto you, The servant is not greater than his lord; neither he that is sent greater than he that sent him. If ye know these things, happy are ye if ye do them." There is in man a disposition to esteem himself more highly than his brother, to work for self, to seek the highest place; and often this results in evil surmisings and bitterness of spirit. The ordinance preceding the Lord's supper, is to clear away these misunderstandings, to bring man out of his selfishness, down from his stilts of self-exaltation, to the humility of heart that will lead him to serve his brother.

The holy Watcher from heaven is present at this season to make it one of soul-searching, of conviction of sin, and of the blessed assurance of sins forgiven. Christ in the fullness of His grace is there to change the current of the thoughts that have been running in selfish channels. The Holy Spirit quickens the sensibilities of those who follow the example of their Lord. As the Saviour's humiliation for us is remembered, thought links with thought; a chain of memories is called up, memories of God's great goodness and of the favor and tenderness of earthly friends. Blessings forgotten, mercies abused, kindnesses slighted, are called to mind. Roots of bitterness that have crowded out the precious plant of love are made manifest. Defects of character, neglect of duties, ingratitude to God, coldness toward our brethren, are called to remembrance. Sin is seen in the light in which God views it. Our thoughts are not thoughts of self-complacency, but of severe self-censure and humiliation. The mind is energized to break down every barrier that has caused alienation. Evil thinking and evil speaking are put away. Sins are confessed, they are forgiven. The subduing grace of Christ comes into the soul, and the love of Christ draws hearts together in a blessed unity.

As the lesson of the preparatory service is thus learned, the desire is kindled for a higher spiritual life. To this desire the divine Witness will respond. The soul will be uplifted. We can partake of the communion with a consciousness of sins forgiven. The sunshine of Christ's righteousness will fill the chambers of the mind and the soul temple. We "behold the Lamb of God, which taketh away the sin of the world." John 1:29.

To those who receive the spirit of this service, it can never become a mere ceremonial. Its constant lesson will be, "By love serve one another." Galatians 5:13. In washing the feet of His disciples, Christ gave evidence that He would do any service, however humble, that would make them heirs with Him of the eternal wealth of heaven's treasure. His disciples, in performing the same rite, pledge themselves in like manner to serve their brethren. Whenever this ordinance is rightly celebrated, the children of God are brought into a holy relationship, to help and bless each other. They covenant that the life shall be given to unselfish ministry. And this, not only for one another. Their field of labor is as wide as their Master's was. The world is full of those who need our ministry. The poor, the helpless, the ignorant, are on every hand. Those who have communed with Christ in the upper chamber, will go forth to minister as He did.

Jesus, the served of all, came to be the servant of all. And because He ministered to all, He will again be served and honored by all. And those who would partake of His divine attributes, and share with Him the joy of seeing souls redeemed, must follow His example of unselfish ministry.

All this was comprehended in the words of Jesus, "I have given you an example, that ye should do as I have done to you." This was the intent of the service He established. And He says, "If ye know these things," if you know the purpose of His lessons, "happy are ye if ye do them."

"In Remembrance of Me"

The Lord Jesus the same night in which He was betrayed took bread: and when He had given thanks, He brake it, and said, Take, eat: this is My body, which is broken for you: this do in remembrance of Me. After the same manner also He took the cup, when He had supped, saying, This cup is the new testament in My blood: this do ye, as oft as ye drink it, in remembrance of Me. For as often as ye eat this bread, and drink this cup, ye do show the Lord's death till He come." 1 Corinthians 2:23-26.

Christ was standing at the point of transition between two economies and their two great festivals. He, the spotless Lamb of God, was about to present Himself as a sin offering, and He would thus bring to an end the system of types and ceremonies that for four thousand years had pointed to His death. As He ate the Passover with His disciples, He instituted in its place the service that was to be the memorial of His great sacrifice. The national festival of the Jews was to pass away forever. The service which Christ established was to be observed by His followers in all lands and through all ages.

The Passover was ordained as a commemoration of the deliverance of Israel from Egyptian bondage. God had directed that, year by year, as the children should ask the meaning of this ordinance, the history should be repeated. Thus the wonderful deliverance was to be kept fresh in the minds of all. The ordinance of the Lord's supper was given to commemorate the great deliverance wrought out as the result of the death of Christ. Till He shall come the second time in power and glory, this ordinance is to be celebrated. It is the means by which His great work for us is to be kept fresh in our minds.

At the time of their deliverance from Egypt, the children of Israel ate the Passover supper standing, with their loins girded, and with their staves in their hands, ready for their journey. The manner in which they celebrated this ordinance harmonized with their condition; for they were about to be thrust out of the land of Egypt, and were to begin a painful and difficult journey through the wilderness. But in Christ's time the condition of things had changed. They were not now about to be thrust out of a strange country, but were dwellers in their own land. In harmony with the rest that had been given them, the people then partook of the Passover supper in a reclining position. Couches were placed about the table, and the guests lay upon them, resting upon the left arm, and having the right hand free for use in eating. In this position a guest could lay his head upon the breast of the one who sat next above him. And the feet, being at the outer edge of the couch, could be washed by one passing around the outside of the circle.

Christ is still at the table on which the paschal supper has been spread. The unleavened cakes used at the Passover season are before Him. The Passover wine, untouched by fermentation, is on the table. These emblems Christ employs to represent His own unblemished sacrifice. Nothing corrupted by fermentation, the symbol of sin and death, could represent the "Lamb without blemish and without spot." 1 Peter 1:19.

"And as they were eating, Jesus took bread, and blessed it, and brake it, and gave it to the disciples, and said, Take, eat: this is My body. And He took the cup, and gave thanks, and gave it to them, saying, Drink ye all of it; for this is My blood of the new testament, which is shed for many for the remission of sins. But I say unto you, I will not drink henceforth of this fruit of the vine, until that day when I drink it new with you in My Father's kingdom."

Judas the betrayer was present at the sacramental service. He received from Jesus the emblems of His broken body and His spilled blood. He heard the words, "This do in remembrance of Me." And sitting there in the very presence of the Lamb of God, the betrayer brooded upon his own dark purposes, and cherished his sullen, revengeful thoughts.

At the feet washing, Christ had given convincing proof that He understood the character of Judas. "Ye are not all clean," John 13:11. He said. These words convinced the false disciple that Christ read his secret purpose. Now Christ spoke out more plainly. As they were seated at the table He said, looking upon His disciples, "I speak not of you all: I know whom I have chosen; but that the scripture may be fulfilled, He that eateth bread with Me, hath lifted up his heel against Me."

Even now the disciples did not suspect Judas. But they saw that Christ appeared greatly troubled. A cloud settled over them all, a premonition of some dreadful calamity, the nature of which they did not understand. As they ate in silence, Jesus said, "Verily, I say unto you, that one of you shall betray Me." At these words amazement and consternation seized them. They could not comprehend how any one of them could deal treacherously with their divine Teacher. For what cause could they betray Him? and to whom? Whose heart could give birth to such a design? Surely not one of the favored Twelve, who had been privileged above all others to hear His teachings, who had shared His wonderful love, and for whom He had shown such great regard by bringing them into close communion with Himself!

As they realized the import of His words, and remembered how true His sayings were, fear and self-distrust seized them. They began to search their own hearts to see if one thought against their Master were harbored there. With the most painful emotion, one after another inquired, "Lord, is it I?" But Judas sat silent. John in deep distress at last inquired, "Lord, who is it?" And Jesus answered, "He that dippeth his hand with Me in the dish, the same shall betray Me. The Son of man goeth as it is written of Him: but woe unto that man by whom the Son of man is betrayed; it had been good for that man if he had not been born." The disciples had searched one another's faces closely as they asked, "Lord, is it I?" And now the silence of Judas drew all eyes to him. Amid the confusion of questions and expressions of astonishment, Judas had not heard the words of Jesus in answer to John's question. But now, to escape the scrutiny of the disciples, he asked as they had done, "Master, is it I?" Jesus solemnly replied, "Thou hast said."

In surprise and confusion at the exposure of his purpose, Judas rose hastily to leave the room. "Then said Jesus unto him, That thou doest, do quickly. . . . He then having received the sop went immediately out: and it was night." Night it was to the traitor as he turned away from Christ into the outer darkness.

Until this step was taken, Judas had not passed beyond the possibility of repentance. But when he left the presence of his Lord and his fellow disciples, the final decision had been made. He had passed the boundary line.

Wonderful had been the long-suffering of Jesus in His dealing with this tempted soul. Nothing that could be done to save Judas had been left undone. After he had twice covenanted to betray his Lord, Jesus still gave him opportunity for repentance. By reading the secret purpose of the traitor's heart, Christ gave to Judas the final, convincing

---

❝When your duties appear stern and severe, and your burdens too heavy to bear, remember that for your sake I endured the cross . . . When your heart shrinks from the trying ordeal, remember that your Redeemer liveth to make intercession for you.❞

---

evidence of His divinity. This was to the false disciple the last call to repentance. No appeal that the divine-human heart of Christ could make had been spared. The waves of mercy, beaten back by stubborn pride, returned in a stronger tide of subduing love. But although surprised and alarmed at the discovery of his guilt, Judas became only the more determined. From the sacramental supper he went out to complete the work of betrayal.

In pronouncing the woe upon Judas, Christ also had a purpose of mercy toward His disciples. He thus gave them the crowning evidence of His Messiahship. "I tell you before it come," He said, "that when it is come to pass, ye may believe that I Am." Had Jesus remained silent, in apparent ignorance of what was to come upon Him, the disciples might have thought that their Master had not divine foresight, and had been surprised and betrayed into the hands of the murderous mob. A year before, Jesus had told the disciples that He had chosen twelve, and that one was a devil. Now His words to Judas, showing that his treachery was fully known to his Master, would strengthen the faith of Christ's true followers during His humiliation. And when Judas should have come to his dreadful end,

they would remember the woe that Jesus had pronounced upon the betrayer.

And the Saviour had still another purpose. He had not withheld His ministry from him whom He knew to be a traitor. The disciples did not understand His words when He said at the feet washing, "Ye are not all clean," nor yet when at the table He declared, "He that eateth bread with Me hath lifted up his heel against Me." John 13:11, 18. But afterward, when His meaning was made plain, they had something to consider as to the patience and mercy of God toward the most grievously erring.

Though Jesus knew Judas from the beginning, He washed his feet. And the betrayer was privileged to unite with Christ in partaking of the sacrament. A long-suffering Saviour held out every inducement for the sinner to receive Him, to repent, and to be cleansed from the defilement of sin. This example is for us. When we suppose one to be in error and sin, we are not to divorce ourselves from him. By no careless separation are we to leave him a prey to temptation, or drive him upon Satan's battleground. This is not Christ's method. It was because the disciples were erring and faulty that He washed their feet, and all but one of the Twelve were thus brought to repentance.

Christ's example forbids exclusiveness at the Lord's supper. It is true that open sin excludes the guilty. This the Holy Spirit plainly teaches. 1 Corinthians 5:11. But beyond this none are to pass judgment. God has not left it with men to say who shall present themselves on these occasions. For who can read the heart? Who can distinguish the tares from the wheat? "Let a man examine himself, and so let him eat of that bread, and drink of that cup." For "whosoever shall eat this bread, and drink this cup of the Lord, unworthily, shall be guilty of the body and blood of the Lord." "He that eateth and drinketh unworthily, eateth and drinketh damnation to himself, not discerning the Lord's body." 1 Corinthians 11:28, 27, 29.

When believers assemble to celebrate the ordinances, there are present messengers unseen by human eyes. There may be a Judas in the company, and if so, messengers from the prince of darkness are there, for they attend all who refuse to be controlled by the Holy Spirit. Heavenly angels also are present. These unseen visitants are present on every such occasion. There may come into the company persons who are not in heart servants of truth and holiness, but who may wish to take part in the service. They should not be forbidden. There are witnesses present who were present when Jesus washed the feet of the disciples and of Judas. More than human eyes beheld the scene.

Christ by the Holy Spirit is there to set the seal to His own ordinance. He is there to convict and soften the heart. Not a look, not a thought of contrition, escapes His notice. For the repentant, brokenhearted one He is waiting. All things are ready for that soul's reception. He who washed the feet of Judas, longs to wash every heart from the stain of sin.

None should exclude themselves from the communion because some who are unworthy may be present. Every disciple is called upon to participate publicly, and thus bear witness that he accepts Christ as a personal Saviour. It is at these, His own appointments, that Christ meets His people, and energizes them by His presence. Hearts and hands that are unworthy may even administer the ordinance, yet Christ is there to minister to His children. All who come with their faith fixed upon Him will be greatly blessed. All who neglect these seasons of divine privilege will suffer loss. Of them it may appropriately be said, "Ye are not all clean."

In partaking with His disciples of the bread and wine, Christ pledged Himself to them as their Redeemer. He committed to them the new covenant, by which all who receive Him become children of God, and joint heirs with Christ. By this covenant every blessing that heaven could bestow for this life and the life to come, was theirs. This covenant deed was to be ratified with the blood of Christ. And the administration of the sacrament was to keep before the disciples the infinite sacrifice made for each of them individually as a part of the great whole of fallen humanity.

But the communion service was not to be a season of sorrowing. This was not its purpose. As the Lord's disciples gather about His table, they are not to remember and lament their shortcomings. They are not to dwell upon their past religious experience, whether that experience has been elevating or depressing. They are not to recall the differences between them and their brethren. The preparatory service has embraced all this. The self-examination, the confession of sin, the reconciling of differences, has all been done. Now they come to meet with Christ. They are not to stand in the shadow of the cross, but in its saving light. They are to open the soul to the bright beams of the Sun of Righteousness. With hearts cleansed by Christ's most precious blood, in full consciousness of His presence, although unseen, they are to hear His words, "Peace I leave with you, My peace I give unto you; not as the world giveth, give I unto you." John 14:27.

Our Lord says, Under conviction of sin, remember that I died for you. When oppressed and persecuted and afflicted for My sake and the gospel's, remember My love, so great that for you I gave My life. When your duties appear stern and severe, and your burdens too heavy to bear, remember that for your sake I endured the cross, despising the shame. When your heart shrinks from the trying ordeal, remember that your Redeemer liveth to make intercession for you.

The communion service points to Christ's second coming. It was designed to keep this hope vivid in the minds of the disciples. Whenever they met together to commemorate His death, they recounted how "He took the cup, and gave thanks, and gave it to them, saying, Drink ye all of it; for this is My blood of the new testament, which is shed for many for the remission of sins. But I say unto you, I will not drink henceforth of this fruit of the vine, until that day when I drink it new with you in My Father's kingdom." In their tribulation they found comfort in the hope of their Lord's return. Unspeakably precious to them was the thought, "As often as ye eat this bread, and drink this cup, ye do show the Lord's death till He come." 1 Corinthians 11:26.

These are the things we are never to forget. The love of Jesus, with its constraining power, is to be kept fresh in our memory. Christ has instituted this service that it may speak to our senses of the love of God that has been expressed in our behalf. There can be no union between our souls and God except through Christ. The union and love between brother and brother must be cemented and rendered eternal by the love of Jesus. And nothing less than the death of Christ could make His love efficacious for us. It is only because of His death that we can look with joy to His second coming. His sacrifice is the center of our hope. Upon this we must fix our faith.

The ordinances that point to our Lord's humiliation and suffering are regarded too much as a form. They were instituted for a purpose. Our senses need to be quickened to lay hold of the mystery of godliness. It is the privilege of all to comprehend, far more than we do, the expiatory sufferings of Christ. "As Moses lifted up the serpent in the wilderness," even so has the Son of man been lifted up, "that whosoever believeth in Him should not perish, but have eternal life." John 3:14, 15. To the cross of Calvary, bearing a dying Saviour, we must look. Our eternal interests demand that we show faith in Christ.

Our Lord has said, "Except ye eat the flesh of the Son of man, and drink His blood, ye have no life in you. . . . For My flesh is meat indeed, and My blood is drink indeed." John 6:53-55. This is true of our physical nature. To the death of Christ we owe even this earthly life. The bread we eat is the purchase of His broken body. The water we drink is bought by His spilled blood. Never one, saint or sinner, eats his daily food, but he is nourished by the body and the blood of Christ. The cross of Calvary is stamped on every loaf. It is reflected in every water spring. All this Christ has taught in appointing the emblems of His great sacrifice. The light shining from that communion service in the upper chamber makes sacred the provisions for our daily life. The family board becomes as the table of the Lord, and every meal a sacrament.

And how much more are Christ's words true of our spiritual nature. He declares, "Whoso eateth My flesh and drinketh My blood hath eternal life." It is by receiving the life for us poured out on Calvary's cross, that we can live the life of holiness. And this life we receive by receiving His word, by doing those things which He has commanded. Thus we become one with Him. "He that eateth My flesh," He says, "and drinketh My blood, dwelleth in Me, and I in him. As the living Father hath sent Me, and I live by the Father; so he that eateth Me, even he shall live by Me." John 6:54, 56, 57. To the holy communion this scripture in a special sense applies. As faith contemplates our Lord's great sacrifice, the soul assimilates the spiritual life of Christ. That soul will receive spiritual strength from every communion. The service forms a living connection by which the believer is bound up with Christ, and thus bound up with the Father. In a special sense it forms a connection between dependent human beings and God.

As we receive the bread and wine symbolizing Christ's broken body and spilled blood, we in imagination join in the scene of communion in the upper chamber. We seem to be passing through the garden consecrated by the agony of Him who bore the sins of the world. We witness the struggle by which our reconciliation with God was obtained. Christ is set forth crucified among us.

Looking upon the crucified Redeemer, we more fully comprehend the magnitude and meaning of the sacrifice made by the Majesty of heaven. The plan of salvation is glorified before us, and the thought of Calvary awakens living and sacred emotions in our hearts. Praise to God and the Lamb will be in our hearts and on our lips; for pride and self-worship cannot flourish in the soul that keeps fresh in memory the scenes of Calvary.

He who beholds the Saviour's matchless love, will be elevated in thought, purified in heart, transformed in character. He will go forth to be a light to the world, to reflect in some degree this mysterious love. The more we contemplate the cross of Christ, the more fully shall we adopt the language of the apostle when he said, "God forbid that I should glory, save in the cross of our Lord Jesus Christ, by whom the world is crucified unto me, and I unto the world." Galatians 6:14.

"Let Not Your Heart Be Troubled"

Looking upon His disciples with divine love and with the tenderest sympathy, Christ said, "Now is the Son of man glorified, and God is glorified in Him." Judas had left the upper chamber, and Christ was alone with the eleven. He was about to speak of His approaching separation from them; but before doing this He pointed to the great object of His mission. It was this that He kept ever before Him. It was His joy that all His humiliation and suffering would glorify the Father's name. To this He first directs the thoughts of His disciples.

Then addressing them by the endearing term, "Little children," He said, "Yet a little while I am with you. Ye shall seek Me; and as I said unto the Jews, Whither I go, ye cannot come; so now I say to you."

The disciples could not rejoice when they heard this. Fear fell upon them. They pressed close about the Saviour. Their Master and Lord, their beloved Teacher and Friend, He was dearer to them than life. To Him they had looked for help in all their difficulties, for comfort in their sorrows and disappointments. Now He was to leave them, a lonely, dependent company. Dark were the forebodings that filled their hearts.

But the Saviour's words to them were full of hope. He knew that they were to be assailed by the enemy, and that Satan's craft is most successful against those who are depressed by difficulties. Therefore He pointed them away from "the things which are seen," to "the things which are not seen." 2 Corinthians 4:18. From earthly exile He turned their thoughts to the heavenly home.

"Let not your heart be troubled," He said; "ye believe in God, believe also in Me. In My Father's house are many mansions; if it were not so, I would have told you. I go to prepare a place for you. And if I go and prepare a place for you, I will come again, and receive you unto Myself; that were I am, there ye may be also. And whither I go ye know, and the way ye know." For your sake I came into the world. I am working in your behalf. When I go away, I shall still work earnestly for you. I came into the world to reveal Myself to you, that you might believe. I go to the Father to co-operate with Him in your behalf. The object of Christ's departure was the opposite of what the disciples feared. It did not mean a final separation. He was going to prepare a place for them, that He might come again, and receive them unto Himself. While He was building mansions for them, they were to build characters after the divine similitude.

Still the disciples were perplexed. Thomas, always troubled by doubts, said, "Lord, we know not whither Thou goest; and how can we know the way? Jesus saith unto him, I am the Way, the Truth, and the life; no man cometh unto the Father, but by Me. If ye had known Me, ye should have known My Father also: and from henceforth ye know Him, and have seen Him."

There are not many ways to heaven. Each one may not choose his own way. Christ says, "I am the way. . . . No man cometh unto the Father but by Me." Since the first gospel sermon was preached, when in Eden it was declared that the seed of the woman should bruise the serpent's head, Christ had been uplifted as the way, the truth, and the life. He was the way when Adam lived, when Abel presented to God the blood of the slain lamb, representing the blood of the Redeemer. Christ was the way by which patriarchs and prophets were saved. He is the way by which alone we can have access to God.

"If ye had known Me," Christ said, "ye should have known My Father also; and from henceforth ye know Him, and have seen Him." But not yet did the disciples understand. "Lord, show us the Father," exclaimed Philip, "and it sufficeth us."

Amazed at his dullness of comprehension, Christ asked with pained surprise, "Have I been so long time with you, and yet hast thou not known Me, Philip?" Is it possible that you do not see the Father in the works He does through Me? Do you not believe that I came to testify of the Father? "How sayest thou then, Show us the Father?" "He that hath seen Me hath seen the Father." Christ had not ceased to be God when he became man. Though He had humbled Himself to humanity, the Godhead was still His own. Christ alone could represent the Father to humanity, and this representation the disciples had been privileged to behold for over three years.

"Believe Me that I am in the Father, and the Father in Me; or else believe Me for the very works' sake." Their faith might safely rest on the evidence given in Christ's works, works that no man, of himself, ever had done, or ever could do. Christ's works testified to His divinity. Through Him the Father had been revealed.

If the disciples believed this vital connection between the Father and the Son, their faith would not forsake them when they saw Christ's suffering and death to save a perishing world. Christ was seeking to lead them from their low condition of faith to the experience they might receive if they truly realized what He was,—God in human flesh. He desired them to see that their faith must lead up to God, and be anchored there. How earnestly and perseveringly our compassionate Saviour sought to prepare His disciples for the storm of temptation that was soon to beat upon them. He would have them hid with Him in God.

As Christ was speaking these words, the glory of God was shining from His countenance, and all present felt a sacred awe as they listened with rapt attention to His words. Their hearts were more decidedly drawn to Him; and as they were drawn to Christ in greater love, they were drawn to one another. They felt that heaven was very near, and that the words to which they listened were a message to them from their Heavenly Father.

"Verily, verily, I say unto you," Christ continued, "He that believeth on Me, the works that I do shall he do also." The Saviour was deeply anxious for His disciples to understand for what purpose His divinity was united to humanity. He came to the world to display the glory of God, that man might be uplifted by its restoring power. God was manifested in Him that He might be manifested in them. Jesus revealed no qualities, and exercised no powers, that men may not have through faith in Him. His perfect humanity is that which all His followers may possess, if they will be in subjection to God as He was.

"And greater works than these shall he do; because I go unto My Father." By this Christ did not mean that the disciples' work would be of a more exalted character than His, but that it would have greater extent. He did not refer merely to miracle working, but to all that would take place under the working of the Holy Spirit.

After the Lord's ascension, the disciples realized the fulfillment of His promise. The scenes of the crucifixion, resurrection, and ascension of Christ were a living reality to them. They saw that the prophecies had been literally fulfilled. They searched the Scriptures, and accepted their teaching with a faith and assurance unknown before. They knew that the divine Teacher was all that He had claimed

---

"He came to the world to display the glory of God, that man might be uplifted by its restoring power. . . . Jesus revealed no qualities, and exercised no powers, that men may not have through faith in Him. His perfect humanity is that which all His followers may possess, if they will be in subjection to God as He was."

---

to be. As they told their experience, and exalted the love of God, men's hearts were melted and subdued, and multitudes believed on Jesus.

The Saviour's promise to His disciples is a promise to His church to the end of time. God did not design that His wonderful plan to redeem men should achieve only insignificant results. All who will go to work, trusting not in what they themselves can do, but in what God can do for and through them, will certainly realize the fulfillment of His promise. "Greater works than these shall ye do," He declares: "because I go unto my Father."

As yet the disciples were unacquainted with the Saviour's unlimited resources and power. He said to them, "Hitherto have ye asked nothing in My name." John 16:24. He explained that the secret of their success would be in asking for strength and grace in His name. He would be present before the Father to make request for them. The prayer of the humble suppliant He presents as His own desire in that soul's behalf. Every sincere prayer is heard in heaven. It may not be fluently expressed; but if the heart is in it, it will ascend to the sanctuary where Jesus ministers, and He will present it to the Father without one awkward, stammering word, beautiful and fragrant with the incense of His own perfection.

The path of sincerity and integrity is not a path free from obstruction, but in every difficulty we are to see a call to prayer. There is no one living who has any power that he has not received from God, and the source whence it comes is open to the weakest human being. "Whatsoever ye shall ask in My name," said Jesus, "that will I do, that the Father may be glorified in the Son. If ye shall ask anything in My name, I will do it."

"In My name," Christ bade His disciples pray. In Christ's name His followers are to stand before God. Through the value of the sacrifice made for them, they are of value in the Lord's sight. Because of the imputed righteousness of Christ they are accounted precious. For Christ's sake the Lord pardons those that fear Him. He does not see in them the vileness of the sinner. He recognizes in them the likeness of His Son, in whom they believe.

The Lord is disappointed when His people place a low estimate upon themselves. He desires His chosen heritage to value themselves according to the price He has placed upon them. God wanted them, else He would not have sent His Son on such an expensive errand to redeem them. He has a use for them, and He is well pleased when they make the very highest demands upon Him, that they may glorify His name. They may expect large things if they have faith in His promises.

But to pray in Christ's name means much. It means that we are to accept His character, manifest His spirit, and work His works. The Saviour's promise is given on condition. "If ye love Me," He says, "keep My commandments." He saves men, not in sin, but from sin; and those who love Him will show their love by obedience.

All true obedience comes from the heart. It was heart-work with Christ. And if we consent, He will so identify Himself with our thoughts and aims, so blend our hearts and minds into conformity to His will, that when obeying Him we shall be but carrying out our own impulses. The will, refined and sanctified, will find its highest delight in doing His service. When we know God as it is our privilege to know Him, our life will be a life of continual obedience. Through an appreciation of the character of Christ, through communion with God, sin will become hateful to us.

As Christ lived the law in humanity, so we may do if we will take hold of the Strong for strength. But we are not to place the responsibility of our duty upon others, and wait for them to tell us what to do. We cannot depend for counsel upon humanity. The Lord will teach us our duty just as willingly as He will teach somebody else. If we come to Him in faith, He will speak His mysteries to us personally. Our hearts will often burn within us as One

draws nigh to commune with us as He did with Enoch. Those who decide to do nothing in any line that will displease God, will know, after presenting their case before Him, just what course to pursue. And they will receive not only wisdom, but strength. Power for obedience, for service, will be imparted to them, as Christ has promised. Whatever was given to Christ, — the "all things" to supply the need of fallen men, — was given to Him as the head and representative of humanity. And "whatsoever we ask, we receive of Him, because we keep His commandments, and do those things that are pleasing in His sight." John 3:22.

Before offering Himself as the sacrificial victim, Christ sought for the most essential and complete gift to bestow upon His followers, a gift that would bring within their reach the boundless resources of grace. "I will pray the Father," He said, "and He shall give you another Comforter, that He may abide with you forever; even the Spirit of truth; whom the world cannot receive, because it seeth Him not, neither knoweth Him; but ye know Him; for He dwelleth with you, and shall be in you. I will not leave you orphans: I will come to you." John 14:16-18, margin.

Before this the Spirit had been in the world; from the very beginning of the work of redemption He had been moving upon men's hearts. But while Christ was on earth, the disciples had desired no other helper. Not until they were deprived of his presence would they feel their need of the Spirit, and then He would come.

The Holy Spirit is Christ's representative, but divested of the personality of humanity, and independent thereof. Cumbered with humanity, Christ could not be in every place personally. Therefore it was for their interest that He should go to the Father, and send the Spirit to be His successor on earth. No one could then have any advantage because of his location or his personal contact with Christ. By the Spirit the Saviour would be accessible to all. In this sense He would be nearer to them than if He had not ascended on high.

"He that loveth Me, shall be loved of My Father, and I will love him, and will manifest Myself to him." Jesus read the future of His disciples. He saw one brought to the scaffold, one to the cross, one to exile among the lonely rocks of the sea, others to persecution and death. He encouraged them with the promise that in every trial He would be with them. That promise has lost none of its force. The Lord knows all about His faithful servants who for His sake are lying in prison or who are banished to lonely islands. He comforts them with His own presence. When for the truth's sake the believer stands at the bar of unrighteous tribunals, Christ stands by his side. All the reproaches that fall upon him, fall upon Christ. Christ is condemned over again in the person of His disciple. When one is incarcerated in prison walls, Christ ravishes the heart with His love. When one suffers death for His sake, Christ says, "I am He that liveth, and was dead; and, behold, I am alive forevermore, . . . and have the keys of hell and of death." Revelation 1:18. The life that is sacrificed for Me is preserved unto eternal glory.

At all times and in all places, in all sorrows and in all afflictions, when the outlook seems dark and the future perplexing, and we feel helpless and alone, the Comforter will be sent in answer to the prayer of faith. Circumstances may separate us from every earthly friend; but no circumstance, no distance, can separate us from the heavenly Comforter. Wherever we are, wherever we may go, He is always at our right hand to support, sustain, uphold, and cheer.

The disciples still failed to understand Christ's words in their spiritual sense, and again He explained His meaning. By the Spirit, He said He would manifest Himself to them. "The Comforter, which is the Holy Ghost, whom the Father will send in My name, He shall teach you all things." No more will you say, I cannot comprehend. No longer will you see through a glass, darkly. You shall "be able to comprehend with all saints, what is the breadth, and length, and depth, and height, and to know the love of Christ, which passeth knowledge." Ephesians 3:18, 19.

The disciples were to bear witness to the life and work of Christ. Through their word He was to speak to all the people on the face of the earth. But in the humiliation and death of Christ they were to suffer great trial and disappointment. That after this experience their word might be accurate, Jesus promised that the Comforter should "bring all things to your remembrance, whatsoever I have said unto you."

"I have yet many things to say unto you," He continued, "but ye cannot bear them now. Howbeit when He, the Spirit of truth, is come, He will guide you into all truth: for He shall not speak of Himself; but whatsoever He shall hear, that shall He speak: and He will show you things to come. He shall glorify Me: for He shall receive of Mine, and shall show it unto you." Jesus had opened before His disciples a vast tract of truth. But it was most difficult for them to keep His lessons distinct from the traditions and maxims of the scribes and Pharisees. They had been educated to accept the teaching of the rabbis as the voice of God, and it still held a power over their minds, and molded their sentiments. Earthly ideas, temporal things, still had a large place in their thoughts. They did not understand the spiritual nature of Christ's kingdom, though He had so often explained it to them. Their minds had become confused. They did not comprehend the value of the scriptures Christ presented. Many of His lessons seemed almost lost upon them. Jesus saw that they did not lay hold of the real meaning of His words. He compassionately promised that the Holy Spirit should recall these sayings to their minds. And He had left unsaid many things that could not be comprehended by the disciples. These also would be opened to them by the Spirit. The Spirit was to quicken their understanding, that they might have an appreciation of heavenly things. "When He, the Spirit of truth, is come," said Jesus, "He will guide you into all truth."

The Comforter is called "the Spirit of truth." His work is to define and maintain the truth. He first dwells in the heart as the Spirit of truth, and thus He becomes the Comforter. There is comfort and peace in the truth, but no real peace or comfort can be found in falsehood. It is through false theories and traditions that Satan gains his power over the mind. By directing men to false standards, he misshapes the character. Through the Scriptures the Holy Spirit speaks to the mind, and impresses truth upon the heart. Thus He exposes error, and expels it from the soul. It is by the Spirit of truth, working through the word of God, that Christ subdues His chosen people to Himself.

In describing to His disciples the office work of the Holy Spirit, Jesus sought to inspire them with the joy and hope that inspired His own heart. He rejoiced because of the abundant help He had provided for His church. The Holy Spirit was the highest of all gifts that He could solicit from His Father for the exaltation of His people. The Spirit was to be given as a regenerating agent, and without this the sacrifice of Christ would have been of no avail. The power of evil had been strengthening for centuries, and the submission of men to this Satanic captivity was amazing. Sin could be resisted and overcome only through the mighty agency of the third person of the Godhead, who would come with no modified energy, but in the fullness of divine power. It is the Spirit that makes effectual what has been wrought out by the world's Redeemer. It is by the Spirit that the heart is made pure. Through the Spirit the believer becomes a partaker of the divine nature. Christ has given His Spirit as a divine power to overcome all hereditary and cultivated tendencies to evil, and to impress His own character upon His church.

Of the Spirit Jesus said, "He shall glorify Me." The Saviour came to glorify the Father by the demonstration of His love; so the Spirit was to glorify Christ by revealing His grace to the world. The very image of God is to be reproduced in humanity. The honor of God, the honor of Christ, is involved in the perfection of the character of His people.

"When He [the Spirit of truth] is come, He will reprove the world of sin, and of righteousness, and of judgment." The preaching of the word will be of no avail without the continual presence and aid of the Holy Spirit. This is the only effectual teacher of divine truth. Only when the truth is accompanied to the heart by the Spirit, will it quicken the conscience or transform the life. One might be able to present the letter of the word of God, he might be familiar with all its commands and promises; but unless the Holy Spirit sets home the truth, no souls will fall on the Rock and be broken. No amount of education, no advantages, however great, can make one a channel of light without the co-operation of the Spirit of God. The sowing of the gospel seed will not be a success unless the seed is quickened into life by the dew of heaven. Before one book of the New Testament was written, before one gospel sermon had been preached after Christ's ascension, the Holy Spirit came upon the praying apostles. Then the testimony of their enemies was, "Ye have filled Jerusalem with your doctrine." Acts 5:28.

Christ has promised the gift of the Holy Spirit to His church, and the promise belongs to us as much as to the first disciples. But like every other promise, it is given on conditions. There are many who believe and profess to claim the Lord's promise; they talk *about* Christ and *about* the Holy Spirit, yet receive no benefit. They do not surrender the soul to be guided and controlled by the divine agencies. We cannot use the Holy Spirit. The Spirit is to use us. Through the Spirit God works in His people "to will and to do of His good pleasure." Philippians 2:13. But many will not submit to this. They want to manage themselves. This is why they do not receive the heavenly gift. Only to those who wait humbly upon God, who watch for His guidance and grace, is the Spirit given. The power of God awaits their demand and reception. This promised blessing, claimed by faith, brings all other blessings in its train. It is given according to the riches of the grace of Christ, and He is ready to supply every soul according to the capacity to receive.

In His discourse to the disciples, Jesus made no mournful allusion to His own sufferings and death. His last legacy to them was a legacy of peace. He said, "Peace I leave with you, My peace I give unto you; not as the world giveth, give I unto you. Let not your heart be troubled, neither let it be afraid."

Before leaving the upper chamber, the Saviour led His disciples in a song of praise. His voice was heard, not in the strains of some mournful lament, but in the joyful notes of the Passover hallel: —

"O praise the Lord, all ye nations;
Praise Him all ye people.
For His merciful kindness is great toward us,
And the truth of the Lord endureth forever.
Praise ye the Lord." Psalm 117.

After the hymn, they went out. Through the crowded streets they made their way, passing out of the city gate toward the Mount of Olives. Slowly they proceeded, each busy with his own thoughts. As they began to descend toward the mount, Jesus said, in a tone of deepest sadness, "All ye shall be offended because of Me this night; for it is written, I will smite the shepherd, and the sheep of the flock shall be scattered abroad." Matthew 26:31. The disciples listened in sorrow and amazement. They remembered how in the synagogue at Capernaum, when Christ spoke of Himself as the Bread of Life, many had been offended, and had turned away from Him. But the Twelve had not shown themselves unfaithful. Peter, speaking for his brethren, had then declared his loyalty to Christ. Then the Saviour had said, "Have not I chosen you Twelve, and one of you is a devil?" John 6:70. In the upper chamber Jesus said that one of the Twelve would betray Him, and that Peter would deny Him. But now His words include them all.

Now Peter's voice is heard vehemently protesting, "Although all shall be offended, yet will not I." Mark 14:29, 30, 31. In the upper chamber he had declared, "I will lay down my life for Thy sake." Jesus had warned him that he would that very night deny his Saviour. Now Christ repeats the warning: "Verily I say unto thee, That this day, even in this night, before the cock crow twice, thou shalt deny Me thrice." But Peter only "spake the more vehemently, If I should die with Thee, I will not deny Thee in any wise. Likewise also said they all." Mark 14:29, 30, 31. In their self-confidence they denied the repeated statement of Him who knew. They were unprepared for the test; when temptation should overtake them, they would understand their own weakness.

When Peter said he would follow his Lord to prison and to death, he meant it, every word of it; but he did not know himself. Hidden in his heart were elements of evil that circumstances would fan into life. Unless he was made conscious of his danger, these would prove his eternal ruin. The Saviour saw in him a self-love and assurance that would overbear even his love for Christ. Much of infirmity, of unmortified sin, carelessness of spirit, unsanctified temper, heedlessness in entering into temptation, had been revealed in his experience. Christ's solemn warning was a call to heart searching. Peter needed to distrust himself, and to have a deeper faith in Christ. Had he in humility received the warning, he would have appealed to the Shepherd of the flock to keep His sheep. When on the Sea of Galilee he was about to sink, he cried, "Lord, save me." Matthew 14:30. Then the hand of Christ was outstretched to grasp his hand. So now if he had cried to Jesus, Save me from myself, he would have been kept. But Peter felt that he was distrusted, and he thought it cruel. He was already offended, and he became more persistent in his self-confidence.

Jesus looks with compassion on His disciples. He cannot save them from the trial, but He does not leave them comfortless. He assures them that He is to break the fetters of the tomb, and that His love for them will not fail. "After I am risen again," He says, "I will go before you into Galilee." Matthew 26:32. Before the denial, they have the assurance of forgiveness. After His death and resurrection, they knew that they were forgiven, and were dear to the heart of Christ.

Jesus and his disciples were on the way to Gethsemane, at the foot of Mount Olivet, a retired spot which He had often visited for meditation and prayer. The Saviour had been explaining to His disciples His mission to the world, and the spiritual relation to Him which they were to sustain. Now He illustrates the lesson. The moon is shining bright, and reveals to Him a flourishing grapevine. Drawing the attention of the disciples to it, He employs it as a symbol.

"I am the true Vine," He says. Instead of choosing the graceful palm, the lofty cedar, or the strong oak, Jesus takes the vine with its clinging tendrils to represent Himself. The palm tree, the cedar, and the oak stand alone. They require no support. But the vine entwines about the trellis, and thus climbs heavenward. So Christ in His humanity was dependent upon divine power. "I can of Mine own self do nothing," He declared. John 5:30.

"I am the true Vine." The Jews had always regarded the vine as the most noble of plants, and a type of all that was powerful, excellent, and fruitful. Israel had been represented as a vine which God had planted in the promised land. The Jews based their hope of salvation on the fact of their connection with Israel. But Jesus says, I am the real Vine. Think not that through a connection with Israel you may become partakers of the life of God, and inheritors of His promise. Through Me alone is spiritual life received.

"I am the true Vine, and My Father is the husbandman." On the hills of Palestine our Heavenly Father had planted this goodly Vine, and He Himself was the husbandman. Many were attracted by the beauty of this Vine, and declared its heavenly origin. But to the leaders in Israel it appeared as a root out of a dry ground. They took the plant, and bruised it, and trampled it under their unholy feet. Their thought was to destroy it forever. But the heavenly husbandman never lost sight of His plant. After men thought they had killed it, He took it, and replanted it on the other side of the wall. The vine stock was to be no longer visible. It was hidden from the rude assaults of men. But the branches of the Vine hung over the wall. They were to represent the Vine. Through them grafts might still be united to the Vine. From them fruit has been obtained. There has been a harvest which the passers-by have plucked.

"I am the Vine; ye are the branches," Christ said to His disciples. Though He was about to be removed from them, their spiritual union with Him was to be unchanged. The connection of the branch with the vine, He said, represents the relation you are to sustain to Me. The scion is engrafted into the living vine, and fiber by fiber, vein by vein, it grows into the vine stock. The life of the vine becomes the life of the branch. So the soul dead in trespasses and sins receives life through connection with Christ. By faith in Him as a personal Saviour the union is formed. The sinner unites his weakness to Christ's strength, his emptiness to Christ's fullness, his frailty to Christ's enduring might. Then he has the mind of Christ. The humanity of Christ has touched our humanity, and our humanity has touched divinity. Thus through the agency of the Holy Spirit man becomes a partaker of the divine nature. He is accepted in the Beloved.

This union with Christ, once formed, must be maintained. Christ said, "Abide in Me, and I in you. As the branch cannot bear fruit of itself, except it abide in the vine, no more can ye, except ye abide in Me." This is no casual touch, no off-and-on connection. The branch becomes a part of the living vine. The communication of life, strength, and fruitfulness from the root to the branches is unobstructed and constant. Separated from the vine, the branch cannot live. No more, said Jesus, can you live apart from Me. The life you have received from Me can be preserved only by continual communion. Without Me you cannot overcome one sin, or resist one temptation.

"Abide in Me, and I in you." Abiding in Christ means a constant receiving of His Spirit, a life of unreserved surrender to His service. The channel of communication must be open continually between man and his God. As the vine branch constantly draws the sap from the living vine, so are we to cling to Jesus, and receive from Him by faith the strength and perfection of His own character.

The root sends its nourishment through the branch to the outermost twig. So Christ communicates the current of spiritual strength to every believer. So long as the soul is united to Christ, there is no danger that it will wither or decay.

The life of the vine will be manifest in fragrant fruit on the branches. "He that abideth in Me," said Jesus, "and I in him, the same bringeth forth much fruit; for without Me ye can do nothing." When we live by faith on the Son of God, the fruits of the Spirit will be seen in our life; not one will be missing.

"My Father is the husbandman. Every branch in Me that beareth not fruit, He taketh away." While the graft is outwardly united with the vine, there may be no vital connection. Then there will be no growth or fruitfulness. So there may be an apparent connection with Christ, without a real union with Him by faith. A profession of religion places men in the church, but the character and conduct show whether they are in connection with Christ. If they bear no fruit, they are false branches. Their separation from Christ involves a ruin as complete as that represented by the dead branch. "If a man abide not in Me," said Christ, "he is cast forth as a branch, and is withered, and men gather them, and cast them into the fire, and they are burned."

"And every branch that beareth fruit, He purgeth [pruneth] it, that it may bring forth more fruit." From the chosen Twelve who had followed Jesus, one as a withered branch was about to be taken away, the rest were to pass under the pruning knife of bitter trial. Jesus with solemn tenderness explained the purpose of the husbandman. The pruning will cause pain, but it is the Father who applies the knife. He works with no wanton hand or indifferent heart. There are branches trailing upon the ground; these must be cut loose from the earthly supports to which their tendrils are fastening. They are to reach heavenward, and find their support in God. The excessive foliage that draws away the life current from the fruit, must be pruned off. The overgrowth must be cut out, to give room for the healing beams of the Sun of Righteousness. The husbandman prunes away the harmful growth, that the fruit may be richer and more abundant.

"Herein is My Father glorified," said Jesus, "that ye bear much fruit." God desires to manifest through you the holiness, the benevolence, the compassion of His own character. Yet the Saviour does not bid the disciples labor to bear fruit. He tells them to abide in Him. "If ye abide in Me," He says, "and My words abide in you, ye shall ask what ye will, and it shall be done unto you." It is through the word that Christ abides in His followers. This is the same vital union that is represented by eating His flesh and drinking His blood. The words of Christ are spirit and life. Receiving them, you receive the life of the Vine. You live "by every word that proceedeth out of the mouth of God." Matthew 4:4. The life of Christ in you produces the same

---

"The Lord is disappointed when His people place a low estimate upon themselves. He desires His chosen heritage to value themselves according to the price He has placed upon them. God wanted them, else He would not have sent His Son on such an expensive errand to redeem them. . . . They may expect large things if they have faith in His promises."

---

fruits as in Him. Living in Christ, adhering to Christ, supported by Christ, drawing nourishment from Christ, you bear fruit after the similitude of Christ.

In this last meeting with His disciples, the great desire which Christ expressed for them was that they might love one another as He had loved them. Again and again He spoke of this. "These things I command you," He said repeatedly, "that ye love one another." His very first injunction when alone with them in the upper chamber was, "A new commandment I give unto you, That ye love one another; as I have loved you, that ye also love one another." To the disciples this commandment was new; for they had not loved one another as Christ had loved them. He saw that new ideas and impulses must control them; that new principles must be practiced by them; through His

life and death they were to receive a new conception of love. The command to love one another had a new meaning in the light of His self-sacrifice. The whole work of grace is one continual service of love, of self-denying, self-sacrificing effort. During every hour of Christ's sojourn upon the earth, the love of God was flowing from Him in irrepressible streams. All who are imbued with His spirit will love as He loved. The very principle that actuated Christ will actuate them in all their dealing one with another.

This love is the evidence of their discipleship. "By this shall all men know that ye are My disciples," said Jesus, "if ye have love one to another." When men are bound together, not by force or self-interest, but by love, they show the working of an influence that is above every human influence. Where this oneness exists, it is evidence that the image of God is being restored in humanity, that a new principle of life has been implanted. It shows that there is power in the divine nature to withstand the supernatural agencies of evil, and that the grace of God subdues the selfishness inherent in the natural heart.

This love, manifested in the church, will surely stir the wrath of Satan. Christ did not mark out for His disciples an easy path. "If the world hate you." He said, "ye know that it hated Me before it hated you. If ye were of the world, the world would love his own; but because ye are not of the world, but I have chosen you out of the world, therefore the world hateth you. Remember the word that I said unto you, The servant is not greater than his lord. If they have persecuted Me, they will also persecute you; if they have kept My saying, they will keep yours also. But all these things will they do unto you for My name's sake, because they know not Him that sent Me." The gospel is to be carried forward by aggressive warfare, in the midst of opposition, peril, loss, and suffering. But those who do this work are only following in their Master's steps.

As the world's Redeemer, Christ was constantly confronted with apparent failure. He, the messenger of mercy to our world, seemed to do little of the work He longed to do in uplifting and saving. Satanic influences were constantly working to oppose His way. But He would not be discouraged. Through the prophecy of Isaiah He declares, "I have labored in vain, I have spent My strength for naught, and in vain; yet surely My judgment is with the Lord, and My work with My God. . . . Though Israel be not gathered, yet shall I be glorious in the eyes of the Lord, and My God shall be My strength." It is to Christ that the promise is given, "Thus saith the Lord, the Redeemer of Israel, and His Holy One, to Him whom man despiseth, to Him whom the nation abhorreth; . . . thus saith the Lord: . . . I will preserve Thee, and give Thee for a covenant of the people, to establish the earth, to cause to inherit the desolate heritages; that Thou mayest say to the prisoners, Go forth; to them that are in darkness, Show yourselves. . . . They shall not hunger nor thirst; neither shall the heat nor sun smite them: for He that hath mercy on them shall lead them, even by the springs of water shall He guide them." Isaiah 49:4, 5, 7-10.

Upon this word Jesus rested, and He gave Satan no advantage. When the last steps of Christ's humiliation were to be taken, when the deepest sorrow was closing about His soul, He said to His disciples, "The prince of this world cometh, and hath nothing in Me." "The prince of this world is judged." Now shall he be cast out. John 14:30; 16:11; 12:31. With prophetic eye Christ traced the scenes to take place in His last great conflict. He knew that when He should exclaim, "It is finished," all heaven would triumph. His ear caught the distant music and the shouts of victory in the heavenly courts. He knew that the knell of Satan's empire would then be sounded, and the name of Christ would be heralded from world to world throughout the universe.

Christ rejoiced that He could do more for His followers than they could ask or think. He spoke with assurance, knowing that an almighty decree had been given before the world was made. He knew that truth, armed with the omnipotence of the Holy Spirit, would conquer in the contest with evil; and that the bloodstained banner would wave triumphantly over His followers. He knew that the life of His trusting disciples would be like His, a series of uninterrupted victories, not seen to be such here, but recognized as such in the great hereafter.

"These things I have spoken unto you," He said, "that in Me ye might have peace. In the world ye shall have tribulation; but be of good cheer; I have overcome the world." Christ did not fail, neither was He discouraged, and His followers are to manifest a faith of the same enduring nature. They are to live as He lived, and work as He worked, because they depend on Him as the great Master Worker. Courage, energy, and perseverance they must possess. Though apparent impossibilities obstruct their way, by His grace they are to go forward. Instead of deploring difficulties, they are called upon to surmount them. They are to despair of nothing, and to hope for everything. With the golden chain of His matchless love, Christ has bound them to the throne of God. It is His purpose that the highest influence in the universe, emanating from the source of all power, shall be theirs. They are to have power to resist evil, power that neither earth, nor death, nor hell can master, power that will enable them to overcome as Christ overcame.

Christ designs that heaven's order, heaven's plan of government, heaven's divine harmony, shall be represented in His church on earth. Thus in His people He is glorified. Through them the Sun of Righteousness will shine in undimmed luster to the world. Christ has given to His church ample facilities, that He may receive a large revenue of glory from His redeemed, purchased possession. He has bestowed upon His people capabilities and blessings that they may represent His own sufficiency. The church, endowed with the righteousness of Christ, in His depositary, in which the riches of His mercy, His grace, and His love, are to appear in full and final display. Christ looks upon His people in their purity and perfection, as the reward of His humiliation, and the supplement of His glory, — Christ, the great Center, from whom radiates all glory.

With strong, hopeful words the Saviour ended His instruction. Then He poured out the burden of His soul in prayer for His disciples. Lifting His eyes to heaven, He said, "Father, the hour is come; glorify Thy Son, that Thy Son also may glorify Thee: as Thou hast given Him power over all flesh, that He should give eternal life to as many as Thou hast given Him. And this is life eternal, that they might know Thee the only true God, and Jesus Christ, whom Thou hast sent."

Christ had finished the work that was given Him to do. He had glorified God on the earth. He had manifested the Father's name. He had gathered out those who were to continue His work among men. And He said, "I am glorified in them. And now I am no more in the world, but these are in the world, and I come to Thee. Holy Father, keep through Thine own name those whom Thou hast given Me, that they may be one, as We are." "Neither pray I for these alone, but for them also which shall believe on Me through their word; that they all may be one; . . . I in them, and Thou in Me, that they may be made perfect in one; and that the world may know that Thou hast sent Me, and hast loved them, as Thou hast loved Me."

Thus in the language of one who has divine authority, Christ gives His elect church into the Father's arms. As a consecrated high priest He intercedes for His people. As a faithful shepherd He gathers His flock under the shadow of the Almighty, in the strong and sure refuge. For Him there waits the last battle with Satan, and He goes forth to meet it.

Gethsemane

In company with His disciples, the Saviour slowly made His way to the garden of Gethsemane. The Passover moon, broad and full, shone from a cloudless sky. The city of pilgrims' tents was hushed into silence.

Jesus had been earnestly conversing with His disciples and instructing them; but as He neared Gethsemane, He became strangely silent. He had often visited this spot for meditation and prayer; but never with a heart so full of sorrow as upon this night of His last agony. Throughout His life on earth He had walked in the light of God's presence. When in conflict with men who were inspired by the very spirit of Satan, He could say, "He that sent Me is with Me; the Father hath not left Me alone; for I do always those things that please Him." John 8:29. But now He seemed to be shut out from the light of God's sustaining presence. Now He was numbered with the transgressors. The guilt of fallen humanity He must bear. Upon Him who knew no sin, must be laid the iniquity of us all. So dreadful does sin appear to Him, so great is the weight of guilt which He must bear, that He is tempted to fear it will shut Him out forever from His Father's love. Feeling how terrible is the wrath of God against transgression, He exclaims, "My soul is exceeding sorrowful, even unto death."

As they approached the garden, the disciples had marked the change that came over their Master. Never before had they seen Him so utterly sad and silent. As He proceeded, this strange sadness deepened; yet they dared not question Him as to the cause. His form swayed as if he were about to fall. Upon reaching the garden, the disciples looked anxiously for His usual place of retirement, that their Master might rest. Every step that He now took was with labored effort. He groaned aloud, as if suffering under the pressure of a terrible burden. Twice His companions supported Him, or He would have fallen to the earth.

Near the entrance to the garden, Jesus left all but three of the disciples, bidding them pray for themselves and for Him. With Peter, James, and John, He entered its secluded recesses. These three disciples were Christ's closest companions. They had beheld His glory on the mount of transfiguration; they had seen Moses and Elijah talking with Him; they had heard the voice from heaven; now in His great struggle, Christ desired their presence near Him. Often they had passed the night with Him in this retreat. On these occasions, after a season of watching and prayer, they would sleep undisturbed at a little distance from their Master, until He awoke them in the morning to go forth anew to labor. But now He desired them to spend the night with Him in prayer. Yet He could not bear that even they should witness the agony He was to endure.

"Tarry ye here," He said, "and watch with Me."

He went a little distance from them — not so far but that they could both see and hear Him — and fell prostrate upon the ground. He felt that by sin He was being separated from His Father. The gulf was so broad, so black, so deep, that His spirit shuddered before it. This agony He must not exert His divine power to escape. As man He must suffer the consequences of man's sin. As man He must endure the wrath of God against transgression.

Christ was now standing in a different attitude from that in which He had ever stood before. His suffering can best be described in the words of the prophet, "Awake, O sword, against My shepherd, and against the man that is My fellow, saith the Lord of hosts." Zechariah 13:7. As the substitute and surety for sinful man, Christ was suffering under divine justice. He saw what justice meant.

(685-686)   This chapter is based on Matthew 26:36-56; Mark 14:32-50; Luke 22:39-53; John 18:1-12.   123

Hitherto He had been as an intercessor for others; now He longed to have an intercessor for Himself.

As Christ felt His unity with the Father broken up, He feared that in His human nature He would be unable to endure the coming conflict with the powers of darkness. In the wilderness of temptation the destiny of the human race had been at stake. Christ was then conqueror. Now the tempter had come for the last fearful struggle. For this he had been preparing during the three years of Christ's ministry. Everything was at stake with him. If he failed here, his hope of mastery was lost; the kingdoms of the world would finally become Christ's; he himself would be overthrown and cast out. But if Christ could be overcome, the earth would become Satan's kingdom, and the human race would be forever in his power. With the issues of the conflict before Him, Christ's soul was filled with dread of separation from God. Satan told Him that if He became the surety for a sinful world, the separation would be eternal. He would be identified with Satan's kingdom, and would never more be one with God.

And what was to be gained by this sacrifice? How hopeless appeared the guilt and ingratitude of men! In its hardest features Satan pressed the situation upon the Redeemer: "The people who claim to be above all others in temporal and spiritual advantages have rejected you. They are seeking to destroy you, the foundation, the center and seal of the promises made to them as a peculiar people. One of your own disciples, who has listened to your instruction, and has been among the foremost in church activities, will betray you. One of your most zealous followers will deny you. All will forsake you." Christ's whole being abhorred the thought. That those whom He had undertaken to save, those whom He loved so much, should unite in the plots of Satan, this pierced His soul. The conflict was terrible. Its measure was the guilt of His nation, of His accusers and betrayer, the guilt of a world lying in wickedness. The sins of men weighed heavily upon Christ, and the sense of God's wrath against sin was crushing out His life.

Behold Him contemplating the price to be paid for the human soul. In His agony He clings to the cold ground, as if to prevent Himself from being drawn farther from God. The chilling dew of night falls upon His prostrate form, but He heeds it not. From His pale lips comes the bitter cry, "O My Father, if it be possible, let this cup pass from Me." Yet even now He adds, "Nevertheless not as I will, but as Thou wilt."

The human heart longs for sympathy in suffering. This longing Christ felt to the very depths of His being. In the supreme agony of His soul He came to His disciples with a yearning desire to hear some words of comfort from those whom He had so often blessed and comforted, and shielded in sorrow and distress. The One who had always had words of sympathy for them was now suffering superhuman agony, and He longed to know that they were praying for Him and for themselves. How dark seemed the malignity of sin. Terrible was the temptation to let the human race bear the consequences of its own guilt, while He stood innocent before God. If He could only know that His disciples understood and appreciated this, He would be strengthened.

Rising with painful effort, He staggered to the place where He had left His companions. But He "findeth them asleep." Had He found them praying, He would have been relieved. Had they been seeking refuge in God, that Sa-

---

"The fate of humanity trembled in the balance. Christ might even now refuse to drink the cup apportioned to guilty man. It was not yet too late. He might wipe the bloody sweat from His brow, and leave man to perish in his iniquity. He might say, Let the transgressor receive the penalty of his sin, and I will go back to My Father. . . . Will the innocent suffer the consequences of the curse of sin, to save the guilty?"

---

tanic agencies might not prevail over them, He would have been comforted by their steadfast faith. But they had not heeded the repeated warning, "Watch and pray." At first they had been much troubled to see their Master, usually so calm and dignified, wrestling with a sorrow that was beyond comprehension. They had prayed as they heard the strong cries of the sufferer. They did not intend to forsake their Lord, but they seemed paralyzed by a stupor which they might have shaken off if they had continued pleading with God. They did not realize the necessity of watchfulness and earnest prayer in order to withstand temptation.

Just before He bent His footsteps to the garden, Jesus had said to the disciples, "All ye shall be offended because of

Me this night." They had given Him the strongest assurance that they would go with Him to prison and to death. And poor, self-sufficient Peter had added, "Although all shall be offended, yet will not I." Mark 14:27, 29. But the disciples trusted to themselves. They did not look to the mighty helper as Christ had counseled them to do. Thus when the Saviour was most in need of their sympathy and prayers, they were found asleep. Even Peter was sleeping.

And John, the loving disciple who had leaned upon the breast of Jesus, was asleep. Surely, the love of John for his Master should have kept him awake. His earnest prayers should have mingled with those of his loved Saviour in the time of His supreme sorrow. The Redeemer had spent entire nights praying for His disciples, that their faith might not fail. Should Jesus now put to James and John the question He had once asked them, "Are ye able to drink of the cup that I shall drink of, and to be baptized with the baptism that I am baptized with?" they would not have ventured to answer, "We are able." Matthew 20:22.

The disciples awakened at the voice of Jesus, but they hardly knew Him, His face was so changed by anguish. Addressing Peter, Jesus said, "Simon, sleepest thou? couldst not thou watch one hour? Watch ye and pray, lest ye enter into temptation. The spirit truly is ready, but the flesh is weak." The weakness of His disciples awakened the sympathy of Jesus. He feared that they would not be able to endure the test which would come upon them in His betrayal and death. He did not reprove them, but said, "Watch ye and pray, lest ye enter into temptation." Even in His great agony, He was seeking to excuse their weakness. "The spirit truly is ready," He said, "but the flesh is weak."

Again the Son of God was seized with superhuman agony, and fainting and exhausted, He staggered back to the place of His former struggle. His suffering was even greater than before. As the agony of soul came upon Him, "His sweat was as it were great drops of blood falling down to the ground." The cypress and palm trees were the silent witnesses of His anguish. From their leafy branches dropped heavy dew upon His stricken form, as if nature wept over its Author wrestling alone with the powers of darkness.

A short time before, Jesus had stood like a mighty cedar, withstanding the storm of opposition that spent its fury upon Him. Stubborn wills, and hearts filled with malice and subtlety, had striven in vain to confuse and overpower Him. He stood forth in divine majesty as the Son of God. Now He was like a reed beaten and bent by the angry storm. He had approached the consummation of His work a conqueror, having at each step gained the victory over the powers of darkness. As one already glorified, He had claimed oneness with God. In unfaltering accents He had poured out His songs of praise. He had spoken to His disciples in words of courage and tenderness. Now had come the hour of the power of darkness. Now His voice was heard on the still evening air, not in tones of triumph,

but full of human anguish. The words of the Saviour were borne to the ears of the drowsy disciples, "O My Father, if this cup may not pass away from Me, except I drink it, Thy will be done."

The first impulse of the disciples was to go to Him; but He had bidden them tarry there, watching unto prayer. When Jesus came to them, He found them still sleeping. Again He had felt a longing for companionship, for some words from His disciples which would bring relief, and break the spell of darkness that well-nigh overpowered Him. But their eyes were heavy; "neither wist they what to answer Him." His presence aroused them. They saw His face marked with the bloody sweat of agony, and they were filled with fear. His anguish of mind they could not understand. "His visage was so marred more than any man, and His form more than the sons of men." Isaiah 52:14.

Turning away, Jesus sought again His retreat, and fell prostrate, overcome by the horror of a great darkness. The humanity of the Son of God trembled in that trying hour. He prayed not now for His disciples that their faith might not fail, but for His own tempted, agonized soul. The awful moment had come, — that moment which was to decide the destiny of the world. The fate of humanity trembled in the balance. Christ might even now refuse to drink the cup apportioned to guilty man. It was not yet too late. He might wipe the bloody sweat from His brow, and leave man to perish in his iniquity. He might say, Let the transgressor receive the penalty of his sin, and I will go back to My Father. Will the Son of God drink the bitter cup of humiliation and agony? Will the innocent suffer the consequences of the curse of sin, to save the guilty? The words fall tremblingly from the pale lips of Jesus, "O My Father, if this cup may not pass away from Me, except I drink it, Thy will be done."

Three times has He uttered that prayer. Three times has humanity shrunk from the last, crowning sacrifice. But now the history of the human race comes up before the world's Redeemer. He sees that the transgressors of the law, if left to themselves, must perish. He sees the helplessness of man. He sees the power of sin. The woes and lamentations of a doomed world rise before Him. He beholds its impending fate, and His decision is made. He will save man at any cost to Himself. He accepts His baptism of blood, that through Him perishing millions may gain everlasting life. He has left the courts of heaven, where all is purity, happiness, and glory, to save the one lost sheep, the one world that has fallen by transgression. And He will not turn from His mission. He will become the propitiation of a race that has willed to sin. His prayer now breathes only submission: "If this cup may not pass away from Me, except I drink it, Thy will be done."

Having made the decision, He fell dying to the ground from which He had partially risen. Where now were His disciples, to place their hands tenderly beneath the head of their fainting Master, and bathe that brow, marred indeed more than the sons of men? The Saviour trod the wine-press alone, and of the people there was none with Him.

But God suffered with His Son. Angels beheld the Saviour's agony. They saw their Lord enclosed by legions of Satanic forces, His nature weighed down with a shuddering, mysterious dread. There was silence in heaven. No harp was touched. Could mortals have viewed the amazement of the angelic host as in silent grief they watched the Father separating His beams of light, love, and glory from His beloved Son, they would better understand how offensive in His sight is sin.

The worlds unfallen and the heavenly angels had watched with intense interest as the conflict drew to its close. Satan and his confederacy of evil, the legions of apostasy, watched intently this great crisis in the work of redemption. The powers of good and evil waited to see what answer would come to Christ's thrice-repeated prayer. Angels had longed to bring relief to the divine sufferer, but this might not be. No way of escape was found for the Son of God. In this awful crisis, when everything was at stake, when the mysterious cup trembled in the hand of the sufferer, the heavens opened, a light shone forth amid the stormy darkness of the crisis hour, and the mighty angel who stands in God's presence, occupying the position from which Satan fell, came to the side of Christ. The angel came not to take the cup from Christ's hand, but to strengthen Him to drink it, with the assurance of the Father's love. He came to give power to the divine-human suppliant. He pointed Him to the open heavens, telling Him of the souls that would be saved as the result of His sufferings. He assured Him that His Father is greater and more powerful than Satan, that His death would result in the utter discomfiture of Satan, and that the kingdom of this world would be given to the saints of the Most High. He told Him that He would see of the travail of His soul, and be satisfied, for He would see a multitude of the human race saved, eternally saved.

Christ's agony did not cease, but His depression and discouragement left Him. The storm had in no wise abated, but He who was its object was strengthened to meet its fury. He came forth calm and serene. A heavenly peace rested upon His bloodstained face. He had borne that which no human being could ever bear; for He had tasted the sufferings of death for every man.

The sleeping disciples had been suddenly awakened by the light surrounding the Saviour. They saw the angel bending over their prostrate Master. They saw him lift the Saviour's head upon his bosom, and point toward heaven. They heard his voice, like sweetest music, speaking words of comfort and hope. The disciples recalled the scene upon the mount of transfiguration. They remembered the glory that in the temple had encircled Jesus, and the voice of God that spoke from the cloud. Now that same glory was again revealed, and they had no further fear for their Master. He was under the care of God; a mighty angel had been sent to protect Him. Again the disciples in their weariness yield to the strange stupor that overpowers them. Again Jesus finds them sleeping.

Looking sorrowfully upon them He says, "Sleep on now, and take your rest; behold, the hour is at hand, and the Son of man is betrayed into the hands of sinners."

Even as He spoke these words, He heard the footsteps of the mob in search of Him, and said, "Rise, let us be going; behold, he is at hand that doth betray Me."

No traces of His recent agony were visible as Jesus stepped forth to meet His betrayer. Standing in advance of His disciples He said, "Whom seek ye?" They answered, "Jesus of Nazareth." Jesus replied, "I am He." As these words were spoken, the angel who had lately ministered to Jesus, moved between Him and the mob. A divine light illuminated the Saviour's face, and a dovelike form over-shadowed Him. In the presence of this divine glory, the murderous throng could not stand for a moment. They staggered back. Priests, elders, soldiers, and even Judas, fell as dead men to the ground.

The angel withdrew, and the light faded away. Jesus had opportunity to escape, but He remained, calm and self-possessed. As one glorified He stood in the midst of that hardened band, now prostrate and helpless at His feet. The disciples looked on, silent with wonder and awe.

But quickly the scene changed. The mob started up. The Roman soldiers, the priests and Judas, gathered about Christ. They seemed ashamed of their weakness, and fearful that He would yet escape. Again the question was asked by the Redeemer, "Whom seek ye?" They had had evidence that He who stood before them was the Son of God, but they would not be convinced. To the question, "Whom seek ye?" again they answered, "Jesus of Nazareth." The Saviour then said, "I have told you that I am He. If therefore ye seek Me, let these go their way" — pointing to the disciples. He knew how weak was their faith, and He sought to shield them from temptation and trial. For them He was ready to sacrifice Himself.

Judas the betrayer did not forget the part he was to act. When the mob entered the garden, he had led the way, closely followed by the high priest. To the pursuers of Jesus he had given a sign, saying, "Whomsoever I shall kiss, that same is He; hold Him fast." Matthew 26:48. Now he pretends to have no part with them. Coming close to Jesus, he takes His hand as a familiar friend. With the words, "Hail, Master," he kisses Him repeatedly, and appears to weep as if in sympathy with Him in His peril.

Jesus said to him, "Friend, wherefore art thou come?" His voice trembled with sorrow as He added, "Judas, betrayest thou the Son of man with a kiss?" This appeal should have aroused the conscience of the betrayer, and touched his stubborn heart; but honor, fidelity, and human tenderness had forsaken him. He stood bold and defiant, showing no disposition to relent. He had given himself up to Satan, and he had no power to resist him. Jesus did not refuse the traitor's kiss.

The mob grew bold as they saw Judas touch the person of Him who had so recently been glorified before their eyes. They now laid hold of Jesus, and proceeded to bind those precious hands that had ever been employed in doing good.

The disciples had thought that their Master would not suffer Himself to be taken. For the same power that had caused the mob to fall as dead men could keep them helpless, until Jesus and His companions should escape. They were disappointed and indignant as they saw the cords brought forward to bind the hands of Him whom they loved. Peter in his anger rashly drew his sword and tried to defend his Master, but he only cut off an ear of the high priest's servant. When Jesus saw what was done, He released His hands, though held firmly by the Roman soldiers, and saying, "Suffer ye thus far," He touched the wounded ear, and it was instantly made whole. He then said to Peter, "Put up again thy sword into his place; for all they that take the sword shall perish with the sword. Thinkest thou that I cannot now pray to My Father, and He shall presently give Me more than twelve legions of angels?" — a legion in place of each one of the disciples. O why, the disciples thought, does He not save Himself and us? Answering their unspoken thought He added, "But how then shall the scriptures be fulfilled, that thus it must be?" "The cup which my Father hath given Me, shall I not drink it?"

The official dignity of the Jewish leaders had not prevented them from joining in the pursuit of Jesus. His arrest was too important a matter to be trusted to subordinates; the wily priests and elders had joined the temple police and the rabble in following Judas to Gethsemane. What a company for those dignitaries to unite with, — a mob that was eager for excitement, and armed with all kinds of implements, as if in pursuit of a wild beast.

Turning to the priests and elders, Christ fixed upon them His searching glance. The words He spoke they would never forget as long as life should last. They were as the sharp arrows of the Almighty. With dignity He said: You come out against Me with swords and staves as you would against a thief or a robber. Day by day I sat teaching in the temple. You had every opportunity of laying hands upon Me, and you did nothing. The night is better suited to your work. "This is your hour, and the power of darkness."

The disciples were terrified as they saw Jesus permit Himself to be taken and bound. They were offended that He should suffer this humiliation to Himself and them. They could not understand His conduct, and they blamed Him for submitting to the mob. In their indignation and fear, Peter proposed that they save themselves. Following this suggestion, "they all forsook Him, and fled." But Christ had foretold this desertion, "Behold," He had said, "the hour cometh, yea, is now come, that ye shall be scattered, every man to his own, and shall leave Me alone; and yet I am not alone, because the Father is with Me." John 16:32.

Before Annas and the Court of Caiaphas

Over the brook Kedron, past gardens and olive groves, and through the hushed streets of the sleeping city, they hurried Jesus. It was past midnight, and the cries of the hooting mob that followed Him broke sharply upon the still air. The Saviour was bound and closely guarded, and He moved painfully. But in eager haste His captors made their way with Him to the palace of Annas, the ex-high priest.

Annas was the head of the officiating priestly family, and in deference to his age he was recognized by the people as high priest. His counsel was sought and carried out as the voice of God. He must first see Jesus a captive to priestly power. He must be present at the examination of the prisoner, for fear that the less-experienced Caiaphas might fail of securing the object for which they were working. His artifice, cunning, and subtlety must be used on this occasion; for at all events, Christ's condemnation must be secured.

Christ was to be tried formally before the Sanhedrim; but before Annas He was subjected to a preliminary trial. Under the Roman rule the Sanhedrin could not execute the sentence of death. They could only examine a prisoner, and pass judgment, to be ratified by the Roman authorities. It was therefore necessary to bring against Christ charges that would be regarded as criminal by the Romans. An accusation must also be found which would condemn Him in the eyes of the Jews. Not a few among the priests and rulers had been convicted by Christ's teaching, and only fear of excommunication prevented them from confessing Him. The priests well remembered the question of Nicodemus "Doth our law judge any man, before it hear him, and know what he doeth?" John 7:51. This question had for the time broken up the council, and thwarted their plans. Joseph of Arimathea and Nicodemus were not now to be summoned, but there were others who might dare to speak in favor of justice. The trial must be so conducted as to unite the members of the Sanhedrim against Christ. There were two charges which the priests desired to maintain. If Jesus could be proved a blasphemer, He would be condemned by the Jews. If convicted of sedition, it would secure His condemnation by the Romans. The second charge Annas tried first to establish. He questioned Jesus concerning His disciples and His doctrines, hoping the prisoner would say something that would give him material upon which to work. He thought to draw out some statement to prove that He was seeking to establish a secret society, with the purpose of setting up a new kingdom. Then the priests could deliver Him to the Romans as a disturber of the peace and a creator of insurrection.

Christ read the priest's purpose as an open book. As if reading the inmost soul of His questioner, He denied that there was between Him and His followers any secret bond of union, or that He gathered them secretly and in the darkness to conceal His designs. He had no secrets in regard to His purpose or doctrines. "I spake openly to the world," He answered; "I ever taught in the synagogue, and in the temple, whither the Jews always resort; and in secret have I said nothing."

The Saviour contrasted His own manner of work with the methods of His accusers. For months they had hunted Him, striving to entrap Him and bring Him before a secret tribunal, where they might obtain by perjury what it was impossible to gain by fair means. Now they were carrying out their purpose. The midnight seizure by a mob, the mockery and abuse before He was condemned, or even accused, was their manner of work, not His. Their action

This chapter is based on Matthew 26:57-75; 27:1;
Mark 14:53-72; 15:1; Luke 22:54-71; John 18:13-27.

was in violation of the law. Their own rules declared that every man should be treated as innocent until proved guilty. By their own rules the priests stood condemned.

Turning upon His questioner, Jesus said, "Why askest thou Me?" Had not the priests and rulers sent spies to watch His movements, and report His every word? Had not these been present at every gathering of the people, and carried to the priests information of all His sayings and doings? "Ask them which heard Me, what I have said unto them," replied Jesus; "behold, they know what I said."

Annas was silenced by the decision of the answer. Fearing that Christ would say something regarding his course of action that he would prefer to keep covered up, he said nothing more to Him at this time. One of his officers, filled with wrath as he saw Annas silenced, struck Jesus on the face, saying, "Answerest Thou the high priest so?"

Christ calmly replied, "If I have spoken evil, bear witness of the evil; but if well, why smitest thou Me?" He spoke no burning words of retaliation. His calm answer came from a heart sinless, patient, and gentle, that would not be provoked.

Christ suffered keenly under abuse and insult. At the hands of the beings whom He had created, and for whom He was making an infinite sacrifice, He received every indignity. And He suffered in proportion to the perfection of His holiness and His hatred of sin. His trial by men who acted as fiends was to Him a perpetual sacrifice. To be surrounded by human beings under the control of Satan was revolting to Him. And He knew that in a moment, by the flashing forth of His divine power, He could lay His cruel tormentors in the dust. This made the trial the harder to bear.

The Jews were looking for a Messiah to be revealed in outward show. They expected Him, by one flash of over-mastering will, to change the current of men's thoughts, and force from them an acknowledgment of His supremacy. Thus, they believed, He was to secure His own exaltation, and gratify their ambitious hopes. Thus when Christ was treated with contempt, there came to Him a strong temptation to manifest His divine character. By a word, by a look, He could compel His persecutors to confess that He was Lord above kings and rulers, priests and temple. But it was His difficult task to keep to the position He had chosen as one with humanity.

The angels of heaven witnessed every movement made against their loved Commander. They longed to deliver Christ. Under God the angels are all-powerful. On one occasion, in obedience to the command of Christ, they slew of the Assyrian army in one night one hundred and eighty-five thousand men. How easily could the angels, beholding the shameful scene of the trial of Christ, have testified their indignation by consuming the adversaries of God. But they were not commanded to do this. He who could have doomed His enemies to death bore with their cruelty. His love for His Father, and His pledge, made from the foundation of the world, to become the Sin-

bearer, led Him to endure uncomplainingly the coarse treatment of those He came to save. It was a part of His mission to bear, in His humanity, all the taunts and abuse that men could heap upon Him. The only hope of humanity was in this submission of Christ to all that He could endure from the hands and hearts of men.

Christ had said nothing that could give His accusers an advantage; yet He was bound, to signify that He was condemned. There must, however, be a pretense of justice. It was necessary that there should be the form of a legal trial. This the authorities were determined to hasten. They knew the regard in which Jesus was held by the people, and feared that if the arrest were noised abroad, a rescue

> **"Christ suffered keenly under abuse and insult. At the hands of the beings whom He had created, and for whom He was making an infinite sacrifice, He received every indignity."**

would be attempted. Again, if the trial and execution were not brought about at once, there would be a week's delay on account of the celebration of the Passover. This might defeat their plans. In securing the condemnation of Jesus they depended largely upon the clamor of the mob, many of them the rabble of Jerusalem. Should there be a week's delay, the excitement would abate, and a reaction would be likely to set in. The better part of the people would be aroused in Christ's favor; many would come forward with testimony in His vindication, bringing to light the mighty works He had done. This would excite popular indignation against the Sanhedrim. Their proceedings would be condemned, and Jesus would be set free, to receive new homage from the multitudes. The priests and rulers therefore determined that before their purpose could become known, Jesus should be delivered into the hands of the Romans.

But first of all, an accusation was to be found. They had gained nothing as yet. Annas ordered Jesus to be taken to Caiaphas. Caiaphas belonged to the Sadducees, some of whom were now the most desperate enemies of Jesus. He himself, though wanting in force of character, was fully as severe, heartless, and unscrupulous as was Annas. He would leave no means untried to destroy Jesus. It was now early morning, and very dark; by the light of torches and lanterns the armed band with their prisoner proceeded to the high priest's palace. Here, while the members of the Sanhedrin were coming together, Annas and Caiaphas again questioned Jesus, but without success.

When the council had assembled in the judgment hall, Caiaphas took his seat as presiding officer. On either side were the judges, and those specially interested in the trial. The Roman soldiers were stationed on the platform below the throne. At the foot of the throne stood Jesus. Upon Him the gaze of the whole multitude was fixed. The excitement was intense. Of all the throng He alone was calm and serene. The very atmosphere surrounding Him seemed pervaded by a holy influence.

Caiaphas had regarded Jesus as his rival. The eagerness of the people to hear the Saviour, and their apparent readiness to accept His teachings, had aroused the bitter jealousy of the high priest. But as Caiaphas now looked upon the prisoner, He was struck with admiration for His noble and dignified bearing. A conviction came over him that this man was akin to God. The next instant he scornfully banished the thought. Immediately his voice was heard in sneering, haughty tones demanding that Jesus work one of His mighty miracles before them. But his words fell upon the Saviour's ears as though He heard them not. The people compared the excited and malignant deportment of Annas and Caiaphas with the calm, majestic bearing of Jesus. Even in the minds of that hardened multitude arose the question, Is this man of Godlike presence to be condemned as a criminal?

Caiaphas, perceiving the influence that was obtaining, hastened the trial. The enemies of Jesus were in great perplexity. They were bent on securing His condemnation, but how to accomplish this they knew not. The numbers of the council were divided between the Pharisees and the Sadducees. There was bitter animosity and controversy between them; certain disputed points they dared not approach for fear of a quarrel. With a few words Jesus could have excited their prejudices against each other, and thus have averted their wrath from Himself. Caiaphas knew this, and he wised to avoid stirring up a contention. There were plenty of witnesses to prove that Christ had denounced the priests and scribes, that He had called them hypocrites and murderers; but this testimony it was not expedient to bring forward. The Sadducees in their sharp contentions with the Pharisees had used to them similar language. And such testimony would have no weight with the Romans, who were themselves disgusted with the pretensions of the Pharisees. There was abundant evidence that Jesus had disregarded the traditions of the Jews, and had spoken irreverently of many of their ordinances; but in regard to tradition the Pharisees and Sadducees were at swords' points; and this evidence also would have no weight with the Romans. Christ's enemies dared not accuse Him of Sabbathbreaking, lest an examination should reveal the character of His work. If His miracles of healing were brought to light, the very object of the priests would be defeated.

False witnesses had been bribed to accuse Jesus of inciting rebellion and seeking to establish a separate government. But their testimony proved to be vague and contradictory. Under examination they falsified their own statements.

Early in His ministry Christ had said, "Destroy this temple, and in three days I will raise it up." In the figurative language of prophecy, He had thus foretold His own death and resurrection. "He spake of the temple of His body." John 2:19, 21. These words the Jews had understood in a literal sense, as referring to the temple at Jerusalem. Of all that Christ had said, the priests could find nothing to use against Him save this. By misstating these words they hoped to gain an advantage. The Romans had engaged in rebuilding and embellishing the temple, and they took great pride in it; any contempt shown to it would be sure to excite their indignation. Here Romans and Jews, Pharisees and Sadducees, could meet; for all held the temple in great veneration. On this point two witnesses were found whose testimony was not so contradictory as that of the others had been. One of them, who had been bribed to accuse Jesus, declared, "This fellow said, I am able to destroy the temple of God, and to build it in three days." Thus Christ's words were misstated. If they had been reported exactly as He spoke them, they would not have secured His condemnation even by the Sanhedrin. Had Jesus been a mere man, as the Jews claimed, His declaration would only have indicated an unreasonable, boastful spirit, but could not have been construed into blasphemy. Even as misrepresented by the false witnesses, His words contained nothing which would be regarded by the Romans as a crime worthy of death.

Patiently Jesus listened to the conflicting testimonies. No word did He utter in self-defense. At last His accusers were entangled, confused, and maddened. The trial was making no headway: it seemed that their plottings were to fail. Caiaphas was desperate. One last resort remained; Christ must be forced to condemn Himself. The high priest started from the judgment seat, his face contorted with passion, his voice and demeanor plainly indicating that were it in his power he would strike down the prisoner before him. "Answerest Thou nothing?" he exclaimed; "what is it which these witness against Thee?"

Jesus held His peace. "He was oppressed, and He was afflicted yet He opened not His mouth. He is brought as a lamb to the slaughter, and as a sheep before her shearers is dumb, so He openeth not His mouth." Isaiah 53:7.

At last, Caiaphas, raising his right hand toward heaven, addressed Jesus in the form of a solemn oath: "I adjure Thee by the living God, that Thou tell us whether Thou be the Christ, the Son of God."

To this appeal Christ could not remain silent. There was a time to be silent, and a time to speak. He had not spoken until directly questioned. He knew that to answer now would make His death certain. But the appeal was made by the highest acknowledged authority of the nation, and in the name of the Most High. Christ would not fail to show proper respect for the law. More than this, His own relation to the Father was called in question. He must plainly declare His character and mission. Jesus had said to His disciples, "Whosoever therefore shall confess Me before men, him will I confess also before My Father which is in heaven." Matthew 10:32. Now by His own example He repeated the lesson.

Every ear was bent to listen, and every eye was fixed on His face as He answered, "Thou hast said." A heavenly light seemed to illuminate His pale countenance as He added, "Nevertheless I say unto you, Hereafter shall ye see the Son of man sitting on the right hand of power, and coming in the clouds of heaven."

For a moment the divinity of Christ flashed through His guise of humanity. The high priest quailed before the penetrating eyes of the Saviour. That look seemed to read his hidden thoughts, and burn into his heart. Never in afterlife did he forget that searching glance of the persecuted Son of God.

"Hereafter," said Jesus, "shall ye see the Son of man sitting on the right hand of power, and coming in the clouds of heaven." In these words Christ presented the reverse of the scene then taking place. He, the Lord of life and glory, would be seated at God's right hand. He would be the judge of all the earth, and from His decision there could be no appeal. Then every secret thing would be set in the light of God's countenance, and judgment be passed upon every man according to his deeds.

The words of Christ startled the high priest. The thought that there was to be a resurrection of the dead, when all would stand at the bar of God, to be rewarded according to their works, was a thought of terror to Caiaphas. He did not wish to believe that in future he would receive sentence according to his works. There rushed before his mind as a panorama the scenes of the final Judgment. For a moment he saw the fearful spectacle of the graves giving up their dead, with the secrets he had hoped were forever hidden. For a moment he felt as if standing before the eternal Judge, whose eye, which sees all things, was reading his soul, bringing to light mysteries supposed to be hidden with the dead.

The scene passed from the priest's vision. Christ's words cut him, the Sadducee, to the quick. Caiaphas had denied the doctrine of the resurrection, the Judgment, and a future life. Now he was maddened by Satanic fury. Was this man, a prisoner before him, to assail his most cherished theories? Rending his robe, that the people might see his pretended horror, he demanded that without further preliminaries the prisoner be condemned for blasphemy. "What further need have we of witnesses?" he said; "behold, now ye have heard His blasphemy. What think ye?" And they all condemned Him.

Conviction mingled with passion led Caiaphas to do as he did. He was furious with himself for believing Christ's words, and instead of rending his heart under a deep sense of truth, and confessing that Jesus was the Messiah, he rent his priestly robes in determined resistance. This act was deeply significant. Little did Caiaphas realize its meaning. In this act, done to influence the judges and secure Christ's condemnation, the high priest had condemned himself. By the law of God he was disqualified for the priesthood. He had pronounced upon himself the death sentence.

A high priest was not to rend his garments. By the Levitical law, this was prohibited under sentence of death. Under no circumstances, on no occasion, was the priest to rend his robe. It was the custom among the Jews for the garments to be rent at the death of friends, but this custom the priests were not to observe. Express command had been given by Christ to Moses concerning this. Leviticus 10:6.

Everything worn by the priest was to be whole and without blemish. By those beautiful official garments was represented the character of the great antitype, Jesus Christ. Nothing but perfection, in dress and attitude, in word and spirit, could be acceptable to God. He is holy, and His glory and perfection must be represented by the earthly service. Nothing but perfection could properly represent the sacredness of the heavenly service. Finite man might rend his own heart by showing a contrite and humble spirit. This God would discern. But no rent must be made in the priestly robes, for this would mar the representation of heavenly things. The high priest who dared to appear in holy office, and engage in the service of the sanctuary, with a rent robe, was looked upon as having severed himself from God. By rending his garment he cut himself off from being a representative character. He was no longer accepted by God as an officiating priest. This course of action, as exhibited by Caiaphas, showed human passion, human imperfection.

By rending his garments, Caiaphas made of no effect the law of God, to follow the tradition of men. A man-made law provided that in case of blasphemy a priest might rend his garments in horror at the sin, and be guiltless. Thus the law of God was made void by the laws of men.

Each action of the high priest was watched with interest by the people; and Caiaphas thought for effect to display his piety. But in this act, designed as an accusation against Christ, he was reviling the One of whom God had said, "My name is in Him." Exodus 23:21. He himself was committing blasphemy. Standing under the condemnation of God, he pronounced sentence upon Christ as a blasphemer.

When Caiaphas rent his garment, his act was significant of the place that the Jewish nation as a nation would thereafter occupy toward God. The once favored people of God were separating themselves from Him, and were fast becoming a people disowned by Jehovah. When Christ upon the cross cried out, "It is finished," (John

19:30.) and the veil of the temple was rent in twain, the Holy Watcher declared that the Jewish people had rejected Him who was the antitype of all their types, the substance of all their shadows. Israel was divorced from God. Well might Caiaphas then rend his official robes, which signified that he claimed to be a representative of the great High Priest; for no longer had they any meaning for him or for the people. Well might the high priest rend his robes in horror for himself and for the nation.

"When the condemnation of Jesus was pronounced by the judges, a satanic fury took possession of the people. The roar of voices was like that of wild beasts. The crowd made a rush toward Jesus, crying, He is guilty, put Him to death! Had it not been for the Roman soldiers, Jesus would not have lived to be nailed to the cross of Calvary. He would have been torn in pieces before His judges."

The Sanhedrin had pronounced Jesus worthy of death; but it was contrary to the Jewish law to try a prisoner by night. In legal condemnation nothing could be done except in the light of day and before a full session of the council. Notwithstanding this, the Saviour was now treated as a condemned criminal, and given up to be abused by the lowest and vilest of human kind. The palace of the high priest surrounded an open court in which the soldiers and the multitude had gathered. Through this court, Jesus was taken to the guardroom, on every side meeting with mockery of His claim to be the Son of God. His own words, "sitting on the right hand of power," and, "coming in the clouds of heaven," were jeeringly repeated. While in the guardroom, awaiting His legal trial, He was not protected.

The ignorant rabble had seen the cruelty with which He was treated before the council, and from this they took license to manifest all the Satanic elements of their nature. Christ's very nobility and Godlike bearing goaded them to madness. His meekness, His innocence, His majestic patience, filled them with hatred born of Satan. Mercy and justice were trampled upon. Never was criminal treated in so inhuman a manner as was the Son of God.

But a keener anguish rent the heart of Jesus; the blow that inflicted the deepest pain no enemy's hand could have dealt. While He was undergoing the mockery of an examination before Caiaphas, Christ had been denied by one of His own disciples.

After deserting their Master in the garden, two of the disciples had ventured to follow, at a distance, the mob that had Jesus in charge. These disciples were Peter and John. The priests recognized John as a well-known disciple of Jesus, and admitted him to the hall, hoping that as he witnessed the humiliation of his leader, he would scorn the idea of such a one being the Son of God. John spoke in favor of Peter, and gained an entrance for him also.

In the court a fire had been kindled; for it was the coldest hour of the night, being just before the dawn. A company drew about the fire, and Peter presumptuously took his place with them. He did not wish to be recognized as a disciple of Jesus. By mingling carelessly with the crowd, he hoped to be taken for one of those who had brought Jesus to the hall.

But as the light flashed upon Peter's face, the woman who kept the door cast a searching glance upon him. She had noticed that he came in with John, she marked the look of dejection on his face, and thought that he might be a disciple of Jesus. She was one of the servants of Caiaphas' household, and was curious to know. She said to Peter, "Art not thou also one of this man's disciples?" Peter was startled and confused; the eyes of the company instantly fastened upon him. He pretended not to understand her, but she was persistent, and said to those around her that this man was with Jesus. Peter felt compelled to answer, and said angrily, "Woman, I know Him not." This was the first denial, and immediately the cock crew. O Peter! so soon ashamed of thy Master! so soon to deny thy Lord!

The disciple John, upon entering the judgment hall, did not try to conceal the fact that he was a follower of Jesus. He did not mingle with the rough company who were reviling his Master. He was not questioned; for he did not assume a false character, and thus lay himself liable to suspicion. He sought a retired corner secure from the notice of the mob, but as near Jesus as it was possible for him to be. Here he could see and hear all that took place at the trial of his Lord.

Peter had not designed that his real character should be known. In assuming an air of indifference he had placed himself on the enemy's ground, and he became an easy prey to temptation. If he had been called to fight for his Master, he would have been a courageous soldier; but when the finger of scorn was pointed at him, he proved himself a coward. Many who do not shrink from active warfare for their Lord, are driven by ridicule to deny their faith. By associating with those whom they should avoid, they place themselves in the way of temptation. They invite the enemy to tempt them, and are led to say and do that of which under other circumstances they would never have been guilty. The disciple of Christ who in our day disguises his faith through dread of suffering or reproach, denies his Lord as really as did Peter in the judgment hall.

Peter tried to show no interest in the trial of his Master, but his heart was wrung with sorrow as he heard the cruel taunts, and saw the abuse He was suffering. More than this, he was surprised and angry that Jesus should humiliate Himself and His followers by submitting to such treatment. In order to conceal his true feelings, he endeavored to join with the persecutors of Jesus in their untimely jests. But his appearance was unnatural. He was acting a lie, and while seeking to talk unconcernedly he could not restrain expressions of indignation at the abuse heaped upon his Master.

Attention was called to him the second time, and he was again charged with being a follower of Jesus. He now declared with an oath, "I do not know the man." Still another opportunity was given him. An hour had passed, when one of the servants of the high priest, being a near kinsman of the man whose ear Peter had cut off, asked him, "Did not I see thee in the garden with Him?" "Surely thou art one of them; for thou art a Galilean, and thy speech agreeth thereto." At this Peter flew into a rage. The disciples of Jesus were noted for the purity of their language, and in order fully to deceive his questioners, and justify his assumed character, Peter now denied his Master with cursing and swearing. Again the cock crew. Peter heard it then, and he remembered the words of Jesus, "Before the cock crow twice, thou shalt deny me thrice." Mark 14:30.

While the degrading oaths were fresh upon Peter's lips, and the shrill crowing of the cock was still ringing in his ears, the Saviour turned from the frowning judges, and looked full upon His poor disciple. At the same time Peter's eyes were drawn to his Master. In that gentle countenance he read deep pity and sorrow, but there was no anger there.

The sight of that pale, suffering face, those quivering lips, that look of compassion and forgiveness, pierced his heart like an arrow. Conscience was aroused. Memory was active. Peter called to mind his promise of a few short hours before that he would go with his Lord to prison and to death. He remembered his grief when the Saviour told him in the upper chamber that he would deny his Lord thrice that same night. Peter had just declared that he knew not Jesus, but he now realized with bitter grief how well his Lord knew him, and how accurately He had read his heart, the falseness of which was unknown even to himself.

A tide of memories rushed over him. The Saviour's tender mercy, His kindness and longsuffering, His gentleness and patience toward His erring disciples, — all was remembered. He recalled the caution, "Simon, behold, Satan hath desired to have you, that he may sift you as wheat. But I have prayed for thee, that thy faith fail not." Luke 22:31,32. He reflected with horror upon his own ingratitude, his falsehood, his perjury. Once more he looked at his Master, and saw a sacrilegious hand raised to smite Him in the face. Unable longer to endure the scene, he rushed, heartbroken, from the hall.

He pressed on in solitude and darkness, he knew not and cared not whither. At last he found himself in Gethsemane. The scene of a few hours before came vividly to his mind. The suffering face of his Lord, stained with bloody sweat and convulsed with anguish, rose before him. He remembered with bitter remorse that Jesus had wept and agonized in prayer alone, while those who should have united with Him in that trying hour were sleeping. He remembered His solemn charge, "Watch and pray, that ye enter not into temptation." Matthew 26:41. He witnessed again the scene in the judgment hall. It was torture to his bleeding heart to know that he had added the heaviest burden to the Saviour's humiliation and grief. On the very spot where Jesus had poured out His soul in agony to His Father, Peter fell upon his face, and wished that he might die.

It was in sleeping when Jesus bade him watch and pray that Peter had prepared the way for his great sin. All the disciples, by sleeping in that critical hour, sustained a great loss. Christ knew the fiery ordeal through which they were to pass. He knew how Satan would work to paralyze their senses that they might be unready for the trial. Therefore it was that He gave them warning. Had those hours in the garden been spent in watching and prayer, Peter would not have been left to depend upon his own feeble strength. He would not have denied his Lord. Had the disciples watched with Christ in His agony, they would have been prepared to behold His suffering upon the cross. They would have understood in some degree the nature of His overpowering anguish. They would have been able to recall His words that foretold His sufferings, His death, and His resurrection. Amid the gloom of the most trying hour, some rays of hope would have lighted up the darkness and sustained their faith.

As soon as it was day, the Sanhedrin again assembled, and again Jesus was brought into the council room. He had declared Himself the Son of God, and they had construed His words into a charge against Him. But they could not condemn Him on this, for many of them had not been present at the night session, and they had not heard His words. And they knew that the Roman tribunal would find in them nothing worthy of death. But if from His own lips they could all hear those words repeated, their object might be gained. His claim to the Messiahship they might construe into a seditious political claim.

134

"Art Thou the Christ?" they said, "tell us." But Christ remained silent. They continued to ply Him with questions. At last in tones of mournful pathos He answered, "If I tell you, ye will not believe; and if I also ask you, ye will not answer Me, nor let Me go." But that they might be left without excuse He added the solemn warning, "Hereafter shall the Son of man sit on the right hand of the power of God.

"Art Thou then the Son of God?" they asked with one voice. He said unto them, "Ye say that I am." They cried out, "What need we any further witness? for we ourselves have heard of His own mouth."

And so by the third condemnation of the Jewish authorities, Jesus was to die. All that was now necessary, they thought, was for the Romans to ratify this condemnation, and deliver Him into their hands.

Then came the third scene of abuse and mockery, worse even than that received from the ignorant rabble. In the very presence of the priests and rulers, and with their sanction, this took place. Every feeling of sympathy or humanity had gone out of their hearts. If their arguments were weak, and failed to silence His voice, they had other weapons, such as in all ages have been used to silence heretics, — suffering, and violence, and death.

When the condemnation of Jesus was pronounced by the judges, a Satanic fury took possession of the people. The roar of voices was like that of wild beasts. The crowd made a rush toward Jesus, crying, He is guilty, put Him to death!

Had it not been for the Roman soldiers, Jesus would not have lived to be nailed to the cross of Calvary. He would have been torn in pieces before His judges, had not Roman authority interfered, and by force of arms restrained the violence of the mob.

Heathen men were angry at the brutal treatment of one against whom nothing had been proved. The Roman officers declared that the Jews in pronouncing condemnation upon Jesus were infringing upon the Roman power, and that it was even against the Jewish law to condemn a man to death upon his own testimony. This intervention brought a momentary lull in the proceedings; but the Jewish leaders were dead alike to pity and to shame.

Priests and rulers forgot the dignity of their office, and abused the Son of God with foul epithets. They taunted Him with His parentage. They declared that His presumption in proclaiming Himself the Messiah made Him deserving of the most ignominious death. The most dissolute men engaged in infamous abuse of the Saviour. An old garment was thrown over His head, and His persecutors struck Him in the face, saying, "Prophesy unto us, Thou Christ, Who is he that smote Thee?" When the garment was removed, one poor wretch spat in His face.

The angels of God faithfully recorded every insulting look, word, and act, against their beloved Commander. One day the base men who scorned and spat upon the calm, pale face of Christ, will look upon it in its glory, shining brighter than the sun.

Judas

The history of Judas presents the sad ending of a life that might have been honored of God. Had Judas died before his last journey to Jerusalem, he would have been regarded as a man worthy of a place among the Twelve, and one who would be greatly missed. The abhorrence which has followed him through the centuries would not have existed, but for the attributes revealed at the close of his history. But it was for a purpose that his character was laid open to the world. It was to be a warning to all who, like him, should betray sacred trusts.

A little before the Passover, Judas had renewed his contract with the priests to deliver Jesus into their hands. Then it was arranged that the Saviour should be taken at one of His resorts for meditation and prayer. Since the feast at the house of Simon, Judas had had opportunity to reflect upon the deed which he had covenanted to perform, but his purpose was unchanged. For thirty pieces of silver — the price of a slave — he sold the Lord of Glory to ignominy and death.

Judas had naturally a strong love for money; but he had not always been corrupt enough to do such a deed as this. He had fostered the evil spirit of avarice until it had become the ruling motive of his life. The love of mammon overbalanced his love for Christ. Through becoming the slave of one vice he gave himself to Satan, to be driven to any lengths in sin.

Judas had joined the disciples when multitudes were following Christ. The Saviour's teaching moved their hearts as they hung entranced upon His words, spoken in the synagogue, by the seaside, upon the mount. Judas saw the sick, the lame, the blind, flock to Jesus from the towns and cities. He saw the dying laid at His feet. He witnessed the Saviour's mighty works in healing the sick, casting out devils, and raising the dead. He felt in his own person the evidence of Christ's power. He recognized the teaching of Christ as superior to all that he had ever heard. He loved the great Teacher, and desired to be with Him. He felt a desire to be changed in character and life, and he hoped to experience this through connecting himself with Jesus. The Saviour did not repulse Judas. He gave him a place among the Twelve. He trusted him to do the work of an evangelist. He endowed him with power to heal the sick and to cast out devils. But Judas did not come to the point of surrendering himself fully to Christ. He did not give up his worldly ambition or his love of money. While he accepted the position of a minister of Christ, he did not bring himself under the divine molding. He felt that he could retain his own judgment and opinions, and he cultivated a disposition to criticize and accuse.

Judas was highly regarded by the disciples, and had great influence over them. He himself had a high opinion of his own qualifications, and looked upon his brethren as greatly inferior to him in judgment and ability. They did not see their opportunities, he thought, and take advantage of circumstances. The church would never prosper with such short-sighted men as leaders. Peter was impetuous; he would move without consideration. John, who was treasuring up the truths that fell from Christ's lips, was looked upon by Judas as a poor financier. Matthew, whose training had taught him accuracy in all things, was very particular in regard to honesty, and he was ever contemplating the words of Christ, and became so absorbed in them that, as Judas thought, he could not be trusted to do sharp, far-seeing business. Thus Judas summed up all the disciples, and flattered himself that the church would often be brought into perplexity and embarrassment if it were

136   (716-717)

not for his ability as a manager. Judas regarded himself as the capable one, who could not be overreached. In his own estimation he was an honor to the cause, and as such he always represented himself.

Judas was blinded to his own weakness of character, and Christ placed him where he would have an opportunity to see and correct this. As treasurer for the disciples, he was called upon to provide for the needs of the little company, and to relieve the necessities of the poor. When in the Passover chamber Jesus said to him, "That thou doest, do quickly" (John 13:27), the disciples thought He had bidden him buy what was needed for the feast, or give something to the poor. In ministering to others, Judas might have developed an unselfish spirit. But while listening daily to the lessons of Christ and witnessing His unselfish life, Judas indulged his covetous disposition. The small sums that came into his hands were a continual temptation. Often when he did a little service for Christ, or devoted time to religious purposes, he paid himself out of this meager fund. In his own eyes these pretexts served to excuse his action; but in God's sight he was a thief.

Christ's oft-repeated statement that His kingdom was not of this world offended Judas. He had marked out a line upon which he expected Christ to work. He had planned that John the Baptist should be delivered from prison. But lo, John was left to be beheaded. And Jesus, instead of asserting His royal right and avenging the death of John, retired with His disciples into a country place. Judas wanted more aggressive warfare. He thought that if Jesus would not prevent the disciples from carrying out their schemes, the work would be more successful. He marked the increasing enmity of the Jewish leaders, and saw their challenge unheeded when they demanded from Christ a sign from heaven. His heart was open to unbelief, and the enemy supplied thoughts of questioning and rebellion. Why did Jesus dwell so much upon that which was discouraging? Why did He predict trial and persecution for Himself and for His disciples? The prospect of having a high place in the new kingdom had led Judas to espouse the cause of Christ. Were his hopes to be disappointed? Judas had not decided that Jesus was not the Son of God; but he was questioning, and seeking to find some explanation of His mighty works.

Notwithstanding the Saviour's own teaching, Judas was continually advancing the idea that Christ would reign as king in Jerusalem. At the feeding of the five thousand he tried to bring this about. On this occasion Judas assisted in distributing the food to the hungry multitude. He had an opportunity to see the benefit which it was in his power to impart to others. He felt the satisfaction that always comes in service to God. He helped to bring the sick and suffering from among the multitude to Christ. He saw what relief, what joy and gladness, come to human hearts through the healing power of the Restorer. He might have comprehended the methods of Christ. But he was blinded by his own selfish desires. Judas was first to take advantage of the enthusiasm excited by the miracle of the loaves. It was he who set on foot the project to take Christ by force and make Him king. His hopes were high. His disappointment was bitter.

Christ's discourse in the synagogue concerning the bread of life was the turning point in the history of Judas. He heard the words, "Except ye eat the flesh of the Son of man, and drink His blood, ye have no life in you." John 6:53. He saw that Christ was offering spiritual rather than worldly good. He regarded himself as far-sighted, and thought he could see that Jesus would have no honor, and that He could bestow no high position upon His followers. He determined not to unite himself so closely to Christ but that he could draw away. He would watch. And he did watch.

From that time he expressed doubts that confused the disciples. He introduced controversies and misleading sentiments, repeating the arguments urged by the scribes and Pharisees against the claims of Christ. All the little and large troubles and crosses, the difficulties and the apparent hindrances to the advancement of the gospel, Judas interpreted as evidences against its truthfulness. He would introduce texts of Scripture that had no connection with the truths Christ was presenting. These texts, separated from their connection, perplexed the disciples, and increased the discouragement that was constantly pressing upon them. Yet all this was done by Judas in such a way as to make it appear that he was conscientious. And while the disciples were searching for evidence to confirm the words of the great Teacher, Judas would lead them almost imperceptibly on another track. Thus in a very religious, and apparently wise way, he was presenting matters in a different light from that in which Jesus had given them, and attaching to His words a meaning that He had not conveyed. His suggestions were constantly exciting an ambitious desire for temporal preferment, and thus turning the disciples from the important things they should have considered. The dissension as to which of them should be greatest was generally excited by Judas.

When Jesus presented to the rich young ruler the condition of discipleship, Judas was displeased. He thought that a mistake had been made. If such men as this ruler could be connected with the believers, they would help sustain Christ's cause. If Judas were only received as a counselor, he thought, he could suggest many plans for the advantage of the little church. His principles and methods would differ somewhat from Christ's, but in these things he thought himself wiser than Christ.

In all that Christ said to His disciples, there was something with which, in heart, Judas disagreed. Under his influence the leaven of disaffection was fast doing its work. The disciples did not see the real agency in all this; but Jesus saw that Satan was communicating his attributes to Judas, and thus opening up a channel through which to influence the other disciples. This, a year before the betrayal, Christ declared. "Have not I chosen you twelve," He said, "and one of you is a devil?" John 6:70.

Yet Judas made no open opposition, nor seemed to question the Saviour's lessons. He made no outward murmur until the time of the feast in Simon's house. When Mary anointed the Saviour's feet, Judas manifested his covetous disposition. At the reproof from Jesus his very spirit seemed turned to gall. Wounded pride and desire for

---

"Judas now cast himself at the feet of Jesus, acknowledging Him to be the Son of God, and entreating Him to deliver Himself. The Saviour did not reproach His betrayer. . . . his confession was forced from his guilty soul by an awful sense of condemnation . . . but he felt no deep, heartbreaking grief that he had betrayed the spotless Son of God . . . Yet Jesus spoke no word of condemnation. He looked pityingly upon Judas, and said, 'For this hour came I into the world.'"

---

revenge broke down the barriers, and the greed so long indulged held him in control. This will be the experience of every one who persists in tampering with sin. The elements of depravity that are not resisted and overcome, respond to Satan's temptation, and the soul is led captive at his will.

But Judas was not yet wholly hardened. Even after he had twice pledged himself to betray the Saviour, there was opportunity for repentance. At the Passover supper Jesus proved His divinity by revealing the traitor's purpose. He tenderly included Judas in the ministry to the disciples. But the last appeal of love was unheeded. Then the case of Judas was decided, and the feet that Jesus had washed, went forth to the betrayer's work.

Judas reasoned that if Jesus was to be crucified, the event must come to pass. His own act in betraying the Saviour would not change the result. If Jesus was not to die, it would only force Him to deliver Himself. At all events, Judas would gain something by his treachery. He counted that he had made a sharp bargain in betraying his Lord.

Judas did not, however, believe that Christ would permit Himself to be arrested. In betraying Him, it was his purpose to teach Him a lesson. He intended to play a part that would make the Saviour careful thenceforth to treat him with due respect. But Judas knew not that he was giving Christ up to death. How often, as the Saviour taught in parables, the scribes and Pharisees had been carried away with His striking illustrations. How often they had pronounced judgment against themselves. Often when the truth was brought home to their hearts, they had been filled with rage, and had taken up stones to cast at Him; but again and again He had made His escape. Since He had escaped so many snares, thought Judas, He certainly would not allow Himself to be taken.

Judas decided to put the matter to the test. If Jesus really was the Messiah, the people, for whom He had done so much, would rally about Him, and would proclaim Him king. This would forever settle many minds that were now in uncertainty. Judas would have the credit of having placed the king on David's throne. And this act would secure to him the first position, next to Christ, in the new kingdom.

The false disciple acted his part in betraying Jesus. In the garden, when he said to the leaders of the mob, "Whomsoever I shall kiss, that same is He; hold Him fast" (Matthew 26:48), he fully believed that Christ would escape out of their hands. Then if they should blame him, he could say, Did I not tell you to hold Him fast?

Judas beheld the captors of Christ, acting upon his words, bind Him firmly. In amazement he saw that the Saviour suffered Himself to be led away. Anxiously he followed Him from the garden to the trial before the Jewish rulers. At every movement he looked for Him to surprise His enemies, by appearing before them as the Son of God, and setting at naught all their plots and power. But as hour after hour went by, and Jesus submitted to all the abuse heaped upon Him, a terrible fear came to the traitor that he had sold his Master to His death.

As the trial drew to a close, Judas could endure the torture of his guilty conscience no longer. Suddenly a hoarse voice rang through the hall, sending a thrill of terror to all hearts: He is innocent; spare Him, O Caiaphas!

The tall form of Judas was now seen pressing through the startled throng. His face was pale and haggard, and great drops of sweat stood on his forehead. Rushing to the throne of judgment, he threw down before the high priest the pieces of silver that had been the price of his Lord's betrayal. Eagerly grasping the robe of Caiaphas, he implored him to release Jesus, declaring that He had done nothing worthy of death. Caiaphas angrily shook him off, but was confused, and knew not what to say. The perfidy of the priests was revealed. It was evident that they had bribed the disciple to betray his Master.

"I have sinned," again cried Judas, "in that I have betrayed the innocent blood." But the high priest, regaining his self-possession, answered with scorn, "What is that to us? See thou to that. Matthew 27:4. The priests had been willing to make Judas their tool; but they despised his baseness. When he turned to them with confession, they spurned him.

Judas now cast himself at the feet of Jesus, acknowledging Him to be the Son of God, and entreating Him to deliver Himself. The Saviour did not reproach His betrayer. He knew that Judas did not repent; his confession was forced from his guilty soul by an awful sense of condemnation and a looking for of judgment, but he felt no deep, heartbreaking grief that he had betrayed the spotless Son of God, and denied the Holy One of Israel. Yet Jesus spoke no word of condemnation. He looked pityingly upon Judas, and said, "For this hour came I into the world."

A murmur of surprise ran through the assembly. With amazement they beheld the forbearance of Christ toward His betrayer. Again there swept over them the conviction that this man was more than mortal. But if He was the Son of God, they questioned, why did He not free Himself from His bonds, and triumph over His accusers?

Judas saw that his entreaties were in vain, and he rushed from the hall exclaiming, It is too late! It is too late! He felt that he could not live to see Jesus crucified, and in despair went out and hanged himself.

Later that same day, on the road from Pilate's hall to Calvary, there came an interruption to the shouts and jeers of the wicked throng who were leading Jesus to the place of crucifixion. As they passed a retired spot, they saw at the foot of a lifeless tree, the body of Judas. It was a most revolting sight. His weight had broken the cord by which he had hanged himself to the tree. In falling, his body had been horribly mangled, and dogs were now devouring it. His remains were immediately buried out of sight; but there was less mockery among the throng, and many a pale face revealed the thoughts within. Retribution seemed already visiting those who were guilty of the blood of Jesus.

In Pilate's Judgment Hall

In the judgment hall of Pilate, the Roman governor, Christ stands bound as a prisoner. About Him are the guard of soldiers, and the hall is fast filling with spectators. Just outside the entrance are the judges of the Sanhedrin, priests, rulers, elders, and the mob.

After condemning Jesus, the council of the Sanhedrin had come to Pilate to have the sentence confirmed and executed. But these Jewish officials would not enter the Roman judgment hall. According to their ceremonial law they would be defiled thereby, and thus prevented from taking part in the feast of the Passover. In their blindness they did not see that murderous hatred had defiled their hearts. They did not see that Christ was the real Passover lamb, and that, since they had rejected Him, the great feast had for them lost its significance.

When the Saviour was brought into the judgment hall, Pilate looked upon Him with no friendly eyes. The Roman governor had been called from his bedchamber in haste, and he determined to do his work as quickly as possible. He was prepared to deal with the prisoner with magisterial severity. Assuming his severest expression, he turned to see what kind of man he had to examine, that he had been called from his repose at so early an hour. He knew that it must be some one whom the Jewish authorities were anxious to have tried and punished with haste.

Pilate looked at the men who had Jesus in charge, and then his gaze rested searchingly on Jesus. He had had to deal with all kinds of criminals; but never before had a man bearing marks of such goodness and nobility been brought before him. On His face he saw no sign of guilt, no expression of fear, no boldness or defiance. He saw a man of calm and dignified bearing, whose countenance bore not the marks of a criminal, but the signature of heaven.

Christ's appearance made a favorable impression upon Pilate. His better nature was roused. He had heard of Jesus and His works. His wife had told him something of the wonderful deeds performed by the Galilean prophet, who cured the sick and raised the dead. Now this revived as a dream in Pilate's mind. He recalled rumors that he had heard from several sources. He resolved to demand of the Jews their charges against the prisoner.

Who is this man, and wherefore have ye brought Him? he said. What accusation bring ye against Him? The Jews were disconcerted. Knowing that they could not substantiate their charges against Christ, they did not desire a public examination. They answered that He was a deceiver called Jesus of Nazareth.

Again Pilate asked, "What accusation bring ye against this man?" The priests did not answer his question, but in words that showed their irritation, they said. "If He were not a malefactor, we would not have delivered Him up unto thee." When those composing the Sanhedrin, the first men of the nation, bring to you a man they deem worthy of death, is there need to ask for an accusation against him? They hoped to impress Pilate with a sense of their importance, and thus lead him to accede to their request without going through many preliminaries. They were eager to have their sentence ratified; for they knew that the people who had witnessed Christ's marvelous works could tell a story very different from the fabrication they themselves were now rehearsing.

The priests thought that with the weak and vacillating Pilate they could carry through their plans without trouble. Before this he had signed the death warrant hastily, condemning to death men they knew were not worthy of death. In his estimation the life of a prisoner was of little

This chapter is based on Matthew 27:2, 11-31;
Mark 15: 1-20; Luke 23:1-25; John 18:28-40; 19:1-16.

account; whether he were innocent or guilty was of no special consequence. The priests hoped that Pilate would now inflict the death penalty on Jesus without giving Him a hearing. This they besought as a favor on the occasion of their great national festival.

But there was something in the prisoner that held Pilate back from this. He dared not do it. He read the purpose of the priests. He remembered how, not long before, Jesus had raised Lazarus, a man that had been dead four days; and he determined to know, before signing the sentence of condemnation, what were the charges against Him, and whether they could be proved.

If your judgment is sufficient, he said, why bring the prisoner to me? "Take ye Him, and judge Him according to your law." Thus pressed, the priests said that they had already passed sentence upon Him, but that they must have Pilate's sentence to render their condemnation valid. What is your sentence? Pilate asked. The death sentence, they answered, but it is not lawful for us to put any man to death. They asked Pilate to take their word as to Christ's guilt, and enforce their sentence. They would take the responsibility of the result.

Pilate was not a just or a conscientious judge; but weak though he was in moral power, he refused to grant this request. He would not condemn Jesus until a charge had been brought against Him.

The priests were in a dilemma. They saw that they must cloak their hypocrisy under the thickest concealment. They must not allow it to appear that Christ had been arrested on religious grounds. Were this put forward as a reason, their proceedings would have no weight with Pilate. They must make it appear that Jesus was working against the common law; then He could be punished as a political offender. Tumults and insurrection against the Roman government were constantly arising among the Jews. With these revolts the Romans had dealt very rigorously, and they were constantly on the watch to repress everything that could lead to an outbreak.

Only a few days before this the Pharisees had tried to entrap Christ with the question, "Is it lawful for us to give tribute unto Caesar?" But Christ had unveiled their hypocrisy. The Romans who were present had seen the utter failure of the plotters, and their discomfiture at His answer, "Render therefore unto Caesar the things which be Caesar's." Luke 20:22-25.

Now the priests thought to make it appear that on this occasion Christ had taught what they hoped He would teach. In their extremity they called false witnesses to their aid, "and they began to accuse Him, saying, We found this fellow perverting the nation, and forbidding to give tribute to Caesar, saying that He Himself is Christ a king." Three charges, each without foundation. The priests knew this, but they were willing to commit perjury could they but secure their end.

Pilate saw through their purpose. He did not believe that the prisoner had plotted against the government. His meek and humble appearance was altogether out of harmony with the charge. Pilate was convinced that a deep plot had been laid to destroy an innocent man who stood in the way of the Jewish dignitaries. Turning to Jesus he asked, "Art Thou the King of the Jews?" The Saviour answered, "Thou sayest it." And as He spoke, His countenance lighted up as if a sunbeam were shining upon it.

When they heard His answer, Caiaphas and those that were with him called Pilate to witness that Jesus had admitted the crime with which He was charged. With noisy cries, priests, scribes, and rulers demanded that He be sentenced to death. The cries were taken up by the mob, and the uproar was deafening. Pilate was confused. Seeing that Jesus made no answer to His accusers, Pilate said to Him, "Answerest Thou nothing? behold how many things they witness against Thee. But Jesus yet answered nothing."

Standing behind Pilate, in view of all in the court, Christ heard the abuse; but to all the false charges against Him, He answered not a word. His whole bearing gave evidence of conscious innocence. He stood unmoved by the fury of the waves that beat about Him. It was as if the heavy surges of wrath, rising higher and higher, like the waves of the boisterous ocean, broke about Him, but did not touch Him. He stood silent, but His silence was eloquence. It was a light shining from the inner to the outer man.

Pilate was astonished at His bearing. Does this man disregard the proceedings because He does not care to save His life? he asked himself. As he looked at Jesus, bearing insult and mockery without retaliation, he felt that He could not be as unrighteous and unjust as were the clamoring priests. Hoping to gain the truth from Him and to escape the tumult of the crowd, Pilate took Jesus aside with him, and again questioned, "Art Thou the King of the Jews?"

Jesus did not directly answer this question. He knew that the Holy Spirit was striving with Pilate, and He gave him opportunity to acknowledge his conviction. "Sayest thou this thing of thyself," He asked, "or did others tell it thee of Me?" That is, was it the accusations of the priests, or a desire to receive light from Christ, that prompted Pilate's question? Pilate understood Christ's meaning; but pride arose in his heart. He would not acknowledge the conviction that pressed upon him. "Am I a Jew?" he said. "Thine own nation and the chief priests have delivered Thee unto me. What hast Thou done?"

Pilate's golden opportunity had passed. Yet Jesus did not leave him without further light. While He did not directly answer Pilate's question, He plainly stated His own mission. He gave Pilate to understand that He was not seeking an earthly throne.

"My kingdom is not of this world," He said; "if My kingdom were of this world, then would My servants fight, that I should not be delivered to the Jews; but now is My kingdom not from hence. Pilate therefore said unto Him, Art Thou a king then? Jesus answered, Thou sayest that I am a king. To this end was I born, and for this cause came I into the world, that I should bear witness unto the truth. Every one that is of the truth heareth My voice."

Christ affirmed that His word was in itself a key which would unlock the mystery to those who were prepared to receive it. It had a self-commending power, and this was the secret of the spread of His kingdom of truth. He desired Pilate to understand that only by receiving and appropriating truth could his ruined nature be reconstructed.

Pilate had a desire to know the truth. His mind was confused. He eagerly grasped the words of the Saviour, and his heart was stirred with a great longing to know what it really was, and how he could obtain it. "What is truth?" he inquired. But he did not wait for an answer. The tumult outside recalled him to the interests of the hour; for the priests were clamorous for immediate action. Going out to the Jews, he declared emphatically, "I find in Him no fault at all."

These words from a heathen judge were a scathing rebuke to the perfidy and falsehood of the rulers of Israel who were accusing the Saviour. As the priests and elders heard this from Pilate, their disappointment and rage knew no bounds. They had long plotted and waited for this opportunity. As they saw the prospect of the release of Jesus, they seemed ready to tear Him in pieces. They loudly denounced Pilate, and threatened him with the censure of the Roman government. They accused him of refusing to condemn Jesus, who, they affirmed had set Himself up against Caesar.

Angry voices were now heard, declaring that the seditious influence of Jesus was well known throughout the country. The priests said, "He stirreth up the people, teaching throughout all Jewry, beginning from Galilee to this place."

Pilate at this time had no thought of condemning Jesus. He knew that the Jews had accused Him through hatred and prejudice. He knew what his duty was. Justice demanded that Christ should be immediately released. But Pilate dreaded the ill will of the people. Should he refuse to give Jesus into their hands, a tumult would be raised, and this he feared to meet. When he heard that Christ was from Galilee, he decided to send Him to Herod, the ruler of that province, who was then in Jerusalem. By this course, Pilate thought to shift the responsibility of the trial from himself to Herod. He also thought this a good opportunity to heal an old quarrel between himself and Herod. And so it proved. The two magistrates made friends over the trial of the Saviour.

Pilate delivered Jesus again to the soldiers, and amid the jeers and insults of the mob He was hurried to the judgment hall of Herod. "When Herod saw Jesus, he was exceeding glad." He had never before met the Saviour, but "he was desirous to see Him of a long season, because he had heard many things of Him; and he hoped to have seen some miracle done by Him." This Herod was he whose hands were stained with the blood of John the Baptist. When Herod first heard of Jesus, he was terror-stricken, and said, "It is John, whom I beheaded; he is risen from the dead;" "therefore mighty works do show forth themselves in him." Mark 6:16; Matthew 14:2. Yet Herod desired to see Jesus. Now there was opportunity to save the life of this prophet, and the king hoped to banish forever from his mind the memory of that bloody head brought to him in a charger. He also desired to have his curiosity gratified, and thought that if Christ were given any prospect of release, He would do anything that was asked of Him.

A large company of the priests and elders had accompanied Christ to Herod. And when the Saviour was brought in, these dignitaries, all speaking excitedly, urged their

> ❝Pilate had a desire to know the truth. His mind was confused. He eagerly grasped the words of the Saviour, and his heart was stirred with a great longing to know what it really was, and how he could obtain it. 'What is truth?' he inquired.❞

accusations against Him. But Herod paid little regard to their charges. He commanded silence, desiring an opportunity to question Christ. He ordered that the fetters of Christ should be unloosed, at the same time charging His enemies with roughly treating Him. Looking with compassion into the serene face of the world's Redeemer, he read in it only wisdom and purity. He as well as Pilate was satisfied that Christ had been accused through malice and envy.

Herod questioned Christ in many words, but throughout the Saviour maintained a profound silence. At the command of the king, the decrepit and maimed were then called in, and Christ was ordered to prove His claims by working a miracle. Men say that Thou canst heal the sick, said Herod. I am anxious to see that Thy widespread fame has not been belied. Jesus did not respond, and Herod still continued to urge: If Thou canst work miracles for others, work them now for Thine own good, and it will serve Thee a good purpose. Again he commanded, Show us a sign that

142

Thou hast the power with which rumor hath accredited Thee. But Christ was as one who heard and saw not. The Son of God had taken upon Himself man's nature. He must do as man must do in like circumstances. Therefore He would not work a miracle to save Himself the pain and humiliation that man must endure when placed in a similar position.

Herod promised that if Christ would perform some miracle in his presence, He should be released. Christ's accusers had seen with their own eyes the mighty works wrought by His power. They had heard Him command the grave to give up its dead. They had seen the dead come forth obedient to His voice. Fear seized them lest He should now work a miracle. Of all things they most dreaded an exhibition of His power. Such a manifestation would prove a deathblow to their plans, and would perhaps cost them their lives. Again the priests and rulers, in great anxiety, urged their accusations against Him. Raising their voices, they declared, He is a traitor, a blasphemer. He works His miracles through the power given Him by Beelzebub, the prince of the devils. The hall became a scene of confusion, some crying one thing and some another.

Herod's conscience was now far less sensitive than when he had trembled with horror at the request of Herodias for the head of John the Baptist. For a time he had felt the keen stings of remorse for his terrible act; but his moral perceptions had become more and more degraded by his licentious life. Now his heart had become so hardened that he could even boast of the punishment he had inflicted upon John for daring to reprove him. And he now threatened Jesus, declaring repeatedly that he had power to release or to condemn Him. But no sign from Jesus gave evidence that He heard a word.

Herod was irritated by this silence. It seemed to indicate utter indifference to his authority. To the vain and pompous king, open rebuke would have been less offensive than to be thus ignored. Again he angrily threatened Jesus, who still remained unmoved and silent.

The mission of Christ in this world was not to gratify idle curiosity. He came to heal the brokenhearted. Could He have spoken any word to heal the bruises of sin-sick souls, He would not have kept silent. But He had no words for those who would but trample the truth under their unholy feet.

Christ might have spoken words to Herod that would have pierced the ears of the hardened king. He might have stricken him with fear and trembling by laying before him the full iniquity of his life, and the horror of his approaching doom. But Christ's silence was the severest rebuke that He could have given. Herod had rejected the truth spoken to him by the greatest of the prophets, and no other message was he to receive. Not a word had the Majesty of Heaven for him. That ear that had ever been open to human woe, had no room for Herod's commands. Those eyes that had ever rested upon the penitent sinner in pitying, forgiv-

ing love, had no look to bestow upon Herod. Those lips that had uttered the most impressive truth, that in tones of tenderest entreaty had pleaded with the most sinful and the most degraded, were closed to the haughty king who felt no need of a Saviour.

Herod's face grew dark with passion. Turning to the multitude, he angrily denounced Jesus as an impostor. Then to Christ he said, If you will give no evidence of your claim, I will deliver you up to the soldiers and the people. They may succeed in making you speak. If you are an impostor, death at their hands is only what you merit; if you are the Son of God, save yourself by working a miracle.

No sooner were these words spoken, than a rush was made for Christ. Like wild beasts, the crowd darted upon their prey. Jesus was dragged this way and that, Herod joining the mob in seeking to humiliate the Son of God. Had not the Roman soldiers interposed, and forced back the maddened throng, the Saviour would have been torn in pieces.

"Herod with his men of war set Him at naught, and mocked Him, and arrayed Him in a gorgeous robe." The Roman soldiers joined in this abuse. All that these wicked, corrupt soldiers, helped on by Herod and the Jewish dignitaries, could instigate, was heaped upon the Saviour. Yet His divine patience failed not.

Christ's persecutors had tried to measure His character by their own; they had represented Him as vile as themselves. But back of all the present appearance another scene intruded itself, — a scene which they will one day see in all its glory. There were some who trembled in Christ's presence. While the rude throng were bowing in mockery before Him, some who came forward for that purpose turned back, afraid and silenced. Herod was convicted. The last rays of merciful light were shining upon his sin-hardened heart. He felt that this was no common man; for divinity had flashed through humanity. At the very time when Christ was encompassed by mockers, adulterers, and murderers, Herod felt that he was beholding a God upon His throne.

Hardened as he was, Herod dared not ratify the condemnation of Christ. He wished to relieve himself of the terrible responsibility, and he sent Jesus back to the Roman judgment hall.

Pilate was disappointed and much displeased. When the Jews returned with their prisoner, he asked impatiently what they would have him do. He reminded them that he had already examined Jesus, and found no fault in Him; he told them that they had brought complaints against Him, but they had not been able to prove a single charge. He had sent Jesus to Herod, the tetrarch of Galilee, and one of their own nation, but he also had found in Him nothing worthy of death. "I will therefore chastise Him," Pilate said, "and release Him."

Here Pilate showed his weakness. He had declared that Jesus was innocent, yet he was willing for Him to be scourged to pacify His accusers. He would sacrifice justice and principle, in order to compromise with the mob. This placed him at a disadvantage. The crowd presumed upon his indecision, and clamored the more for the life of the prisoner. If at the first Pilate had stood firm, refusing to condemn a man whom he found guiltless, he would have broken the fatal chain that was to bind him in remorse and guilt as long as he lived. Had he carried out his convictions of right, the Jews would not have presumed to dictate to him. Christ would have been put to death, but the guilt would not have rested upon Pilate. But Pilate had taken step after step in the violation of his conscience. He had excused himself from judging with justice and equity, and he now found himself almost helpless in the hands of the priests and rulers. His wavering and indecision proved his ruin.

Even now Pilate was not left to act blindly. A message from God warned him from the deed he was about to commit. In answer to Christ's prayer, the wife of Pilate had been visited by an angel from heaven, and in a dream she had beheld the Saviour and conversed with Him. Pilate's wife was not a Jew, but as she looked upon Jesus in her dream, she had no doubt of His character or mission. She knew Him to be the Prince of God. She saw Him on trial in the judgment hall. She saw the hands tightly bound as the hands of a criminal. She saw Herod and his soldiers doing their dreadful work. She heard the priests and rulers, filled with envy and malice, madly accusing. She heard the words, "We have a law, and by our law He ought to die." She saw Pilate give Jesus to the scourging, after he had declared, "I find no fault in Him." She heard the condemnation pronounced by Pilate, and saw him give Christ up to His murderers. She saw the cross uplifted on Calvary. She saw the earth wrapped in darkness, and heard the mysterious cry, "It is finished." Still another scene met her gaze. She saw Christ seated upon the great white cloud, while the earth reeled in space, and His murderers fled from the presence of His glory. With a cry of horror she awoke, and at once wrote to Pilate words of warning.

While Pilate was hesitating as to what he should do, a messenger pressed through the crowd, and handed him the letter from his wife, which read, —

"Have thou nothing to do with that just man; for I have suffered many things this day in a dream because of Him."

Pilate's face grew pale. He was confused by his own conflicting emotions. But while he had been delaying to act, the priests and rulers were still further inflaming the minds of the people. Pilate was forced to action. He now bethought himself of a custom which might serve to secure Christ's release. It was customary at this feast to release some one prisoner whom the people might choose. This custom was of pagan invention; there was not a shadow of justice in it, but it was greatly prized by the Jews. The Roman authorities at this time held a prisoner named Barabbas, who was under sentence of death. This man had claimed to be the Messiah. He claimed authority to estab-

lish a different order of things, to set the world right. Under Satanic delusion he claimed that whatever he could obtain by theft and robbery was his own. He had done wonderful things through Satanic agencies, he had gained a following among the people, and had excited sedition against the Roman government. Under cover of religious enthusiasm he was a hardened and desperate villain, bent on rebellion and cruelty. By giving the people a choice between this man and the innocent Saviour, Pilate thought to arouse them to a sense of justice. He hoped to gain their sympathy for Jesus in opposition to the priests and rulers. So, turning to the crowd, he said with great earnestness, "Whom will ye that I release unto you? Barabbas, or Jesus which is called Christ?"

Like the bellowing of wild beasts came the answer of the mob, Release unto us Barabbas. Louder and louder swelled the cry, Barabbas! Barabbas! Thinking that the people had not understood his question, Pilate asked, "Will ye that I release unto you the King of the Jews?" But they cried out again, "Away with this man, and release unto us Barabbas!" "What shall I do then with Jesus which is called Christ." Pilate asked. Again the surging multitude roared like demons. Demons themselves, in human form, were in the crowd, and what could be expected but the answer, "Let Him be crucified"?

Pilate was troubled. He had not thought it would come to that. He shrank from delivering an innocent man to the most ignominious and cruel death that could be inflicted. After the roar of voices had ceased, he turned to the people, saying, "Why, what evil hath He done?" But the case had gone too far for argument. It was not evidence of Christ's innocence that they wanted, but His condemnation.

Still Pilate endeavored to save Him. "He said unto them the third time, Why, what evil hath He done? I have found no cause of death in Him. I will therefore chastise Him, and let Him go." But the very mention of His release stirred the people to a tenfold frenzy. "Crucify Him, crucify Him," they cried. Louder and louder swelled the storm that Pilate's indecision had called forth.

Jesus was taken, faint with weariness and covered with wounds, and scourged in the sight of the multitude. "And the soldiers led Him into the hall, called Praetorium, and they call together the whole band. And they clothed Him with purple, and platted a crown of thorns, and put it about His head, and began to salute Him, Hail, King of the Jews. And they . . . did spit upon Him, and bowing their knees worshiped Him." Occasionally some wicked hand snatched the reed that had been placed in His hand, and struck the crown upon His brow, forcing the thorns into His temples, and sending the blood trickling down His face and beard.

Wonder, O heavens! and be astonished, O earth! Behold the oppressor and the oppressed. A maddened throng enclose the Saviour of the world. Mocking and jeering are mingled with the coarse oaths of blasphemy. His lowly birth and humble life are commented upon by the unfeel-

ing mob. His claim to be the Son of God is ridiculed, and the vulgar jest and insulting sneer are passed from lip to lip.

Satan led the cruel mob in its abuse of the Saviour. It was his purpose to provoke Him to retaliation if possible, or to drive Him to perform a miracle to release Himself, and thus break up the plan of salvation. One stain upon His human life, one failure of His humanity to endure the terrible test, and the Lamb of God would have been an imperfect offering, and the redemption of man a failure. But He who by a command could bring the heavenly host to His aid, — He who could have driven that mob in terror from His sight by the flashing forth of His divine majesty, — submitted with perfect calmness to the coarsest insult and outrage.

Christ's enemies had demanded a miracle as evidence of His divinity. They had evidence far greater than any they had sought. As their cruelty degraded His torturers below humanity into the likeness of Satan, so did His meekness and patience exalt Jesus above humanity, and prove His kinship to God. His abasement was the pledge of His exaltation The blood drops of agony that from His wounded temples flowed down His face and beard were the pledge of His anointing with "the oil of gladness" (Hebrews 1:9.) as our great High Priest.

Satan's rage was great as he saw that all the abuse inflicted upon the Saviour had not forced the least murmur from His lips. Although He had taken upon Him the nature of man, He was sustained by a Godlike fortitude, and departed in no particular from the will of His Father.

When Pilate gave Jesus up to be scourged and mocked, he thought to excite the pity of the multitude. He hoped they would decide that this was sufficient punishment. Even the malice of the priests, he thought, would now be satisfied. But with keen perception the Jews saw the weakness of thus punishing a man who had been declared innocent. They knew that Pilate was trying to save the life of the prisoner, and they were determined that Jesus should not be released. To please and satisfy us, Pilate has scourged Him, they thought, and if we press the matter to a decided issue, we shall surely gain our end.

Pilate now sent for Barabbas to be brought into the court. He then presented the two prisoners side by side, and pointing to the Saviour he said in a voice of solemn entreaty, "Behold the man." "I bring Him forth to you, that ye may know that I find no fault in Him."

There stood the Son of God, wearing the robe of mockery and the crown of thorns. Stripped to the waist, His back showed the long, cruel stripes, from which the blood flowed freely. His face was stained with blood, and bore the marks of exhaustion and pain; but never had it appeared more beautiful than now. The Saviour's visage was not marred before His enemies. Every feature expressed gentleness and resignation and the tenderest pity for His cruel foes. In His manner there was no cowardly weakness, but the strength and dignity of longsuffering. In striking contrast was the prisoner at His side. Every line of the countenance of Barabbas proclaimed him the hardened ruffian that he was. The contrast spoke to every beholder. Some of the spectators were weeping. As they looked upon Jesus, their hearts were full of sympathy. Even the priests and rulers were convicted that He was all that He claimed to be.

The Roman soldiers that surrounded Christ were not all hardened; some were looking earnestly into His face for one evidence that He was a criminal or dangerous character. From time to time they would turn and cast a look of contempt upon Barabbas. It needed no deep insight to read him through and through. Again they would turn to the One upon trial. They looked at the divine sufferer with feelings of deep pity. The silent submission of Christ stamped upon their minds the scene, never to be effaced until they either acknowledged Him as the Christ, or by rejecting Him decided their own destiny.

Pilate was filled with amazement at the uncomplaining patience of the Saviour. He did not doubt that the sight of this man, in contrast with Barabbas, would move the Jews to sympathy. But he did not understand the fanatical hatred of the priests for Him, who, as the light of the world, had made manifest their darkness and error. They had moved the mob to a mad fury, and again priests, rulers, and people raised that awful cry, "Crucify Him! crucify Him!" At last, losing all patience with their unreasoning cruelty, Pilate cried out despairingly, "Take ye Him, and crucify Him; for I find no fault in Him."

The Roman governor, though familiar with cruel scenes, was moved with sympathy for the suffering prisoner, who, condemned and scourged, with bleeding brow and lacerated back, still had the bearing of a king upon his throne. But the priests declared, "We have a law, and by our law He ought to die, because He made Himself the Son of God."

Pilate was startled. He had no correct idea of Christ and His mission; but he had an indistinct faith in God and in beings superior to humanity. A thought that had once before passed through his mind now took more definite shape. He questioned whether it might not be a divine being that stood before him, clad in the purple robe of mockery, and crowned with thorns.

Again he went into the judgment hall, and said to Jesus, "Whence art thou?" But Jesus gave him no answer. The Saviour had spoken freely to Pilate, explaining His own mission as a witness to the truth. Pilate had disregarded the light. He had abused the high office of judge by yielding his principles and authority to the demands of the mob. Jesus had no further light for him. Vexed at His silence, Pilate said haughtily: —

"Speakest Thou not unto me? knowest Thou not that I have power to crucify Thee, and have power to release Thee?"

Jesus answered, "Thou couldst have no power at all against Me, except it were given thee from above; therefore he that delivered Me unto thee hath the greater sin."

Thus the pitying Saviour, in the midst of His intense suffering and grief, excused as far as possible the act of the Roman governor who gave Him up to be crucified. What a scene was this to hand down to the world for all time! What a light it sheds upon the character of Him who is the Judge of all the earth!

> **"**Jesus was taken, faint with weariness and covered with wounds, and scourged in the sight of the multitude. . . . Occasionally some wicked hand snatched the reed that had been placed in His hand, and struck the crown upon His brow, forcing the thorns into His temples, and sending the blood trickling down His face and beard. Wonder, O heavens! and be astonished, O earth!**"**

"He that delivered Me unto thee," said Jesus, "hath the greater sin." By this Christ meant Caiaphas, who, as high priest, represented the Jewish nation. They knew the principles that controlled the Roman authorities. They had had light in the prophecies that testified of Christ, and in His own teachings and miracles. The Jewish judges had received unmistakable evidence of the divinity of Him whom they condemned to death. And according to their light would they be judged.

The greatest guilt and heaviest responsibility belonged to those who stood in the highest places in the nation, the depositaries of sacred trusts that they were basely betraying. Pilate, Herod, and the Roman soldiers were comparatively ignorant of Jesus. They thought to please the priests and rulers by abusing Him. They had not the light which the Jewish nation had so abundantly received. Had the light been given to the soldiers, they would not have treated Christ as cruelly as they did.

Again Pilate proposed to release the Saviour. "But the Jews cried out saying, If thou let this man go, thou art not Caesar's friend." Thus these hypocrites pretended to be jealous for the authority of Caesar. Of all the opponents of the Roman rule, the Jews were most bitter. When it was safe for them to do so, they were most tyrannical in enforcing their own national and religious requirements; but when they desired to bring about some purpose of cruelty, they exalted the power of Caesar. To accomplish the destruction of Christ, they would profess loyalty to the foreign rule which they hated.

"Whosoever maketh himself a king," they continued, "speaketh against Caesar." This was touching Pilate in a weak point. He was under suspicion by the Roman government, and he knew that such a report would be ruin to him. He knew that if the Jews were thwarted, their rage would be turned against him. They would leave nothing undone to accomplish their revenge. He had before him an example of the persistence with which they sought the life of One whom they hated without reason.

Pilate then took his place on the judgment seat, and again presented Jesus to the people, saying, "Behold your King." Again the mad cry was heard, "Away with Him! crucify Him!" In a voice that was heard far and near, Pilate asked, "Shall I crucify your King?" But from profane, blasphemous lips went forth the words, "We have no king but Caesar."

Thus by choosing a heathen ruler, the Jewish nation had withdrawn from the theocracy. They had rejected God as their king. Henceforth they had no deliverer. They had no king but Caesar. To this the priests and teachers had led the people. For this, with the fearful results that followed, they were responsible. A nation's sin and a nation's ruin were due to the religious leaders.

"When Pilate saw that he could prevail nothing, but that rather a tumult was made, he took water, and washed his hands before the multitude, saying, I am innocent of the blood of this just person; see ye to it." In fear and self-condemnation Pilate looked upon the Saviour. In the vast sea of upturned faces, His alone was peaceful. About His head a soft light seemed to shine. Pilate said in his heart, He is a God. Turning to the multitude he declared, I am clear of His blood. Take ye Him, and crucify Him. But mark ye, priests and rulers, I pronounce Him a just man. May He whom He claims as His Father judge you and not me for this day's work. Then to Jesus he said, Forgive me for this act; I cannot save you. And when he had again scourged Jesus, he delivered Him to be crucified.

Pilate longed to deliver Jesus. But he saw that he could not do this, and yet retain his own position and honor. Rather than lose his worldly power, he chose to sacrifice an innocent life. How many, to escape loss or suffering, in like manner sacrifice principle. Conscience and duty point one way, and self-interest points another. The current sets strongly in the wrong direction, and he who compromises with evil is swept away into the thick darkness of guilt.

Pilate yielded to the demands of the mob. Rather than risk losing his position, he delivered Jesus up to be crucified. But in spite of his precautions, the very thing he dreaded afterward came upon him. His honors were stripped from him, he was cast down from his high office, and, stung by remorse and wounded pride, not long after the crucifixion he ended his own life. So all who compromise with sin will gain only sorrow and ruin. "There is a way which seemeth right unto a man, but the end thereof are the ways of death." Proverbs 14:12.

When Pilate declared himself innocent of the blood of Christ, Caiaphas answered defiantly, "His blood be on us, and on our children." The awful words were taken up by the priests and rulers, and echoed by the crowd in an inhuman roar of voices. The whole multitude answered and said, "His blood be on us, and on our children."

The people of Israel had made their choice. Pointing to Jesus they had said, "Not this man, but Barabbas." Barabbas, the robber and murderer, was the representative of Satan. Christ was the representative of God. Christ had been rejected; Barabbas had been chosen. Barabbas they were to have. In making this choice they accepted him who from the beginning was a liar and a murderer. Satan was their leader. As a nation they would act out his dictation. His works they would do. His rule they must endure. That people who chose Barabbas in the place of Christ were to feel the cruelty of Barabbas as long as time should last.

Looking upon the smitten Lamb of God, the Jews had cried, "His blood be on us, and on our children." That awful cry ascended to the throne of God. That sentence, pronounced upon themselves, was written in heaven. That prayer was heard. The blood of the Son of God was upon their children and their children's children, a perpetual curse.

Terribly was it realized in the destruction of Jerusalem. Terribly has it been manifested in the condition of the Jewish nation for eighteen hundred years, — a branch severed from the vine, a dead, fruitless branch, to be gathered up and burned. From land to land throughout the world, from century to century, dead, dead in trespasses and sins!

Terribly will that prayer be fulfilled in the great Judgment day. When Christ shall come to the earth again, not as a prisoner surrounded by a rabble will men see Him. They will see Him then as heaven's King. Christ will come in His own glory, in the glory of His Father, and the glory of the holy angels. Ten thousand times ten thousand, and thousands of thousands of angels, the beautiful and triumphant sons of God, possessing surpassing loveliness and glory, will escort Him on His way. Then shall He sit upon the throne of His glory, and before Him shall be gathered all nations. Then every eye shall see Him, and they also that pierced Him. In the place of a crown of thorns, He will wear a crown of glory, — a crown within a crown. In place of that old purple kingly robe, He will be clothed in raiment of whitest white, "so as no fuller on earth can white them." Mark 9:3. And on His venture and on His thigh a name will be written, "King of kings, and Lord of lords." Revelation 19:16. Those who mocked and smote Him will be there. The priests and rulers will behold again the scene in the judgment hall. Every circumstance will appear before them, as if written in letters of fire. Then those who prayed, "His blood be on us, and on our children," will receive the answer to their prayer. Then the whole world will know and understand. They will realize who and what they, poor, feeble, finite beings, have been warring against. In awful agony and horror they will cry to the mountains and rocks, "Fall on us, and hide us from the face of Him that sitteth on the throne, and from the wrath of the Lamb; for the great day of His wrath is come, and who shall be able to stand?" Revelation 6:16, 17.

Calvary

And when they were come to the place, which is called Calvary, there they crucified Him."

"That He might sanctify the people with His own blood," Christ "suffered without the gate." Hebrews 13:12. For transgression of the law of God, Adam and Eve were banished from Eden. Christ, our substitute, was to suffer without the boundaries of Jerusalem. He died outside the gate, where felons and murderers were executed. Full of significance are the words, "Christ hath redeemed us from the curse of the law, being made a curse for us." Galatians 3:13.

A vast multitude followed Jesus from the judgment hall to Calvary. The news of His condemnation had spread throughout Jerusalem, and people of all classes and all ranks flocked toward the place of crucifixion. The priests and rulers had been bound by a promise not to molest Christ's followers if He Himself were delivered to them, and the disciples and believers from the city and the surrounding region joined the throng that followed the Saviour.

As Jesus passed the gate of Pilate's court, the cross which had been prepared for Barabbas was laid upon His bruised and bleeding shoulders. Two companions of Barabbas were to suffer death at the same time with Jesus, and upon them also crosses were placed. The Saviour's burden was too heavy for Him in His weak and suffering condition. Since the Passover supper with His disciples, he had taken neither food nor drink. He had agonized in the garden of Gethsemane in conflict with Satanic agencies. He had endured the anguish of the betrayal, and had seen His disciples forsake Him and flee. He had been taken to Annas, then to Caiaphas, and then to Pilate. From Pilate He had been sent to Herod, then sent again to Pilate. From insult to renewed insult, from mockery to mockery, twice tortured by the scourge,—all that night there had been scene after scene of a character to try the soul of man to the uttermost. Christ had not failed. He had spoken no word but that tended to glorify God. All through the disgraceful farce of a trial He had borne Himself with firmness and dignity. But when after the second scourging the cross was laid upon Him, human nature could bear no more. He fell fainting beneath the burden.

The crowd that followed the Saviour saw His weak and staggering steps, but they manifested no compassion. They taunted and reviled Him because He could not carry the heavy cross. Again the burden was laid upon Him, and again He fell fainting to the ground. His persecutors saw that it was impossible for Him to carry His burden farther. They were puzzled to find any one who would bear the humiliating load. The Jews themselves could not do this, because the defilement would prevent them from keeping the Passover. None even of the mob that followed Him would stoop to bear the cross.

At this time a stranger, Simon a Cyrenian, coming in from the country, meets the throng. He hears the taunts and ribaldry of the crowd; he hears the words contemptuously repeated, Make way for the King of the Jews. He stops in astonishment at the scene; and as he expresses his compassion, they seize him and place the cross upon his shoulders.

Simon had heard of Jesus. His sons were believers in the Saviour, but he himself was not a disciple. The bearing of the cross to Calvary was a blessing to Simon, and he was ever after grateful for this providence. It led him to take upon himself the cross of Christ from choice, and ever cheerfully stand beneath its burden.

Not a few women are in the crowd that follow the Uncondemned to His cruel death. Their attention is fixed upon Jesus. Some of them have seen Him before. Some have carried to Him their sick and suffering ones. Some have themselves been healed. The story of the scenes that have taken place is related. They wonder at the hatred of the crowd toward Him for whom their own hearts are melting and ready to break. And notwithstanding the action of the maddened throng, and the angry words of the priests and rulers, these women give expression to their sympathy. As Jesus falls fainting beneath the cross, they break forth into mournful wailing.

This was the only thing that attracted Christ's attention. Although full of suffering, while bearing the sins of the world, He was not indifferent to the expression of grief. He looked upon these women with tender compassion. They were not believers in Him; He knew that they were not lamenting Him as one sent from God, but were moved by feelings of human pity. He did not despise their sympathy, but it awakened in His heart a deeper sympathy for them. "Daughters of Jerusalem," He said, "weep not for Me, but weep for yourselves, and for your children." From the scene before Him, Christ looked forward to the time of Jerusalem's destruction. In that terrible scene, many of those who were now weeping for Him, were to perish with their children.

From the fall of Jerusalem the thoughts of Jesus passed to a wider judgment. In the destruction of the impenitent city He saw a symbol of the final destruction to come upon the world. He said, "Then shall they begin to say to the mountains, Fall on us; and to the hills, Cover us. For if they do these things in a green tree, what shall be done in the dry?" By the green tree, Jesus represented Himself, the innocent Redeemer. God suffered His wrath against transgression to fall on His beloved Son. Jesus was to be crucified for the sins of men. What suffering, then, would the sinner bear who continued in sin? All the impenitent and unbelieving would know a sorrow and misery that language would fail to express.

Of the multitude that followed the Saviour to Calvary, many had attended Him with joyful hosannas and the waving of palm branches, as He rode triumphantly into Jerusalem. But not a few who had then shouted His praise because it was popular to do so, now swelled the cry of "Crucify Him! crucify Him!" When Christ rode into Jerusalem, the hopes of the disciples had been raised to the highest pitch. They had pressed close about their Master, feeling that it was a high honor to be connected with Him. Now in His humiliation they followed Him at a distance. They were filled with grief, and bowed down with disappointed hopes. How were the words of Jesus verified: "All ye shall be offended because of Me this night; for it is written, I will smite the shepherd, and the sheep of the flock shall be scattered abroad." Matthew 26:31.

Arriving at the place of execution, the prisoners were bound to the instruments of torture. The two thieves wrestled in the hands of those who placed them on the cross; but Jesus made no resistance. The mother of Jesus, supported by John the beloved disciple, had followed the steps of her Son to Calvary. She had seen Him fainting under the burden of the cross, and had longed to place a supporting hand beneath His wounded head, and to bathe that brow which had once been pillowed upon her bosom. But she was not permitted this mournful privilege. With the

---

"The cross was laid upon His bruised and bleeding shoulders. ... The Saviour's burden was too heavy for Him ... all that night there had been scene after scene of a character to try the soul of man to the uttermost. Christ had not failed.... But when the cross was laid upon Him, human nature could bear no more. He fell fainting beneath the burden."

---

disciples she still cherished the hope that Jesus would manifest His power, and deliver Himself from His enemies. Again her heart would sink as she recalled the words in which He had foretold the very scenes that were then taking place. As the thieves were bound to the cross, she looked on with agonizing suspense. Would He who had given life to the dead, suffer Himself to be crucified? Would the Son of God suffer Himself to be thus cruelly slain? Must she give up her faith that Jesus was the Messiah? Must she witness His shame and sorrow, without even the privilege of ministering to Him in His distress? She saw His hands stretched upon the cross; the hammer and the nails were brought, and as the spikes were driven through the tender flesh, the heart-stricken disciples bore away from the cruel scene the fainting form of the mother of Jesus.

The Saviour made no murmur of complaint. His face remained calm and serene, but great drops of sweat stood upon His brow. There was no pitying hand to wipe the death dew from His face, nor words of sympathy and unchanging fidelity to stay His human heart. While the soldiers were doing their fearful work, Jesus prayed for His enemies, "Father, forgive them; for they know not what they do." His mind passed from His own suffering to the sin of His persecutors, and the terrible retribution that would be theirs. No curses were called down upon the soldiers who were handling Him so roughly. No vengeance was invoked upon the priests and rulers, who were gloating over the accomplishment of their purpose. Christ pitied them in their ignorance and guilt. He breathed only a plea for their forgiveness, — "for they know not what they do."

Had they known that they were putting to torture One who had come to save the sinful race from eternal ruin, they would have been seized with remorse and horror. But their ignorance did not remove their guilt; for it was their privilege to know and accept Jesus as their Saviour. Some of them would yet see their sin, and repent, and be converted. Some by their impenitence would make it an impossibility for the prayer of Christ to be answered for them. Yet just the same God's purpose was reaching its fulfilment. Jesus was earning the right to become the advocate of men in the Father's presence.

That prayer of Christ for His enemies embraced the world. It took in every sinner that had lived or should live, from the beginning of the world to the end of time. Upon all rests the guilt of crucifying the Son of God. To all, forgiveness is freely offered. "Whosoever will" may have peace with God, and inherit eternal life.

As soon as Jesus was nailed to the cross, it was lifted by strong men, and with great violence thrust into the place prepared for it. This caused the most intense agony to the Son of God. Pilate then wrote an inscription in Hebrew, Greek, and Latin, and placed it upon the cross, above the head of Jesus. It read, "Jesus of Nazareth the King of the Jews." This inscription irritated the Jews. In Pilate's court they had cried, "Crucify Him!" "We have no king but Caesar." John 19:15. They had declared that whoever should acknowledge any other king was a traitor. Pilate wrote out the sentiment they had expressed. No offense was mentioned, except that Jesus was the King of the Jews. The inscription was a virtual acknowledgment of the allegiance of the Jews to the Roman power. It declared that whoever might claim to be the King of Israel, would be judged by them worthy of death. The priests had overreached themselves. When they were plotting the death of Christ, Caiaphas had declared it expedient that one man should die to save the nation. Now their hypocrisy was revealed. In order to destroy Christ, they had been ready to sacrifice even their national existence.

The priests saw what they had done, and asked Pilate to change the inscription. They said, "Write not, The King of the Jews; but that He said, I am King of the Jews." But Pilate was angry with himself because of his former weakness, and he thoroughly despised the jealous and artful priests and rulers. He replied coldly, "What I have written I have written."

A higher power than Pilate or the Jews had directed the placing of that inscription above the head of Jesus. In the providence of God it was to awaken thought, and investigation of the Scriptures. The place where Christ was crucified was near to the city. Thousands of people from all lands were then at Jerusalem, and the inscription declaring Jesus of Nazareth the Messiah would come to their notice. It was a living truth, transcribed by a hand that God had guided.

In the sufferings of Christ upon the cross, prophecy was fulfilled. Centuries before the crucifixion, the Saviour had foretold the treatment He was to receive. He said, "Dogs have compassed Me: the assembly of the wicked have enclosed Me; they pierced My hands and My feet. I may tell all My bones; they look and stare upon Me. They part My garments among them, and cast lots upon My vesture." Psalms 22:16-18. The prophecy concerning His garments was carried out without counsel or interference from the friends or the enemies of the Crucified One. To the soldiers who had placed Him upon the cross, His clothing was given. Christ heard the men's contention as they parted the garments among them. His tunic was woven throughout without seam, and they said, "Let us not rend it, but cast lots for it, whose it shall be."

In another prophecy the Saviour declared, "Reproach hath broken My heart; and I am full of heaviness: and I looked for some to take pity, but there was none; and for comforters, but I found none. They gave me also gall for My meat; and in My thirst they gave Me vinegar to drink." Psalms 69:20,21. To those who suffered death by the cross, it was permitted to give a stupefying potion, to deaden the sense of pain. This was offered to Jesus; but when He had tasted it, He refused it. He would receive nothing that could becloud His mind. His faith must keep fast hold upon God. This was His only strength. To becloud His senses would give Satan an advantage.

The enemies of Jesus vented their rage upon Him as He hung upon the cross. Priests, rulers, and scribes joined with the mob in mocking the dying Saviour. At the baptism and at the transfiguration the voice of God had been heard proclaiming Christ as His Son. Again, just before Christ's betrayal, the Father had spoken, witnessing to His divinity. But now the voice from heaven was silent. No testimony in Christ's favor was heard. Alone He suffered abuse and mockery from wicked men.

"If Thou be the Son of God," they said, "come down from the cross." "Let Him save Himself, if He be Christ, the chosen of God." In the wilderness of temptation Satan had declared, "If Thou be the Son of God, command that these stones be made bread." "If Thou be the Son of God, cast Thyself down" from the pinnacle of the temple. Matthew 4:3,6. And Satan with his angels, in human form, was present at the cross. The archfiend and his hosts were co-operating with the priests and rulers. The teachers of the people had stimulated the ignorant mob to pronounce judgment against One upon whom many of them had never looked, until urged to bear testimony against Him. Priests, rulers, Pharisees, and the hardened rabble were confederated together in a Satanic frenzy. Religious rulers united with Satan and his angels. They were doing his bidding.

Jesus, suffering and dying, heard every word as the priests declared, "He saved others; Himself He cannot save. Let Christ the King of Israel descend now from the cross, that we may see and believe." Christ could have come down from the cross. But it is because He would not save Himself that the sinner has hope of pardon and favor with God.

In their mockery of the Saviour, the men who professed to be the expounders of prophecy were repeating the very words which inspiration had foretold they would utter upon this occasion. Yet in their blindness they did not see that they were fulfilling the prophecy. Those who in derision uttered the words, "He trusted in God; let Him deliver Him now, if He will have Him; for He said, I am the Son of God," little thought that their testimony would sound down the ages. But although spoken in mockery, these words led men to search the Scriptures as they had never done before. Wise men heard, searched, pondered, and prayed. There were those who never rested until, by comparing scripture with scripture, they saw the meaning of Christ's mission. Never before was there such a general knowledge of Jesus as when He hung upon the cross. Into the hearts of many who beheld the crucifixion scene, and who heard Christ's words, the light of truth was shining.

To Jesus in His agony on the cross there came one gleam of comfort. It was the prayer of the penitent thief. Both the men who were crucified with Jesus had at first railed upon Him; and one under his suffering, only became more desperate and defiant. But not so with his companion. This man was not a hardened criminal; he had been led astray by evil associations, but he was less guilty than many of those who stood beside the cross reviling the Saviour. He had seen and heard Jesus, and had been convicted by His teaching, but he had been turned away from Him by the priests and rulers. Seeking to stifle conviction, he had plunged deeper and deeper into sin, until he was arrested, tried as a criminal, and condemned to die on the cross. In the judgment hall and on the way to Calvary he had been in company with Jesus. He had heard Pilate declare, "I find no fault in Him." John 19:4. He had marked His Godlike bearing, and His pitying forgiveness of His tormentors. On the cross he sees the many great religionists shoot out the tongue with scorn, and ridicule the Lord Jesus. He sees the wagging heads. He hears the upbraiding speeches taken up by his companion in guilt: "If Thou be Christ, save Thyself and us." Among the passers-by he hears many defending Jesus. He hears them repeat His words, and tell of His works. The conviction comes back to him that this is the Christ. Turning to his fellow criminal he says, "Dost thou not fear God, seeing thou art in the same condemnation?" The dying thieves have no longer anything to fear from man. But upon one of them presses the conviction that there is a God to fear, a future to cause him to tremble. And now, all sin-polluted as it is, his life history is about to close. "And we indeed justly," he moans; "for we receive the due reward of our deeds; but this man hath done nothing amiss."

There is no question now. There are no doubts, no reproaches. When condemned for his crime, the thief had become hopeless and despairing; but strange, tender thoughts now spring up. He calls to mind all he has heard of Jesus, how He has healed the sick and pardoned sin. He has heard the words of those who believed in Jesus and followed Him weeping. He has seen and read the title above the Saviour's head. He has heard the passers-by repeat it, some with grieved, quivering lips, others with jesting and mockery. The Holy Spirit illuminates his mind, and little by little the chain of evidence is joined together. In Jesus, bruised, mocked, and hanging upon the cross, he sees the Lamb of God, that taketh away the sin of the world. Hope is mingled with anguish in his voice as the helpless, dying soul casts himself upon a dying Saviour. "Lord, remember me," he cries, "when Thou comest into Thy kingdom."

Quickly the answer came. Soft and melodious the tone, full of love, compassion, and power the words: Verily I say unto thee today, Thou shalt be with Me in Paradise.

For long hours of agony, reviling and mockery have fallen upon the ears of Jesus. As He hangs upon the cross, there floats up to Him still the sound of jeers and curses. With longing heart He has listened for some expression of faith from His disciples. He has heard only the mournful words, "We trusted that it had been He which should have redeemed Israel." How grateful then to the Saviour was the utterance of faith and love from the dying thief. While the leading Jews deny Him, and even the disciples doubt His divinity, the poor thief, upon the brink of eternity, calls Jesus Lord. Many were ready to call Him Lord when He wrought miracles, and after He had risen from the grave; but none acknowledged Him as He hung dying upon the cross save the penitent thief who was saved at the eleventh hour.

The bystanders caught the words as the thief called Jesus Lord. The tone of the repentant man arrested their attention. Those who at the foot of the cross had been quarreling over Christ's garments, and casting lots upon His vesture, stopped to listen. Their angry tones were hushed. With bated breath they looked upon Christ, and waited for the response from those dying lips.

As He spoke the words of promise, the dark cloud that seemed to enshroud the cross was pierced by a bright and living light. To the penitent thief came the perfect peace of acceptance with God. Christ in His humiliation was glorified. He who in all other eyes appeared to be con-

152

quered, was a Conqueror. He was acknowledged as the Sinbearer. Men may exercise power over His human body. They may pierce the holy temples with the crown of thorns. They may strip from Him His raiment, and quarrel over its division. But they cannot rob Him of His power to forgive sins. In dying He bears testimony to His own divinity and to the glory of the Father. His ear is not heavy

---

❝The mother of Jesus . . . had followed the steps of her Son to Calvary. She had seen Him fainting under the burden of the cross . . . Would the Son of God suffer Himself to be thus cruelly slain? . . . She saw His hands stretched upon the cross; the hammer and the nails were brought, and as the spikes were driven through the tender flesh, the heart-stricken disciples bore away from the cruel scene the fainting form of the mother of Jesus.❞

---

that it cannot hear, neither His arm shortened that it cannot save. It is His royal right to save unto the uttermost all who come unto God by Him.

I say unto thee today, Thou shalt be with Me in Paradise. Christ did not promise that the thief should be with Him in Paradise that day. He Himself did not go that day to Paradise. He slept in the tomb, and on the morning of the resurrection He said, "I am not yet ascended to My Father." John 20:17. But on the day of the crucifixion, the day of apparent defeat and darkness, the promise was given. "Today," while dying upon the cross as a malefactor, Christ assures the poor sinner, "Thou shalt be with Me in Paradise."

The thieves crucified with Jesus were placed "on either side one, and Jesus in the midst." This was done by the direction of the priests and rulers. Christ's position between the thieves was to indicate that He was the greatest criminal of the three. Thus was fulfilled the scripture, "He was numbered with the transgressors." Isaiah 53:12. But the full meaning of their act the priests did not see. As Jesus, crucified with the thieves, was placed "in the midst," so His cross was placed in the midst of a world lying in sin. And the words of pardon spoken to the penitent thief, kindled a light that will shine to the earth's remotest bounds.

With amazement the angels beheld the infinite love of Jesus, who, suffering the most intense agony of mind and body, thought only of others, and encouraged the penitent soul to believe. In His humiliation He as a prophet had addressed the daughters of Jerusalem; as priest and advocate He had pleaded with the Father to forgive His murderers; as a loving Saviour He had forgiven the sins of the penitent thief.

As the eyes of Jesus wandered over the multitude about Him, one figure arrested His attention. At the foot of the cross stood His mother, supported by the disciple John. She could not endure to remain away from her Son; and John, knowing that the end was near, had brought her again to the cross. In His dying hour, Christ remembered His mother. Looking into her grief-stricken face and then upon John, He said to her, "Woman, behold thy son;" then to John, "Behold thy mother." John understood Christ's words, and accepted the trust. He at once took Mary to his home, and from that hour cared for her tenderly. O pitiful, loving Saviour; amid all His physical pain and mental anguish, He had a thoughtful care for His mother. He had no money with which to provide for her comfort; but He was enshrined in the heart of John, and He gave His mother to him as a precious legacy. Thus He provided for her that which she most needed, — the tender sympathy of one who loved her because she loved Jesus. And in receiving her as a sacred trust, John was receiving a great blessing. She was a constant reminder of his beloved Master.

The perfect example of Christ's filial love shines forth with undimmed luster from the mist of ages. For nearly thirty years Jesus by His daily toil had helped bear the burdens of the home. And now, even in His last agony, He remembers to provide for His sorrowing, widowed mother. The same spirit will be seen in every disciple of our Lord. Those who follow Christ will feel that it is a part of their religion to respect and provide for their parents. From the heart where His love is cherished, father and mother will never fail of receiving thoughtful care and tender sympathy.

And now the Lord of Glory was dying, a ransom for the race. In yielding up His precious life, Christ was not upheld by triumphant joy. All was oppressive gloom. It was not the dread of death that weighed upon Him. It was not the pain and ignominy of the cross that caused His inexpressible agony. Christ was the prince of sufferers; but His suffering was from a sense of the malignity of sin, a knowledge that through familiarity with evil, man had become blinded to its enormity. Christ saw how deep is the hold of sin upon the human heart, how few would be willing to break from its power. He knew that without help from God, humanity must perish, and He saw multitudes perishing within reach of abundant help.

Upon Christ as our substitute and surety was laid the iniquity of us all. He was counted a transgressor, that He

---

"Had they known that they were putting to torture One who had come to save the sinful race from eternal ruin, they would have been seized with remorse and horror. But their ignorance did not remove their guilt; for it was their privilege to know and accept Jesus as their Saviour.... Yet, just the same, God's purpose was reaching its fulfillment."

---

might redeem us from the condemnation of the law. The guilt of every descendant of Adam was pressing upon His heart. The wrath of God against sin, the terrible manifestation of His displeasure because of iniquity, filled the soul of His Son with consternation. All His life Christ had been publishing to a fallen world the good news of the Father's mercy and pardoning love. Salvation for the chief of sinners was His theme. But now with the terrible weight of guilt He bears, He cannot see the Father's reconciling face. The withdrawal of the divine countenance from the Saviour in this hour of supreme anguish pierced His heart with a sorrow that can never be fully understood by man. So great was this agony that His physical pain was hardly felt.

Satan with his fierce temptations wrung the heart of Jesus. The Saviour could not see through the portals of the tomb. Hope did not present to Him His coming forth from

the grave a conqueror, or tell Him of the Father's acceptance of the sacrifice. He feared that sin was so offensive to God, that their separation was to be eternal. Christ felt the anguish which the sinner will feel when mercy shall no longer plead for the guilty race. It was the sense of sin, bringing the Father's wrath upon Him as man's substitute, that made the cup He drank so bitter, and broke the heart of the Son of God.

With amazement angels witnessed the Saviour's despairing agony. The hosts of heaven veiled their faces from the fearful sight. Inanimate nature expressed sympathy with its insulted and dying Author. The sun refused to look upon the awful scene. Its full, bright rays were illuminating the earth at midday, when suddenly it seemed to be blotted out. Complete darkness, like a funeral pall, enveloped the cross. "There was darkness over all the land until the ninth hour." There was no eclipse or other natural cause for this darkness, which was as deep as midnight without moon or stars. It was a miraculous testimony given by God that the faith of after generations might be confirmed.

In that thick darkness God's presence was hidden. He makes darkness His pavilion, and conceals His glory from human eyes. God and His holy angels were beside the cross. The Father was with His Son. Yet His presence was not revealed. Had His glory flashed forth from the cloud, every human beholder would have been destroyed. And in that dreadful hour Christ was not to be comforted with the Father's presence. He trod the wine press alone, and of the people there was none with Him.

In the thick darkness, God veiled the last human agony of His Son. All who had seen Christ in His suffering had been convicted of His divinity. That face, once beheld by humanity, was never forgotten. As the face of Cain expressed his guilt as a murderer, so the face of Christ revealed innocence, serenity, benevolence, — the image of God. But His accusers would not give heed to the signet of heaven. Through long hours of agony Christ had been gazed upon by the jeering multitude. Now He was mercifully hidden by the mantle of God.

The silence of the grave seemed to have fallen upon Calvary. A nameless terror held the throng that was gathered about the cross. The cursing and reviling ceased in the midst of half-uttered sentences. Men, women, and children fell prostrate upon the earth. Vivid lightnings occasionally flashed forth from the cloud, and revealed the cross and the crucified Redeemer. Priests, rulers, scribes, executioners, and the mob, all thought that their time of retribution had come. After a while some whispered that Jesus would now come down from the cross. Some attempted to grope their way back to the city, beating their breasts and wailing in fear.

At the ninth hour the darkness lifted from the people but still enveloped the Saviour. It was a symbol of the agony and horror that weighed upon His heart. No eye could pierce the gloom that surrounded the cross, and none could penetrate the deeper gloom that enshrouded the suffering soul of Christ. The angry lightnings seemed to be hurled at Him as He hung upon the cross. Then "Jesus cried with a loud voice, saying, Eloi, Eloi, lama sabachthani?" "My God, my God, why hast Thou forsaken Me?" As the outer gloom settled about the Saviour, many voices exclaimed, "The vengeance of Heaven is upon Him. The bolts of God's wrath are hurled at Him, because He claimed to be the Son of God." Many who believed on Him heard His despairing cry. Hope left them. If God had forsaken Jesus, in what could His followers trust?

When the darkness lifted from the oppressed spirit of Christ, He revived to a sense of physical suffering, and said, "I thirst." One of the Roman soldiers, touched with pity as he looked at the parched lips, took a sponge on a stalk of hyssop, and dipping it in a vessel of vinegar, offered it to Jesus. But the priests mocked at His agony. When darkness covered the earth, they had been filled with fear; as their terror abated, the dread returned that Jesus would yet escape them. His words, "Eloi, Eloi, lama sabachthani," they had misinterpreted. With bitter contempt and scorn they said, "This man calleth for Elias." The last opportunity to relieve His sufferings they refused. "Let be," they said, "let us see whether Elias will come to save Him."

The spotless Son of God hung upon the cross, His flesh lacerated with stripes; those hands so often reached out in blessing, nailed to the wooden bars; those feet so tireless on ministries of love, spiked to the tree; that royal head pierced by the crown of thorns; those quivering lips shaped to the cry of woe. And all that He endured,—the blood drops that flowed from His head, His hands, His feet, the agony that racked His frame, and the unutterable anguish that filled His soul at the hiding of His Father's face,—speaks to each child of humanity, declaring, It is for thee that the Son of God consents to bear this burden of guilt; for thee He spoils the domain of death, and opens the gates of Paradise. He who stilled the angry waves and walked the foam-capped billows, who made devils tremble and disease flee, who opened blind eyes, and called forth the dead to life,—offers Himself upon the cross as a sacrifice, and this from love to thee. He, the Sinbearer, endures the wrath of divine justice, and for thy sake becomes sin itself.

In silence the beholders watched for the end of the fearful scene. The sun shone forth; but the cross was still enveloped in darkness. Priests and rulers looked toward Jerusalem; and lo, the dense cloud had settled over the city, and the plains of Judea. The Sun of Righteousness, the Light of the world, was withdrawing His beams from the once favored city of Jerusalem. The fierce lightnings of God's wrath were directed against the fated city.

Suddenly the gloom lifted from the cross, and in clear, trumpetlike tones, that seemed to resound throughout creation, Jesus cried, "It is finished." "Father, into Thy hands I commend My spirit." A light encircled the cross, and the face of the Saviour shone with a glory like the sun. He then bowed His head upon His breast, and died.

Amid the awful darkness, apparently forsaken of God, Christ had drained the last dregs in the cup of human woe. In those dreadful hours He had relied upon the evidence of His Father's acceptance heretofore given Him. He was acquainted with the character of His Father; He understood His justice, His mercy, and His great love. By faith He rested in Him whom it had ever been His joy to obey. And as in submission He committed Himself to God, the sense of the loss of His Father's favor was withdrawn. By faith, Christ was victor.

Never before had the earth witnessed such a scene. The multitude stood paralyzed, and with bated breath gazed upon the Saviour. Again darkness settled upon the earth, and a hoarse rumbling, like heavy thunder, was heard. There was a violent earthquake. The people were shaken together in heaps. The wildest confusion and consternation ensued. In the surrounding mountains, rocks were rent asunder, and went crashing down into the plains. Sepulchers were broken open, and the dead were cast out of their tombs. Creation seemed to be shivering to atoms. Priests, rulers, soldiers, executioners, and people, mute with terror, lay prostrate upon the ground.

When the loud cry, "It is finished," came from the lips of Christ, the priests were officiating in the temple. It was the hour of the evening sacrifice. The lamb representing Christ had been brought to be slain. Clothed in his significant and beautiful dress, the priest stood with lifted knife, as did Abraham when he was about to slay his son. With intense interest the people were looking on. But the earth trembles and quakes; for the Lord Himself draws near. With a rending noise the inner veil of the temple is torn from top to bottom by an unseen hand, throwing open to the gaze of the multitude a place once filled with the presence of God. In this place the Shekinah had dwelt. Here God had manifested His glory above the mercy seat. No one but the high priest ever lifted the veil separating this apartment from the rest of the temple. He entered in once a year to make an atonement for the sins of the people. But lo, this veil is rent in twain. The most holy place of the earthly sanctuary is no longer sacred.

All is terror and confusion. The priest is about to slay the victim; but the knife drops from his nerveless hand, and the lamb escapes. Type has met antitype in the death of God's Son. The great sacrifice has been made. The way into the holiest is laid open. A new and living way is prepared for all. No longer need sinful, sorrowing humanity await the coming of the high priest. Henceforth the Saviour was to officiate as priest and advocate in the heaven of heavens. It was as if a living voice had spoken to the worshipers: There is now an end to all sacrifices and offerings for sin. The Son of God is come according to His word, "Lo, I come (in the volume of the book it is written of Me,) to do Thy will, O God." "By His own blood" He entereth "in once into the holy place, having obtained eternal redemption for us." Hebrews 10:17; 9:12.

"It Is Finished"

Christ did not yield up His life till He had accomplished the work which He came to do, and with His parting breath He exclaimed, "It is finished." John 19:30. The battle had been won. His right hand and His holy arm had gotten Him the victory. As a Conqueror He planted His banner on the eternal heights. Was there not joy among the angels? All heaven triumphed in the Saviour's victory. Satan was defeated, and knew that his kingdom was lost.

To the angels and the unfallen worlds the cry, "It is finished," had a deep significance. It was for them as well as for us that the great work of redemption had been accomplished. They with us share the fruits of Christ's victory.

Not until the death of Christ was the character of Satan clearly revealed to the angels or to the unfallen worlds. The archapostate had so clothed himself with deception that even holy beings had not understood his principles. They had not clearly seen the nature of his rebellion.

It was a being of wonderful power and glory that had set himself against God. Of Lucifer the Lord says, "Thou sealest up the sum, full of wisdom, and perfect in beauty." Ezekiel 28:12. Lucifer had been the covering cherub. He had stood in the light of God's presence. He had been the highest of all created beings, and had been foremost in revealing God's purposes to the universe. After he had sinned, his power to deceive was the more deceptive, and the unveiling of his character was the more difficult, because of the exalted position he had held with the Father.

God could have destroyed Satan and his sympathizers as easily as one can cast a pebble to the earth; but He did not do this. Rebellion was not to be overcome by force. Compelling power is found only under Satan's govern-

ment. The Lord's principles are not of this order. His authority rests upon goodness, mercy, and love; and the presentation of these principles is the means to be used. God's government is moral, and truth and love are to be the prevailing power.

It was God's purpose to place things on an eternal basis of security, and in the councils of heaven it was decided that time must be given for Satan to develop the principles which were the foundation of his system of government. He had claimed that these were superior to God's principles. Time was given for the working of Satan's principles, that they might be seen by the heavenly universe.

Satan led men into sin, and the plan of redemption was put in operation. For four thousand years, Christ was working for man's uplifting, and Satan for his ruin and degradation. And the heavenly universe beheld it all.

When Jesus came into the world, Satan's power was turned against Him. From the time when He appeared as a babe in Bethlehem, the usurper worked to bring about His destruction. In every possible way he sought to prevent Jesus from developing a perfect childhood, a faultless manhood, a holy ministry, and an unblemished sacrifice. But he was defeated. He could not lead Jesus into sin. He could not discourage Him, or drive Him from a work He had come on earth to do. From the desert to Calvary, the storm of Satan's wrath beat upon Him, but the more mercilessly it fell, the more firmly did the Son of God cling to the hand of His Father, and press on in the bloodstained path. All the efforts of Satan to oppress and overcome Him, only brought out in a purer light His spotless character.

All heaven and the unfallen worlds had been witnesses to the controversy. With what intense interest did they follow the closing scenes of the conflict. They beheld the Saviour enter the garden of Gethsemane, His soul bowed down with the horror of a great darkness. They heard His bitter cry, "Father, if it be possible, let this cup pass from Me." Matthew 26:39. As the Father's presence was withdrawn, they saw Him sorrowful with a bitterness of sorrow exceeding that of the last great struggle with death. The bloody sweat was forced from His pores, and fell in drops upon the ground. Thrice the prayer for deliverance was wrung from His lips. Heaven could no longer endure the sight, and a messenger of comfort was sent to the Son of God.

Heaven beheld the Victim betrayed into the hands of the murderous mob, and with mockery and violence hurried from one tribunal to another. It heard the sneers of His persecutors because of His lowly birth. It heard the denial with cursing and swearing by one of His best-loved disciples. It saw the frenzied work of Satan, and his power over the hearts of men. O, fearful scene! the Saviour seized at midnight in Gethsemane, dragged to and fro from palace to judgment hall, arraigned twice before the priests, twice before the Sanhedrin, twice before Pilate, and once before Herod, mocked, scourged, condemned, and led out to be crucified, bearing the heavy burden of the cross, amid the wailing of the daughters of Jerusalem and the jeering of the rabble.

Heaven viewed with grief and amazement Christ hanging upon the cross, blood flowing from His wounded temples, and sweat tinged with blood standing upon His brow. From His hands and feet the blood fell, drop by drop, upon the rock drilled for the foot of the cross. The wounds made by the nails gaped as the weight of His body dragged upon His hands. His labored breath grew quick and deep, as His soul panted under the burden of the sins of the world. All heaven was filled with wonder when the prayer of Christ was offered in the midst of His terrible suffering, — "Father, forgive them; for they know not what they do." Luke 23:34. Yet there stood men, formed in the image of God, joining to crush out the life of His only begotten Son. What a sight for the heavenly universe!

The principalities and powers of darkness were assembled around the cross, casting the hellish shadow of unbelief into the hearts of men. When the Lord created these beings to stand before His throne, they were beautiful and glorious. Their loveliness and holiness were in accordance with their exalted station. They were enriched with the wisdom of God, and girded with the panoply of heaven. They were Jehovah's ministers. But who could recognize in the fallen angels the glorious seraphim that once ministered in the heavenly courts?

Satanic agencies confederated with evil men in leading the people to believe Christ the chief of sinners, and to make Him the object of detestation. Those who mocked Christ as He hung upon the cross were imbued with the spirit of the first great rebel. He filled them with vile and loathsome speeches. He inspired their taunts. But by all this he gained nothing.

Could one sin have been found in Christ, had He in one particular yielded to Satan to escape the terrible torture, the enemy of God and man would have triumphed. Christ bowed His head and died, but He held fast His faith and His submission to God. "And I heard a loud voice saying in heaven, Now is come salvation, and strength, and the kingdom of our God, and the power of His Christ; for the accuser of our brethren is cast down, which accused them before our God day and night." Revelation 12:10.

Satan saw that his disguise was torn away. His administration was laid open before the unfallen angels and before the heavenly universe. He had revealed himself as a murderer. By shedding the blood of the Son of God, he had uprooted himself from the sympathies of the heavenly beings. Henceforth his work was restricted. Whatever attitude he might assume, he could no longer await the angels as they came from the heavenly courts, and before them accuse Christ's brethren of being clothed with the garments of blackness and the defilement of sin. The last link of sympathy between Satan and the heavenly world was broken.

Yet Satan was not then destroyed. The angels did not even then understand all that was involved in the great controversy. The principles at stake were to be more fully revealed. And for the sake of man, Satan's existence must be continued. Man as well as angels must see the contrast between the Prince of Light and the prince of darkness. He must choose whom he will serve.

In the opening of the great controversy, Satan had declared that the law of God could not be obeyed, that justice was inconsistent with mercy, and that, should the law be broken, it would be impossible for the sinner to be pardoned. Every sin must meet its punishment, urged Satan; and if God should remit the punishment of sin, He would not be a God of truth and justice. When men broke the law of God, and defied His will, Satan exulted. It was proved, he declared, that the law could not be obeyed; man could not be forgiven. Because he, after his rebellion, had been banished from heaven, Satan claimed that the human race must be forever shut out from God's favor. God could not be just, he urged, and yet show mercy to the sinner.

But even as a sinner, man was in a different position from that of Satan. Lucifer in heaven had sinned in the light of God's glory. To him as to no other created being was given a revelation of God's love. Understanding the character of God, knowing His goodness, Satan chose to follow his own selfish, independent will. This choice was final. There was no more that God could do to save him. But man was deceived; his mind was darkened by Satan's sophistry. The height and depth of the love of God he did not know. For him there was hope in a knowledge of God's love. By beholding His character he might be drawn back to God.

Through Jesus, God's mercy was manifested to men; but mercy does not set aside justice. The law reveals the attributes of God's character, and not a jot or tittle of it could be changed to meet man in his fallen condition. God did not change His law, but He sacrificed Himself, in Christ, for man's redemption. "God was in Christ, reconciling the world unto Himself." 2 Corinthians 5:19.

The law requires righteousness, — a righteous life, a perfect character; and this man has not to give. He cannot meet the claims of God's holy law. But Christ, coming to the earth as man, lived a holy life, and developed a perfect character. These He offers as a free gift to all who will receive them. His life stands for the life of men. Thus they have remission of sins that are past, through the forbear-

---

"The warfare against God's law, which was begun in heaven, will be continued until the end of time. Every man will be tested. . . . All will be called to choose between the law of God and the laws of men . . . Then the end will come. God will vindicate His law and deliver His people."

---

ance of God. More than this, Christ imbues men with the attributes of God. He builds up the human character after the similitude of the divine character, a goodly fabric of spiritual strength and beauty. Thus the very righteousness of the law is fulfilled in the believer in Christ. God can "be just, and the justifier of him which believeth in Jesus." Romans 3:26

God's love has been expressed in His justice no less than in His mercy. Justice is the foundation of His throne, and the fruit of His love. It had been Satan's purpose to divorce mercy from truth and justice. He sought to prove that the righteousness of God's law is an enemy to peace. But Christ shows that in God's plan they are indissolubly joined together; the one cannot exist without the other. "Mercy and truth are met together; righteousness and peace have kissed each other." Psalms 85:10.

By His life and His death, Christ proved that God's justice did not destroy His mercy, but that sin could be forgiven, and that the law is righteous, and can be perfectly

obeyed. Satan's charges were refuted. God had given man unmistakable evidence of His love.

Another deception was now to be brought forward. Satan declared that mercy destroyed justice, that the death of Christ abrogated the Father's law. Had it been possible for the law to be changed or abrogated, then Christ need not have died. But to abrogate the law would be to immortalize transgression, and place the world under Satan's control. It was because the law was changeless, because man could be saved only through obedience to its precepts, that Jesus was lifted up on the cross. Yet the very means by which Christ established the law, Satan represented as destroying it. Here will come that last conflict of the great controversy between Christ and Satan.

That the law which was spoken by God's own voice is faulty, that some specification has been set aside, is the claim which Satan now puts forward. It is the last great deception that he will bring upon the world. He needs not to assail the whole law; if he can lead men to disregard one precept, his purpose is gained. For "whosoever shall keep the whole law, and yet offend in one point, he is guilty of all." James 2:10. By consenting to break one precept, men are brought under Satan's power. By substituting human law for God's law, Satan will seek to control the world. This work is foretold in prophecy. Of the great apostate power which is the representative of Satan, it is declared, "He shall speak great words against the Most High, and shall wear out the saints of the Most High, and think to change times and laws; and they shall be given into his hand." Daniel 7:25.

Men will surely set up their laws to counterwork the laws of God. They will seek to compel the consciences of others, and in their zeal to enforce these laws they will oppress their fellow men.

The warfare against God's law, which was begun in heaven, will be continued until the end of time. Every man will be tested. Obedience or disobedience is the question to be decided by the whole world. All will be called to choose between the law of God and the laws of men. Here the dividing line will be drawn. There will be but two classes. Every character will be fully developed; and all will show whether they have chosen the side of loyalty or that of rebellion.

Then the end will come. God will vindicate His law and deliver His people. Satan and all who have joined him in rebellion will be cut off. Sin and sinners will perish, root and branch, (Malachi 4:1) — Satan the root, and his followers the branches. The word will be fulfilled to the prince of evil. "Because thou hast set thine heart as the heart of God; . . . I will destroy thee, O covering cherub, from the midst of the stones of fire. . . . Thou shalt be a terror, and never shalt thou be any more." Then "the wicked shall not be; yea, thou shalt diligently consider his place, and it shall not be;" "they shall be as though they had not been." Ezekiel 28:6-19.

This is not an act of arbitrary power on the part of God. The rejecters of His mercy reap that which they have sown. God is the fountain of life; and when one chooses the service of sin, he separates from God, and thus cuts himself off from life. He is "alienated from the life of God." Christ says, "All they that hate Me love death." Ephesians 4:18; Proverbs 8:36. God gives them existence for a time that they may develop their character and reveal their principles. This accomplished, they receive the results of their own choice. By a life of rebellion, Satan and all who unite with him place themselves so out of harmony with God that His very presence is to them a consuming fire. The glory of Him who is love will destroy them.

At the beginning of the great controversy, the angels did not understand this. Had Satan and his host then been left to reap the full result of their sin, they would have perished; but it would not have been apparent to heavenly beings that this was the inevitable result of sin. A doubt of God's goodness would have remained in their minds as evil seed, to produce its deadly fruit of sin and woe.

But not so when the great controversy shall be ended. Then, the plan of redemption having been completed, the character of God is revealed to all created intelligences. The precepts of His law are seen to be perfect and immutable. Then sin has made manifest its nature, Satan his character. Then the extermination of sin will vindicate God's love and establish His honor before a universe of beings who delight to do His will, and in whose heart is His law.

Well, then, might the angels rejoice as they looked upon the Saviour's cross; for though they did not then understand all, they knew that the destruction of sin and Satan was forever made certain, that the redemption of man was assured, and that the universe was made eternally secure. Christ Himself fully comprehended the results of the sacrifice made upon Calvary. To all these He looked forward when upon the cross He cried out, "It is finished."

In Joseph's Tomb

At last Jesus was at rest. The long day of shame and torture was ended. As the last rays of the setting sun ushered in the Sabbath, the Son of God lay in quietude in Joseph's tomb. His work completed, His hands folded in peace, He rested through the sacred hours of the Sabbath day.

In the beginning the Father and the Son had rested upon the Sabbath after their work of creation. When "the heavens and the earth were finished, and all the host of them," (Genesis 2:1.) the Creator and all heavenly beings rejoiced in contemplation of the glorious scene. "The morning stars sang together, and all the sons of God shouted for joy." Job 38:7. Now Jesus rested from the work of redemption; and though there was grief among those who loved Him on earth, yet there was joy in heaven. Glorious to the eyes of heavenly beings was the promise of the future. A restored creation, a redeemed race, that having conquered sin could never fall, — this, the result to flow from Christ's completed work, God and angels saw. With this scene the day upon which Jesus rested is forever linked. For "His work is perfect;" and "whatsoever God doeth, it shall be forever." Deuteronomy 32:4; Ecclesiastes 3:14. When there shall be a "restitution of all things which God hath spoken by the mouth of all His holy prophets since the world began," (Acts 3:21.) the creation Sabbath, the day on which Jesus lay at rest on Joseph's tomb, will still be a day of rest and rejoicing. Heaven and earth will unite in praise, as "from one Sabbath to another," (Isaiah 66:23.) the nations of the saved shall bow in joyful worship to God and the Lamb.

In the closing events of the crucifixion day, fresh evidence was given of the fulfillment of prophecy, and new witness borne to Christ's divinity. When the darkness had lifted from the cross, and the Saviour's dying cry had been uttered, immediately another voice was heard, saying, "Truly this was the Son of God."

These words were said in no whispered tones. All eyes were turned to see whence they came. Who had spoken? It was the centurion, the Roman soldier. The divine patience of the Saviour, and His sudden death, with the cry of victory upon His lips, had impressed this heathen. In the bruised, broken body hanging upon the cross, the centurion recognized the form of the Son of God. He could not refrain from confessing his faith. Thus again evidence was given that our Redeemer was to see of the travail of His soul. Upon the very day of His death, three men, differing widely from one another, had declared their faith, — he who commanded the Roman guard, he who bore the cross of the Saviour, and he who died upon the cross at His side.

As evening drew on, an unearthly stillness hung over Calvary. The crowd dispersed, and many returned to Jerusalem greatly changed in spirit from what they had been in the morning. Many had flocked to the crucifixion from curiosity, and not from hatred toward Christ. Still they believed the accusations of the priests, and looked upon Christ as a malefactor. Under an unnatural excitement they had united with the mob in railing against Him. But when the earth was wrapped in blackness, and they stood accused by their own consciences, they felt guilty of a great wrong. No jest or mocking laughter was heard in the midst of that fearful gloom; and when it was lifted, they made their way to their homes in solemn silence. They were convinced that the charges of the priests were false, that Jesus was no pretender; and a few weeks later, when Peter preached upon the day of Pentecost, they were among the thousands who became converts to Christ.

160

(769-770)

But the Jewish leaders were unchanged by the events they had witnessed. Their hatred of Jesus had not abated. The darkness that had mantled the earth at the crucifixion was not more dense than that which still enveloped the minds of the priests and rulers. At His birth the star had known Christ, and had guided the wise men to the manger where He lay. The heavenly hosts had known Him, and had sung His praise over the plains of Bethlehem. The sea had known His voice, and had obeyed His command. Disease and death had recognized His authority, and had yielded to Him their prey. The sun had known Him, and at the sight of His dying anguish, had hidden its face of light. The rocks had known Him, and had shivered into fragments at His cry. Inanimate nature had known Christ, and had borne witness to His divinity. But the priests and rulers of Israel knew not the Son of God.

Yet the priests and rulers were not at rest. They had carried out their purpose in putting Christ to death; but they did not feel the sense of victory they had expected. Even in the hour of their apparent triumph, they were harassed with doubts as to what would next take place. They had heard the cry, "It is finished." "Father, into Thy hands I commend My spirit." John 19:30; Luke 23:46. They had seen the rocks rent, and had felt the mighty earthquake, and they were restless and uneasy.

They had been jealous of Christ's influence with the people when living; they were jealous of Him even in death. They dreaded the dead Christ more, far more, than they had ever feared the living Christ. They dreaded to have the attention of the people directed any further to the events attending His crucifixion. They feared the results of that day's work. Not on any account would they have had His body remain on the cross during the Sabbath. The Sabbath was now drawing on, and it would be a violation of its sanctity for the bodies to hang upon the cross. So, using this as a pretext, the leading Jews requested Pilate that the death of the victims might be hastened, and their bodies be removed before the setting of the sun.

Pilate was as unwilling as they for the body of Jesus to remain upon the cross. His consent having been obtained, the legs of the two thieves were broken to hasten their death; but Jesus was found to be already dead. The rude soldiers had been softened by what they had heard and seen of Christ, and they were restrained from breaking His limbs. Thus in the offering of the Lamb of God was fulfilled the law of the Passover, "They shall leave none of it unto the morning, nor break any bone of it; according to all the ordinances of the Passover they shall keep it." Numbers 9:12.

The priests and rulers were amazed to find that Christ was dead. Death by the cross was a lingering process; it was difficult to determine when life had ceased. It was an unheard-of thing for one to die within six hours of crucifixion. The priests wished to make sure of the death of Jesus, and at their suggestion a soldier thrust a spear into the Saviour's side. From the wound thus made, there flowed two copious and distinct streams, one of blood, the other of water. This was noted by all the beholders, and John states the occurrence very definitely. He says, "One of the soldiers with a spear pierced His side, and forthwith came there out blood and water. And he that saw it bare record, and his record is true; and he knoweth that he saith true, that ye might believe. For these things were done, that the scripture should be fulfilled, A bone of Him shall not be broken. And again another scripture saith, They shall look on Him whom they pierced." John 19:34-37.

"At last Jesus was at rest. The long day of shame and torture was ended. As the last rays of the setting sun ushered in the Sabbath, the Son of God lay in quietude in Joseph's tomb. His work completed, His hands folded in peace, He rested through the sacred hours of the Sabbath day."

After the resurrection the priests and rulers circulated the report that Christ did not die upon the cross, that He merely fainted, and was afterward revived. Another report affirmed that it was not a real body of flesh and bone, but the likeness of a body, that was laid in the tomb. The action of the Roman soldiers disproves these falsehoods. They broke not His legs, because He was already dead. To satisfy the priests, they pierced His side. Had not life been already extinct, this wound would have caused instant death.

But it was not the spear thrust, it was not the pain of the cross, that caused the death of Jesus. That cry, uttered "with a loud voice," (Matthew 27:50; Luke 23:46.) at the moment of death, the stream of blood and water that flowed from His side, declared that He died of a broken heart. His heart was broken by mental anguish. He was slain by the sin of the world.

With the death of Christ the hopes of His disciples perished. They looked upon His closed eyelids and drooping head, his hair matted with blood, His pierced hands and feet, and their anguish was indescribable. Until the last they had not believed that He would die; they could hardly believe that He was really dead. Overwhelmed with sorrow, they did not recall His words foretelling this very scene. Nothing that He had said, now gave them comfort. They saw only the cross and its bleeding victim. The future seemed dark with despair. Their faith in Jesus had perished; but never had they loved their Lord as now. Never before had they so felt His worth, and their need of His presence.

Even in death, Christ's body was very precious to His disciples. They longed to give Him an honored burial, but knew not how to accomplish this. Treason against the Roman government was the crime for which Jesus was condemned, and persons put to death for this offense were consigned to a burial ground especially provided for such criminals. The disciple John with the women from Galilee had remained at the cross. They could not leave the body of their Lord to be handled by the unfeeling soldiers, and buried in a dishonored grave. Yet they could not prevent it. They could obtain no favors from the Jewish authorities, and they had no influence with Pilate.

In this emergency, Joseph of Arimathea and Nicodemus came to the help of the disciples. Both these men were members of the Sanhedrin, and were acquainted with Pilate. Both were men of wealth and influence. They were determined that the body of Jesus should have an honorable burial.

Joseph went boldly to Pilate, and begged from him the body of Jesus. For the first time, Pilate learned that Jesus was really dead. Conflicting reports had reached him in regard to the events attending the crucifixion, but the knowledge of Christ's death had been purposely kept from him. Pilate had been warned by the priests and rulers against deception by Christ's disciples in regard to His body. Upon hearing Joseph's request, he therefore sent for the centurion who had charge at the cross, and learned for a certainty of the death of Jesus. He also drew from him an account of the scenes of Calvary, confirming the testimony of Joseph.

The request of Joseph was granted. While John was troubled about the burial of his Master, Joseph returned with Pilate's order for the body of Christ; and Nicodemus came bringing a costly mixture of myrrh and aloes, of about a hundred pounds' weight, for His embalming. The most honored in all Jerusalem could not have been shown more respect in death. The disciples were astonished to see these wealthy rulers as much interested as they themselves in the burial of their Lord.

Neither Joseph nor Nicodemus had openly accepted the Saviour while He was living. They knew that such a step would exclude them from the Sanhedrin, and they hoped to protect Him by their influence in its councils. For a time they had seemed to succeed; but the wily priests, seeing their favor to Christ, had thwarted their plans. In their absence Jesus had been condemned and delivered to be crucified. Now that He was dead, they no longer concealed their attachment to Him. While the disciples feared to show themselves openly as His followers, Joseph and Nicodemus came boldly to their aid. The help of these rich and honored men was greatly needed at this time. They could do for their dead Master what it was impossible for the poor disciples to do; and their wealth and influence protected them, in a great measure, from the malice of the priests and rulers.

Gently and reverently they removed with their own hands the body of Jesus from the cross. Their tears of sympathy fell fast as they looked upon his bruised and lacerated form. Joseph owned a new tomb, hewn in a rock. This he was reserving for himself, but it was near Calvary, and he now prepared it for Jesus. The body, together with the spices brought by Nicodemus, was carefully wrapped in a linen sheet, and the Redeemer was borne to the tomb. There the three disciples straightened the mangled limbs, and folded the bruised hands upon the pulseless breast. The Galilean women came to see that all had been done that could be done for the lifeless form of their beloved Teacher. Then they saw the heavy stone rolled against the entrance of the tomb, and the Saviour was left at rest. The women were last at the cross, and last at the tomb of Christ. While the evening shades were gathering, Mary Magdalene and the other Marys lingered about the resting place of their Lord, shedding tears of sorrow over the fate of Him whom they loved. "And they returned, . . . and rested the Sabbath day, according to the commandment." Luke 23:56.

That was a never-to-be-forgotten Sabbath to the sorrowing disciples, and also to the priests, rulers, scribes, and people. At the setting of the sun on the evening of the preparation day the trumpets sounded, signifying that the Sabbath had begun. The Passover was observed as it had been for centuries, while He to whom it pointed had been slain by wicked hands, and lay in Joseph's tomb. On the Sabbath the courts of the temple were filled with worshipers. The high priest from Golgotha was there, splendidly robed in his sacerdotal garments. White-turbaned priests, full of activity, performed their duties. But some present were not at rest as the blood of bulls and goats was offered for sin. They were not conscious that type had met antitype, that an infinite sacrifice had been made for the sins of the world. They knew not that there was no further value in the performance of the ritual service. But never before had that service been witnessed with such conflicting feelings. The trumpets and musical instruments and the voices of the singers were as loud and clear as usual. But a sense of strangeness pervaded everything. One after another inquired about a strange event that had taken place. Hitherto the most holy place had been sacredly guarded from intrusion. But now it was open to all eyes. The heavy veil of tapestry, made of pure linen, and beautifully wrought with gold, scarlet, and purple, was rent from top to bottom. The place where Jehovah had met with the high priest, to communicate His glory, the place that had been God's sacred audience chamber, lay open to every eye,—a place no longer recognized by the Lord. With gloomy presentiments the priests ministered before the altar. The uncovering of the sacred mystery of the most holy place filled them with dread of coming calamity.

Many minds were busy with thoughts started by the scenes of Calvary. From the crucifixion to the resurrection many sleepless eyes were constantly searching the proph-

---

"But it was not the spear thrust, it was not the pain of the cross, that caused the death of Jesus. That cry, uttered 'with a loud voice', at the moment of death, the stream of blood and water that flowed from His side, declared that He died of a broken heart. His heart was broken by mental anguish. He was slain by the sin of the world."

---

ecies, some to learn the full meaning of the feast they were then celebrating, some to find evidence that Jesus was not what He claimed to be; and others with sorrowful hearts were searching for proofs that He was the true Messiah. Though searching with different objects in view, all were convicted of the same truth,—that prophecy had been fulfilled in the events of the past few days, and that the Crucified One was the world's Redeemer. Many who at that time united in the service never again took part in the paschal rites. Many even of the priests were convicted of the true character of Jesus. Their searching of the prophecies had not been in vain, and after His resurrection they acknowledged Him as the Son of God.

Nicodemus, when he saw Jesus lifted up on the cross, remembered His words spoken by night in the Mount of Olives: "As Moses lifted up the serpent in the wilderness, even so must the Son of man be lifted up; that whosoever believeth in Him should not perish, but have eternal life." John 3:14, 15. On that Sabbath, when Christ lay in the grave, Nicodemus had opportunity for reflection. A clearer light now illuminated his mind, and the words which Jesus had spoken to him were no longer mysterious. He felt that he had lost much by not connecting himself with the Saviour during His life. Now he recalled the events of Calvary. The prayer of Christ for His murderers, and His answer to the petition of the dying thief, spoke to the heart of the learned councilor. Again He looked upon the Saviour in His agony; again he heard that last cry, "It is finished," spoken like the words of a conqueror. Again he beheld the reeling earth, the darkened heavens, the rent veil, the shivered rocks, and his faith was forever established. The very event that destroyed the hopes of the disciples, convinced Joseph and Nicodemus of the divinity of Jesus. Their fears were overcome by the courage of a firm and unwavering faith.

Never had Christ attracted the attention of the multitude as now that He was laid in the tomb. According to their practice, the people brought their sick and suffering ones to the temple courts, inquiring, Who can tell us of Jesus of Nazareth? Many had come from far to find Him who had healed the sick and raised the dead. On every side was heard the cry, We want Christ the Healer. Upon this occasion those who were thought to show indications of the leprosy were examined by the priests. Many were forced to hear their husbands, wives, or children pronounced leprous, and doomed to go forth from the shelter of their homes and the care of their friends, to warn off the stranger with the mournful cry, "Unclean, unclean!" The friendly hands of Jesus of Nazareth, that never refused to touch with healing the loathsome leper, were folded on His breast. The lips that had answered his petition with the comforting words, "I will; be thou clean," (Matthew 8:3.) were now silent. Many appealed to the chief priests and rulers for sympathy and relief, but in vain. Apparently they were determined to have the living Christ among them again. With persistent earnestness they asked for Him. They would not be turned away. But they were driven from the temple courts, and soldiers were stationed at the gates to keep back the multitude that came with their sick and dying, demanding entrance.

The sufferers who had come to be healed by the Saviour, sank under their disappointment. The streets were filled with mourning. The sick were dying for want of the healing touch of Jesus. Physicians were consulted in vain; there was no skill like that of Him who lay in Joseph's tomb.

The mourning cries of the suffering ones brought home to thousands of minds the conviction that a great light had gone out of the world. Without Christ, the earth was blackness and darkness. Many whose voices had swelled the cry of "Crucify Him! crucify Him!" now realized the calamity that had fallen upon them, and would as eagerly have cried, Give us Jesus, had He still been alive.

When the people learned that Jesus had been put to death by the priests, inquiries were made regarding His death. The particulars of His trial were kept as private as possible; but during the time when He was in the grave, His name was on thousands of lips, and reports of His mock trial, and of the inhumanity of the priests and rulers, were circulated everywhere. By men of intellect these priests and rulers were called upon to explain the prophecies of the Old Testament concerning the Messiah, and while trying to frame some falsehood in reply, they became like men insane. The prophecies that pointed to Christ's sufferings and death they could not explain, and many inquirers were convinced that the Scriptures had been fulfilled.

The revenge which the priests had thought would be so sweet, was already bitterness to them. They knew that they were meeting the severe censure of the people, they knew that the very ones whom they had influenced against Jesus were now horrified by their own shameful work. These priests had tried to believe Jesus a deceiver; but it was in vain. Some of them had stood by the grave of Lazarus, and had seen the dead brought back to life. They trembled for fear that Christ would Himself rise from the dead, and again appear before them. They had heard Him declare that He had power to lay down His life and to take it again. They remembered that He had said, "Destroy this temple, and in three days I will raise it up." John 2:19. Judas had told them the words spoken by Jesus to the disciples while on the last journey to Jerusalem: "Behold, we go up to Jerusalem; and the Son of man shall be betrayed unto the chief priests and unto the scribes, and they shall condemn Him to death, and shall deliver Him to the Gentiles, to mock, and to scourge, and to crucify Him. And the third day He shall rise again." Matthew 20:18, 19. When they heard these words, they had mocked and ridiculed. But now they remembered that Christ's predictions had so far been fulfilled. He had said that He would rise again the third day, and who could say that this also would not come to pass? They longed to shut out these thoughts, but they could not. Like their father, the devil, they believed and trembled.

Now that the frenzy of excitement was past, the image of Christ would intrude upon their minds. They beheld Him as He stood serene and uncomplaining before His enemies, suffering without a murmur their taunts and abuse. All the events of His trial and crucifixion came back to them with an overpowering conviction that He was the Son of God. They felt that He might at any time stand before them, the accused to become the accuser, the condemned to condemn, the slain to demand justice in the death of His murderers.

They could rest little upon the Sabbath. Though they would not step over a Gentile's threshold for fear of defilement, yet they held a council concerning the body of Christ. Death and the grave must hold Him whom they had crucified. "The chief priests and Pharisees came together unto Pilate, saying, Sir, we remember that that deceiver said, while He was yet alive, After three days I will rise again. Command therefore that the sepulcher be made sure until the third day, lest His disciples come by night, and steal Him away, and say unto the people, He is risen from the dead. So the last error shall be worse than the first. Pilate said unto them, Ye have a watch; go your way, make it as sure as ye can." Matthew 27:62-65.

The priests gave directions for securing the sepulcher. A great stone had been placed before the opening. Across this stone they placed cords, securing the ends to the solid rock, and sealing them with the Roman seal. The stone could not be moved without breaking the seal. A guard of one hundred soldiers was then stationed around the sepulcher to prevent it from being tampered with. The priests did all they could to keep Christ's body where it had been laid. He was sealed as securely in His tomb as if He were to remain there through all time.

So weak men counseled and planned. Little did these murderers realize the uselessness of their efforts. But by their action God was glorified. The very efforts made to prevent Christ's resurrection are the most convincing arguments in its proof. The greater the number of soldiers placed around the tomb, the stronger would be the testimony that He had risen. Hundreds of years before the death of Christ, the Holy Spirit had declared through the psalmist, "Why do the heathen rage, and the people imagine a vain thing? The kings of the earth set themselves, and the rulers take counsel together, against the Lord, and against His anointed. . . . He that sitteth in the heavens shall laugh; the Lord shall have them in derision." Psalms 2:1-4. Roman guards and Roman arms were powerless to confine the Lord of life within the tomb. The hour of His release was near.

"The Lord Is Risen"

The night of the first day of the week had worn slowly away. The darkest hour, just before daybreak, had come. Christ was still a prisoner in His narrow tomb. The great stone was in its place; the Roman seal was unbroken; the Roman guards were keeping their watch. And there were unseen watchers. Hosts of evil angels were gathered about the place. Had it been possible, the prince of darkness with his apostate army would have kept forever sealed the tomb that held the Son of God. But a heavenly host surrounded the sepulcher. Angels that excel in strength were guarding the tomb, and waiting to welcome the Prince of Life.

"And, behold, there was a great earthquake; for the angel of the Lord descended from heaven." Clothed with the panoply of God, this angel left the heavenly courts. The bright beams of God's glory went before him, and illuminated his pathway. "His countenance was like lightning, and his raiment white as snow. And for fear of him the keepers did shake, and became as dead men."

Now, priests and rulers, where is the power of your guard? — Brave soldiers that have never been afraid of human power, are now as captives taken without sword or spear. The face they look upon is not the face of mortal warrior; it is the face of the mightiest of the Lord's host. This messenger is he who fills the position from which Satan fell. It is he who on the hills of Bethlehem proclaimed Christ's birth. The earth trembles at his approach, the hosts of darkness flee, and as he rolls away the stone, heaven seems to come down to the earth. The soldiers see him removing the stone as he would a pebble, and hear him cry, Son of God, come forth; Thy Father calls Thee. They see Jesus come forth from the grave, and hear Him proclaim over the rent sepulcher, "I am the resurrection and the life." As He comes forth in majesty and glory, the angel host bow low in adoration before the Redeemer, and welcome Him with songs of praise.

An earthquake marked the hour when Christ laid down His life, and another earthquake witnessed the moment when He took it up in triumph. He who had vanquished death and the grave came forth from the tomb with the tread of a conqueror, amid the reeling of the earth, the flashing of lightning, and the roaring of thunder. When He shall come to the earth again, He will shake "not the earth only, but also heaven." Hebrews 12:26. "The earth shall reel to and fro like a drunkard, and shall be removed like a cottage." "The heavens shall be rolled together as a scroll;" "the elements shall melt with fervent heat; the earth also, and the works that are therein, shall be burned up." But "the Lord will be the hope of His people, and the strength of the children of Israel." Isaiah 24:20; 34:4; 2 Peter 3:10; Joel 3:16.

At the death of Jesus the soldiers had beheld the earth wrapped in darkness at midday; but at the resurrection they saw the brightness of the angels illuminate the night, and heard the inhabitants of heaven singing with great joy and triumph: "Thou hast vanquished Satan and the powers of darkness; Thou hast swallowed up death in victory!"

Christ came forth from the tomb glorified, and the Roman guard beheld Him. Their eyes were riveted upon the face of Him whom they had so recently mocked and derided. In this glorified being they beheld the prisoner whom they had seen in the judgment hall, the one for whom they had plaited a crown of thorns. This was the one who had stood unresisting before Pilate and Herod, His form lacerated by the cruel scourge. This was He who had been nailed to the cross, at whom the priests and rulers,

166   This chapter is based on Matthew 28:2-4, 11-15

full of self-satisfaction, had wagged their heads, saying, "He saved others; Himself He cannot save." Matthew 27:42. This was He who had been laid in Joseph's new tomb. The decree of heaven had loosed the captive. Mountains piled upon mountains over His sepulcher could not have prevented Him from coming forth.

At sight of the angels and the glorified Saviour the Roman guard had fainted and become as dead men. When the heavenly train was hidden from their view, they arose to their feet, and as quickly as their trembling limbs could carry them, made their way to the gate of the garden. Staggering like drunken men, they hurried on to the city, telling those whom they met the wonderful news. They were making their way to Pilate, but their report had been carried to the Jewish authorities, and the chief priests and rulers sent for them to be brought first into their presence. A strange appearance those soldiers presented. Trembling with fear, their faces colorless, they bore testimony to the resurrection of Christ. The soldiers told all, just as they had seen it; they had not had time to think or speak anything but the truth. With painful utterance they said, It was the Son of God who was crucified; we have heard an angel proclaiming Him as the Majesty of heaven, the King of Glory.

The faces of the priests were as those of the dead. Caiaphas tried to speak. His lips moved, but they uttered no sound. The soldiers were about to leave the council room, when a voice stayed them. Caiaphas had at last found speech. Wait, wait, he said. Tell no one the things you have seen.

A lying report was then given to the soldiers. "Say ye," said the priests, "His disciples came by night, and stole Him away while we slept." Here the priests overreached themselves. How could the soldiers say that the disciples had stolen the body while they slept? If they were asleep, how could they know? And if the disciples had been proved guilty of stealing Christ's body, would not the priests have been first to condemn them? Or if the sentinels had slept at the tomb, would not the priests have been foremost in accusing them to Pilate?

The soldiers were horrified at the thought of bringing upon themselves the charge of sleeping at their post. This was an offense punishable with death. Should they bear false witness, deceiving the people, and placing their own lives in peril? Had they not kept their weary watch with sleepless vigilance? How could they stand the trial, even for the sake of money, if they perjured themselves?

In order to silence the testimony they feared, the priests promised to secure the safety of the guard, saying that Pilate would not desire to have such a report circulated any more than they did. The Roman soldiers sold their integrity to the Jews for money. They came in before the priests burdened with a most startling message of truth; they went out with a burden of money, and on their tongues a lying report which had been framed for them by the priests.

Meanwhile the report of Christ's resurrection had been carried to Pilate. Though Pilate was responsible for having given Christ up to die, he had been comparatively unconcerned. While he had condemned the Saviour unwillingly, and with a feeling of pity, he had felt no real compunction until now. In terror he now shut himself within his house, determined to see no one. But the priests made their way into his presence, told the story which they had invented, and urged him to overlook the sentinels' neglect of duty. Before consenting to this, he himself privately questioned the guard. They, fearing for their own safety, dared not conceal anything, and Pilate drew from them an account of all that had taken place. He did not prosecute the matter further, but from that time there was no peace for him.

When Jesus was laid in the grave, Satan triumphed. He dared to hope that the Saviour would not take up His life again. He claimed the Lord's body, and set his guard about the tomb, seeking to hold Christ a prisoner. He was bitterly angry when his angels fled at the approach of the heavenly messenger. When he saw Christ come forth in triumph, he knew that his kingdom would have an end, and that he must finally die.

The priests, in putting Christ to death, had made themselves the tools of Satan. Now they were entirely in his power. They were entangled in a snare from which they saw no escape but in continuing their warfare against Christ. When they heard the report of His resurrection, they feared the wrath of the people. They felt that their own lives were in danger. The only hope for them was to prove Christ an impostor by denying that He had risen. They bribed the soldiers, and secured Pilate's silence. They spread their lying reports far and near. But there were witnesses whom they could not silence. Many had heard of the soldiers' testimony to Christ's resurrection. And certain of the dead who came forth with Christ appeared to many, and declared that He had risen. Reports were brought to the priests of persons who had seen these risen ones, and heard their testimony. The priests and rulers were in continual dread, lest in walking the streets, or within the privacy of their own homes, they should come face to face with Christ. They felt that there was no safety for them. Bolts and bars were but poor protection against the Son of God. By day and by night that awful scene in the judgment hall, when they had cried, "His blood be on us, and on our children," (Matthew 27:25.) was before them. Nevermore would the memory of that scene fade from their minds. Nevermore would peaceful sleep come to their pillows.

When the voice of the mighty angel was heard at Christ's tomb, saying, "Thy Father calls Thee," the Saviour came forth from the grave by the life that was in Himself. Now was proved the truth of His words, "I lay down My life, that I might take it again. . . . I have power to lay it down, and I have power to take it again." Now was fulfilled the prophecy He had spoken to the priests and rulers, "Destroy this temple, and in three days I will raise it up." John 10:17, 18; 2:19.

Over the rent sepulcher of Joseph, Christ had proclaimed in triumph, "I am the resurrection and the life." These words could be spoken only by the Deity. All created beings live by the will and power of God. They are dependent recipients of the life of God. From the highest seraph to the humblest animate being, all are replenished from the Source of life. Only He who is one with God could say, I have power to lay down My life, and I have power to take it again. In His divinity, Christ possessed the power to break the bonds of death.

Christ arose from the dead as the first fruits of those that slept. He was the antitype of the wave sheaf, and His resurrection took place on the very day when the wave-sheaf was to be presented before the Lord. For more than a thousand years this symbolic ceremony had been performed. From the harvest fields the first heads of ripened grain were gathered, and when the people went up to Jerusalem to the Passover, the sheaf of first fruits was waved as a thank offering before the Lord. Not until this was presented, could the sickle be put to the grain, and it be gathered into sheaves. The sheaf dedicated to God represented the harvest. So Christ the first fruits represented the great spiritual harvest to be gathered for the kingdom of God. His resurrection is the type and pledge of the resurrection of all the righteous dead. "For if we believe that Jesus died and rose again, even so them also which sleep in Jesus will God bring with Him." 1 Thessalonians 4:14.

As Christ arose, He brought from the grave a multitude of captives. The earthquake at His death had rent open their graves, and when He arose, they came forth with Him. They were those who had been colaborers with God, and who at the cost of their lives had borne testimony to the truth. Now they were to be witnesses for Him who had raised them from the dead.

During His ministry, Jesus had raised the dead to life. He had raised the son of the widow of Nain, and the ruler's daughter and Lazarus. But these were not clothed with immortality. After they were raised, they were still subject to death. But those who came forth from the grave at Christ's resurrection, were raised to everlasting life. They ascended with Him as trophies of His victory over death and the grave. These, said Christ, are no longer the captives of Satan, I have redeemed them. I have brought them from the grave as the first fruits of My power, to be with Me where I am, never more to see death or experience sorrow.

These went into the city, and appeared unto many, declaring, Christ has risen from the dead, and we be risen with Him. Thus was immortalized the sacred truth of the resurrection. The risen saints bore witness to the truth of the words, "Thy dead men shall live; together with My dead body shall they arise." Their resurrection was an illustration of the fulfilment of the prophecy, "Awake and sing, ye that dwell in dust; for thy dew is as the dew of herbs, and the earth shall cast out the dead." Isaiah 26:10.

To the believer, Christ is the resurrection and the life. In our Saviour the life that was lost through sin is restored; for He has life in Himself to quicken whom He will. He is invested with the right to give immortality. The life that He laid down in humanity, He takes up again, and gives to humanity. "I am come," He said, "that they might have life, and that they might have it more abundantly." "Whosoever drinketh of the water that I shall give him, shall never thirst; but the water that I shall give him shall be in him a well of water springing up into everlasting life." "Whoso eateth My flesh, and drinketh My blood, hath eternal life; and I will raise him up at the last day." John 10:10; 4:14; 6:54.

To the believer, death is but a small matter. Christ speaks of it as if it were of little moment. "If a man keep My saying, he shall never see death," "he shall never taste of death." To the Christian, death is but a sleep, a moment of silence and darkness. The life is hid with Christ in God, and "when Christ, who is our life, shall appear, then shall ye also appear with Him in glory." John 8:51, 52; Colossians 3:4.

The voice that cried from the cross, "It is finished," was heard among the dead. It pierced the walls of sepulchers, and summoned the sleepers to arise. Thus will it be when the voice of Christ shall be heard from heaven. That voice will penetrate the graves and unbar the tombs, and the dead in Christ shall arise. At the Saviour's resurrection a few graves were opened, but at His second coming all the precious dead shall hear His voice, and shall come forth to glorious, immortal life. The same power that raised Christ from the dead will raise His church, and glorify it with Him, above all principalities, above all powers, above every name that is named, not only in this world, but also in the world to come.

"Why Weepest Thou?"

The women who had stood by the cross of Christ waited and watched for the hours of the Sabbath to pass. On the first day of the week, very early, they made their way to the tomb, taking with them precious spices to anoint the Saviour's body. They did not think about His rising from the dead. The sun of their hope had set, and night had settled down on their hearts. As they walked, they recounted Christ's works of mercy and His words of comfort. But they remembered not His words, "I will see you again." John 16:22.

Ignorant of what was even then taking place, they drew near the garden, saying as they went, "Who shall roll us away the stone from the door of the sepulcher?" They knew that they could not remove the stone, yet they kept on their way. And lo, the heavens were suddenly alight with glory that came not from the rising sun. The earth trembled. They saw that the great stone was rolled away. The grave was empty.

The women had not all come to the tomb from the same direction. Mary Magdalene was the first to reach the place; and upon seeing that the stone was removed, she hurried away to tell the disciples. Meanwhile the other women came up. A light was shining about the tomb, but the body of Jesus was not there. As they lingered about the place, suddenly they saw that they were not alone. A young man clothed in shining garments was sitting by the tomb. It was the angel who had rolled away the stone. He had taken the guise of humanity that he might not alarm these friends of Jesus. Yet about him the light of the heavenly glory was still shining, and the women were afraid. They turned to flee, but the angel's words stayed their steps. "Fear not ye," he said; "for I know that ye seek Jesus, which was crucified. He is not here; for He is risen, as He said. Come, see the place where the Lord lay. And go quickly, and tell His disciples that He is risen from the dead." Again they look into the tomb, and again they hear the wonderful news. Another angel in human form is there, and he says, "Why seek ye the living among the dead? He is not here, but is risen; remember how He spake unto you when He was yet in Galilee, saying, The Son of man must be delivered into the hands of sinful men, and be crucified, and the third day rise again."

He is risen, He is risen! The women repeat the words again and again. No need now for the anointing spices. The Saviour is living, and not dead. They remember now that when speaking of His death He said that He would rise again. What a day is this to the world! Quickly the women departed from the sepulcher "with fear and great joy, and did run to bring His disciples word."

Mary had not heard the good news. She went to Peter and John with the sorrowful message, "They have taken away the Lord out of the sepulcher, and we know not where they have laid Him." The disciples hurried to the tomb, and found it as Mary had said. They saw the shroud and the napkin, but they did not find their Lord. Yet even here was testimony that He had risen. The grave clothes were not thrown heedlessly aside, but carefully folded, each in a place by itself. John "saw and believed." He did not yet understand the scripture that Christ must rise from the dead; but he now remembered the Saviour's words foretelling His resurrection.

It was Christ Himself who had placed those grave clothes with such care. When the mighty angel came down to the tomb, he was joined by another, who with his company had been keeping guard over the Lord's body. As the angel from heaven rolled away the stone, the other entered the tomb, and unbound the wrappings from the body of Jesus. But it was the Saviour's hand that folded each, and laid it in its place. In His sight who guides alike the star and the atom, there is nothing unimportant. Order and perfection are seen in all His work.

Mary had followed John and Peter to the tomb; when they returned to Jerusalem, she remained. As she looked into the empty tomb, grief filled her heart. Looking in, she saw the two angels, one at the head and the other at the foot where Jesus had lain. "Woman, why weepest thou?" they asked her. "Because they have taken away my Lord,"

"Jesus lives, and because He lives, we shall live also. From grateful hearts, . . . let the glad song ring out, Christ is risen! He lives to make intercession for us. Grasp this hope, and it will hold the soul like a sure, tried anchor. Believe, and thou shalt see the glory of God."

she answered, "and I know not where they have laid Him."

Then she turned away, even from the angels, thinking that she must find someone who could tell her what had been done with the body of Jesus. Another voice addressed her, "Woman, why weepest thou? whom seekest thou?" Through her tear-dimmed eyes, Mary saw the form of a man, and thinking that it was the gardener, she said, "Sir, if thou have borne Him hence, tell me where thou hast laid Him, and I will take Him away." If this rich man's tomb was thought too honorable a burial place for Jesus, she herself would provide a place for Him. There was a grave that Christ's own voice had made vacant, the grave where Lazarus had lain. Might she not there find a burial place for her Lord? She felt that to care for His precious crucified body would be a great consolation to her in her grief.

But now in His own familiar voice Jesus said to her, "Mary." Now she knew that it was not a stranger who was addressing her, and turning she saw before her the living Christ. In her joy she forgot that He had been crucified. Springing toward Him, as if to embrace His feet, she said,

"Rabboni." But Christ raised His hand, saying, Detain Me not; "for I am not yet ascended to My Father; but go to My brethren, and say unto them, I ascend unto My Father, and your Father; and to My God, and your God." And Mary went her way to the disciples with the joyful message.

Jesus refused to receive the homage of His people until He had the assurance that His sacrifice was accepted by the Father. He ascended to the heavenly courts, and from God Himself heard the assurance that His atonement for the sins of men had been ample, that through His blood all might gain eternal life. The Father ratified the covenant made with Christ, that He would receive repentant and obedient men, and would love them even as He loves His Son. Christ was to complete His work, and fulfill His pledge to "make a man more precious than fine gold; even a man than the golden wedge of Ophir." Isaiah 13:12. All power in heaven and on earth was given to the Prince of Life, and He returned to His followers in a world of sin, that He might impart to them of His power and glory.

While the Saviour was in God's presence, receiving gifts for His church, the disciples thought upon His empty tomb, and mourned and wept. The day that was a day of rejoicing to all heaven was to the disciples a day of uncertainty, confusion, and perplexity. Their unbelief in the testimony of the women gives evidence of how low their faith had sunk. The news of Christ's resurrection was so different from what they had anticipated, that they could not believe it. It was too good to be true, they thought. They had heard so much of the doctrines and the so-called scientific theories of the Sadducees, that the impression made on their minds in regard to the resurrection was vague. They scarcely knew what the resurrection from the dead could mean. They were unable to take in the great subject.

"Go your way," the angels had said to the women, "tell His disciples and Peter that He goeth before you into Galilee; there shall ye see Him, as He said unto you." These angels had been with Christ as guardian angels throughout His life on earth. They had witnessed His trial and crucifixion. They had heard His words to His disciples. This was shown by their message to the disciples, and should have convinced them of its truth. Such words could have come only from the messengers of their risen Lord.

"Tell His disciples and Peter," the angels said. Since the death of Christ, Peter had been bowed down with remorse. His shameful denial of the Lord, and the Saviour's look of love and anguish, were ever before him. Of all the disciples he had suffered most bitterly. To him the assurance is given that his repentance is accepted and his sin forgiven. He is mentioned by name.

"Tell His disciples and Peter that He goeth before you into Galilee; there shall ye see Him." All the disciples had forsaken Jesus, and the call to meet Him again includes them all. He has not cast them off. When Mary Magdalene told them she had seen the Lord, she repeated the call to the meeting in Galilee. And a third time the message was sent to them. After He had ascended to the Father, Jesus appeared to the other women, saying, "All hail. And they came and held Him by the feet, and worshiped Him. Then said Jesus unto them, Be not afraid; go tell My brethren that they go into Galilee, and there shall they see Me."

Christ's first work on earth after His resurrection was to convince His disciples of His undiminished love and tender regard for them. To give them proof that He was their living Saviour, that He had broken the fetters of the tomb, and could no longer be held by the enemy death; to reveal that He had the same heart of love as when He was with them as their beloved Teacher, He appeared to them again and again. He would draw the bonds of love still closer around them. Go tell My brethren, He said, that they meet Me in Galilee.

As they heard this appointment, so definitely given, the disciples began to think of Christ's words to them foretelling His resurrection. But even now they did not rejoice. They could not cast off their doubt and perplexity. Even when the women declared that they had seen the Lord, The disciples would not believe. They thought them under an illusion.

Trouble seemed crowding upon trouble. On the sixth day of the week they had seen their Master die; on the first day of the next week they found themselves deprived of His body, and they were accused of having stolen it away for the sake of deceiving the people. They despaired of ever correcting the false impressions that were gaining ground against them. They feared the enmity of the priests and the wrath of the people. They longed for the presence of Jesus, who had helped them in every perplexity.

Often they repeated the words, "We trusted that it had been He which should have redeemed Israel." Lonely and sick at heart they remembered His words, "If they do these things in a green tree, what shall be done in the dry?" Luke 24:21; 23:31. They met together in the upper chamber, and closed and fastened the doors, knowing that the fate of their beloved Teacher might at any time be theirs.

And all the time they might have been rejoicing in the knowledge of a risen Saviour. In the garden, Mary had stood weeping, when Jesus was close beside her. Her eyes were so blinded by tears that she did not discern Him. And the hearts of the disciples were so full of grief that they did not believe the angels' message or the words of Christ Himself.

How many are still doing what these disciples did. How many echo Mary's despairing cry, "They have taken away the Lord, . . . and we know not where they have laid Him." To how many might the Saviour's words be spoken, "Why weepest thou? whom seekest thou?" He is close beside them, but their tear-blinded eyes do not discern Him. He speaks to them, but they do not understand.

Oh that the bowed head might be lifted, that the eyes might be opened to behold Him, that the ears might listen to His voice! "Go quickly, and tell His disciples that He is risen." Bid them look not to Joseph's new tomb, that was closed with a great stone, and sealed with the Roman seal. Christ is not there. Look not to the empty sepulcher. Mourn not as those who are hopeless and helpless. Jesus lives, and because He lives, we shall live also. From grateful hearts, from lips touched with holy fire, let the glad song ring out, Christ is risen! He lives to make intercession for us. Grasp this hope, and it will hold the soul like a sure, tried anchor. Believe, and thou shalt see the glory of God.

The Walk to Emmaus

Late in the afternoon of the day of the resurrection, two of the disciples were on their way to Emmaus, a little town eight miles from Jerusalem. These disciples had had no prominent place in Christ's work, but they were earnest believers in Him, They had come to the city to keep the Passover, and were greatly perplexed by the events that had recently taken place. They had heard the news of the morning in regard to the removal of Christ's body from the tomb, and also the report of the women who had seen the angels and had met Jesus. They were now returning to their homes to meditate and pray. Sadly they pursued their evening walk, talking over the scenes of the trial and the crucifixion. Never before had they been so utterly disheartened. Hopeless and faithless, they were walking in the shadow of the cross.

They had not advanced far on their journey when they were joined by a stranger, but they were so absorbed in their gloom and disappointment that they did not observe him closely. They continued their conversation, expressing the thoughts of their hearts. They were reasoning in regard to the lessons that Christ had given, which they seemed unable to comprehend. As they talked of the events that had taken place, Jesus longed to comfort them. He had seen their grief; He understood the conflicting, perplexing ideas that brought to their minds the thought, Can this man, who suffered Himself to be so humiliated, be the Christ? Their grief could not be restrained, and they wept. Jesus knew that their hearts were bound up with Him in love, and He longed to wipe away their tears, and fill them with joy and gladness. But He must first give them lessons they would never forget.

"He said unto them, What manner of communications are these, that ye have one to another, as ye walk, and are sad? And the one of them, whose name was Cleopas, answering said unto Him, Art Thou only a stranger in Jerusalem, and hast not known the things which are come to pass there in these days?" They told Him of their disappointment in regard to their Master, "which was a prophet mighty in deed and word before God and all the people;" but "the chief priests and our rulers," they said, "delivered Him to be condemned to death, and have crucified Him." With hearts sore with disappointment, and with quivering lips, they added, "We trusted that it had been He which should have redeemed Israel. And beside all this, today is the third day since these things were done."

Strange that the disciples did not remember Christ's words, and realize that He had foretold the events which had come to pass. They did not realize that the last part of His disclosure would be just as verily fulfilled as the first part, that the third day He would rise again. This was the part they should have remembered. The priests and rulers did not forget this. On the day "that followed the day of the preparation, the chief priests and Pharisees came together unto Pilate, saying, Sir, we remember that that deceiver said, while He was yet alive, After three days I will rise again." Matthew 27:62, 63. But the disciples did not remember these words.

"Then He said unto them, O fools, and slow of heart to believe all that the prophets have spoken; ought not Christ to have suffered these things, and to enter into His glory?" The disciples wondered who this stranger could be, that He should penetrate to their very souls, and speak with such earnestness, tenderness, and sympathy, and with such hopefulness. For the first time since Christ's betrayal, they began to feel hopeful. Often they looked earnestly at their

This chapter is based on Luke 24:13-33.

companion, and thought that His words were just the words that Christ would have spoken. They were filled with amazement, and their hearts began to throb with joyful expectation.

Beginning at Moses, the very Alpha of Bible history, Christ expounded in all the Scriptures the things concerning Himself. Had He first made Himself known to them, their hearts would have been satisfied. In the fulness of their joy they would have hungered for nothing more. But it was necessary for them to understand the witness borne to Him by the types and prophecies of the Old Testament. Upon these their faith must be established. Christ performed no miracle to convince them, but it was His first work to explain the Scriptures. They had looked upon His death as the destruction of all their hopes. Now He showed from the prophets that this was the very strongest evidence for their faith.

In teaching these disciples, Jesus showed the importance of the Old Testament as a witness to His mission. Many professed Christians now discard the Old Testament, claiming that it is no longer of any use. But such is not Christ's teaching. So highly did He value it, that at one time He said, "If they hear not Moses and the prophets, neither will they be persuaded, though one rose from the dead." Luke 16:31.

It is the voice of Christ that speaks through patriarchs and prophets, from the days of Adam even to the closing scenes of time. The Saviour is revealed in the Old Testament as clearly as in the New. It is the light from the prophetic past that brings out the life of Christ and the teachings of the New Testament with clearness and beauty. The miracles of Christ are a proof of His divinity; but a stronger proof that He is the world's Redeemer is found in comparing the prophecies of the Old Testament with the history of the New.

Reasoning from prophecy, Christ gave his disciples a correct idea of what He was to be in humanity. Their expectation of a Messiah who was to take His throne and kingly power in accordance with the desires of men, had been misleading. It would interfere with a correct apprehension of His descent from the highest to the lowest position that could be occupied. Christ desired that the ideas of His disciples might be pure and true in every specification. They must understand as far as possible in regard to the cup of suffering that had been apportioned to Him. He showed them that the awful conflict which they could not yet comprehend, was the fulfilment of the covenant made before the foundation of the world was laid. Christ must die, as every transgressor of the law must die if he continues in sin. All this was to be, but it was not to end in defeat, but in glorious, eternal victory. Jesus told them that every effort must be made to save the world from sin. His followers must live as He lived, and work as He worked, with intense, persevering effort.

Thus Christ discoursed to His disciples, opening their minds that they might understand the Scriptures. The

disciples were weary, but the conversation did not flag. Words of life and assurance fell from the Saviour's lips. But still their eyes were holden. As He told them of the overthrow of Jerusalem, they looked upon the doomed city with weeping. But little did they yet suspect who their traveling companion was. They did not think that the subject of their conversation was walking by their side; for Christ referred to Himself as though He were another

> **"Many professed Christians now discard the Old Testament, claiming that it is no longer of any use. But such is not Christ's teaching. . . . The miracles of Christ are a proof of His divinity; but a stronger proof that He is the world's Redeemer is found in comparing the prophecies of the Old Testament with the history of the New."**

person. They thought that He was one of those who had been in attendance at the great feast, and who was now returning to his home. He walked as carefully as they over the rough stones, now and then halting with them for a little rest. Thus they proceeded along the mountainous road, while the One who was soon to take His position at God's right hand, and who could say, "All power is given unto Me in heaven and in earth," (Matthew 28:18.) walked beside them.

During the journey the sun had gone down, and before the travelers reached their place of rest, the laborers in the fields had left their work. As the disciples were about to enter their home, the stranger appeared as though He would continue His journey. But the disciples felt drawn to Him. Their souls hungered to hear more from Him. "Abide with us," they said. He did not seem to accept the invitation, but they pressed it upon Him, urging, "It is toward evening, and the day is far spent." Christ yielded to this entreaty and, "went in to tarry with them."

Had the disciples failed to press their invitation, they would not have known that their traveling companion was the risen Lord. Christ never forces His company upon any one. He interests Himself in those who need Him. Gladly will He enter the humblest home, and cheer the lowliest heart. But if men are too indifferent to think of the heavenly guest, or ask Him to abide with them, He passes on. Thus many meet with great loss. They do not know Christ any more than did the disciples as He walked with them by the way.

The simple evening meal of bread is soon prepared. It is placed before the guest, who has taken His seat at the head of the table. Now He puts forth His hands to bless the food. The disciples start back in astonishment. Their companion spreads forth His hands in exactly the same way as their Master used to do. They look again, and lo, they see in His hands the print of nails. Both exclaim at once, It is the Lord Jesus! He has risen from the dead!

They rise to cast themselves at His feet and worship Him, but He has vanished out of their sight. They look at the place which had been occupied by One whose body had lately lain in the grave, and say to each other, "Did not our heart burn within us, while He talked with us by the way, and while He opened to us the Scriptures?"

But with this great news to communicate they cannot sit and talk. Their weariness and hunger are gone. They leave their meal untasted, and full of joy immediately set out again on the same path by which they came, hurrying to tell the tidings to the disciples in the city. In some parts the road is not safe, but they climb over the steep places, slipping on the smooth rocks. They do not see, they do not know, that they have the protection of Him who has traveled the road with them. With their pilgrim staff in hand, they press on, desiring to go faster than they dare. They lose their track, but find it again. Sometimes running, sometimes stumbling, they press forward, their unseen companion close beside them all the way.

The night is dark, but the Sun of Righteousness is shining upon them. Their hearts leap for joy. They seem to be in a new world. Christ is a living Saviour. They no longer mourn over Him as dead. Christ is risen — over and over again they repeat it. This is the message they are carrying to the sorrowing ones. They must tell them the wonderful story of the walk to Emmaus. They must tell who joined them by the way. They carry the greatest message ever given to the world, a message of glad tidings upon which the hopes of the human family for time and for eternity depend.

"Peace Be Unto You"

On reaching Jerusalem the two disciples enter at the eastern gate, which is open at night on festal occasions. The houses are dark and silent, but the travelers make their way through the narrow streets by the light of the rising moon. They go to the upper chamber, where Jesus spent the hours of the last evening before His death. Here they know that their brethren are to be found. Late as it is, they know that the disciples will not sleep till they learn for a certainty what has become of the body of their Lord. They find the door of the chamber securely barred. They knock for admission, but no answer comes. All is still. Then they give their names. The door is carefully unbarred, they enter, and Another, unseen, enters with them. Then the door is again fastened, to keep out spies.

The travelers find all in surprised excitement. The voices of those in the room break out into thanksgiving and praise, saying, "The Lord is risen indeed, and hath appeared to Simon." Then the two travelers, panting with the haste with which they have made their journey, tell the wondrous story of how Jesus has appeared to them. They have just ended, and some are saying that they cannot believe it, for it is too good to be true, when behold, another person stands before them. Every eye is fastened upon the stranger. No one has knocked for entrance. No footstep has been heard. The disciples are startled, and wonder what it means. Then they hear a voice which is no other than the voice of their Master. Clear and distinct the words fall from His lips, "Peace be unto you."

"But they were terrified and affrighted, and supposed that they had seen a spirit. And He said unto them, Why are ye troubled? and why do thoughts arise in your hearts? Behold My hands and My feet, that it is I Myself; handle Me and see; for a spirit hath not flesh and bones, as ye see Me have. And when He had thus spoken, He showed them His hands and His feet."

They beheld the hands and feet marred by the cruel nails. They recognized His voice, like no other they had ever heard. "And while they yet believed not for joy, and wondered, He said unto them, Have ye here any meat? And they give Him a piece of a broiled fish and of an honeycomb. And He took it, and did eat before them." "Then were the disciples glad when they saw the Lord." Faith and joy took the place of unbelief, and with feelings which no words could express they acknowledged their risen Saviour.

At the birth of Jesus the angel announced, Peace on earth, and good will to men. And now at His first appearance to the disciples after His resurrection, the Saviour addressed them with the blessed words, "Peace be unto you." Jesus is ever ready to speak peace to souls that are burdened with doubts and fears. He waits for us to open the door of the heart to Him, and say, Abide with us. He says, "Behold, I stand at the door, and knock; if any man hear My voice, and open the door, I will come in to him, and will sup with him, and he with Me." Revelation 3:20.

The resurrection of Jesus was a type of the final resurrection of all who sleep in Him. The countenance of the risen Saviour, His manner, His speech, were all familiar to His disciples. As Jesus arose from the dead, so those who sleep in Him are to rise again. We shall know our friends, even as the disciples knew Jesus. They may have been deformed, diseased, or disfigured, in this mortal life, and they rise in perfect health and symmetry; yet in the glorified body their identity will be perfectly preserved. Then shall we know even as also we are known. 1 Corinthians 13:12. In the face radiant with the light shining from

the face of Jesus, we shall recognize the lineaments of those we love.

When Jesus met with His disciples, He reminded them of the words He had spoken to them before His death, that all things must be fulfilled which were written in the law of Moses, and in the prophets, and in the Psalms concerning Him. "Then opened He their understanding, that they might understand the Scriptures, and said unto them, Thus it is written, and thus it behooved Christ to suffer, and to rise from the dead the third day; and that repentance and remission of sins should be preached in His name among all nations, beginning at Jerusalem. And ye are witnesses of these things."

The disciples began to realize the nature and extent of their work. They were to proclaim to the world the wonderful truths which Christ had entrusted to them. The events of His life, His death and resurrection, the prophecies that pointed to these events, the sacredness of the law of God, the mysteries of the plan of salvation, the power of Jesus for the remission of sins, — to all these things they were witnesses, and they were to make them known to the world. They were to proclaim the gospel of peace and salvation through repentance and the power of the Saviour.

"And when He had said this, He breathed on them, and saith unto them, Receive ye the Holy Ghost: Whosoever sins ye remit, they are remitted unto them; and whosoever sins ye retain, they are retained." The Holy Spirit was not yet fully manifested; for Christ had not yet been glorified. The more abundant impartation of the Spirit did not take place till after Christ's ascension. Not until this was received could the disciples fulfill the commission to preach the gospel to the world. But the Spirit was now given for a special purpose. Before the disciples could fulfil their official duties in connection with the church, Christ breathed His Spirit upon them. He was committing to them a most sacred trust, and He desired to impress them with the fact that without the Holy Spirit this work could not be accomplished.

The Holy Spirit is the breath of spiritual life in the soul. The impartation of the Spirit is the impartation of the life of Christ. It imbues the receiver with the attributes of Christ. Only those who are thus taught of God, those who possess the inward working of the Spirit, and in whose life the Christ-life is manifested, are to stand as representative men, to minister in behalf of the church.

"Whosoever sins ye remit," said Christ, "they are remitted; . . . and whosoever sins ye retain, they are retained." Christ here gives no liberty for any man to pass judgment upon others. In the sermon on the mount He forbade this. It is the prerogative of God. But on the church in its organized capacity He places a responsibility for the individual members. Toward those who fall into sin, the church has a duty, to warn, to instruct, and if possible to restore. "Reprove, rebuke, exhort," the Lord says, "with all long-suffering and doctrine." 2 Timothy 4:2. Deal faithfully with wrongdoing. Warn every soul that is in danger. Leave none to deceive themselves. Call sin by its right name. Declare what God has said in regard to lying, Sabbath breaking, stealing, idolatry, and every other evil. "They which do such things shall not inherit the kingdom of God." Galatians 5:21. If they persist in sin, the judgment you have declared from God's word is pronounced upon them in heaven. In choosing to sin, they disown Christ; the church must show that she does not sanction their deeds, or she herself dishonors her Lord. She must say about sin what God says about it. She must deal with it as God directs, and her action is ratified in heaven. He who despises the authority of the church, despises the authority of Christ Himself.

But there is a brighter side to the picture. "Whosoever sins ye remit, they are remitted." Let this thought be kept uppermost. In labor for the erring, let every eye be directed to Christ. Let the shepherds have a tender care for the flock of the Lord's pasture. Let them speak to the erring of the forgiving mercy of the Saviour. Let them encourage the sinner to repent, and believe in Him who can pardon. Let them declare, on the authority of God's word, "If we confess our sins, He is faithful and just to forgive us our sins, and to cleanse us from all unrighteousness." 1 John 1:9. All who repent have the assurance, "He will have compassion upon us; He will subdue our iniquities; and Thou wilt cast all their sins into the depths of the sea." Micah 7:19.

Let the repentance of the sinner be accepted by the church with grateful hearts. Let the repenting one be led out from the darkness of unbelief, into the light of faith and righteousness. Let his trembling hand be placed in the loving hand of Jesus. Such a remission is ratified in heaven.

Only in this sense has the church power to absolve the sinner. Remission of sins can be obtained only through the merits of Christ. To no man, to no body of men, is given power to free the soul from guilt. Christ charged His disciples to preach the remission of sins in His name among all nations; but they themselves were not empowered to remove one stain of sin. The name of Jesus is the only "name under heaven given among men, whereby we must be saved." Acts 4:12.

When Jesus first met the disciples in the upper chamber, Thomas was not with them. He heard the reports of the others, and received abundant proof that Jesus had risen; but gloom and unbelief filled his heart. As he heard the disciples tell of the wonderful manifestations of the risen Saviour, it only plunged him in deeper despair. If Jesus had really risen from the dead, there could be no further hope of a literal earthly kingdom. And it wounded his vanity to think that his Master should reveal Himself to all the disciples except him. He was determined not to believe, and for a whole week he brooded over his wretchedness, which seemed all the darker in contrast with the hope and faith of his brethren.

During this time he repeatedly declared, "Except I shall see in His hands the print of the nails, and put my finger into the print of the nails, and thrust my hand into His side, I will not believe." He would not see through the eyes of his brethren, or exercise faith which was dependent upon their testimony. He ardently loved his Lord, but he had allowed jealousy and unbelief to take possession of his mind and heart.

A number of the disciples now made the familiar upper chamber their temporary home, and at evening all except Thomas gathered here. One evening Thomas determined to meet with the others. Notwithstanding his unbelief, he had a faint hope that the good news was true. While the disciples were taking their evening meal, they talked of the evidences which Christ had given them in the prophecies. "Then came Jesus, the doors being shut, and stood in the midst, and said, Peace be unto you."

Turning to Thomas He said, "Reach hither thy finger, and behold My hands; and reach hither thy hand, and thrust it into My side; and be not faithless, but believing." These words showed that He was acquainted with the thoughts and words of Thomas. The doubting disciple knew that none of his companions had seen Jesus for a week. They could not have told the Master of his unbelief. He recognized the One before him as his Lord. He had no desire for further proof. His heart leaped for joy, and he cast himself at the feet of Jesus crying, "My Lord and my God!"

Jesus accepted his acknowledgment, but gently reproved his unbelief: "Thomas, because thou hast seen Me, thou hast believed; blessed are they that have not seen, and yet have believed." The faith of Thomas would have been more pleasing to Christ if he had been willing to believe upon the testimony of his brethren. Should the world now follow the example of Thomas, no one would believe unto salvation; for all who receive Christ must do so through the testimony of others.

Many who are given to doubt excuse themselves by saying that if they had the evidence which Thomas had from his companions, they would believe. They do not realize that they have not only that evidence, but much more. Many who, like Thomas, wait for all cause of doubt to be removed, will never realize their desire. They gradually become confirmed in unbelief. Those who educate themselves to look on the dark side, and murmur and complain, know not what they do. They are sowing the seeds of doubt, and they will have a harvest of doubt to reap. At a time when faith and confidence are most essential, many will thus find themselves powerless to hope and believe.

In His treatment of Thomas, Jesus gave a lesson for His followers. His example shows how we should treat those whose faith is weak, and who make their doubts prominent. Jesus did not overwhelm Thomas with reproach, nor did He enter into controversy with him. He revealed Himself to the doubting one. Thomas had been most unreasonable in dictating the conditions of his faith, but Jesus, by His generous love and consideration, broke down all the barriers. Unbelief is seldom overcome by controversy. It is rather put upon self-defense, and finds new support and excuse. But let Jesus, in His love and mercy, be revealed as the crucified Saviour, and from many once unwilling lips will be heard the acknowledgment of Thomas, "My Lord and my God."

By the Sea
Once More

Jesus had appointed to meet His disciples in Galilee; and soon after the Passover week was ended, they bent their steps thither. Their absence from Jerusalem during the feast, would have been interpreted as disaffection and heresy, therefore they remained till its close; but this over, they gladly turned homeward to meet the Saviour as He had directed.

Seven of the disciples were in company. They were clad in the humble grab of fishermen; they were poor in worldly goods, but rich in the knowledge and practice of the truth, which in the sight of Heaven gave them the highest rank as teachers. They had not been students in the schools of the prophets, but for three years they had been taught by the greatest educator the world has ever known. Under His instruction they had become elevated, intelligent, and refined, agents through whom men might be led to a knowledge of the truth.

Much of the time of Christ's ministry had been passed near the Sea of Galilee. As the disciples gathered in a place where they were not likely to be disturbed, they found themselves surrounded by reminders of Jesus and His mighty works. On this sea, when their hearts were filled with terror, and the fierce storm was hurrying them to destruction, Jesus had walked upon the billows to their rescue. Here the tempest had been hushed by His word. Within sight was the beach where above ten thousand persons had been fed from a few small loaves and fishes. Not far distant was Capernaum, the scene of so many miracles. As the disciples looked upon the scene, their minds were full of the words and deeds of their Saviour.

The evening was pleasant, and Peter, who still had much of his old love for boats and fishing, proposed that they should go out upon the sea and cast their nets. In this plan all were ready to join; they were in need of food and clothing, which the proceeds of a successful night's fishing would supply. So they went out in their boat, but they caught nothing. All night they toiled, without success. Through the weary hours they talked of their absent Lord, and recalled the wonderful events they had witnessed in His ministry beside the sea. They questioned as to their own future, and grew sad at the prospect before them.

All the while a lone watcher upon the shore followed them with His eye, while He Himself was unseen. At length the morning dawned. The boat was but a little way from the shore, and the disciples saw a stranger standing upon the beach, who accosted them with the question, "Children, have ye any meat?" When they answered, "No," "He said unto them, Cast the net on the right side of the ship, and ye shall find. They cast therefore, and now they were not able to draw it for the multitude of fishes."

John recognized the stranger, and exclaimed to Peter, "It is the Lord." Peter was so elated and so glad that in his eagerness he cast himself into the water and was soon standing by the side of his Master. The other disciples came in their boat, dragging the net with fishes. "As soon then as they were come to land, they saw a fire of coals there, and fish laid thereon, and bread."

They were too much amazed to question whence came the fire and the food. "Jesus saith unto them, Bring of the fish which ye have now caught." Peter rushed for the net, which he had dropped, and helped his brethren drag it to the shore. After the work was done, and the preparation made, Jesus bade the disciples come and dine. He broke the food, and divided it among them, and was known and acknowledged by all the seven. The miracle of feeding the five thousand on the mountainside was now brought to their minds; but a mysterious awe was upon them, and in silence they gazed upon the risen Saviour.

Vividly they recalled the scene beside the sea when Jesus had bidden them follow Him. They remembered how, at His command, they had launched out into the deep, and had let down their net, and the catch had been so abundant as to fill the net, even to breaking. Then Jesus had called them to leave their fishing boats, and had promised to make them fishers of men. It was to bring this scene to their minds, and to deepen its impression, that He had again performed the miracle. His act was a renewal of the commission to the disciples. It showed them that the death of their Master had not lessened their obligation to do the work He had assigned them. Though they were to be deprived of His personal companionship, and of the means of support by their former employment, the risen Saviour would still have a care for them. While they were doing His work, He would provide for their needs. And Jesus had a purpose in bidding them cast their net on the right side of the ship. On that side He stood upon the shore. That was the side of faith. If they labored in connection with Him,—His divine power combining with their human effort,—they could not fail of success.

Another lesson Christ had to give, relating especially to Peter. Peter's denial of His Lord had been in shameful contrast to his former professions of loyalty. He had dishonored Christ, and had incurred the distrust of his brethren. They thought he would not be allowed to take his former position among them, and he himself felt that he had forfeited his trust. Before being called to take up again his apostolic work, he must before them all give evidence of his repentance. Without this, his sin, though repented of, might have destroyed his influence as a minister of Christ. The Saviour gave him opportunity to regain the confidence of his brethren, and, so far as possible, to remove the reproach he had brought upon the gospel.

Here is given a lesson for all Christ's followers. The gospel makes no compromise with evil. It cannot excuse sin. Secret sins are to be confessed in secret to God; but for open sin, open confession is required. The reproach of the disciple's sin is cast upon Christ. It causes Satan to triumph, and wavering souls to stumble. By giving proof of repentance, the disciple, so far as lies in his power, is to remove this reproach.

While Christ and the disciples were eating together by the seaside, the Saviour said to Peter, "Simon, son of Jonas, lovest thou Me more than these?" referring to his brethren. Peter had once declared, "Though all men shall be offended because of Thee, yet will I never be offended." Matthew 26:33. But he now put a truer estimate upon himself. "Yea, Lord," he said, "Thou knowest that I love Thee." There is no vehement assurance that his love is greater than that of his brethren. He does not express his own opinion of his devotion. To Him who can read all the motives of the heart he appeals to judge as to his sincerity,—"Thou knowest that I love Thee." And Jesus bids him, "Feed My lambs."

Again Jesus applied the test to Peter, repeating His former words: "Simon, son of Jonas, lovest thou Me?" This time He did not ask Peter whether he loved Him better than did his brethren. The second response was like the first, free from extravagant assurance: "Yea, Lord; Thou knowest that I love Thee." Jesus said to him, "Feed My sheep." Once more the Saviour put the trying question: "Simon, son of Jonas, lovest thou Me?" Peter was grieved; he thought that Jesus doubted his love. He knew that his

> **"How many today are like Peter! They are interested in the affairs of others . . . while they are in danger of neglecting their own. It is our work to look to Christ and follow Him. We shall see mistakes in the lives of others . . . But in Christ we shall find perfection. Beholding Him, we shall become transformed."**

Lord had cause to distrust him, and with an aching heart he answered, "Lord, Thou knowest all things; Thou knowest that I love Thee." Again Jesus said to him, "Feed My sheep."

Three times Peter had openly denied his Lord, and three times Jesus drew from him the assurance of his love and loyalty, pressing home that pointed question, like a barbed arrow to his wounded heart. Before the assembled disciples Jesus revealed the depth of Peter's repentance, and showed how thoroughly humbled was the once boasting disciple.

Peter was naturally forward and impulsive, and Satan had taken advantage of these characteristics to overthrow him. Just before the fall of Peter, Jesus had said to him, "Satan hath desired to have you, that he may sift you as wheat: but I have prayed for thee, that thy faith fail not; and when thou art converted, strengthen thy brethren."

180

Luke 22:31, 32. That time had now come, and the transformation in Peter was evident. The close, testing questions of the Lord had not called out one forward, self-sufficient reply; and because of his humiliation and repentance, Peter was better prepared than ever before to act as shepherd to the flock.

The first work that Christ entrusted to Peter on restoring him to the ministry was to feed the lambs. This was a work in which Peter had little experience. It would require great care and tenderness, much patience and perseverance. It called him to minister to those who were young in the faith, to teach the ignorant, to open the Scriptures to them, and to educate them for usefulness in Christ's service. Heretofore Peter had not been fitted to do this, or even to understand its importance. But this was the work which Jesus now called upon him to do. For this work his own experience of suffering and repentance had prepared him.

Before his fall, Peter was always speaking unadvisedly, from the impulse of the moment. He was always ready to correct others, and to express his mind, before he had a clear comprehension of himself or of what he had to say. But the converted Peter was very different. He retained his former fervor, but the grace of Christ regulated his zeal. He was no longer impetuous, self-confident, and self-exalted, but calm, self-possessed, and teachable. He could then feed the lambs as well as the sheep of Christ's flock.

The Saviour's manner of dealing with Peter had a lesson for him and for his brethren. It taught them to meet the transgressor with patience, sympathy, and forgiving love. Although Peter had denied his Lord, the love which Jesus bore him never faltered. Just such love should the undershepherd feel for the sheep and lambs committed to his care. Remembering his own weakness and failure, Peter was to deal with his flock as tenderly as Christ had dealt with him.

The question that Christ had put to Peter was significant. He mentioned only one condition of discipleship and service. "Lovest thou Me?" He said. This is the essential qualification. Though Peter might possess every other, yet without the love of Christ he could not be a faithful shepherd over the Lord's flock. Knowledge, benevolence, eloquence, gratitude, and zeal are all aids in the good work; but without the love of Jesus in the heart, the work of the Christian minister is a failure.

Jesus walked alone with Peter, for there was something which He wished to communicate to him only. Before His death, Jesus had said to him, "Whither I go, thou canst not follow Me now; but thou shalt follow Me afterward." To this Peter had replied, "Lord, why cannot I follow Thee now? I will lay down my life for Thy sake." John 13:36, 37. When he said this, he little knew to what heights and depths Christ's feet would lead the way. Peter had failed when the test came, but again he was to have opportunity to prove his love for Christ. That he might be strengthened for the final test of his faith, the Saviour opened to him his future. He told him that after living a life of usefulness, when age was telling upon his strength, he would indeed follow his Lord. Jesus said, "When thou wast young, thou girdedst thyself, and walkedst whither thou wouldst; but when thou shalt be old, thou shalt stretch forth thy hands, and another shall gird thee, and carry thee whither thou wouldst not. This spake He, signifying by what death he should glorify God."

Jesus thus made known to Peter the very manner of his death; he even foretold the stretching forth of his hands upon the cross. Again He bade His disciple, "Follow Me." Peter was not disheartened by the revelation. He felt willing to suffer any death for his Lord.

Heretofore Peter had known Christ after the flesh, as many know Him now; but he was no more to be thus limited. He knew Him no more as he had known Him in his association with Him in humanity. He had loved Him as a man, as a heaven-sent teacher; he now loved Him as God. He had been learning the lesson that to him Christ was all in all. Now he was prepared to share in his Lord's mission of sacrifice. When at last brought to the cross, he was, at his own request, crucified with his head downward. He thought it too great an honor to suffer in the same way as his Master did.

To Peter the words "Follow Me" were full of instruction. Not only for his death, but for every step of his life, was the lesson given. Hitherto Peter had been inclined to act independently. He had tried to plan for the work of God, instead of waiting to follow out God's plan. But he could gain nothing by rushing on before the Lord. Jesus bids him, "Follow Me." Do not run ahead of Me. Then you will not have the hosts of Satan to meet alone. Let Me go before you, and you will not be overcome by the enemy.

As Peter walked beside Jesus, he saw that John was following. A desire came over him to know *his* future, and he "saith to Jesus, Lord, and what shall this man do? Jesus saith unto him, If I will that he tarry till I come, what is that to thee? follow thou Me." Peter should have considered that his Lord would reveal to him all that it was best for him to know. It is the duty of every one to follow Christ, without undue anxiety as to the work assigned to others. In saying of John, "If I will that he tarry till I come," Jesus gave no assurance that this disciple should live until the Lord's second coming. He merely asserted His own supreme power, and that even if He should will this to be so, it would in no way affect Peter's work. The future of both John and Peter was in the hands of their Lord. Obedience in following Him was the duty required of each.

How many today are like Peter. They are interested in the affairs of others, and anxious to know their duty, while they are in danger of neglecting their own. It is our work to look to Christ and follow Him. We shall see mistakes in the lives of others, and defects in their character. Humanity is encompassed with infirmity. But in Christ we shall find perfection. Beholding Him, we shall become transformed.

John lived to be very aged. He witnessed the destruction of Jerusalem, and the ruin of the stately temple, — a symbol of the final ruin of the world. To his latest days John closely followed his Lord. The burden of his testimony to the churches was, "Beloved, let us love one another;" "he that dwelleth in love, dwelleth in God, and God in him." 1 John 4:7, 16.

Peter had been restored to his apostleship, but the honor and authority he received from Christ had not given him supremacy over his brethren. This Christ had made plain when in answer to Peter's question, "What shall this man do?" He had said, "What is that to thee? follow thou Me." Peter was not honored as the head of the church. The favor which Christ had shown him in forgiving his apostasy, and entrusting him with the feeding of the flock, and Peter's own faithfulness in following Christ, won for him the confidence of his brethren. He had much influence in the church. But the lesson which Christ had taught him by the Sea of Galilee Peter carried with him throughout his life. Writing by the Holy Spirit to the churches, he said:

"The elders which are among you I exhort, who am also an elder, and a witness of the sufferings of Christ, and also a partaker of the glory that shall be revealed: Feed the flock of God which is among you, taking the oversight thereof, not by constraint, but willingly; not for filthy lucre, but of a ready mind; neither as being lords over God's heritage, but being ensamples to the flock. And when the Chief Shepherd shall appear, ye shall receive a crown of glory that fadeth not away." 1 Peter 5:1-4.]

Go Teach
All Nations

Standing but a step from His heavenly throne, Christ gave the commission to His disciples. "All power is given unto Me in heaven and in earth," He said. "Go ye therefore, and teach all nations." "Go ye into all the world, and preach the gospel to every creature." Mark 16:15. Again and again the words were repeated, that the disciples might grasp their significance. Upon all the inhabitants of the earth, high and low, rich and poor, was the light of heaven to shine in clear, strong rays. The disciples were to be colaborers with their Redeemer in the work of saving the world.

The commission had been given to the twelve when Christ met with them in the upper chamber; but it was now to be given to a larger number. At the meeting on a mountain in Galilee, all the believers who could be called together were assembled. Of this meeting Christ Himself, before His death, had designated the time and place. The angel at the tomb reminded the disciples of His promise to meet them in Galilee. The promise was repeated to the believers who were gathered at Jerusalem during the Passover week, and through them it reached many lonely ones who were mourning the death of their Lord. With intense interest all looked forward to the interview. They made their way to the place of meeting by circuitous routes, coming in from every direction, to avoid exciting the suspicion of the jealous Jews. With wondering hearts they came, talking earnestly together of the news that had reached them concerning Christ.

At the time appointed, about five hundred believers were collected in little knots on the mountainside, eager to learn all that could be learned from those who had seen Christ since His resurrection. From group to group the disciples passed, telling all they had seen and heard of Jesus, and

reasoning from the Scriptures as He had done with them. Thomas recounted the story of his unbelief, and told how his doubts had been swept away. Suddenly Jesus stood among them. No one could tell whence or how He came. Many who were present had never before seen Him; but in His hands and feet they beheld the marks of the crucifixion; His countenance was as the face of God, and when they saw Him, they worshipped Him.

But some doubted. So it will always be. There are those who find it hard to exercise faith, and they place themselves on the doubting side. These lose much because of their unbelief.

This was the only interview that Jesus had with many of the believers after His resurrection. He came and spoke to them saying, "All power is given unto Me in heaven and in earth." The disciples had worshiped Him before He spoke, but His words, falling from lips that had been closed in death, thrilled them with peculiar power. He was now the risen Saviour. Many of them had seen Him exercise His power in healing the sick and controlling Satanic agencies. They believed that He possessed power to set up His kingdom at Jerusalem, power to quell all opposition, power over the elements of nature. He had stilled the angry waters; He had walked upon the white-crested billows; He had raised the dead to life. Now He declared that "all power" was given to Him. His words carried and minds of His hearers above earthly and temporal things to the heavenly and eternal. They were lifted to the highest conception of His dignity and glory.

Christ's words on the mountainside were the announcement that His sacrifice in behalf of man was full and complete. The conditions of the atonement had been fulfilled; the work for which He came to this world had been accomplished. He was on His way to the throne of God, to be honored by angels, principalities, and powers. He had entered upon His mediatorial work. Clothed with boundless authority, He gave His commission to the disciples: "Go ye therefore, and teach all nations," "baptizing them into the name of the Father, and of the Son, and of the Holy Ghost: teaching them to observe all things, whatsoever I commanded you; and, lo, I am with you alway, even unto the end of the world." Matthew 28:19, 20, R. V.

The Jewish people had been made the depositaries of sacred truth; but Pharisaism had made them the most exclusive, the most bigoted of all the human race. Everything about the priests and rulers,—their dress, customs, ceremonies, traditions,—made them unfit to be the light of the world. They looked upon themselves, the Jewish nation, as the world. But Christ commissioned His disciples to proclaim a faith and worship that would have in it nothing of caste or country, a faith that would be adapted to all peoples, all nations, all classes of men.

Before leaving His disciples, Christ plainly stated the nature of His kingdom. He called to their minds what He had previously told them concerning it. He declared that it was not His purpose to establish in this world a temporal, but a spiritual kingdom. He was not to reign as an earthly king on David's throne. Again He opened to them the Scriptures, showing that all He had passed through had been ordained in heaven, in the councils between the Father and Himself. All had been foretold by men inspired by the Holy Spirit. He said, You see that all I have revealed to you concerning My rejection as the Messiah has come to pass. All I have said in regard to the humiliation I should endure and the death I should die, has been verified. On the third day I rose again. Search the Scriptures more diligently, and you will see that in all these things the specifications of prophecy concerning Me have been fulfilled.

Christ commissioned His disciples to do the work He had left in their hands, beginning at Jerusalem. Jerusalem had been the scene of His amazing condescension for the human race. There He had suffered, been rejected and condemned. The land of Judea was His birthplace. There, clad in the garb of humanity, He had walked with men, and few had discerned how near heaven came to the earth when Jesus was among them. At Jerusalem the work of the disciples must begin.

In view of all that Christ had suffered there, and the unappreciated labor He had put forth, the disciples might have pleaded for a more promising field; but they made no such plea. The very ground where He had scattered the seed of truth was to be cultivated by the disciples, and the seed would spring up and yield an abundant harvest. In their work the disciples would have to meet persecution through the jealousy and hatred of the Jews; but this had been endured by their Master, and they were not to flee from it. The first offers of mercy must be made to the murderers of the Saviour.

And there were in Jerusalem many who had secretly believed on Jesus, and many who had been deceived by the priests and rulers. To these also the gospel was to be presented. They were to be called to repentance. The wonderful truth that through Christ alone could remission of sins be obtained, was to be made plain. While all Jerusalem was stirred by the thrilling events of the past few weeks, the preaching of the gospel would make the deepest impression.

But the work was not to stop here. It was to be extended to the earth's remotest bounds. To His disciples Christ said, You have been witnesses of My life of self-sacrifice in behalf of the world. You have witnessed My labors for Israel. Although they would not come unto Me that they might have life, although priests and rulers have done to Me as they listed, although they have rejected Me as the Scriptures foretold, they shall have still another opportunity of accepting the Son of God. You have seen that all who come to Me, confessing their sins, I freely receive. Him that cometh to Me I will in nowise cast out. All who will, may be reconciled to God, and receive everlasting life. To you, My disciples, I commit this message of mercy. It is to be given to Israel first, and then to all nations, tongues, and peoples. It is to be given to Jews and Gentiles. All who believe are to be gathered into one church.

Through the gift of the Holy Spirit the disciples were to receive a marvelous power. Their testimony was to be confirmed by signs and wonders. Miracles would be wrought, not only by the apostles, but by those who received their message. Jesus said, "In My name shall they cast out devils; they shall speak with new tongues; they shall take up serpents; and if they drink any deadly thing, it shall not hurt them; they shall lay hands on the sick, and they shall recover." Mark 16:17, 18.

At that time poisoning was often practiced. Unscrupulous men did not hesitate to remove by this means those who stood in the way of their ambition. Jesus knew that the life of His disciples would thus be imperiled. Many would think it doing God service to put His witnesses to death. He therefore promised them protection from this danger.

The disciples were to have the same power which Jesus had to heal "all manner of sickness and all manner of disease among the people." By healing in His name the diseases of the body, they would testify to His power for the healing of the soul. Matthew 4:23; 9:6. And a new endowment was now promised. The disciples were to preach among other nations, and they would receive power to speak other tongues. The apostles and their associates were unlettered men, yet through the outpouring of the Spirit on the day of Pentecost, their speech, whether in their own or a foreign language, became pure, simple, and accurate, both in word and in accent.

Thus Christ gave His disciples their commission. He made full provision for the prosecution of the work, and

took upon himself the responsibility for its success. So long as they obeyed His word, and worked in connection with Him, they could not fail. Go to all nations, He bade them. Go to the farthest part of the habitable globe, but know that My presence will be there. Labor in faith and confidence, for the time will never come when I will forsake you.

The Saviour's commission to the disciples included all the believers. It includes all believers in Christ to the end of time. It is a fatal mistake to suppose that the work of saving souls depends alone on the ordained minister. All to whom the heavenly inspiration has come, are put in trust with the gospel. All who receive the life of Christ are ordained to work for the salvation of their fellow men. For this work the church was established, and all who take upon themselves its sacred vows are thereby pledged to be co-workers with Christ.

"The Spirit and the bride say, Come. And let him that heareth say, Come." Revelation 22:17. Every one who hears, is to repeat the invitation. Whatever one's calling in life, his first interest should be to win souls for Christ. He may not be able to speak to congregations, but he can work for individuals. To them he can communicate the instruction received from his Lord. Ministry does not consist alone in preaching. Those minister who relieve the sick and suffering, helping the needy, speaking words of comfort to the desponding and those of little faith. Nigh and afar off are souls weighed down by a sense of guilt. It is nor hardship, toil, or poverty that degrades humanity. It is guilt, wrongdoing. This brings unrest and dissatisfaction. Christ would have His servants minister to sin-sick souls.

The disciples were to begin their work where they were. The hardest and most unpromising field was not to be passed by. So every one of Christ's workers is to begin where he is. In our own families may be souls hungry for sympathy, starving for the bread of life. There may be children to be trained for Christ. There are heathen at our very doors. Let us do faithfully the work that is nearest. Then let our efforts be extended as far as God's hand may lead the way. The work of many may appear to be restricted by circumstances; but wherever it is, if performed with faith and diligence it will be felt to the uttermost parts of the earth. Christ's work when upon earth appeared to be confined to a narrow field, but multitudes from all lands heard His message. God often uses the simplest means to accomplish the greatest results. It is His plan that every part of His work shall depend on every other part, as a wheel within a wheel, all acting in harmony. The humblest worker, moved by the Holy Spirit, will touch invisible chords, whose vibrations will ring to the ends of the earth, and make melody through eternal ages.

But the command, "Go ye into all the world," is not to be lost sight of. We are called upon to lift our eyes to the "regions beyond." Christ tears away the wall of partition, the dividing prejudice of nationality, and teaches a love for all the human family. He lifts men from the narrow circle which their selfishness prescribes; He abolishes all territorial lines and artificial distinctions of society. He makes no difference between neighbors and strangers, friends and enemies. He teaches us to look upon every needy soul as our brother, and the world as our field.

When the Saviour said, "Go teach all nations," He said also, "These signs shall follow them that believe: In My name shall they cast out devils; they shall speak with new tongues; they shall take up serpents; and if they drink any deadly thing, it shall not hurt them; they shall lay hands on the sick, and they shall recover." The promise is as far-reaching as the commission. Not that all the gifts are imparted to each believer. The Spirit divides "to every man severally as He will." 1 Corinthians 12:11. But the gifts of the Spirit are promised to every believer according to his need for the Lord's work. The promise is just as strong and trustworthy now as in the days of the apostles. "These signs shall follow them that believe." This is the privilege of God's children, and faith should lay hold on all that it is possible to have as an indorsement of faith.

"They shall lay hands on the sick, and they shall recover." This world is a vast lazar house, but Christ came to heal the sick, to proclaim deliverance to the captives of Satan. He was in Himself health and strength. He imparted His life to the sick, the afflicted, those possessed of demons. He turned away none who came to receive His healing power. He knew that those who petitioned Him for help had brought disease upon themselves; yet He did not refuse to heal them. And when virtue from Christ entered into these poor souls, they were convicted of sin, and many were healed of their spiritual disease, as well as of their physical maladies. The gospel still possesses the same power, and why should we not today witness the same results?

Christ feels the woes of every sufferer. When evil spirits rend a human frame, Christ feels the curse. When fever is burning up the life current, He feels the agony. And He is just as willing to heal the sick now, as when He was personally on earth. Christ's servants are His representatives, the channels for His working. He desires through them to exercise His healing power.

In the Saviour's manner of healing, there were lessons for His disciples. On one occasion He anointed the eyes of a blind man with clay, and bade him, "Go, wash in the pool of Siloam. . . . He went his way therefore, and washed, and came seeing." John 9:7. The cure could be wrought only by the power of the great Healer, yet Christ made use of the simple agencies of nature. While He did not give countenance to drug medication, He sanctioned the use of simple and natural remedies.

To many of the afflicted ones who received healing, Christ said, "Sin no more, lest a worse thing come unto thee." John 5:14. Thus He taught that disease is the result of violating God's laws, both natural and spiritual. The great misery in the world would not exist, did men but live in harmony with the Creator's plan.

Christ had been the guide and teacher of ancient Israel, and He taught them that health is the reward of obedience to the laws of God. The great Physician who healed the sick in Palestine had spoken to His people from the pillar of cloud, telling them what they must do, and what God would do for them. "If thou wilt diligently hearken to the voice of the Lord thy God," He said, "and wilt do that which is right in His sight, and wilt give ear to His commandments, and keep all His statutes, I will put none of these diseases upon thee, which I have brought upon the Egyptians; for I am the Lord that healeth thee." Exodus 15:26. Christ gave to Israel definite instruction in regard to their habits of life, and He assured them, "The Lord will take away from thee all sickness." Deuteronomy 7:15. When they fulfilled the conditions, the promise was verified to them. "There was not one feeble person among their tribes." Psalms 105:37.

These lessons are for us. There are conditions to be observed by all who would preserve health. All should learn what these conditions are. The Lord is not pleased with ignorance in regard to His laws, either natural or spiritual. We are to be workers together with God for the restoration of health to the body as well as to the soul.

And we should teach others how to preserve and to recover health For the sick we should use the remedies which God has provided in nature, and we should point them to Him who alone can restore. It is our work to present the sick and suffering to Christ in the arms of our faith. We should teach them to believe in the great Healer. We should lay hold on His promise, and pray for the manifestation of His power. The very essence of the gospel is restoration, and the Saviour would have us bid the sick, the hopeless, and the afflicted take hold upon His strength.

The power of love was in all Christ's healing, and only by partaking of that love, through faith, can we be instruments for His work. If we neglect to link ourselves in divine connection with Christ, the current of life-giving energy cannot flow in rich streams from us to the people. There were places where the Saviour Himself could not do many mighty works because of their unbelief. So now unbelief separates the church from her divine Helper. Her hold upon eternal realities is weak. By her lack of faith, God is disappointed, and robbed of His glory.

It is in doing Christ's work that the church has the promise of His presence. Go teach all nations, He said; "and, lo, I am with you alway, even unto the end of the world." To take His yoke is one of the first conditions of receiving His power. The very life of the church depends upon her faithfulness in fulfilling the Lord's commission. To neglect this work is surely to invite spiritual feebleness and decay. Where there is no active labor for others, love wanes, and faith grows dim.

Christ intends that His ministers shall be educators of the church in gospel work. They are to teach the people how to seek and save the lost. But is this the work they are doing? Alas, how many are toiling to fan the spark of life in a church that is ready to die! How many churches are tended like sick lambs by those who ought to be seeking for the lost sheep. And all the time millions upon millions without Christ are perishing.

Divine love has been stirred to its unfathomable depths for the sake of men, and angels marvel to behold in the recipients of so great love a mere surface gratitude. Angels marvel at man's shallow appreciation of the love of God. Heaven stands indignant at the neglect shown to the souls of men. Would we know how Christ regards it? How would a father and mother feel, did they know that their child, lost in the cold and the snow, had been passed by, and left to perish, by those who might have saved it? Would they not be terribly grieved, wildly indignant? Would they not denounce those murderers with wrath hot as their tears, intense as their love? The sufferings of every man are the sufferings of God's child, and those who reach out no helping hand to their perishing fellow beings provoke His righteous anger. This is the wrath of the Lamb. To those who claim fellowship with Christ, yet have been indifferent to the needs of their fellow men, He will declare in the great Judgment day, "I know you not whence ye are; depart from Me, all ye workers of iniquity." Luke 13:27.

In the commission to His disciples, Christ not only outlined their work, but gave them their message. Teach the people, He said, "to observe all things whatsoever I have commanded you." The disciples were to teach what Christ had taught. That which He had spoken, not only in person, but through all the prophets and teachers of the Old Testament, is here included. Human teaching is shut out. There is no place for tradition, for man's theories and conclusions, or for church legislation. No laws ordained by ecclesiastical authority are included in the commission. None of these are Christ's servants to teach. "The law and the prophets," with the record of His own words and deeds, are the treasure committed to the disciples to be given to the world. Christ's name is their watchword, their badge of distinction, their bond of union, the authority for their course of action, and the source of their success. Nothing that does not bear His superscription is to be recognized in His kingdom.

The gospel is to be presented, not as a lifeless theory, but as a living force to change the life. God desires that the receivers of His grace shall be witnesses to its power. Those whose course has been most offensive to Him He freely accepts; when they repent, He imparts to them His divine Spirit, places them in the highest positions of trust, and sends them forth into the camp of the disloyal to proclaim His boundless mercy. He would have His servants bear testimony to the fact that through His grace men may possess Christlikeness of character, and may rejoice in the assurance of His great love. He would have us bear testimony to the fact that He cannot be satisfied until the human race are reclaimed and reinstated in their holy privileges as His sons and daughters.

In Christ is the tenderness of the shepherd, the affection of the parent, and the matchless grace of the compassionate Saviour. His blessings He presents in the most alluring terms. He is not content merely to announce these blessings; He presents them in the most attractive way, to excite a desire to possess them. So His servants are to present the riches of the glory of the unspeakable Gift. The wonderful love of Christ will melt and subdue hearts, when the mere reiteration of doctrines would accomplish nothing. "Comfort ye, comfort ye, My people, saith your God." "O Zion, that bringest good tidings, get thee up into the high mountain; O Jerusalem, that bringest good tidings, lift up thy voice with strength; lift it up, be not afraid; say unto the cities of Judah, Behold your God! . . . He shall feed His flock like a shepherd; He shall gather the lambs with His arm, and carry them in His bosom." Isaiah 40:1, 9-11. Tell the people of Him who is "the Chiefest among ten thousand," and the One "altogether lovely." The Song of Solomon 5:10, 16. Words alone cannot tell it. Let it be reflected in the character and manifested in the life. Christ is sitting for His portrait in every disciple. Every one God has predestinated to be "conformed to the image of His Son." Romans 8:29. In every one Christ's longsuffering love, His holiness, meekness, mercy, and truth, are to be manifested to the world.

The first disciples went forth preaching the word. They revealed Christ in their lives. And the Lord worked with them, "confirming the word with signs following." Mark 16:20. These disciples prepared themselves for their work. Before the day of Pentecost they met together, and put away all differences. They were of one accord. They believed Christ's promise that the blessing would be given, and they prayed in faith. They did not ask for a blessing for themselves merely; they were weighted with the burden for the salvation of souls. The gospel was to be carried to the uttermost parts of the earth, and they claimed the endowment o power that Christ had promised. Then it was that the Holy Spirit was poured out, and thousands were converted in a day.

So it may be now. Instead of man's speculations, let the word of God be preached. Let Christians put away their dissensions, and give themselves to God for the saving of the lost. Let them in faith ask for the blessing, and it will come. The outpouring of the Spirit in apostolic days was the "former rain," (Joel 2:23.) and glorious was the result. But the "latter rain" will be more abundant.

All who consecrate soul, body, and spirit to God, will be constantly receiving a new endowment of physical and mental power. The inexhaustible supplies of heaven are at their command. Christ gives them the breath of His own spirit, the life of His own life. The Holy Spirit puts forth its highest energies to work in heart and mind. The grace of God enlarges and multiplies their faculties, and every perfection of the divine nature comes to their assistance in the work of saving souls. Through co-operation with Christ they are complete in Him, and in their human weakness they are enabled to do the deeds of Omnipotence.

The Saviour longs to manifest His grace and stamp His character on the whole world. It is His purchased possession, and He desires to make men free, and pure, and holy. Though Satan works to hinder this purpose, yet through the blood shed for the world there are triumphs to be achieved that will bring glory to God and the Lamb. Christ will not be satisfied till the victory is complete, and "He shall see of the travail of His soul, and shall be satisfied." Isaiah 53:11. All the nations of the earth shall hear the gospel of His grace. Not all will receive His grace; but "a seed shall serve Him; it shall be accounted to the Lord for a generation." Psalms 22:30. "The kingdom and dominion, and the greatness of the kingdom under the whole heaven, shall be given to the people of the saints of the Most High," and "the earth shall be full of the knowledge of the Lord, as the waters cover the sea." "So shall they fear the name of the Lord from the west, and His glory from the rising of the sun." Daniel 7:27; Isaiah 11:9; 59:19.

"How beautiful upon the mountains are the feet of him that bringeth good tidings, that publisheth peace; that bringeth good tidings of good, that publisheth salvation; that saith unto Zion, Thy God reigneth! . . . Break forth into joy, sing together, ye waste places; . . . for the Lord hath comforted His people. . . . The Lord hath made bare His holy arm in the eyes of all the nations, and all the ends of the earth shall see the salvation of our God." Isaiah 52:7-10.

"To My Father, and Your Father"

The time had come for Christ to ascend to His Father's throne. As a divine conqueror He was about to return with the trophies of victory to the heavenly courts. Before His death He had declared to His Father, "I have finished the work which Thou gavest Me to do." John 17:4. After His resurrection He tarried on earth for a season, that His disciples might become familiar with Him in His risen and glorified body. Now He was ready for the leave-taking. He had authenticated the fact that He was a living Saviour. His disciples need no longer associate Him with the tomb. They could think of Him as glorified before the heavenly universe.

As the place of His ascension, Jesus chose the spot so often hallowed by His presence while He dwelt among men. Not Mount Zion, the place of David's city, not Mount Moriah, the temple site, was to be thus honored. There Christ had been mocked and rejected. There the waves of mercy, still returning in a stronger tide of love, had been beaten back by hearts as hard as rock. Thence Jesus, weary and heart-burdened, had gone forth to find rest in the Mount of Olives. The holy Shekinah, in departing from the first temple, had stood upon the eastern mountain, as if loath to forsake the chosen city; so Christ stood upon Olivet, with yearning heart overlooking Jerusalem. The groves and glens of the mountain had been consecrated by His prayers and tears. Its steeps had echoed the triumphant shouts of the multitude that proclaimed Him king. On its sloping descent He had found a home with Lazarus at Bethany. In the garden of Gethsemane at its foot He had prayed and agonized alone. From this mountain He was to ascend to heaven. Upon its summit His feet will rest when He shall come again. Not as a man of sorrows, but as a glorious and triumphant king He will stand upon Olivet, while Hebrew hallelujahs mingle with Gentile hosannas, and the voices of the redeemed as a mighty host shall swell the acclamation, "Crown Him Lord of all."

Now with the eleven disciples, Jesus made His way toward the mountain. As they passed through the gate of Jerusalem, many wondering eyes looked upon the little company, led by One whom a few weeks before the rulers had condemned and crucified. The disciples knew not that this was to be their last interview with their Master. Jesus spent the time in conversation with them, repeating His former instruction. As they approached Gethsemane, He paused, that they might call to mind the lessons He had given them on the night of His great agony. Again He looked upon the vine by which He had then represented the union of His church with Himself and His Father; again He repeated the truths He had then unfolded. All around Him were reminders of His unrequited love. Even the disciples who were so dear to His heart, had, in the hour of His humiliation, reproached and forsaken Him.

Christ had sojourned in the world for thirty-three years; He had endured its scorn, insult, and mockery; He had been rejected and crucified. Now, when about to ascend to His throne of glory—as He reviews the ingratitude of the people He came to save—will He not withdraw from them His sympathy and love? Will not His affections be centered upon that realm where He is appreciated, and where sinless angels wait to do His bidding?—No; His promise to those loved ones whom He leaves on earth is, "I am with you alway, even unto the end of the world." Matthew 28:20

Upon reaching the Mount of Olives, Jesus led the way across the summit, to the vicinity of Bethany. Here He paused, and the disciples gathered about Him. Beams of light seemed to radiate from His countenance as He looked lovingly upon them. He upbraided them not for their faults and failures; words of the deepest tenderness were the last that fell upon their ears from the lips of their Lord. With hands outstretched in blessing, and as if in assurance of His protecting care, He slowly ascended from among them, drawn heavenward by a power stronger than any earthly attraction. As He passed upward, the awestricken disciples looked with straining eyes for the last glimpse of

---

> **"Christ had sojourned in the world for thirty-three years: . . . He had been rejected and crucified. Now, when about to ascend to His throne of glory . . . Will not His affections be centered upon that realm where He is appreciated, and where sinless angels wait to do His bidding? No; His promise to those loved ones whom He leaves on earth is, 'I am with you alway, even unto the end of the world.'"**

---

their ascending Lord. A cloud of glory hid Him from their sight; and the words came back to them as the cloudy chariot of angels received Him, "Lo, I am with you alway, even unto the end of the world." At the same time there floated down to them the sweetest and most joyous music from the angel choir.

While the disciples were still gazing upward, voices addressed them which sounded like richest music. They turned, and saw two angels in the form of men, who spoke to them, saying, "Ye men of Galilee, why stand ye gazing up into heaven? This same Jesus, which is taken up from you into heaven, shall so come in like manner as ye have seen Him go into heaven."

These angels were of the company that had been waiting in a shining cloud to escort Jesus to His heavenly home. The most exalted of the angel throng, they were the two who had come to the tomb at Christ's resurrection, and they had been with Him throughout His life on earth. With eager desire all heaven had waited for the end of His tarrying in a world marred by the curse of sin. The time had now come for the heavenly universe to receive their King. Did not the two angels long to join the throng that welcomed Jesus? But in sympathy and love for those whom He had left, they waited to give them comfort. "Are they not all ministering spirits, sent forth to minister for them who shall be heirs of salvation?" Hebrews 1:14.

Christ had ascended to heaven in the form of humanity. The disciples had beheld the cloud receive Him. The same Jesus who had walked and talked and prayed with them; who had broken bread with them; who had been with them in their boats on the lake; and who had that very day toiled with them up the ascent of Olivet,—the same Jesus had now gone to share His Father's throne. And the angels had assured them that the very One whom they had seen go up into heaven, would come again even as He had ascended. He will come "with clouds; and every eye shall see Him." "The Lord Himself shall descend from heaven with a shout, with the voice of the archangel, and with the trump of God; and the dead in Christ shall rise." "The Son of man shall come in His glory, and all the holy angels with Him, then shall He sit upon the throne of His glory." Revelation 1:7; 1 Thessalonians 4:16; Matthew 25:31. Thus will be fulfilled the Lord's own promise to His disciples: "If I go and prepare a place for you, I will come again, and receive you unto Myself; that where I am, there may ye be also." John 14:3. Well might the disciples rejoice in the hope of their Lord's return.

When the disciples went back to Jerusalem, the people looked upon them with amazement. After the trial and crucifixion of Christ, it had been thought that they would appear downcast and ashamed. Their enemies expected to see upon their faces an expression of sorrow and defeat. Instead of this there was only gladness and triumph. Their faces were aglow with a happiness not born of earth. They did not mourn over disappointed hopes, but were full of praise and thanksgiving to God. With rejoicing they told the wonderful story of Christ's resurrection and is ascension to heaven, and their testimony was received by many.

The disciples no longer had any distrust of the future. They knew that Jesus was in heaven, and that His sympathies were with them still. They knew that they had a friend at the throne of God, and they were eager to present their requests to the Father in the name of Jesus. In solemn awe they bowed in prayer, repeating the assurance, "Whatsoever ye shall ask the Father in My name, He will give it you. Hitherto have ye asked nothing in My name; ask, and ye shall receive, that your joy may be full." John 16:23, 24. They extended the hand of faith higher and higher, with the mighty argument, "It is Christ that died, yea rather, that

190

is risen again, who is even at the right hand of God, who also maketh intercession for us." Romans 8:34. And Pentecost brought them fulness of joy in the presence of the Comforter, even as Christ had promised.

All heaven was waiting to welcome the Saviour to the celestial courts. As He ascended, He led the way, and the multitude of captives set free at His resurrection followed. The heavenly host, with shouts and acclamations of praise and celestial song, attended the joyous train.

As they drew near to the city of God, the challenge is given by the escorting angels, —

"Lift up your heads, O ye gates;
And be ye lift up, ye everlasting doors;
And the King of Glory shall come in!"

Joyfully the waiting sentinels respond, —

"Who is this King of Glory?"

This they say, not because they know not who He is, but because they would hear the answer of exalted praise, —

"The Lord strong and mighty,
The Lord mighty in battle!
Lift up your heads, O ye gates;
Even lift them up, ye everlasting doors;
And the King of Glory shall come in!"

Again is heard the challenge, "Who is this King of Glory?" for the angels never weary of hearing His name exalted. The escorting angels make reply, —

"The Lord of hosts;
He is the King of Glory!" Psalms 24:7-10.

Then the portals of the city of God are opened wide, and the angelic throng sweep through the gates amid a burst of rapturous music.

There is the throne, and around it the rainbow of promise. There are cherubim and seraphim. The commanders of the angel hosts, the sons of God, the representatives of the unfallen worlds, are assembled. The heavenly council before which Lucifer had accused God and His Son, the representatives of those sinless realms over which Satan had thought to establish his dominion, — all are there to welcome the Redeemer. They are eager to celebrate His triumph and to glorify their King.

But He waves them back. Not yet; He cannot now receive the coronet of glory and the royal robe. He enters into the presence of His Father. He points to His wounded head, the pierced side, the marred feet; He lifts His hands, bearing the print of nails. He points to the tokens of His triumph; He presents to God the wave sheaf, those raised with Him as representatives of that great multitude who shall come forth from the grave at His second coming. He

approaches the Father, with whom there is joy over one sinner that repents; who rejoices over one with singing. Before the foundations of the earth were laid, the Father and the Son had united in a covenant to redeem man if he should be overcome by Satan. They had clasped their hands in a solemn pledge that Christ should become the surety for the human race. This pledge Christ has fulfilled. When upon the cross He cried out, "It is finished," He addressed the Father. The compact had been fully carried out. Now He declares, "Father, it is finished. I have done Thy will, O My God. I have completed the work of redemption. If Thy justice is satisfied, 'I will that they also, whom Thou hast given Me, be with Me where I am.' " John 19:30; 17:24.

The voice of God is heard proclaiming that justice is satisfied. Satan is vanquished. Christ's toiling, struggling ones on earth are "accepted in the Beloved." Ephesians 1:6. Before the heavenly angels and the representatives of unfallen worlds, they are declared justified. Where He is, there His church shall be. "Mercy and truth are met together; righteousness and peace have kissed each other." Psalms 85:10. The Father's arms encircle His Son, and the word is given, "Let all the angels of God worship Him." Hebrews 1:6.

With joy unutterable, rulers and principalities and powers acknowledge the supremacy of the Prince of life. The angel host prostrate themselves before Him, while the glad shout fills all the courts of heaven, "Worthy is the Lamb that was slain to receive power, and riches, and wisdom, and strength, and honor, and glory, and blessing!" Revelation 5:12.

Songs of triumph mingle with the music from angel harps, till heaven seems to overflow with joy and praise. Love has conquered. The lost is found. Heaven rings with voices in lofty strains proclaiming, "Blessing, and honor, and glory, and power be unto Him that sitteth upon the throne, and unto the Lamb forever and ever." Revelation 5:13.

From that scene of heavenly joy, there comes back to us on earth the echo of Christ's own wonderful words, "I ascend to My Father, and your Father; and to My God and your God." The family of heaven and the family of earth are one. For us our Lord ascended, and for us He lives. "Wherefore He is able also to save them to the uttermost that come unto God by Him, seeing He ever liveth to make intercession for them."

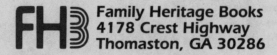